DEFENDING ANIMALS, DISAPPOINTING PEOPLE

ALSO AVAILABLE FROM BLOOMSBURY:

Radical Natural Law, Josephine Donovan

The Discursive Construction of Veganism, Mario Leto

Beyond Animal Rights, Tony Milligan

Living Among Meat Eaters, Carol J. Adams

DEFENDING ANIMALS, DISAPPOINTING PEOPLE

An Ecofeminist Approach

Karen S. Emmerman

BLOOMSBURY ACADEMIC
LONDON • NEW YORK • OXFORD • NEW DELHI • SYDNEY

BLOOMSBURY ACADEMIC
Bloomsbury Publishing Plc, 50 Bedford Square, London, WC1B 3DP, UK
Bloomsbury Publishing Inc, 1359 Broadway, New York, NY 10018, USA
Bloomsbury Publishing Ireland, 29 Earlsfort Terrace, Dublin 2, D02 AY28, Ireland

BLOOMSBURY, BLOOMSBURY ACADEMIC and the Diana logo are trademarks of Bloomsbury Publishing Plc

First published in Great Britain 2026

A catalogue record for this book is available from the British Library.

A catalog record for this book is available from the Library of Congress.

ISBN: HB: 978-1-3504-3534-6
PB: 978-1-3504-3533-9
ePDF: 978-1-3504-3535-3
eBook: 978-1-3504-3536-0

Typeset by Newgen KnowledgeWorks Pvt. Ltd., Chennai, India
Printed and bound in Great Britain

For product safety related questions contact productsafety@bloomsbury.com.

To find out more about our authors and books visit www.bloomsbury.com and sign up for our newsletters

In loving memory of my grandmothers—Freda Goldman,
Ida Emmerman, Lucia Grosso, Françoise Acoulon,
and Harriet Mont Emmerman

CONTENTS

ACKNOWLEDGMENTS

I have a sticky note on the wall of my office that says, "Petit à petit, l'oiseau fait son nit," which translates to "little by little by little the bird makes her nest." It is there to remind me that book writing would take time, require focus and attention, and perhaps more than those things it would demand patience. It turns out to also be a lovely metaphor for how others play a role in the writing process—gathering metaphorical sticks, pieces of fuzz, leaves, and whatnot—bringing them to me as support, ideas to share, helpful feedback, and much-needed connection during what can be a lonely process. I am grateful to all who have helped me build this book, who made it easier to focus, find the time, and be patient.

For nurturing my soul and sense of well-being, I am particularly grateful to the Seabok Crew, Iván Sandoval Cervantes, Brooke Coleman, Rachel Lafer Coppola, John Coppola, Amy Dwyer, Lucretia Koba, Jennifer Mendelson, Ronit Reger, Melanie Skinner, Sarah Clammy Standard, Team Seven, the Lighthouse Club, and the Moranimals. For the gift of both friendship and collaborative thinking, I especially thank Ben Almassi, Monica Aufrecht, Renee Conroy, Asia Ferrin, Jeremy Fischer, Rachel Fredericks, María Elena Garcia, Sara Goering, Diana Goodrich, Mark Hawthorne, J. B. Mulcahy, lauren Ornelas, and Amy Reed-Sandoval. For friendship and our nurturing and laughter-filled writing group, I am thankful for Kris Phillips and Cassie Finley.

I have the good fortune to teach and learn with philosophy students of all ages through my work with the Philosophy Learning and Teaching Organization (PLATO) and the University of Washington. From kindergarten students to graduate students, I have the most wonderful young people with whom to engage in deep thinking, important questions, and the joy of wonder and curiosity. I am so very grateful to each and every student I have had the honor to work with from the youngest philosophers just learning how to be in school to graduate students with whom I have had some of the most enriching discussions imaginable. I am particularly grateful to all the undergraduates and graduate students who have taken my animal ethics courses at the University of Washington (UW) and who have shared their own stories of defending animals and disappointing people. My deep thanks, too, to everyone I have worked with over the years at UW and to the teachers and staff I collaborate with at John Muir and Thurgood Marshall elementary schools. PLATO, too, is a remarkable community of wonderful people doing vitally important work. My heartfelt thanks to Jana Mohr Lone and Debi Talukdar for over a decade of friendship, collaboration, and support. Roberta Israeloff has been a friend, writing mentor, and sounding board. I am grateful to each of them for their wisdom and care.

My thanks to Bloomsbury Academic for believing in this project and to the anonymous reviewers who have pushed me with their generous and valuable feedback, to Lori Gruen and Carol Adams for mentorship, and to the Kline Workshop at the University of Missouri where our wonderful conversations made me see that what I was working on could be a book. Chapter 4 is based in part on my 2019 article "What's Love Got to Do with It? An Ecofeminist Approach to Inter-Animal and Intra-Cultural Conflicts of Interest," published in *Ethical Theory and Moral Practice*. The cover photo, "Betsy and Nutmeg: Mother and Son" is courtesy of Chimpanzee Sanctuary Northwest. I am grateful to them for allowing me to use this beautiful photo and to memorialize Nutmeg Steer in this way.

I have been defending animals and occasionally disappointing people since I was twelve years old. My thanks to my family for hanging in there with me as I learned how to integrate the knowledge of the cruelties animals face into my relationships with the people I love. It was sloppily done at times, I know, but I always and only ever wanted to practice love and respect for the animals and for you.

Of the many animals in the world needing human community and care for their flourishing, I have been so lucky to share my life with Emma, O. J., Ralph, Tiger, Harry, S. Bear Cavinaugh, Brownie, Midnight, Théo, Teddy, Ira, and Paddington. They have all contributed in their own, unique, ways to who I am and to this project. The human animals with whom I share my adult life, Jeremy and Oliver, are my greatest source of joy, laughter, support, creativity, and care. Jeremy has been unfailing in his determination to show up for me in every possible way in this and all endeavors in my life. Oliver makes each and every day better with his passion, creativity, sense of humor, and empathy.

1 INTRODUCTION

Let's begin with an anecdote that may strike a familiar chord.

Rosh Hashannah 1988. The dining table is equipped with its extension leaf to accommodate the extended family, and the table is set with the good dishes miraculously unscathed from their journey to New York during a hasty pogrom-induced departure from the old country. The family gathers to celebrate the start of the Jewish new year. Everyone is in good spirits and feeling festive until I turn away a bowl of my grandmother's chicken soup. The air is sucked from the room. Looks are exchanged. Newly informed about the treatment animals endure in the food system, I have become a vegetarian at the age of thirteen. No one is pleased. It is one thing to eat a veggie burger for lunch and quite another to turn your back on your grandmother's chicken soup at the Rosh Hashannah table. This is the soup of our people and the result of my grandmother's loving labor, the consistent centerpiece of all our holiday gatherings, the healing broth for colds and flus. Feelings are hurt, demands to acquiesce are issued, the idea that meat is murder is explained. The hurt festers for decades as a commitment to vegetarianism becomes a commitment to veganism, further distancing me from the culturally important traditions of my family and community. I remain staunch in my commitment to animals, all the while knowing I have lost ground with my family—I see hurt feelings, a belief I have shown disrespect to my elders, fears I have left them all behind somehow, anger that I have questioned their moral decision-making, and awareness that I have transgressed the norm that we eat animals without question. All the while, I am thinking "I miss and love you, but can't you understand that I can no longer participate in a moral tragedy?" while they are wondering why chickens matter more to me than my most valued relationships and the traditions of our people.

I have defended animals but disappointed people; those same people have at times been defensive and disappointing. This anecdote is autobiographical, but it could just as easily belong to any vegan I encounter—the Iranian vegan rejecting their friends' Persian kebab, the Mexican vegan rejecting the Easter offering of bacalao a la vizcaína, the vegan Gujarati Jain who no longer partakes of the Diwali sweets made with animal products, or the South African vegan who will not participate in a traditional Braais barbecue (Ngqangashe 2019, 152–3).[1] While the traditions and specific foods differ, the scenes that have played out with their families and communities are the same. We all experience the deep pain of defending animals and disappointing people in the process. When one incorporates respect for animals into one's life by adopting veganism or animal advocacy more generally thus rejecting activities that involve animal exploitation, one frequently finds oneself at odds with loved ones and community members who do not share these values. I call these situations "interanimal and intracultural" conflicts because they are between animals (human and other-than-human) and take place within one's own cultural or familial context. This tension often goes unexplored and is certainly undertheorized. This is perhaps because living in a world where animal exploitation and suffering is overwhelmingly ubiquitous tends to make those of us awake to this tragedy yearn to help others see that they should care and that, in caring, they should shift to veganism. We want to paint veganism as the land of plenty it is—full of delicious foods, camaraderie, activities to enjoy, and a sense of peace. Dwelling on what is challenging or heartbreaking will only turn people away with the result that more animals will continue to suffer, earth's climate will continue to change for the worse, and more humans will be harmed by the environmental impacts of industrial animal agriculture and the dangerous work involved in raising and slaughtering animals for consumption. So, we whisper among ourselves about the relational challenges we face or worse, we pretend these challenges do not arise.

Veganism is indeed a land of plenty, especially for those of us who have access to healthy foods easily acquired at local grocery stores and farmers' markets. I know too, however, from my own experience and the experiences of others I have spoken with that veganism can take a relational toll; that in our attempts to defend animals our loved ones sometimes feel hurt, confused, disappointed, angry, or betrayed. These feelings are often dismissed out of hand as evidence that our loved ones feel guilty about their own consumption of animal bodies; that they feel judged by the vegan in their midst; and that they want to avoid reflecting on their own practices at all costs. This may be partially true. I suspect all vegans have experienced the kind of aggressive and defensive posture taken by our meat-eating table companions or the neighbor whose invitation to the zoo we politely decline. However, this explanation is insufficient to explain all that transpires between vegans and their loved ones.

---

[1]My thanks to Atoosa Afshari, Iván Sandoval Cervantes, and Tejas Mehta for sharing their experiences being vegan in their Iranian, Mexican, and Jain communities as well as to the many students who have shared examples from within their own communities, spanning the globe.

This project is a work of ecofeminist animal ethics focusing on conflicts that arise between animal ethics, cultural traditions, and important relationships. Through careful contextual analysis of these conflicts, I shed light on the complexity relationality adds to cases of competing values and offer a relational account, what I call "relational moral attention," of how we might find our way through these ethically and emotionally charged situations without estrangement from either our commitments to animals or our important relationships.

In academic disciplines focused on animal ethics/animal studies and in animal activist circles, there has been considerable discussion about cross-cultural conflicts of interest involving animals. For example, the question of whether Indigenous people should undertake cultural whaling and what, if anything, should be the role of white activists and academics in weighing in on that topic has received substantial attention (Fisher 2011; Gaard 2001; Hawkins 2001; Hogan 1996; Kim 2015). In a similar vein, ecofeminists going back to the 1990s have theorized about "contextual moral vegetarianism," which centers on whether ethical vegetarianism is a universal requirement or a moral response in particular contexts (e.g., Western, industrialized nations where industrialized animal agriculture is the norm and alternatives to animal flesh are readily available) (Curtin 1991, 1992, 2004; Kheel 2004, 2008; Twine 2022.)[2]

Given the keen interest in conflicts between nonhuman animals and human traditions and practices that involve causing animal suffering in the cross-cultural sphere, it is surprising there is so little sustained reflection about conflicts of interest that arise between commitments to nonhuman animals and relationships with loved ones regarding cultural or familial traditions *intraculturally*. What, for example, does animal ethics have to say to the Jewish vegan staring down at a bowl of her grandmother's chicken soup while recognizing the moral impermissibility of both slaughtering chickens for human consumption and disrespecting or acting hurtfully toward her elders? On one reading, someone's nonsubsistence interest in a bowl of chicken soup is a trivial interest in something tasty to eat. Where food is not scarce and resources are plentiful, there is no reason to eat a bowl of chicken soup when one could just as easily enjoy lentil soup. On another reading, the chicken soup is a robust interest in deep familial and cultural traditions and in sustaining important familial relationships. Contextualizing the bowl of soup reveals that it is no small thing for an Ashkenazi Jewish person, for example, to turn her back on a bowl of her grandmother's chicken soup. The refusal undermines the relationship, threatens group harmony, and is interpreted as a moral accusation by those who eat the soup.

[2]Alternatives to animal flesh are not always readily available in the industrialized West. Inequities in access to healthy foods in low-income communities of color render plant-based diets inaccessible to many people living in such communities (Food Empowerment Project, "Food Deserts*").

When we look at some human interests contextually, we see that a tension can arise between two insights: (1) the insight that animals' moral considerability warrants that we not harm them in service of seemingly trivial, nonbasic human interests and (2) the insight that some of our nonbasic interests are nonetheless significantly morally valuable, in particular insofar as they are connected to relationships of love and care and our cultural identities. This tension is the focal point of *Defending Animals, Disappointing People*. Those of us facing this tension confront at least two issues. The first, and more obvious, is the choice about whether to prioritize obligations to and compassion for animals over obligations to and care for our loved ones. Inside of this choice lies yet another dilemma surrounding one's own sense of moral integrity and how that should be weighed when our moral positions set us at odds with loved ones. The second, less obvious and often unacknowledged issue is how to respond once we have made our choice about which value will prevail. I address both issues. Some of the discussion aims at clarifying what is at stake when weighing conflicting values and what considerations can help us make a choice about which should ultimately prevail. Another part of the discussion focuses on what to do once our choice is made. In particular, what to do when we have decided that we will follow our moral principles but that in doing so we may be seen as guilty of another kind of moral failure by turning away from family, friends, and other important relationships in service of those obligations. There is of course a correlated question of what one should do if one opts to weigh relationships more than animals' interests. Most of the book is devoted to the first question.

Often in the animal ethics literature the response to these kinds of conflicts is to note that the human interests involved are so trivial compared to the animals' interests that they simply ought to be given up. This is the recommendation either because the approach is utilitarian, like Peter Singer's, and focuses on weighing interests to resolve conflicts or because the approach is deontological, like Tom Regan's, and focuses on respecting animals' rights. On both approaches it will be absurd to suggest that humans ought to override animals' most important interests or violate their rights to fulfill interests that are neither necessary nor, as some argue, important. Another response that I have encountered in some animal activist circles is to simply wish the dilemmas away by suggesting an easy response to what is actually a complex and sometimes gut-wrenching scenario. Another response is to remain open to hearing that the human interest is, indeed, more robust than originally thought but then use that robustness as a reason to override animals' interest. "Oh!" someone might say, "Traditional foods really are important to your community, and you seem to really love your grandmother. I see now that the interest is not trivial at all. Just go ahead and eat the soup now that it is clear how important it is." I seek a different answer to these dilemmas, one that threads a rather tight needle in an effort to demonstrate that we can see human interests in all their robustness while at the same time recognizing that those interests most often ought not to override animals' interests. Some human interests really are trivial, and no description, however carefully contextualized, will render them any less so. I set those well and truly trivial interests to the side for this project.

Given what I have just said, one might reasonably wonder whether the intention behind this project is simply to defend the claim that the relational vegan ecofeminist approach is better for changing hearts and minds than other approaches or whether there is a deeper argument afoot. While I do think that relational vegan ecofeminism and relational moral attention are more effective when it comes to changing hearts and minds, I make the deeper claim that previous discussions of interspecies conflicts of interest are fundamentally flawed, that they leave out essential ethical details, and that they issue moral edicts and then end the discussion in morally incomplete ways. With few exceptions, they indicate that there is nothing else to say other than that hunting is wrong and you must not do it or that the interest in food is trivial, so you must not eat animal flesh foods. This approach has trickled down through the animal rights movement, enabling activists to label as trivial that which is truly emotionally and ethically wrought. That has a negative practical impact on the efficacy of the animal rights movement resulting in activism that fails to meet people where they are. Such approaches are also deeply *ethically* flawed, failing to attend to the significant part relationality plays in our moral lives. Hence, I defend both the position that for practical reasons of changing hearts and minds relational vegan ecofeminism is an improvement over other approaches and that these other approaches are profoundly ethically problematic.

A related question about scope asks whether the project's focus is on individual change (e.g., persuading a hunter to stop hunting) or effecting local cultural change (e.g., altering animal-exploiting cultural or community traditions). Neither of these options is quite right. With the *Defending Animals, Disappointing People* project, I consider the balance between moral integrity regarding commitments to animals and commitments to loved ones. I do not say much about whether changes in individual behaviors or in local community practices are the priority or about the importance of converting others to veganism and other pro-animal positions. Though I delight in the prospect of ethical veganism gaining in popularity and in pro-animal policies and practices, the focus here is truly on how we manage once we have already taken animals seriously. In this sense, my project is similar to Carol Adams's in *Living Among Meat Eaters* where Adams provides an analysis of why vegans face so much resistance from meat eaters and how they can take care of themselves and meet their own needs in the face of that resistance. In that project Adams does not take the position that vegans must find ways to convince others to adopt veganism. Indeed, she frequently cautions against directly answering questions about the grounds for veganism. As I understand it, her aim was to provide an analysis of why vegans face so much resistance and offer sage guidance to aid vegans in living their lives in a meat-eating society. Along the same lines,

I do not take a position on whether vegans should seek to educate their loved ones in the reasons veganism is an appropriate response to humans' exploitative relationships with other animals. Rather, I emphasize how to think about and how to respond in the face of conflicts between our values that reflect respect and care for both animals and the most important people in our lives.

1 Relational Vegan Ecofeminism

I have named the approach I advocate for Relational Vegan Ecofeminism. Following Greta Gaard, who once wrote about "vegetarian ecofeminism" (Gaard 2002), I use "vegan ecofeminism" to represent ecofeminist positions that advocate strongly for veganism as the appropriate moral response to the question of eating animal flesh and using animals as tools for human purposes. That is perhaps too general a description—there is nuance to the position, which I take up in Chapter 3. For now, "vegan ecofeminism" differentiates the position from ecofeminist theories that leave animals out altogether and those, like Val Plumwood's and Erin McKenna's, who advocate strongly for better moral relationships with animals but whose call for vegetarianism or veganism is not "absolute" (McKenna 2021, 2023; Plumwood 2012).

Ecofeminism is a diverse theory but is generally contextualized, pluralist, and nonhierarchical. Context involves attending closely to the particulars of a situation and the structural and systemic mechanisms in place that both create the moral dilemmas we face and limit the possible responses available. Ecofeminists "*see* the tree; but they also see the logging industry. They see the downed cow in the slaughterhouse pen, but they also see the farming and dairy industry" (Donovan 2007, 192). Ecofeminism is pluralist in several senses: it underscores that moral value and moral considerability stem from a variety of sources rather than one particular capacity or characteristic (e.g., sentience), it notices that both reason and emotion play a vital role in moral deliberation and that justice and care are both integral to the moral life, and it allows for a variety of ethical principles and considerations to factor into our moral thinking rather than positing a one-size-fits-all principle to apply to all situations across all times and places. Some ecofeminism, including my approach, is nonhierarchical in that it rejects fixed hierarchies of life-forms or interests that rank those beings or interests in order of importance. Ecofeminist theory is grounded in the feminist ethics of care, a theory that focuses on meeting the needs of particular others, values rather than rejects emotion as part of the moral life, rejects the primacy of abstract thinking, reconsiders the distinction between private and public life, and conceives of persons as relational rather than individualistic (Held 2006, 10–13). Whereas some feminist care theorizing stopped at the species border, ecofeminism expands our understanding of care and relationality to include other-than-humans. Like many ecofeminists before me, I see veganism as an act of protest against the structures of oppression and domination that normalize and reinforce the exploitation of nature and all the animals dwelling therein (Curtin 1992; Kheel 2004).

One of ecofeminists' main contributions to moral theory is in articulating the joint oppression of women and nature (Adams 1991, 1994, 2010; Donovan 1993; Donovan and Adams 2007; Gaard 2002; Gruen 1993, 2004; Kheel 2004; Warren 1990). The very same conceptual framework that generates beliefs enabling the destruction of the natural world is at the foundation of sexism and misogyny. That pernicious and destructive conceptual framework is patriarchy. Ecofeminists have long identified and argued against the ways that patriarchy marginalizes and others both women and animals (along with other groups who do not meet cisgendered, heteronormative, white, male criteria of inclusion) leading to the objectification, fragmentation, and consumption of all deemed less than (Adams 2010). Patriarchy and, in particular, anthroparchy (systemic, human-centered patriarchal conceptual beliefs) play an important role in this project for it is, as it were, the soup we are all swimming in all day every day, shaping our lives, our choices, and our ways of seeing the world frequently without us even noticing.

The ecofeminist position I offer here is also relational. Much ecofeminism is relational at least inasmuch as it is rooted in a feminist care ethic where relationships of love and care and attentiveness to the other are central to moral life. Much ecofeminism is also relational in the sense of conceiving of humans as in relationship with the natural world and animal others rather than standing apart in a category all our own with nature there as a resource for us. When I use "relational" I mean all those senses of relationality *and* that my approach to interanimal conflicts of interest looks to relationality in the form of relational moral attention as a significant part of adjudicating and responding to interanimal conflicts of interest.

2 Moral Remainders and Relational Moral Attention

The cost of a human life is that our interests will inevitably conflict with others', and we will often do harm to others' interests (cf. Curtin 1991). The reality of interanimal and intracultural conflicts is that no matter how well-navigated, how thoughtfully approached, or how profound our efforts to reduce the impact of our choices on others, more often than not harm will occur. As a result of our choices and actions, sometimes animals will lose, sometimes humans we do not know will lose, and sometimes humans or animals we love and cherish will lose, generating moral remainders. Bernard Williams introduced this term, moral remainders, to capture the regret one feels after resolving a moral conflict but feeling that, however justified one was, moral considerations were left unattended (1965). Moral remainders can be a part of moral life even when we do our very best to mitigate all harms. We can acknowledge that some options are better than others. The options that cause the least harm, demonstrate the most respectful stance toward all sentient animals, and that best acknowledge and address the ways in which exploitation and domination shape the dilemmas we face and the options available for facing them will be better than their alternatives. We may be "justified" in the sense that we pursued the option that is best among all the options. Justification, however, may not mean that we can say "done, clean, finished" once we have chosen the best available alternative. Moral work will likely remain. Margaret Urban Walker noted that our options will often be "imperfect," and that "residues and carry-overs" will be more common than not. "Moral problems," she says, "are nodal points in progressive histories of mutual adjustment and understanding, not 'cases' to be closed by a final verdict of a highest court" (1995, 145). This is not to say that all situations will result in moral remainders. Mercifully, there are times when we can identify the right thing to do, attend to all the needs involved, and feel content in the knowledge that we have set things right.

Still, especially in a world dominated by patriarchal and speciesist ideology, many interanimal and intracultural conflicts of interest will result in moral remainders. Respecting animals can come at a cost to our most important relationships. We disappoint by defending; they disappoint by aggressively rejecting our values. My view is that these moral remainders are an important part of the context of conflicts of interest. Understanding the moral remainders generated by our choices helps us to both determine which is the right choice and know what moral work to undertake once the choice is made. Part of my deliberation over whether or not to eat my grandmother's chicken soup involves the recognition that if I refuse her soup, I generate a moral remainder that requires attention. Here it is reasonable to ask two questions: (1) if this is really more a question of hurt feelings than a *moral* issue. Sure, my grandmother's feelings are hurt, but why would that generate a moral remainder? People's feelings are frequently hurt and not always because we have done something wrong or failed in some way. (2) What generates a moral remainder if a duty or obligation has not been neglected? One is not obligated to eat their grandmother's soup or hunt deer with their uncle. Why would a refusal to do either generate a moral remainder?[3]

The answer to both these questions is similar. Regarding the first question, when we choose to forego the soup or the hunting trip out of an ethical commitment to animals, we disappoint and hurt people we love, compromise our relationships, and alienate ourselves from our families and communities. In turn, people we love

[3]My thanks to Kyle Joannsen who raised this objection when I presented an early version of Chapter 5.

are disappointing; they hurt us with their lack of care, curiosity, and inclusivity. This is more than simply an issue of hurt feelings; it is a moral issue. We come to expect certain things of one another, and our relationships play out according to a narrative that generates and reinforces those expectations (Walker 1995, 142). When I refuse my grandmother's soup, I have not merely hurt her feelings (though it is morally relevant that I have done so), I have also changed the nature of our relationship. As a person in caring relationship with others, part of my job is recognizing the specific details of the relationship and expectations at hand and attending to those in ways that take seriously the damage done by my choices. Those more focused on matters of justice might miss why these are moral matters. From an ethics of care perspective, the answer is clear. Virginia Held wrote that deontological and utilitarian approaches "are not suited for contexts such as family relations and friends, where it is the particularity of persons (not their universal features) that matters most" (2006, 73). Close and loving relationships are not built solely around considerations of justice. Held made this point when she wrote that "when in society individuals treat each other with only the respect that justice requires but no further consideration, the social fabric of trust and concern can be missing or disappearing" (2006, 71; cf. Alvaro 2019). Held noted that the ethics of care views persons as relational:

> The ethic of care ... conceptualizes persons as deeply affected by, and involved in, relations with others; to many care theorists persons are at least partly constituted by their social ties. The ethics of care attends especially to relations between persons, evaluating such relations and valuing relations of care. It does not assume that relations relevant for morality have been entered into voluntarily by free and equal individuals, as do dominant moral theories. It appreciates as well the values of care between persons of unequal power in unchosen relations such as those between parents and children and between members of social groups of various kinds. To the ethics of care, our embeddedness in familial, social, and historical contexts is basic. (46)

This understanding of human relationships is not limited to the realm of feminist care ethics. As Rabbi Rachel Adler wrote:

> Sin in the context of relationship, is not a transgression of an abstract norm, but an injury toward an Other rendered vulnerable by his/her trust. T'Shuvah [return] is turning again to face the Other, not to annul what has occurred, but to sew up the wounds and determine how to go on. Relationships bear scars because they have a memory. As memories accumulate, they carry consequences that bind us. They retell how we must become, what we must recreate, what we must repay. (1983, 93)

Thinking of relationships from the care, rather than the justice, perspective, we can see that when we unilaterally shift what can be expected from a relationship, we potentially undermine trust. Moral life includes assessing and understanding the nature of *relations* and not merely the individuals who make up those relationships (Held 2006, 52–3). Of course, relationships can be modified or ended, but where relationships are healthy, "a caring person will appropriately value caring relations and will seek to modify existing relations to make them more caring" (ibid.). The moral remainders that can arise from defending animals and disappointing loved ones are rooted in this relational conception of the moral life where how we attend to one another, whether we recognize need and offer loving attention, whether we seek to understand one another, and whether we are curious and open to what is happening for the other is a moral matter. Certainly, these matters of care are important for all parties to the relationship. Hence, in Chapters 4–6 I articulate clearly both what the animal advocate must do to address moral remainders and what their loved ones must do to uphold their part in a loving, caring relationship.

The second question asks how a moral remainder can be generated if no specific duty or obligation is ignored or overlooked. Moral life is not fully captured by assessing who has or does not have a duty and what did or did not go wrong in fulfilling one's duties. I likely do not have a *duty* to eat my grandmother's soup, but I still cause relational harm by not eating it. Similarly, the would-be former hunter's father likely does not have a *duty* to refrain from hunting out of respect for his son's love of animals, but something goes wrong from a care perspective when he grabs his rifle and returns with a bloody carcass during his son's visit home from college. Ethics is not entirely encapsulated by reference to duties and obligations. Marti Kheel summed this up when she wrote, "'Rights' or 'interests' are based upon abstract principles, not relations of care. Correct moral conduct, therefore, entails applying rules to concrete situations. By contrast, ecofeminist vegetarian theorists typically focus on the importance of relationships, particularly those based on care" (2008, 233). The idea that the moral life involves more than considerations of justice is contentious to be sure. Engaging with that debate goes beyond the scope of this book. One hope of mine is that, in reading the chapters ahead, those who are skeptical of an ethic that involves both justice and care can find reasons to open their minds. Consulting their own experience as a moral being facing the conflicts I discuss in this work might also help. I think most of us know what it means to feel we have not overlooked an obligation but nevertheless have failed morally from the standpoint of care.

With all of this in mind, relational vegan ecofeminism's approach to interanimal conflicts of interest includes identifying the moral remainders that result when we choose to respect animals' interests in cases of highly valued human interests tied to relationships of love and care. Peter Singer appears optimistic that we can integrate our moral commitments to animals into our existing communities easily, thus relieving the worry of alienation from friends and family with different values (Singer 1990, 182–3). The experience of many vegans does not conform to Singer's easy vision. Sociological research provides empirical backing for the felt experience of many vegans that they are alienated from their communities (Greenebaum 2012; McDonald 2000; Twine 2014, 2016). In most cases of intracultural and interanimal conflicts of interest there will be moral remainders. An adequate theory will have something to say about how to identify and approach these remainders.

Identifying moral remainders is crucial in helping us both adjudicate and resolve conflicts of interest. Knowing what moral remainders might be generated by different actions and understanding what possibilities for addressing those remainders exist is vital to conflict adjudication as well as what actions should follow after we adjudicate. Noticing and attending to what is happening relationally in intracultural and interanimal conflicts of interest aids us in resolving the conflicts by pointing to opportunities for relational moral attention. We both notice the potential for moral remainders while adjudicating, noting what important relational values are at stake as part of that process, and attend to the moral remainders as part of the process post-adjudication. Thus, I introduce the concept of relational moral attention into relational vegan ecofeminism. Relational moral attention integrates elements of Margaret Urban Walker's concept of moral repair, Claire Jean Kim's concept of mutual avowal, and features of virtue ethics and the ethics of care.

As Margaret Urban Walker defines it, "Moral repair is restoring or creating trust and hope in a shared sense of value and responsibility" (Walker 2006: 28). I use the term in a related, but different, way. Walker addresses the moral work that is necessary after considerable wrongdoing. Her paradigmatic cases of moral repair are communities where genocides have occurred. I suggest that the concept also applies to more quotidian situations. I invoke it here because moral repair is work we undertake to sustain moral relationships when they have been damaged. The reparative work in question in the conflicts under discussion here is not a general kind of relationship repair but *moral* repair because relationships have moral valences and there are sometimes morally salient features of relationships that have been damaged in cases where one turns away from one's family and community in favor of other values. This is true even in some cases when the values those communities or families hold are wrong in and of themselves (here I have in mind cases involving speciesist values in particular). This is important. We must not simply go along with the traditions of our people when those traditions are morally problematic. Yet, even where those practices are immoral, our turning away from them, challenging them, or attempting to shift them can cause a moral cost in important relationships. At times, this will manifest in a breach of trust because relationships are built in part on shared expectations of how we will be with one another. When one party to the relationship unilaterally defies those expectations, it can feel like betrayal.[4] Walker's moral repair in the world of genocide, apartheid, and other social atrocities emphasizes a return to shared values and trust in mutually held norms. This is an important part of relational moral attention in the case of intracultural and interanimal conflicts of interest where trust has been eroded and there is a sense that we have lost our shared connection to established moral norms.

Of course, in intracultural and interanimal conflicts of interest, we are not faced with reparative justice for horrific wrongs (or crimes against humanity) requiring all of the elements Walker outlines (2006). Walker's conception of moral repair is relevant insofar as it emphasizes attending to the other, recognizing that where once norms were shared and predictable they no longer are, and contemplating how that impacted and continues to impact others. It involves thinking about trust, how it has been broken or wounded, and how to undertake repair. Another difference in the cases Walker and I consider is that in situations of gross injustice, reparative work in the form of listening to and understanding others' pain, offering some form or reparation, and attempting to reinstate trust involves more active work by the wrongdoer or their representatives than the wronged. In intracultural conflicts about asserting one's commitment to animals over the interests our loved ones have in shared traditions and practices, however, the reparative work necessitates bidirectional repair.[5] The vegan must engage in reparative efforts with his loved ones, and the loved ones must engage in reparative efforts with the vegan. Often, there is not one party that is more responsible than the other for the relational harms. This is quite different from cases of genocide, for example.

Relational moral attention also includes mutual avowal. As Claire Kim articulates it, mutual avowal means an "open and active acknowledgment of connection with other struggles. … If disavowal is a closing off, a repudiation, a turning away from, avowal is an opening, a recognition, a turning toward" (2015, 20). In her work, Kim is specifically discussing others' social justice struggles, for example, Michael Vick's status as a Black man facing systemic racism and how that intersected with animal advocates' critique of his dogfighting operation. In that case, animal advocates willfully refused to see the ways anti-Black racism intersected with public discourse about Vick. At the same time, Vick's defenders refused to engage with the speciesism and domination central to the cruelty of dog fighting. When parties practice mutual avowal, according to Kim, they acknowledge and seek to understand the social justice claims of those with whom

---

[4]A literary example of such a case is Nick Hornby's novel *How to Be Good* in which a hitherto selfish and grouchy man suddenly decides to follow a stringent moral commitment to not possessing anything more than is absolutely needed to survive much to the horror of his physician wife and one of their children.

[5]Twine (2016, 260).

they disagree. Kim is clear that this does not rule out critique. One can practice mutual avowal while also offering critiques of a practice (182).

In intracultural conflicts, the issue may not manifest in the necessity to practice mutual avowal of this specific form. Intraculturally there may be issues of differing social justice claims between the parties, but there may not. Mutual avowal remains relevant to relational moral attention, however, in its insistence on taking up the other's issues as one's own; in refusing the urge to tell ourselves "this has nothing to do with me" (20). One way we show loving attention to one another in relationships is not only by acknowledging the struggles of those we love but also in acknowledging and showing respect for their values (where those values are worthy of respect—more on that later). Disavowal only drives us further apart. Where relationships or values are pernicious, disavowal may be necessary. Where there is love and care, however, avowal is crucial. Again, as Kim rightly notes, this need not rule out critique. I can acknowledge and make my business that which is important to you without endorsing it. I can turn toward rather than away while also rejecting my loved one's values. Indeed, critique can demonstrate relationality, care, and inclusiveness by showing someone that they are important enough to warrant difficult and uncomfortable conversations.

Relational moral attention is deeply rooted in an ethic of care, attending to the other, taking seriously their status as an individual with their particular needs and perspectives. We look toward the other and see what a loving response will entail. This does not necessitate reneging on our moral commitments just as lovingly responding to young children in our lives does not mean relenting to their demands. Sometimes in life you just have to put your shoes on even when you are three years old and seriously object to the concept. We can insist on that truth while acknowledging that it is cause for frustration and a sense of lack of agency. We can lovingly hold that frustration, even sometimes patiently awaiting a tantrum to end, while insisting on the necessity of footwear when going to the park. Similarly, I will not relent in my veganism to join a friend on a fishing expedition, but I can acknowledge and attend to his feelings and seek other ways to address the need for connection with me. He should do that for me by realizing that inviting me to fish with him is akin to inviting me to bash people in the knees with a baseball bat. There is no way I am going to do it. I find it morally repugnant and deeply upsetting. Responding lovingly to my particularity means learning to invite me for a walk or a kayaking adventure on the lake without rods and reels.

Finally, relational moral attention will involve identifying and exhibiting the virtues of compassion, patience, curiosity, and respect for others. Relational moral attention involves asking ourselves who we want to be and how we want to behave in this moment. Does a compassionate person respond to my grandmother's distress about my refusing her soup with lectures and arguments about chickens' moral status or does she turn toward my grandmother with love and mutual avowal? Does a person with respect for others plan a family hunting trip when one of the family members is a stalwart animal advocate? We must all ask ourselves what sort of person we want to be and whether we are living up to that expectation for ourselves. This may sound simplistic, but truly so many difficulties vegans encounter with their communities and loved ones would be far less charged if all parties would ask themselves this. Remembering who we are and what virtues we wish to embody goes a long way toward helping us provide the best kind of relational moral attention to one another. If we do not want to be a party to cruelty, reminding ourselves of this fact will enable us to better meet others where they are with compassion and care.

I say much more about relational moral attention in Part 2. As I emphasize there, in cases where such attention is warranted and desirable, caching out what that process involves will depend on the details. What is possible with my grandmother may not be possible with yours. The norms of one's family, the personalities and histories of the parties involved, and the details of the various background conditions all matter. Relationships take many forms and have different power dynamics. The ethics of care and the work or repair is about particular individuals with distinct relationships. Put another way, care ethics involves more than addressing type (human) by attending to token (*this* human—my mother Janet, my father Michael) with all their individual particularities. There are needs humans have qua humans (food, water, shelter, opportunities for creativity, etc.), and then there are needs individuals have because of who they are specifically. Janet does not require scuba diving to be happy, but Michael certainly does. Therefore, the nature of this approach precludes offering one standard for how to address the need for relational moral attention.

Two crucial questions arise about relational moral attention. First, so far, my discussion of relational moral attention has focused solely on relationships between humans. As this is an animal ethics book, one might ask whether there is an opportunity for relational moral attention between humans and other animals and what role, if any, that would play in understanding and responding to conflicts of interest. Second, one might wonder whether the work of relational moral attention must be undertaken in *all* cases. If our relatives are rude, cantankerous, misogynistic, and so forth, must we address moral remainders or engage in relational moral attention at all?

With respect to the first question about whether relational moral attention is possible and important between humans and other animals, I believe it is. It is certainly possible to practice relational moral attention with other animals, as we see in the very best kind of care for them in true sanctuaries and other settings where humans care for and relate to animals in ways that practice repair, avowal, care, and the virtues of compassion, humility, respect, and so forth (Donaldson and Kymlicka 2015; Doyle 2017; Emmerman 2014; Jones 2014). Moreover, thinking and feeling our way through our relationships with other animals is crucial for contextualizing interanimal conflicts of interest for those relationships shape and create the conflicts we face. Perhaps most importantly, however, I maintain that relational moral attention and the recognition of its limitations in the cross-species setting must factor into how we adjudicate conflicts in the first place.

I have said cross-species relational moral attention is certainly possible and necessary, but it is also limited. It is often far more difficult to undertake the work of addressing moral remainders across species than it is within our own. Acts of relational moral attention can appear as acts of aggression to some animals, for example, inducing extreme fear. They do not necessarily understand our intentions. Our ministrations may be unwelcomed intrusions. We may not be in a position to do reparative work with the individual animals harmed. If we override animals' interests, we may do so in ways that provide material support for their continued suffering as when we fuel the exploitation of animals by purchasing their flesh for consumption—our dollars reinforcing demand for animal products. Relational moral attention in such cases seems impossible for we are not in direct relationship with, nor can we attend to the needs of, the specific animals involved. We can perhaps undertake actions to expiate what we have done (e.g., giving money to a sanctuary caring for similar animals), but that will do nothing for the animals hurt now.

This is a different situation than we find ourselves in with the beloved humans in our lives. They are sometimes right in front of us, communicating in the same ways we do, able to see actions grounded in relational moral attention for the expressions of care they are. They can receive immediately our work of avowal and the results of our commitment to being just, compassionate, and respectful. This may not result in uptake on their part, but the opportunity is available and the possibility for repair open. Since this is often not the case when we override other animals' interests it is one reason to think that we ought to resolve our intracultural and interanimal conflicts of interest in the animals' favor. Whether and how much relational moral repair is possible is one contextual feature to consider when facing such conflicts. The impossibility of repair for animals in many cases will explain why for vegans these intracultural conflicts often involve defending the animals rather than overriding their interests in service of our important relationships.

The second question regarding whether we owe relational moral attention to all people with whom we are in some sort of relationship no matter how pernicious their values or how awfully they treat us requires a longer response. I address this in various places in Part 2, in Chapters 4 and 6 in particular. The quick answer to the question of whether we owe relational moral attention to all people we are in relationship with when we choose obligations to animals over culturally or relationally important practices (or in other scenarios where conflicts in values arise) is no. As usual, however, the details of the relationships—whether they are themselves toxic, whether the parties can reasonably be expected to communicate openly and compassionately with one another, whether violence has taken place, and so forth—will matter considerably here. We are not obligated to undertake the work of moral repair with every distant, grouchy relative who finds our moral commitments an affront to their sense of tradition. In the context of this project, relational moral attention is the work we undertake to address the moral remainders generated by our choices to respect animal's moral value rather than our families' important traditions. While feminist ethics identifies the importance of caring relationships, it also recognizes that some relationships are pernicious and, therefore, not of the morally valuable sort (Gruen 1999). Some relationships are damaging in ways that call for significant revision and some must be given up altogether (Held 2006, 49–50). Peter Railton once noted that some forms of "social criticism or cultural innovation" may require that individuals or groups alienate themselves from their social context (1984, 148). With respect to some relatives, there may be no moral remainder either because of a lack of relationship or because the existing relationship is unhealthy. Similarly, there may be no place for relational moral attention because there is no functional relationship to which we can attend or because the values espoused by our loved ones are hateful. Though even in the latter case all hope is not necessarily lost. Turning toward one another and meeting people where they are while holding them to account can affect significant and lasting change (Saslow).

3 Is Allowing for Compromise Speciesist?

As readers will see, the deeply contextual and relational nature of relational vegan ecofeminism means there may be situations in which it is appropriate or permissible to compromise one's veganism in service of relationships of love and care. It may be appropriate at times to defend people and disappoint animals. I intend for these situations to be rare and result in overriding animals' interests only after careful contextual consideration. There is much nuance to the matter of defending people and disappointing animals that I hope is clarified over the course of the book. For now, I address one worry about the space I create for outcomes that prioritize relationships over animals' interests.

In particular, one might wish to ask why we would take this approach to vegan values, an approach that includes flexibility and the potential for compromising those values, when we would not in other kinds of moral cases like stealing, actively polluting the environment, or committing acts of racism, transphobia, or misogyny. If the family tradition were to gather annually to rob and then burn down a random neighbor's house no compromise would be possible no matter how much we love and care for our family members. Burglary and arson are a hard pass ethically. Is that because they involve harm to humans? Am I for occasional compromise with actions concerning animals due to speciesism? Is compromise only available because somewhere, deep down inside even the most committed vegan lies acceptance of the moral inferiority of other-than-human animals?[6]

The availability of some limited compromise when it comes to interanimal and intracultural conflicts of interest does not reveal a deep-seated speciesist worldview. Rather, it points to the complex and unique nature of the context surrounding these kinds of conflicts and the epistemic states most people are in with respect to human relationships with other animals. As I will argue in Chapter 4 regarding traditional and culturally important foods, in many situations where these conflicts arise the animal is already slaughtered and cooked, for example. This is unlike the annual burglary/arson tradition in that the harm has already been done. My refusing to partake of the soup makes no difference at all to the animal harmed for the meal. Therefore, there is room for the relational issues to take precedence on *some rare occasions*. My grandmother might be dying, so this could be a situation where compromise is possible (more on this in Chapter 4). As I argue in Chapter 5, since recreational hunting involves killing an animal who would otherwise survive, compromise is not available in that case. The details of the situation are significant to adjudicating conflicts, as are the possibilities for relational moral attention toward those who are harmed as a result of our choices.

Moreover, people are in different positions epistemically regarding speciesism than they are with respect to other forms of marginalization. Notwithstanding the political climate in the United States in 2026, there has been considerable open discussion about some other "isms" (e.g., racism, sexism, ableism, heterosexism). Conversations around speciesism are comparatively far behind. There are no lessons in schools detailing animal exploitation and abuse or tying human consumer choices to that exploitation and abuse, for example. Though I believe at least some people living in industrial societies are culpable for their ignorance about animals' suffering at human hands, it is undeniably true that public discussion of the "animal issue" is in a very different place than it is about other sorts of social justice issues. For example, there is wide public disagreement over issues involving racism and transphobia but very little regarding our treatment of animals. Thus, decisions about whether to defend animals or defend people must include consideration of what we can reasonably expect our loved ones to know and understand in an anthroparchal world. Similarly, these decisions will reflect recognition of issues of dependency and whether the individuals in question depend on one another in ways that influence the options available to them. An adolescent being raised by her grandmother is in a different situation than one who visits her grandmother

[6]My thanks to participants at the Kline workshop for raising this important issue and to Bob Fischer and Asia Ferrin in particular for helpful discussions about this issue. I am grateful to Bob for raising the issue of the different epistemic states people are in with regarding to speciesism versus some other "isms," discussed later.

on occasional weekends and holidays. Depending on the details, that difference may render it more or less difficult for the adolescent to challenge familial norms. Sunaura Taylor makes the important point that absolutism about veganism can marginalize people with disabilities. It is possible, she notes, to care deeply for animal rights while physiologically requiring animal protein for survival (2017, 200–4). Again, we see how important the particulars are.

Finally, and perhaps most controversially for animal advocates, I posit that we are kidding ourselves if we say that a real vegan never compromises or never chooses other considerations over animals. This is a grief-inducing realization for many of us, but it is undeniably true. Again, I explain this in detail in the remainder of the book but will briefly address it here. Every time we take a medication tested on animals, hop on an airplane for an "unnecessary trip" to visit distant loved ones, buy produce from farms exploiting their farmworkers or using farming methods deadly to field animals, and so forth we are either compromising vegan values or at least allowing other considerations to override those values. This is not because we are horrible people or that we secretly endorse speciesism. Rather, it is because (1) some conflicts just are not satisfactorily resolvable at this point in time—most medications we take are tested on animals no matter how much we wish that were not true, justice for farmworkers is a lengthy political battle, and so on; and (b) some actions are incredibly important from the relational point of view and contextual details reveal that prioritizing those relationships might be necessary or permissible in a given case.

I take my migraine medication despite it having been tested on animals. I fed my premature son infant formula that included nonvegan vitamin D3 when he was in neonatal intensive care because, of the options available to me at the time, it was the one I could manage (Emmerman 2022), I have certainly consumed vegetables and fruits harvested by exploited workers, and I travel to visit friends in need and even for fun occasionally though I know doing so negatively impacts the planet for all living beings. I do all these things not because I disvalue animal lives but because the moral life is complex. Thus, I invite readers to remember that even the most committed vegan makes compromises in their values or prioritizes other values over vegan commitments from time to time. This is not indicative of speciesism on our part. Rather, it highlights the way the world is arranged during late-stage capitalism, how complicated it is to live a human life with all the competing values we face, and how considering relationships of love and care with others complicates (and enriches!) our moral worlds. My sincere hope is that relational vegan ecofeminism with its focus on relational moral attention will significantly reduce the number of situations where it might be appropriate to disappoint animals rather than loved ones. Declaring by fiat that such outcomes must never arise, however, fails to grasp contextual complexity and perpetuates the falsity that if we simply will it to be so we can always—in all times, across all situations—prioritize the animals we love so much. Claims to that kind of moral purity are profoundly suspicious.

4 Animal Use and Abuse

In a world that systematically devalues and exploits living beings an awakening must occur in order to take them seriously. A person needs to be jolted out of the unnoticed conceptual framework supporting this objectification and exploitation long enough to see that what we do to animals all day every day, day after day, warrants significant concern and attention. The facts of animal abuse are largely unchallenged by the industries that bear the responsibility for animal exploitation. Contentiousness arises when we question whether that abuse is warranted, justified, permissible, and necessary. The sheer number of animals harmed and killed by humans on an annual basis is staggering. In the United States alone we raise and slaughter 10 billion animals annually for human consumption, we use approximately 100 million for animal research, and we hunt and kill somewhere on the order of 100 million animals yearly. Animal agriculture contributes significantly to climate change and environmental destruction (Adams and Gruen 2022; MacDonald 2022; Twine 2021, 2024). Marginalized humans are significantly harmed and sometimes killed in the industries that bring us ubiquitous and cheap animal flesh foods (Food Empowerment Project, "Slaughterhouse Workers"; Pachirat 2011; Schlosser 2001).

Access to detailed information about animal suffering is one excellent way to awaken to the truth of humans' domination over those animals' lives and welfare. Thus, many books concerning animal ethics commence with a detailed discussion of animal use and abuse. This one does not. My starting place is that caring about animals' suffering is important, and that humans should feel deep species shame for our unjustified use and abuse of our Earth fellows. There are plentiful resources available for learning about animal exploitation. If readers need to be convinced that animals matter, that the way we humans treat them is morally reprehensible, and that this must change I invite them to avail themselves of these resources. An excellent start is Mark Hawthorne's *Bleating Hearts: The Hidden World of Animal Suffering* (2013), Peter Singer's *Animal Liberation* (first published in the 1970s but the information he provides sadly remains largely unchanged), Jo-Anne McArthur's stunning photojournalism, the many excellent documentaries and websites accessible on the internet, and the large volume of excellent academic research and writing on the topic. I will gesture at the realities of how humans treat other animals throughout the book, but my focus is on the relational moral complications that stem from taking other-than-human animals seriously rather than on arguing for why they matter morally. I therefore leave it to others to provide the specifics of our deeply entangled and problematic relationships with fellow creatures. If readers cannot relate to a person who adopts veganism as an act of resistance, care, and commitment to nonviolence, I wholeheartedly welcome them to substitute some other strong ethical stance that does resonate with them. The ethical approach I articulate is applicable to most situations in which one's principled objections to the harms in the world and commitment to making our planet a kinder, more compassionate place set them at odds with the traditions of their families and communities.

5 Notes on Terminology

There are several terms, some common some less common, used in the animal ethics literature that warrant brief explanation before readers begin Part 1. Jargon can be off-putting and unnecessarily intimidating, so I avoid it as much as possible. At the same time, there exist specific words for specific concepts or phenomena that are helpful to thinking together about important ideas. Among those I use are:

Animal—More recently, some animal ethicists including myself have shifted toward using the language of "other-than-human animals" or "animal others" to highlight the absurdity and dangers of the false human/animal binary. Humans are animals just like bears, hares, and mares are animals. I use "animal others" and "other-than-human animals" in places but primarily use "animals" to refer to our other-than-human Earth fellows. This is simply due to prioritizing brevity.

Speciesism—Whereas "carnism" (see definition later) refers specifically to the belief system grounding conceptions around which animals are for eating and why, "speciesism" refers more generally to an unwarranted bias for members of one's own species. Coined originally by Richard Ryder, the term is most often associated with Peter Singer. "Speciesism" is used broadly in the animal ethics literature to refer to preferencing human interests over animals' interests even in cases where the human interests at issue are the same as or significantly less important than the animals' interests. Speciesism is often grounded in a belief in human exceptionalism or superiority.

Anthroparchy—Less common than "speciesism," "anthroparchy" refers to "'human domination'" and "a social system, a complex and relatively stable set of relationships in which 'the environment' is dominated through formations of social organization which privilege the human" (Calvo 2008, 33). It is used in place of "anthropocentrism" and "speciesism" to highlight the structural and systemic nature of the oppression and exploitation of nature and animals. Readers can think about the distinction between "patriarchy" and "sexism" where the former refers to an oppressive belief system that systematically devalues women and anything associated with the feminine whereas the latter points to a limited problem of discrimination or even an individual instance of sex-based discrimination that may simply be a personal failing rather than indicative of a broader set of systemically discriminatory beliefs. I will use "speciesism" when discussing Singer and "anthroparchy" on other occasions.

Carnist/carnism—Coined by Melanie Joy, carnism refers to "the belief system that conditions us to eat certain animals" and expresses an ideology of shared beliefs and related practices that are often invisible to us (Joy 2010, 29–31). These beliefs and practices are unquestioned, seen as the norm, and often go unnoticed. I will use "carnism" when referring to the practice of eating animal flesh and "carnist" to refer to those who eat animal flesh in this unquestioning way.

Farmed/zooed—I refer to animals used in farming as "farmed animals" and animals held captive in zoos as "zooed animals." This highlights the reality that there is no such thing as a "farm" or a "zoo" animal in nature. The terms naturalize that which is the result of human decision-making.[7]

Vegan—When I refer to veganism, I refer specifically to ethical veganism, which "is a commitment to try to abstain from consuming products derived from animals including meat, dairy, and eggs, as well as products derived from or containing animal products as an ingredient" (Gruen and Jones 2016). In particular, the paradigmatic vegan at the heart of this book is one for whom animals' moral standing is a considerable factor. Ethical veganism is distinguished from other forms of veganism centered on health concerns rather than ethical commitments. In addition to the dietary commitments of ethical veganism described earlier, part of an ethical vegan framework includes a commitment to abstain from the use of animal products in clothing and accessories and a refusal to support recreational endeavors that exploit animals (e.g., zoos and rodeos). Some ethical vegans' reasons center on environmental ethical considerations rather than on animal welfare. Those who are vegan for health reasons and perhaps those whose veganism is rooted in concern for the environment may not feel the defending animals/disappointing people dilemma at all or as acutely as ethical vegans whose moral considerations include animal well-being as a significant concern.[8]

---

[7]For a discussion of verbal activism and an argument in favor of using "anymal" instead of "animal" as an act of verbal activism, see Kemmerer (2006).

[8]Research suggests that those who are vegetarian for health reasons face less significant social challenges than ethical vegetarians (Amato and Partridge 1989, 180–5).

6 Chapter Outline

Part 1: Theorizing Interanimal Conflicts of Interest

In Part 1, I focus on ethical theory, considering different approaches to interanimal and intracultural conflicts of interest. In Chapter 2, "Interests, Special Relations, and Context: Approaches to Interanimal Conflicts of Interest," I discuss the distinction between basic and nonbasic interests and several methods for adjudicating interanimal conflicts of interest. I begin with approaches centered on prioritizing interests—Peter Singer's, Paul Taylor's, Gary Varner's, and MaryAnne Warren's—arguing that they are inadequate. I then turn to "special relations" accounts of conflicts of interest, focusing on Nel Noddings and Mary Midgley, both of whom argued that there are ethically defensible reasons humans can prioritize humans' interests when conflicts arise. Midgley's position is more animal-centric than Nodding's, but in the end neither is appropriate for resolving interanimal conflicts of interest. Finally, I consider contextual approaches in the form of Carlo Alvaro's virtue ethics and Elisa Aaltola's multipronged approach steeped heavily in contextual understanding. Though my own approach is contextual, it differs from Alvaro's and Aaltola's.

In Chapter 3, "Relational Vegan Ecofeminism," I introduce and situate ecofeminist theory, discuss contextual moral vegetarianism, and differentiate between vegan ecofeminism and other forms of ecofeminist theory that center animals but do not advocate for strict veganism. I lay out the contextualized, pluralist, nonhierarchical, and relational features of relational vegan ecofeminism and explain how relational moral attention is vital to approaching interanimal and intracultural conflicts of interest. Like many feminist theories, my approach seeks to strike a balance between abstract principles and the particulars of cases (Curtin 1991; Donovan and Adams 2007a; Gruen 1993; Held 1995; Walker 1995). Rather than positing a fixed hierarchy of interests or life-forms, I offer a methodology that moves between the details of a case and guiding principles. I argue for taking relationships of love and care seriously in understanding humans' interests. The ecofeminist approach is deeply contextualized, taking social, political, economic, and other factors into account. It also takes seriously that what matters about animals is not simply their sentience (Singer, Varner) or their inherent worth (Regan, Taylor) but also their relationships of love and care, their desire to live their own lives according to their species-typical behaviors, and their status as individuals in and of themselves irrespective of their utility for humans. This leads us to Part 2 of the book where I discuss specific conflicts, how traditional animal ethics theories approach the issue, and how relational vegan ecofeminism employs relational moral attention to help mitigate conflicts where in defending animals we disappoint the people we love.

Part 2: Applying Relational Vegan Ecofeminism

In Part 2, I illuminate how relational vegan ecofeminism approaches conflicts of interest without setting out fixed rules for resolving conflicts instead illuminating important contextual considerations and offering options for a way forward. There are several questions that linger in the background of each of these conflicts. These questions center on when it is recommended to cut ties with loved ones whose values differ considerably from one's own, whether/when it might be permissible to set aside obligations to animals in service of maintaining loving relationships, what responsibilities those of us who adopt values antithetic to those held by the people we love might have to our loved ones when conflicts occur, and what responsibilities they might have to us.

Cultural foodways contribute extensively to identity. As Cathryn Bailey argues, "Ethnic foodways are not merely ornamental; rather, the reproduction of ethnic identity is, in part, dependent on their maintenance" (Bailey 2007, 47). Margaret Robinson wrestles with balancing veganism with a desire for cultural authenticity in Mi'kmaq culture (Robinson 2013). One could argue that much of Jonathan Safran Foer's *Eating Animals* is a meditation on the way food contributes to familial, cultural, and community identity (2009). Thus, in Chapter 4 I focus on conflicts between obligations to animals and familial and cultural traditions centered on food. Using the autobiographical example of being a Jewish vegan faced with a bowl of my grandmother's chicken soup, I demonstrate how the ecofeminist approach contextualizes the interest in the soup by recognizing the intersections of love, care, class, and gender embedded in the interest. I argue that, while certainly robust when fully contextualized, the interest in culturally important foods prepared by people we love most often should not override animals' interests. I discuss contexts where making an exception to veganism and eating those foods might be occasionally appropriate. Since most situations will involve defending animals and disappointing loved ones, I then show how my relational approach requires attending to the potentially damaging implications of that adjudication for the relationships of love and care tied to the interest in traditional foods. Expressing care, loving curiosity, and willingness to shift traditions are crucial elements of this work. The chapter ends with a discussion of complications including the complexity of identifying shared values, the argument that social obligations might occasionally require vegans to consume animal flesh (Fensmire 2015, 2024; Hare; Rubio), and consequentialist concerns around role modeling and negative social contagion (Almassi; Fischer).

Most animal activists and most animal ethicists are opposed to recreational hunting (i.e., hunting for sport). In Chapter 5, "The Buck (Killing) Stops Here: Contextualizing Recreational Hunting," I take up the dilemma posed by recreational, non-Indigenous, hunting in North America when it is steeped in relationships of love and care. I discuss the fifth-generation hunter as a stand-in for any person who has grown up in a family where recreational hunting is part of their family history and present. What does the fifth-generation hunter do when he awakens to animals' moral considerability and turns away from the family tradition? Ecofeminist theory has typically focused on describing hunting as an act rooted in patriarchal conceptions of value, dominance, and violence. While I agree with this analysis of recreational hunting, I argue that it obscures the important relational elements of hunting for many people socialized to hunting since youth and relies on an essentialized conception of masculinity (Littlefield 2006, 2010; Littlefield and Ozanne 2011; Marks 1991). How does a feminist theory that takes relationships, love, and care to be central to ethical deliberation handle a case where the interest in causing animals suffering and death is tied to important relationships and deeply held familial and cultural values? This case poses different questions than in Chapter 3 because activities involving killing animals take on an immediacy that may not be present in situations where, for example, the chicken used to make a traditional soup was slaughtered weeks ago and nothing we can do while sitting at the holiday table can change that. While recreational hunting is always impermissible on ecofeminist grounds, a fully contextualized understanding of some hunters' interests in hunting reveals important ethical dimensions for a feminist theory. After offering a deep dive into the context around recreational hunting, I take up the question of whether a moderated interest (e.g., wildlife photography rather than hunting with a gun) can count as fulfilling the interest in question as well as what relational moral attention looks like in these kinds of conflicts.

In Chapter 6, "No Zoo for You! Vegan Families in a Speciesist World," I discuss the moral dimensions of raising children as vegans. Rather than focusing on issues already covered in the literature (i.e., nutritional worries and how couples where only one parent is vegan should approach their child's diet) I look carefully at potential social and relational harms that vegan children face, how veganism can separate them from others in their families, and what relational moral attention can do to mitigate these issues. There is a tendency among vegan activists and theorists to either ignore or seriously understate the kinds of relational moral difficulties that arise in raising vegan children in a carnist and anthroparchal world.[9] My hope with this chapter is to provide a realistic consideration of at least some of the relational challenges and then point to opportunities for relational

[9]Peter Singer and Jim Mason, for example, devote an entire chapter of *The Ethics of What We Eat* to the ethics or raising vegan children without ever addressing issues of relationality (2006).

moral attention that can ease the burdens on children raised vegan, their parents, and their extended families. I take up the question of whether vegans should compromise on their vegan values when raising vegan children (by allowing their children to eat traditional foods or go to the zoo with their classmates, for example). In doing so, I point to the reasons vegan parents might consider compromise and the deeply contextual nature of such decisions.

In the concluding chapter, I take up two important questions. The first asks whether relational moral attention is plausible as an approach to mitigating these entrenched and complex conflicts of interest. This concern is especially poignant in 2026 when it feels as though much productive dialog over differences in values and ways of seeing the world has ceased. Still, I remain optimistic and hopeful for many reasons including that everyday expressions of care and loving attention are overlooked or undervalued on a regular basis while still making a profound difference in relationships. Second, given the deep challenges involved in resolving interanimal and intracultural conflicts of interest, one might wonder why we would even expect people to go so far beyond the boundaries of common morality to defend animals. It seems like far too much to ask. Finally, I point to opportunities to move the relational vegan ecofeminist project forward in future work.

My aim is to communicate thoughts and ideas in a way nonexperts can understand and relate to. Thus, I hope the entire book is interesting and relevant to all who read it including those not trained in academic philosophy. That said, I have structured the book so that readers more interested in application than in theory can start with Part 2, skipping over Part 1. This approach may require flipping back to Chapter 3 to understand the nuances of ecofeminism but should nevertheless work just fine, enabling readers to focus on what is most important to them.

Something I wish to flag for readers to keep in mind as they read is that the identification of which traditions are thought central to a group is not a value-neutral process. So many of the interanimal and intracultural conflicts we face arise because at some point particular practices were identified as central whereas others were marginalized. It is disappointing but unsurprising in an anthroparchal system that many of the traditions identified as central involve violence or domination of some sort. Why, for example, does recreational hunting appear more central an activity in some families than, say, a long-standing tradition of quilt-making? I discuss this in some detail in Chapter 4, but it warrants attention throughout the book. A question we must ask ourselves is why the more violent or exploitative practices are so often deemed more important than the ones involving artistry or care or compassion and how that shapes the dilemmas we face. Defending animals would be far less likely to disappoint people were traditions centered on artistry, creativity, care, and compassion considered just as or more important than traditions centered on domination and violence.

As we turn now to Chapter 2, I leave off with the words of Marti Kheel who articulated so beautifully the perspective she brought to her work and that I bring to mine:

> I bring to my critical work a perspective informed by (1) an ethical orientation that emphasizes the centrality of feelings of attachment and care; (2) a view of human maturity that entails deepening, not transcending, these feelings; (3) a vision of a post-patriarchal world that affirms diversity, not dualism; (4) an affirmation of the individual integrity of other-than-humans; (5) a belief in the importance of forging cross-generational links in nonviolent ways; and (6) an affirmation of the repetitive cycles of nature, including life and death. (2008, 15)

With this perspective guiding the way, with attention to the particulars of individual situations and relationships, and with a focus on care and loving attention it is possible to both defend animals and rather than merely not disappoint people, perhaps even delight them.

PART ONE

THEORIZING INTERANIMAL CONFLICTS OF INTEREST

2 INTERESTS, SPECIAL RELATIONS, AND CONTEXT: APPROACHES TO INTERANIMAL CONFLICTS OF INTEREST

Most philosophers who think about the moral status of animals must at some point confront the question of what to do when human and animal interests conflict. Once we take animals seriously as part of the moral community, we are flooded with interanimal conflicts. Our lives are intertwined with animals' lives to such an extent that our interests conflict quite regularly. Often, these conflicts are mundane to the point where they barely register for us—perhaps our cat desperately wants to sit on our computer keyboard as we work frantically toward a deadline. Sometimes the conflicts are of a moderate nature—as when our community wants to build a new library and the most affordable site is home to a family of otters or rabbits. Some conflicts are matters of life or death: someone enjoying a hike in the woods encounters a bear protecting her cubs. Others involve determining whether humans should raise and slaughter animals for food, medical experimentation, and entertainment. Unless a human faces an apex predator in the wild, more often than not it is the animals' lives on the line with humans holding their fate in our hands.

In what follows, I will consider several different approaches to interanimal conflicts of interest and explain why they are inadequate. I group the approaches according to the root structure their theory relies on for articulating how to make ethical decisions in cases of conflict. The first group I consider is the "Categorization and Prioritization of Interests Approaches." This is by far the dominant system for approaching conflicts of interest, and it relies on determining what kind of interests are at stake and providing a theory for how they should be understood and hierarchized. I call the second group "Relations-Based Approaches." Rather than focusing on a detailed discussion of interests, these approaches think more about the role our relationships play in determining priority in conflicts. Finally, I consider the "Contextual Approaches" where interests play a role at times, but the focus is on either (1) understanding the particularities of situations rather than on building static hierarchies or (2) cultivating the right kinds of virtues so that one's moral character is reliably capable of making good decisions when conflicts arise. Before turning to the Categorization and Prioritization of Interests Approaches, I will say a few words about interests generally and about the distinction commonly made between basic and nonbasic interests in particular.

At times, when we use "interests" we mean things that are good for us (e.g., the interest in adequate nutrition). Other times, we use "interests" more colloquially to indicate things that we want or that capture our attention (e.g., the interest in going to a movie). Yet, interests do not always fall cleanly into either category. The object of our interest might both captivate our attention and be a necessary part of a good life. Alternatively, the object of our interest might not be something we find captivating but is nevertheless good for us. My interest in regular trips to the dentist is in this category. As I demonstrate in this book, some of the interests in play when vegans wrestle with commitments to animals and relationships with loved ones are of a more complicated kind. My interest in my grandmother's chicken soup counts as an interest in the colloquial sense of something I am interested in, for example, but it also needs to be understood as an interest in the deeper sense because of its role in my identity and important relationships.

As a result of the ubiquity of conflicts that arise when we take animals seriously, most philosophers working in animal ethics include discussions of priority in their work. One very common way to adjudicate competing claims is to point to a difference between basic and nonbasic interests and claim that categorizing interests according to that binary serves as a normative guide in helping resolve conflicts. As Peter Singer describes them, basic interests are related to our subsistence conditions. Basic interests are those interests whose satisfaction is a necessary condition for the satisfaction of further interests. For humans, they are limited to food, shelter, medical care, and some form of education. Nonbasic interests are those related to anything beyond what humans require to survive (Singer 1979a, 161).[1] There may be some minor disagreement about how much

[1]Cf. Singer (1972). Many, though not all, ethicists accept the idea of basic interests as the most fundamental subsistence conditions necessary to live. Feminist theory has much more to say about love and care being essential for human thriving. For other, more robust conceptions of basic interests see Scheffler (1992, 122) and Williams (1973, 1981).

education counts as a basic interest, for example, but the base conditions for sustaining life are generally agreed upon. Nonbasic interests, however, are more contentious. The taxonomy of nonbasic interests, how we think about them and what importance they have, varies quite a bit among animal ethicists who think about prioritization. It is this difference in approach to nonbasic interests that differentiates the Categorization and Prioritization of Interests approaches from one another.

1 Categorization and Prioritization of Interests Approaches

1.1 Peter Singer's Utilitarian Approach

I begin with Peter Singer's utilitarian view because his presents the most straightforwardly minimalist conception of human interests. I call his a "minimalist" conception because he has a very thin idea of what counts as a basic interest for human beings that he combines with an unnuanced view of humans' nonbasic interests. In particular, Singer thinks humans have a basic interest in adequate food, shelter, and medical care as well as some minimal amount of education. These are, as he says, the "basic necessities of life" (1979a, 161.). All other human interests are nonbasic. He argues that nonbasic interests should not override basic interests. Anyone reading his work is quickly struck by the numerous ways in which animals' basic interests are violated regularly in service of humans' nonbasic interests. Factory farming, circuses, zoos, and rodeos are just a few of the pursuits we engage in that cause significant harm to animals to fulfill humans' comparatively less important interests. Reading Singer, one is left with the impression that there is considerable work to be done toward improving our treatment of animals. Indeed, there is. There is much to be grateful for in Singer's many contributions to raising awareness of animal suffering and of humans' obligations to end practices responsible for that suffering.

Yet, as I will show, Singer's minimalist account errs on the side of trivializing humans' nonbasic interests. In doing so, his theory does not provide a way for moral agents to address some of the deep complexity they face when interests attached to relationships of love, care, identity, and cultural traditions conflict with animals' basic interests. I have two concerns about Singer's categorization and hierarchy of interests: (1) that his taxonomy of interests appears quite clear but is in fact ambiguous and (2) that his decontextualization of humans' nonbasic interests is deeply problematic.

In *Animal Liberation* Singer offered his argument for the moral considerability of animals. Following Bentham and Mill in their utilitarian framework, Singer argued that the only morally relevant characteristic is whether or not a being has interests and, in particular, an interest in not suffering. Since animals do have an interest in avoiding unnecessary suffering, it would be wrong to dismiss animals morally. The reason we cannot kick kittens for pure enjoyment is that kittens are sentient creatures and we are required to take their suffering into consideration when we deliberate about which actions we will pursue. Equal consideration of interests involves treating like interests alike regardless of who they belong to. Singer tells us that "the basic principle of equality does not require equal or identical treatment; it requires equal consideration" (Singer 1990, 3).[2] Chimpanzees do not have an interest in taking in a Broadway show, so I do nothing wrong when I give my extra ticket to my best friend instead of to the chimpanzee at the sanctuary nearby. Chimpanzees do, however, have an interest in not suffering. Thus, I do something very wrong if I do not give equal consideration to the chimpanzee's suffering when I deliberate over whether to subject her or my neighbor to a life in captivity for human entertainment and edification.[3]

Singer tags as "speciesist" all positions that grant precedence to human interests on the sole basis that the interests at stake belong to humans. In doing so, these views pick out a morally irrelevant characteristic (membership in the species *Homo sapiens*) and employ it to settle moral questions. Singer likens speciesism to racism and sexism (1990, 9). Just as the sexist employs the morally irrelevant characteristic of one's sex to settle conflicts of interest, the speciesist employs the morally irrelevant characteristic of species. Singer enjoins us to take all suffering into consideration no matter whose suffering it is, and he argues that failing to do so is to draw moral boundaries in the wrong places. We do not perform invasive research on cognitively impaired humans despite their impaired reasoning ability, so why, Singer asks, would we be justified in causing the same amount of pain to a chimpanzee or another animal with similar cognitive capacities? On Singer's view, only a speciesist perspective, one in which we do not give equal consideration to like interests, would allow us to harm the animals but not the human.[4]

It is interesting to note that Singer defines speciesism in terms of how one resolves conflicts of interest. In a system requiring equal consideration of interests, where like interests must be treated alike, much of the work of morality reduces to how we handle conflicts between interests—how we categorize and prioritize the

---

[2]Cf. Singer (1979b, 1989, 1996).

[3]See Gruen (2011, 130–62) and Gruen (2014) for an in-depth discussion of the moral complications involving captive animals.

[4]Singer rather frequently makes the point that there is significant variation in cognitive function in human beings in an attempt to show that there is no moral justification for treating a cognitively disabled human with more moral consideration than a fully functional great ape, for example. Singer has rightfully been charged with both ableism and further marginalizing an already marginalized portion of the human population with these comments and claims. See, for example, Johnson (2003) and Kittay (2009). For more on the intersection of disability and animal ethics, see Taylor (2017).

interests at stake. The test of whether we are correctly assessing which actions to carry out is, to a large extent, a test of whether we accurately weighed the interests involved.

To do this characterizing and prioritizing of interests accurately in interanimal conflicts of interest, we need both a clear understanding of humans' and animals' interests. I will return to human interests in a moment. Singer asserts that animals, as sentient creatures, have a basic interest in not suffering unnecessarily. This presumably would involve sufficient food, shelter, and medical care (where appropriate) that meet an animals' species-typical needs.[5] Sentient animals are not a homogenous group, however, so there will be differences both in what is needed for them to survive and variation in their cognitive capacities. We know, for example, that cetaceans and great apes possess high levels of cognitive function, and we think that other creatures, like fish, have more rudimentary cognitive function.[6] Hence, it is reasonable to ask if some sentient creatures might, in addition to having a basic interest in avoiding pain, also have a basic interest in continued life because, like humans, they have a sense of the future.

Singer's answer to this question is "sometimes." In the human case, "killing a person who prefers to continue living is … wrong, other things being equal" (Singer 1993 94). Inasmuch as some animals have the cognitive capacity to conceive of "themselves as distinct beings with a past and a future … the case against killing is strong, as strong as the case against killing permanently intellectually disabled human beings at a similar mental level" (131–2). He notes that as far as we know this most likely applies to the great apes (ibid.). Singer doubts whether chickens have self-consciousness (1979b, 153), and he is not completely sure about bovines (Singer and Mason 2006, 253). Whether a being has an interest in continued life is determined by whether the being is self-conscious. Only creatures who have a conception of themselves as existing over time or possessing a future can have a preference for continued life (Singer 1979b, 151). Therefore, there is nothing directly immoral about painlessly killing a non-self-conscious being so long as you replace them with another non-self-conscious being who will live just as pleasant a life (this is known as the "replacement theory").[7]

What is important about this for our purposes is that, as far as Singer is concerned, all sentient animals have a basic interest in not suffering gratuitously, but only the

[5]Access to medical care will not necessarily be relevant to a wild lion but would be highly relevant for a companion animal. It is not species-typical for a turtle to require access to tall trees for survival, but it is for many large wild cats.

[6]I say, "we know," but it turns out that humans are not very good at assessing the cognition of other animals (de Waal 2016), so I am hesitant to name with any certainty which animals have lower cognition than others.

[7]There could be indirect reasons for not killing such a being. They might be someone's beloved companion animal, for example, thus exposing them to the pain of grief and loss if they should be killed.

self-conscious have a basic interest in continued life. When we are in doubt about whether a being is self-conscious, we should err on the side of caution (Singer 1993, 119). Killing a self-conscious animal is morally wrong unless there are conflicting interests that outweigh the particular animal's basic interest in not dying. Causing unnecessary suffering to any animal is wrong unless there are conflicting interests that outweigh the particular animal's basic interest in not suffering gratuitously.

On Singer's system of weighing interests many of the activities we take for granted that involve animals are, in fact, morally impermissible. Singer takes a firm stance on the issue of eating animal flesh from factory farms, for example. He claims that we have an obligation to abstain from eating nearly all animal flesh because doing so fulfills an interest of ours that can hardly compare to the interest an animal has in not suffering. In *Practical Ethics*, Singer says, "If animals count in their own right, our use of animals for food becomes questionable—especially when animal flesh is a luxury rather than a necessity" (Singer 1993, 62). In "All Animals Are Equal," Singer notes that factory farming caters only to "our pleasures of taste ... our practice of rearing and killing animals in order to eat them is a clear instance of the sacrifice of the most important interests of those other beings in order to satisfy *trivial* interests of our own" (Singer 1989, 79–90, italics mine). In a lifeboat situation involving a dog and a cognitively typical adult human there may be human interests at stake that weigh more heavily than the dog's interests (i.e., a preference for continued life), leading us to sacrifice the dog (Singer 1979c, 195–6). When we consider the diet of people in industrialized nations, however, we see that the balance tips in the opposite direction because the animals' interests weigh more heavily than the humans'. We cannot put our "trivial" interest in pleasures of the palate ahead of the interest in not suffering.

This weighing of interests applies equally to using animals for experimentation (Singer 1990, 53–5) and entertainment. Animal research for cosmetic products and household goods is ruled out for the most part on the grounds that invasive tests on animals to provide us with yet another bleach or lipstick is impermissible. Circuses, rodeos, and most other uses of animals for entertainment meet a similar fate. Where the human interest at stake carries less weight than the animals' interests (perhaps because the humans' interest is nonbasic and the animals' basic), the animals will win over the humans. One of the appeals of Singer's approach is its simple, action-guiding nature. It demands much of us with regard to our treatment of animals, but it does so in a way that provides an uncomplicated map of the moral terrain.

Among those interested in interanimal conflicts, Singer has been targeted for making mountains out of what they believe should be moral molehills. Donald VanDeVeer, for instance, wrote that Singer "lost some hard-won credibility" when he suggested, in the essay "Animal Liberation," that there was a genuine conflict of interests at play in situations where rats are biting "slum children" (VanDeVeer 1979, 22).[8] I am less concerned about these worries than I am about concerns

[8]For Singer's discussion of rats and "slum children" see Singer (1973).

about Singer's stance on partiality for loved ones, the confusing nature of his taxonomy of interests, and his decontextualized descriptions of nonbasic interests.

Regarding the concern about partiality, Deborah Slicer has argued that Singer's discussion of biomedical research on animals is flawed because he relies on an "essentialist" approach to moral considerability (Slicer 1991). That is, he "propose[s] a single capacity—the possession of interests—for being owed moral consideration" (110). Slicer objects to this essentialist approach on several grounds, but most important for our purposes is her claim that it "renders inessential and unimportant certain relationships—familial relationships or friendships, for example—that do seem essential and important to many of the rest of us" (111).[9] In talking through Singer's arguments against animal experimentation, Slicer highlights his rejection of any kind of partialist considerations when working through conflicts of interest. She notes that he assumes that our "allegiance to principled demands will and should cut cleanly through any preexisting emotional or other bonds we might have to members of our own species, community, friends, family, or lovers who may suffer as a result of Singer's … recommendations" (119). Slicer is not arguing that these bonds must and will always override animals' interests, but that they ought to be considered part of the conversation. It is morally dubious to require people to weigh interests impartially, as if they have no connections to any of the parties.

Singer is deeply wary of introducing bonds of care into moral deliberation because he believes that when we do so, animals' interests will nearly always win out. As he puts it, "The emotional appeal of saving a dying child will always outweigh an appeal to the interests of a rodent, or even a million rodents" (Singer 1994, 38). I appreciate his concern. Those of us attuned to animal suffering and the prevalence of speciesism know that animals nearly always lose when an emotional appeal to human suffering is made. At the same time, I join Erin McKenna in her assertion that the kind of impartiality Singer demands of us—weighing interests with no appeal to emotions, affect, relationality, and so forth—is both undesirable and, very likely, impossible to achieve (McKenna 1994). As McKenna argues, Singer's theoretical commitment to impartial reasoning puts limits on our moral imagination. As I hope to show in this book, it need not be the case that animals' interests lose out to the relational and emotional ties we humans have to others. Rather than reject partiality as a part of our moral world, what if we were to embrace it and work with it in ways that do not have to involve humans' attachments always overriding animals' lives?

In his work on global poverty, Singer made a concession to partiality in which he rather grudgingly observed that some partiality is justifiable because enabling people to care for their nearest and dearest before seeing to the needs of others

[9]Cf. Midgley (1983), in particular chapter 9, and Warren (1997), chapter 5.

may prove to maximize happiness.[10] If I have only one bowl of rice left and we are starving, I can give it to my son instead of my neighbor's starving son because at the end of the day the world is a better place when parents show their children love and make it clear that their safety is the parents' primary concern (Singer 1993, 233). It is permissible to show enough partiality that we can ensure achievement of the goods of love and safety (Singer 2002, 164).

Lori Gruen has charged that this partialist concession dilutes the action-guiding nature of Singer's view (Gruen 1999). With the partialist concession in play, instead of impartially weighing the interests at stake in a conflict, we are now juggling the interests as well as our relationship to the interest bearer, what that relationship requires in terms of partiality, our understanding of the importance of the role the interest plays in that person's life, and so forth. We are now well past the realm of any clear distinction Singer once made between basic interests and frivolities. I agree with Gruen that Singer's partialist concession diminishes somewhat the action-guiding nature of his view. However, I think this is a step in the right direction rather than a problem. To the extent that Singer is embracing more complexity in humans' interests, he is moving his view closer to accurately capturing what is at stake for us in some conflicts. He is recognizing what Slicer notes is essential to human life but that he has hitherto not included in his approach. Some action-guidance needs to be sacrificed in service of accuracy. Activists, in particular, are sometimes loath to embrace the complexity that diminishes a theory's ability to provide action-guidance. I hope to show over the course of this work that we can embrace complexity while maintaining strong obligations toward animals. It is true, though, that doing some involves some loss of clear guidance.

Interestingly, Singer does not appear to make the partialist concession in his writing on animal ethics. Still, Gruen is concerned that making that concession in the global poverty literature will have an ill effect on the strong stance Singer takes regarding animal liberation (Gruen 1999, 145). Her concern is that once Singer concedes that we can put our relationships with loved ones ahead of others' needs or interests we might fail to do right by animals when their interests conflict with the interests of those with whom we are in relationships of love and care. With the partialist concession in hand, for example, I might just eat my grandmother's chicken soup or even drive to the store and buy the chicken for her. This is not the result Singer wants and would constitute a rather huge loss of the gains he made with his arguments for animal liberation. More recently, Gruen has written that personal relationships can complicate commitments to animal welfare because sometimes interests tied to these relationships can be "personally challenging" to manage when they conflict with obligations to animals (Gruen 2011, 93). Like

[10]I say "grudgingly" because Singer's tone when he discusses the way Israeli mothers on kibbutzim snuck into the communal nurseries to hold and nurture their own babies is best described as regretful (Singer 1999, 300).

me, Gruen seeks an approach that accounts for the bonds of love and friendship while also noting the claims animals make on us are real and very important. I am hopeful that striking that balance is possible when we think contextually and relationally.

I'll now leave concerns about the partialist concession behind and turn instead to what I think are two more pressing flaws in Singer's categorization and prioritization system: an ambiguous taxonomy and the decontextualization of nonbasic interests. We will begin with his problematic taxonomy. In "Famine, Affluence, and Morality" Singer drew what appeared to be a very clear line between basic and nonbasic interests. In defending the principle that we should give to more needy others up until the point of marginal utility he made clear that affluent Westerners could give no weight to interests beyond their most basic necessities (1972). Still, over the course of many years of writing, his discussion of the kinds of interests at stake in conflicts between humans or between humans and animals is overwhelmingly diverse. He refers at times to: "basic needs," "essential needs," "luxuries," "frivolities," "major interests," "minor interests," "important interests," "less important interests," "mere wants," "mere enjoyments," "bare essentials," "basic necessities," and "trivial interests."[11]

Now, it could be argued that some of these terms are clearly synonymous with one another. "Mere wants" certainly sounds like the same type of thing as a "luxury," and "frivolities" might easily be paired with "mere enjoyment." Along the same lines, "bare essentials" could cover the same category of interests as "basic necessities." Even if we grant the ways in which some of Singer's terminology might be synonymous, his taxonomy of interests remains unclear. Is "major interests" synonymous with "basic necessities"? Does Singer have some kind of scale in mind where basic needs are at one end, luxuries at the other, and then major interests somewhere in between? It is difficult to tell, yet clarity on this point is necessary in order to know how we are meant to adjudicate conflicts of interest.

We can tell a story where "major" interests are synonymous with "basic interests" quite easily. The interest the people of Flint, Michigan, have in access to a clean water supply is clearly basic in the sense that clean water is a necessary condition for survival. Thus, one might indeed call Flint residents' interest in clean water a "major" interest. Alternatively, it is easy to tell a story where major interests are not the same as basic interests. The Makah Native American Indian tribe has a major interest in reestablishing their cultural tradition of whale hunting. Some people think deprivation of that interest would constitute a significant loss for the Makah.[12] Do we want to say that their major interest is on par with a basic

[11]These references are culled from various sources including Singer 1979a, 1979c, 1989, 1993, 1996, 2002).

[12]With respect to the Makah, it remains unclear whether whaling is in fact an integral part of their cultural practice. Appeals to cultural tradition, like the Makah claim to recommence whale hunting, are profoundly complex and highly controversial. For example, Ronnie Hawkins notes that there is

interest in access to clean water? I suspect not, but Singer allows the ambiguity to persist. The issue becomes even more complex when we realize that the kind of interest that might be considered "major" need not be as historical and rich as the Makah tribe's interest in whale hunting. Many people have interests that matter significantly to them but not to the point where deprivation of the interests would cause them to lose the means of survival. An example could be something as simple as an interest in completing one's book project or any other endeavor that counts as what Bernard Williams called a "ground project," which he defined as a "project or set of projects which are closely related to [one's] existence and which to a significant degree give meaning to [one's] life" (Williams 1981, 5).

When Singer says that "the principle of equal consideration of interests does not allow for major interests to be sacrificed for minor interests" (Singer 1979a, 55) he is attempting to provide us with action-guiding information. Yet, if a "major interest" can be something like carrying out a cultural practice tied to deeply held beliefs like the Makah whale hunt or the fifth-generation hunter facing a hunting outing with their grandfather, it is unclear exactly what people ought to do when their major interest comes up against the whales' or deer's basic interest in not suffering from the acute pain of being hunted and killed. Here, Singer may want to express some justified frustration because regardless of the ambiguities, there are also plentiful situations in which it is very clear that the human interests involved in an interanimal conflict do not carry nearly the same weight as the animals' interests. We can quibble over the edge cases, but we will be busy enough sorting through the clear ones to occupy us for some time. Once one has been fully educated on the realities of modern industrial farming, for example, it is difficult to have patience with interests that amount to "tastiness" or "I just really like barbequing ribs."

At first, this frustration appears reasonable. There are indeed quite a lot of clear cases where our "trivial" or "minor" interests are quickly identifiable as such, and we need only accept what that means for our relationship with animals, do that, and move on. Still, I have concerns. Singer is unclear about whether interests ought to be described in isolation or comparatively. Consider, for example, my interest in eating my grandmother's chicken soup. We might judge this interest a major interest when we consider it apart from the chickens' interests. As I will do in Chapter 4, we can describe all of the cultural nuances surrounding Jewish life and chicken soup, my very close relationship with my grandmother, and the fact that insulting her at the end of her life would demonstrate considerable lack of respect.

---

some evidence that the Makah's interest in reinstating the whale hunt was driven at least in part by pressure from commercial whaling organizations (Hawkins 2001, 288). Linda Fisher, a member of the Ojibway nation, argues that focusing on hunting as a way to preserve traditional ways of life is in deep tension with American Indian traditions of respect for nonhumans (Fisher 2011). Claire Kim offers an in-depth analysis of the complexity of the Makah whaling case in Kim (2015). I will assume for the moment that whale hunting serves an important cultural purpose for the Makah.

We might, however, deem that my interest in her chicken soup is trivial when compared to the interest chickens raised and slaughtered to make that soup have in not having lived confined to tiny and filthy cages, deprived of daylight and fresh air, and subjected to debeaking without the courtesy of anesthesia. While basic interests might be a clear enough category if limited to those things necessary for survival, we can wonder whether minor interests are minor in and of themselves or only when compared to another creature's interests.

From Singer's treatment of conflicting interests, I believe he wants us to engage in a process of comparison. He says,

> In considering the ethics of the use of animal flesh for human food in industrialized societies, we are considering a situation in which a relatively minor human interest must be balanced against the lives and welfare of the animals involved. The principle of equal consideration of interests does not allow major interests to be sacrificed for minor interests. (Singer 1993, 63)

When he discusses our minor interest in pleasing our palates he does so as a comparison with a cow's interest in not suffering in a factory farm. This is sensible because comparisons are the only way to judge relative weight, but we encounter problems when we look at interests in this purely relative way. First, we miss the importance that the interest has for the individual involved. It is true that someone's interest in a tasty bowl of hot chicken soup might pale in comparison with the chickens' interest in avoiding the abject suffering and premature death involved in raising and slaughtering chickens for human consumption. When we label that interest as "minor," however, we fail to see the person's interest for what it is *for her*. My interest in the chicken soup may not be trivial at all given my love for my grandmother and the role her soup has played in the traditions and festivals of my family. This may strike one as a purely pragmatic problem, namely that in failing to look at what an interest means to an individual Singer weakens the persuasive powers of his position and, therefore, fails to reach as many people as he could. I do think he has a pragmatic problem insofar as his view is meant to change hearts and minds, but I submit that the issue is more complex than just one of strategizing about how best to reach people and convince them to change their behavior. This brings me to my second concern about Singer's account: his decontextualization of humans' nonbasic interests.

When Singer talks about interests in this comparative way (the chicken's interest is basic and the humans' nonbasic), he does so by decontextualizing the interest not only from the individual's attachment to the object or activity but also from the interest's role in the individual's ethnic and cultural practices. In doing so, he paints the interest with too broad a brush. Describing my interest in my grandmother's chicken soup as trivial and related to pleasing my palate paints an inaccurate picture of the interests at stake for me when faced with a bowl of her soup. As I argue in Chapter 4, my interest encompasses much that goes beyond enjoying a bowl of delicious soup.

The decontextualized description of the interest does not allow room for understanding the robustness of the interests at stake in some of our choices. Deborah Slicer makes this point about decontextualized interests nicely when she notes that the kinds of "delimited descriptions" Singer provides leave unexplored the "historical, social, economic, familial, and other details that seem crucial to an assessment of a situation, a decision, or a character" (Slicer 1991, 113). Marti Kheel referred to such decontextualized descriptions as "truncated narratives" and warned against their use in moral deliberation (Kheel 1993, 255–9). Singer has stripped important contextual details of certain nonbasic interests in service of providing a straightforward categorization and prioritization process. Decontextualizing nonbasic interests, however, is deeply problematic because, as Slicer rightly notes, context is crucial to assessments of the moral decisions we face and to understanding the nature of the moral character of the decision-maker. I appreciate that Slicer includes character in her list of assessments that may be skewed when we think of interests in a decontextualized way. For, decontextualized, the fifth-generation hunter's interest in hunting with her grandfather makes her look like a jerk who likes to kill innocent animals for pleasure.

Contextualized, while we might think she is mistaken in how to relate to wild animals, our assessment of her character might be softened somewhat when we consider how difficult it is to find oneself at odds with one's family traditions and what it could cost her relationally to distance herself from the family's hunting practices (a topic I take up in Chapter 5). What is at stake here is not merely the pragmatic concern that Singer could reach more people if he thought about interests contextually. Our assessment of people's moral character and their decision-making skills is also at stake. How we describe people and their moral decisions matters even if we ultimately think their decisions are morally unjustifiable. I do not condone recreational hunting, but to describe the fifth-generation hunter's situation as one in which she cannot properly distinguish between a trivial interest and a basic interest is unfair and simplistic in some cases.

I have often wished that Singer's system for categorizing and prioritizing interests would be the one we could rely on for making the requisite changes in our practices regarding interanimal conflicts of interest. The system has simplicity on its side as well as first-glance persuasiveness. It is easy to characterize my interest in my grandmother's chicken soup (as well as her interest in watching me eat it) as trivial, point to the horrific suffering endured by the chickens, and then conclude that we must not make and eat the soup. Indeed, I agree that we must not make and eat the soup. We cannot choose a system of adjudicating conflicts simply because it results in the kinds of obligations we endorse, however. The system must characterize the interests at stake correctly, in all their richness. Singer's minimalist conception of human interests, his decontextualizing of interests, and his ambiguous taxonomy provide reasons to wonder if his view is really the best we can do. Someone who I believe does better is Paul Taylor. We turn now to his categorization and prioritization approach to interanimal conflicts of interest.

1.2 Paul Taylor's Deontological Approach

Whereas Singer's approach to conflicts of interest is rooted in a utilitarian framework and ultimately results in a hierarchy of life-forms (beings with higher cognition have more value that beings with lower cognition when push comes to shove), Paul Taylor's approach stems from a deontic (duty-based) framework and, at least in theory, does not rely on a hierarchy of life-forms. Whether or not Taylor ultimately does endorse some kind of hierarchy is a subject of much debate, but it does not matter for our purposes here.[13] Of interest to us is his approach to categorization and prioritization in situations where animals' and humans' interests conflict. Taylor's theory, respect for nature, is a rich and complex normative guide for human actions with respect to the nonhuman world.

Taylor's theory is of particular interest because, like Singer, he relies on the distinction between basic and nonbasic interests to adjudicate interanimal conflicts of interest. Unlike Singer, however, Taylor does not draw the conclusion that human nonbasic interests must yield to animals' basic interests in cases of conflict. Rather, he takes a nuanced approach to human interests by noting that some nonbasic interests are linked to highly valued ends whereas others are not. In interanimal conflicts where the human nonbasic interest falls into the former category and is consistent with the attitude of respect for nature, Taylor allows for the pursuit of the nonbasic interest even when doing so involves harmful consequences for nonhuman lives. Taylor makes a distinction between nonbasic interests that really are trivial (e.g., an interest in owning figures carved from elephants' ivory) and those that are not properly characterized as trivial (e.g., a community's interest in building a new library). There is much to appreciate about Taylor's detailed and carefully constructed approach. Like Taylor, I reject the notion of human superiority, and, like Taylor, I think of humans' nonbasic interests as far more nuanced than Singer presents them. There is also a spirit to Taylor's work that I wholeheartedly appreciate. For example, he insists through his Principle of Restitution that when humans' nonbasic interests are permitted to override animals' basic interests humans must make restitution. I have not encountered another environmental or animal ethicist who includes a requirement for restitution in their work. Unfortunately, his approach to interanimal conflicts

[13]Those interested in the debate can read French (1995); Norton (1987); Spitler (1982); and Sterba (1995).

of interest is flawed in ways that cause me to look to other adjudication systems, but readers will likely hear some echoes of Taylor in the pages of Chapters 3–6.

Before turning to Taylor's categorization and prioritization of interests approach, I will very briefly give an account of his general framework. Taylor is a biocentric egalitarian. His views are biocentric in two senses. First, he is concerned with moral relations between humans and all living things (not, as with Singer, only other sentient life). Strictly speaking, that means that when discussing conflicts of interest, Taylor is talking about interspecies conflicts, not merely interanimal conflicts. I will use "interanimal" for the sake of consistency. Second, the attitude of respect for nature that moral agents are meant to adopt is based on a scientifically informed understanding of the planet's ecosystems and humans' role as part of a very large whole. Taylor calls this understanding the "biocentric outlook," a set of beliefs that recognize the interconnectedness of all living things, the fact that humans are one species among many, that all living organisms have a well-being of their own, and that rejects the idea of human superiority over other species (Taylor 1986, 99–168). This is how his view comes to be *egalitarian*. For the biocentric egalitarian like Taylor, all living beings have equal inherent worth and inherent worth does not admit of degrees; one either has inherent worth or one does not (1984, 152–6). The biocentric outlook, Taylor argues, helps us see that all living things are teleological centers of life and no living thing is superior to any other. Therefore, moral agents have an obligation to treat all living things as equal members of the biotic community (129–56, 172–92). Taylor argues that this move is parallel to a similar move in interhuman morality. He notes that once we recognize that all persons are autonomous centers of life, we see that treating them as having equal inherent worth is the only way of treating them that is compatible with this recognition of their rationality (79). Thus, respect for nature parallels respect for persons. It is easy to see how a biocentric egalitarian would require a robust system for approaching conflicts of interest; we cannot move from our homes to our jobs without harming at least some plants if not some animals (if we factor in the long-term effects of our reliance on oil, etc.). On such a view conflicts abound.

Taylor's approach to conflict adjudication relies on a multistep process. First, we must identify what kind of interests are at stake in the conflict. Second, we look to see which of his detailed priority principles applies to that situation. If the interests on both sides of the conflict are basic, step one goes fairly easily. If, however, the human interests are nonbasic, additional attention is necessary. We need to determine what kind of nonbasic interest it is and also whether or not it is compatible with respect for nature. From there, we can move to applying the appropriate priority principle. Let's begin with how to identify interests.

Taylor begins his discussion of interests by noting that they can have different degrees of importance to an organism depending on how much of a deprivation nonfulfillment of the interest will be for that organism. He points out that "the most important interests are those whose fulfillment is needed by an organism if it is to remain alive" (1986, 271). It is in my dog, Paddington's, interests to have sufficient food and it is also in his interest to have ample opportunities for play (though truthfully, he prefers napping). The former is of comparatively more importance for Paddington than the latter since, without sufficient food, Paddington will die. This is true according to Paddington's teleology rather than simply his perspective. Taylor's account of interests includes no requirement that the organism in question be conscious at all (271). This means the entity need not possess a subjective value concept. For an entity to have interests, it is sufficient that we can speak of it as having a good that can be benefited or harmed by events or actions whether or not the entity itself is conscious of those interests (1986, 65).[14] On Taylor's view it is perfectly sensible to speak of the Japanese maple tree in my front yard as having an interest in water whereas on Singer's account this would not be the appropriate use of the concept of interests.

When discussing humans' basic interests, Taylor says:

> I might note that with reference to humans, basic interests are what rational and factually enlightened people would value as an essential part of their very existence *as persons*. They are what people need if they are going to be able to pursue those goals and purposes that make life meaningful and worthwhile. Thus for human persons their basic interests are those interests which, when morally legitimate, they have a *right* to have fulfilled. … We do not have a right to whatever will make us happy or contribute to the realization of our value system; we do have a right to the necessary conditions for maintenance and development of our personhood. These conditions include subsistence and security ("the right to life"), autonomy, and liberty. (1986, 272)

Taylor does not list exactly what would count as a basic interest for humans—what is essential to "subsistence and security, autonomy, and liberty"—but such a list would no doubt include food, shelter, and adequate medical care. It is a question whether the list would include such things as projects and relationships that give meaning to our lives. The passage quoted earlier is not decisive between whether these things *are* basic interests or whether what we need in order to pursue them (as necessary conditions of the possibility of pursuing them) are basic interests. Clarity on this question of what specifically counts as a basic interest is paramount to accurate use of Taylor's priority principles. This ambiguity is thus problematic. I suspect that Taylor would not include anything on the list of basic interests that Singer would not include. For, if Taylor conceives of basic interests broadly such that they include meaningful projects and relationships then we are led to wonder

[14]Taylor does not believe that artifacts (items made by humans or other animals) have interests (Taylor 1986, 61, 271).

why, as we will see later, he carves out a category of nonbasic interests that are tied to highly valued ends.[15]

Taylor's conception of nonbasic interests is that they are "the particular ends we consider worth seeking and the means we consider best for achieving them that make up our individual value systems. The nonbasic interests of humans thus vary from person to person, while basic interests are common to all." (273) While food and shelter are interests common to all beings, my interests in reading the works of Anthony Trollope or attending a Bruce Springsteen concert are not. Taylor's conception of human nonbasic interests includes the recognition that some nonbasic interests matter more to people than others. He offers three subcategories of nonbasic interests:

1. Community interests related to the values a community takes to be central to its identity and civilization;
2. Individual interests linked to ends that we take to be central to a life worth living; and
3. Interests that do not fall in categories 1 and 2.

Community interests concern those integral to a community's conception of its "highest values" (Taylor 1986, 281). These relate to the ways in which communities achieve and maintain a "high level of culture" and "a high level of civilized life" (ibid.). Taylor gives the examples of building libraries, museums, and hospitals as well as constructing transportation systems and making new public parks (280). The interests encompassed in this category are highly valued by communities and are unlikely to be interests easily given up. They relate to our sense of identity and achievement as a community and are central to our understanding of who we are and who we want to be.

Category 2 interests are similarly highly valued and unlikely to be easily foregone. These are akin to category 1 interests, but they reflect what is highly valued by individuals rather than groups. Some interests have special value for us due to the "central place they occupy in people's rational conception of their own true good" (Taylor 1986, 281). It is appropriate to think of these category 2 interests as along the lines of Williams's conception of ground projects. They are the sorts of interests that are integral to having a sense of living a worthwhile life. Someone's commitment to a career can be a category 2 interest, as would a parent's interest in seeing their child thrive or an avid hiker's interest in being outdoors.

[15]It is open to Taylor to claim that achieving autonomy requires relationships of love and care in addition to sufficient security and nutrition. Nothing in his writing suggests to me that he has this relational view of autonomy that is most commonly found in feminist literature. See, for example, Friedman (2003) and Mackenzie and Stoljar (2000).

The third category of nonbasic interests includes interests that fall neither into the category of a community's most cherished values nor those interests that contribute to an individual's sense of flourishing. Interests of this sort proliferate. For most people, it includes things like having new clothes, buying new cars, and enjoying hot chocolate. For communities they may include such interests as putting up decorations around Halloween or building functional but not particularly architecturally iconic housing.

We can see already that Taylor's conception of human interests is more refined than Singer's. Where Singer does not differentiate between nonbasic interests that are crucial to our identity as either individuals or groups and those that are not, this differentiation is central to Taylor's adjudication system. For, Taylor wants to take seriously that humans have nonbasic interests that are still of vital importance to their conception of themselves and that these interests will factor differently in interanimal conflicts of interest than the more trivial sorts of nonbasic interests Singer focuses on.

Step one of Taylor's approach to interanimal conflicts of interest is to identify which kind of interest it at stake. This will be necessary to determine for both the animals and the humans. Briefly, I have some concerns about this process of identification. First, Taylor does not believe animals have nonbasic interests.[16] It is not difficult to conceive of nonbasic interests in animals. Martha Nussbaum, for example, discusses imagination and play alongside more subsistence-related issues when she discusses animals' capabilities that are important to consider when facing questions of interspecific justice (2004, 314–17). Though I will not delve deeper into this issue here, I will note that it is a flaw in Taylor's account that when considering the kinds of interests involved in a conflict, we only have basic interests to choose from for animals. Second, Taylor is vague about how broadly he conceives of humans' basic interests. As I mentioned earlier, it is unclear whether he considers meaningful relationships and projects as part of basic interests. Though I believe he does not, he does not answer the question himself despite it being information vital to correct use of his priority principles. On Taylor's account there is both ambiguity about exactly what counts as a basic interest for humans and also whether animals have nonbasic interests at all. If they do, his adjudication system is silent about how to proceed when those kinds of animal interests conflict with humans' interests. Third, Taylor says nothing about relationships of love and care when he discusses category 1 and 2 interests. No doubt, these kinds of relationships can be included in what people take to be crucial for a flourishing life, but he never explicitly mentions this. When discussing human values, he leaves relationships out altogether.[17] Moreover, the ways these relationships can

[16]Taylor (1986, 279). In his chart of priority principles, there is no mention of animals' nonbasic interests.

[17]See Taylor (1986, 258–9), for example.

complicate our interests get no attention in Taylor's account. This is a significant deficiency considering how much of our moral lives involve relationality.

In part one of Taylor's adjudication procedure, we determine whether the human interest is basic or nonbasic. If it is the latter, we then determine whether it is a category 1, 2, or 3 interest (i.e., we ask if the interest is tied to a highly valued end for either an individual or a community). If the interest is indeed connected to a highly valued end, we must turn to the business of determining whether it is intrinsically incompatible with the attitude of respect for nature. An interest is intrinsically incompatible with the attitude of respect for nature when the project itself embodies a failure to respect the inherent worth of another organism insofar as it exemplifies an "exploitative" attitude that recognizes wildlife as having merely instrumental value (Taylor 1984; 1986, 274, 278–80, 309). These are interests that "would be given up by anyone who had respect for nature since the kind of actions and intentions involved in satisfying them directly would embody or express an exploitative attitude towards nature" (273). His examples of such interests include killing elephants to sell their tusks, killing rhinoceroses for their horns, picking rare wildflowers for a private collection, and recreational hunting (274). Interests that are intrinsically incompatible with the attitude of respect for nature are those that (1) are nonbasic and (2) involve an exploitative attitude toward plants and animals thus treating them as mere means. It is important to note that the status of the interest as nonbasic is relevant to the judgment of the interest's intrinsic incompatibility with the attitude of respect for nature. Presumably, then, killing a bear in self-defense while hiking would not be intrinsically incompatible with the attitude of respect for nature (assuming the bear presented a lethal threat and there were no means of escape) even though great harm comes to the bear in doing so. As an action taken alone, pulling out wildflowers for the purposes of putting them in a private collection is indistinguishable from pulling out wildflowers to create a new public park. Both involve someone leaning over and pulling out the flower, thus harming it, when they do not strictly need to do so. Hence, the difference between interests that are intrinsically incompatible with the attitude of respect for nature and those that are not rests on what interest the action is fulfilling and not the intrinsic features of the action itself.

Interests that are not intrinsically incompatible with the attitude of respect for nature are those that do not involve an exploitative attitude. They may indeed bring harm to living beings in their fulfillment, but the attitude behind them is not itself exploitative. Taylor lists activities such as building libraries, hospitals, roads, and parks in areas that will either destroy or seriously damage animals or ecosystems as examples of such interests (1986, 276). In the Pacific Northwest of the United States, for example, we might think about building a Mount Rainier education center. The project itself does not reflect the attitude that wildlife has merely instrumental value. Still, Taylor is clear that the person with the attitude of respect for nature will deliberate carefully about whether the interest at stake is indeed highly valued enough to justify the deleterious consequences of its pursuit for nonhumans. If it is not, the person with respect for nature will forego the interest (1986, 276–7).

This brings us to the end of part one of Taylor's adjudication procedure for conflicts of interest. We identify specifically what kind of interest is at stake for the humans (basic or nonbasic, if nonbasic then whether it is intrinsically incompatible with the attitude of respect for nature). With this information in hand, we can move to step two, which involves identifying and utilizing the correct priority principle to determine the right action to take. The priority principles are the Principle of Self-Defense, the Principle of Proportionality, the Principle of Minimum Wrong, the Principle of Distributive Justice, and the Principle of Restitutive Justice (1986, 256–303). An in-depth discussion of these principles would take us too far afield, so I will point to a few features that are of particular interest as we think about interanimal conflicts of interest.[18]

The Principle of Proportionality applies in situations where an animals' basic interests are in conflict with a human's nonbasic interest that is inherently incompatible with the attitude of respect for nature. It tells us that we must not allow nonbasic interests of this kind to override animals' basic interests. Concretely, consider a hunter's interest in recreational hunting. The hunter uses Taylor's adjudication system to determine what they ought to do about their upcoming hunting trip. Taylor's system will tell the hunter to note that their interest is both nonbasic and inherently incompatible with the attitude of respect for nature (it is exploitative and fails to respect the equal inherent worth of all living beings). The principle in turn tells the hunter that in such a conflict, this kind of nonbasic interest must not override the animals' basic interests in survival. The interest in hunting must give way to the other beings' basic interests.

The Principle of Minimum Wrong involves cases where the human interest is not intrinsically incompatible with respect for nature, that is, it does not in and of itself involve an exploitative attitude. With such interests, we may determine that they are not indeed sufficiently highly valued to justify the consequences for animals and thus abandon the interest. In situations where even a rational person who has adopted the attitude of respect for nature "will not be willing to relinquish the pursuit of those interests even when they take into account the undesirable consequences for wildlife," we turn to the Principle of Minimum Wrong (1986, 280). This principle instructs us that it is permissible to pursue category 1 and 2 interests in such cases but only "so long as doing so involves fewer wrongs (violations of duties) than any other alternative way of pursuing those values" (282). If building our Mount Rainier education center can be accomplished either by building a viewing deck around its summit and running cable cars up the sides

[18]For a deep dive into Taylor's priority principles, see Emmerman (2012).

or by putting it at the base of the mountain where there is already a parking lot, then we must pursue the latter course assuming it involves fewer violations of duties than the former.

Taylor's Principle of Restitutive Justice applies to situations where we have followed the Principle of Minimum Wrong—we have caused harm to wild animals and plants in service of highly valued ends that are compatible with respect for nature. If we have properly adopted the attitude of respect for nature, we will recognize that when we have caused harm, we have an obligation to make reparations (304). As Taylor puts it, we need a principle of restitution because "the actions of moral agents will always fall short of treating each organism, human or nonhuman, with perfect equality of consideration" (ibid.). I mention this principle here because whether or not interanimal restitution is indeed possible factors into my approach to conflicts of interest. It is a beautiful thing that Taylor includes the obligation to practice restitutive justice. He anticipates moral remainders and includes a principle requiring us to attend to those moral debts. He does not, however, address the idea that we might have moral work to do with our loved ones when we forego interests tied to relationships of love and care or community traditions.

Taylor takes seriously that nonbasic interests come in a variety of forms and have differing degrees of depth and importance in our lives. Much of *Respect for Nature* is devoted to carefully considering interanimal conflicts of interest and threading the very fine needle of how to show respect for the inherent worth of living beings while allowing for flourishing human lives. Despite his efforts, there are some issues with Taylor's view that are sufficiently problematic to warrant searching for other methods of adjudication. Most importantly, Taylor does not recognize the possibility that we might have a highly valued nonbasic interest that is also exploitative and, thus, incompatible with respect for nature. The Principle of Minimum Wrong permits the pursuit of nonbasic interests that are not incompatible with the attitude of respect for nature. The Principle of Proportionality, however, rules out satisfaction of interests that are incompatible with respect for nature without acknowledging that they are sometimes complex and highly valued. As I discuss in Chapter 5, a hunter's interest in recreational hunting can be both highly valued and exploitative. While I do not advocate making such interests permissible, an adequate account of interanimal conflicts of interest must have something to say about them.

Taylor explains that when an interest is intrinsically incompatible with the attitude of respect for nature it is an interest whose pursuit "would be given up by anyone who had respect for nature since the kind of actions and intentions involved in satisfying them directly would embody or express an exploitative attitude towards nature" (1986, 273). Those who participate in these activities or enjoy the goods obtained through them "cannot be said to have genuine respect for nature" (274–5). He goes on to note that all of the interests underlying these practices are nonbasic and, therefore, not related to humans' subsistence needs (275). They simply are not important enough to warrant the harm done to other living beings in their pursuit and a person with genuine respect for nature will see that. They are understood as a category 3 interest rather than as belonging to categories 1 or 2. Just as Singer did a disservice in describing my interest in my grandmother's chicken soup as "nonbasic" in the sense of being unimportant, Taylor risks erring in the same way. He wants to think of recreational hunting as serving nonbasic interests that are not terribly important. I would love it if this were the case, but as I will show in Chapter 5, it sometimes is not. Some people who grew up hunting and for whom it has become a crucial means of communing with loved ones would argue that Taylor is just as dismissive of their hunting interest as Singer is of my soup interest. How does Taylor make this mistake?

I believe the explanation lies in the Kantian roots of his view. Taylor says his account is meant to be rationally grounded (Taylor 1981, 197; 1986, 9). In his writings he does not address emotions and relationships or how they can inform moral thinking as well as complicate our interests.[19] Even when Taylor does list interests that are highly valued by individuals and communities, they are always the sort of things that can be understood as somehow contributing to the development of our personhood where personhood is understood in the traditional sense of the Kantian rational agent—someone who deliberates alone and entirely without emotion. Despite his efforts to show the complexity of human interests, love and care are missing from his discussion. As a result, he provides an incomplete picture of some kinds of interests and thus misses their important features. The Principle of Proportionality simply rules out such interests without acknowledging that they exist and their abandonment may require attention to the moral elements of love and care. My discussion of recreational hunting in Chapter 5 seeks to avoid these problems by recognizing the way emotion can inform our sense of what matters about nonhumans' lives but also how relationships of love and care can complicate our interests in ways that must be addressed. Relational vegan ecofeminism does not condone recreational hunting. It prohibits it while paying acute attention to the relational elements of the interest in hunting and offers a way to think about how to cope with the damage done to those elements when the interest is, as it must be, abandoned. This is accomplished in large part by thinking about restitution in the interhuman context just as Taylor advocates for in the human-animal context.

Taylor's system is appealing in part because he acknowledges a spectrum of nonbasic interests. I worry, however, whether the various distinctions he requires in order to use his priority principles can be clearly determined most of the time.

---

[19]See Kheel (1985, 142) for a discussion of Taylor's reliance on rationality. Taylor also believes that the adoption of the attitude of respect for nature will be achieved through reason alone. As Rosalind Hursthouse argued, this is an oversimplification of how such an attitude would be adopted given how demanding it is once taken seriously (2007, 163–4).

Even in his attempt to take humans' nonbasic interests seriously, Taylor ended up trivializing some potentially important human interests. It may seem reasonable to think that a person with respect for nature would automatically reject an interest in recreational hunting as too unimportant to justify killing innocent animals—that she will classify the hunting as a category 3 interest rather than a category 1 or 2 interest. I am not so sure, though, because the relational elements of hunting could make that shift rather challenging. Adjudicating conflicts of interest with truncated narratives can lead to these sorts of problems. Taylor's way of approaching interests can be seen as a partial step away from abstraction, but it does not come far enough.

1.3 Gary Varner's Two-Level Utilitarian Approach

We arrive now at the more robust view articulated by Gary Varner (2012). I call Varner's account of interanimal conflicts of interest robust because of all the systems that categorize and prioritize interests, his takes the complexity of humans' nonbasic interests the most seriously. Operating within a Harean two-level utilitarianism, Varner offers an approach to conflicts of interest that involves hierarchies of interests and life-forms.[20] His is the most highly contextualized approach to nonbasic interests of the views we have considered so far. Varner also takes animals very seriously as moral subjects. Unfortunately, his view is insufficiently protective of animals' interests in large part because he relies heavily on a hierarchy of life-forms and because he introduces context in the wrong way.

Varner argues that sentience is sufficient for moral standing, but that there are different levels of moral significance depending on what kind of sentient creature a being is (2012, 22–4, 105–221). In this sense his view is reflective of Singer's, not Taylor's, which is unsurprising since both Varner and Singer are utilitarians. On Varner's hierarchy, the beings with the most moral significance are "persons" followed by "near-persons," and the "merely sentient" at the bottom. Varner argues that the special moral significance of persons is grounded in their capacity for storytelling, which is tightly linked to ground projects since it is through these projects that we create a narrative of who we are, where we have been, and what future we desire. The added value comes not from the storytelling itself, but rather that the capacity for storytelling points to having a biographical sense of self. Beings with the capacity for storytelling can understand their lives as unfolding over time, they can both experience and "author" their own life stories by setting goals for the future, making choices about what sorts of people they want to be,

[20]Harean Two-Level Utilitarianism involves developing easily accessible rules for governing our day-to-day moral lives (e.g., do not lie) and then a critical level of reflection that both justifies those rules and enables us to think through novel cases (e.g., complicated moral situations where a rule like "do not lie" conflicts with another moral rule such as "do not cause unnecessary harm").

and deciding which features of their story make for decisive information about who they are (134–9). Persons have an interest in "how their life-as-a-whole-goes" (174). Beings with a biographical sense of self have the most moral significance because they have all the value contained in the experiences of both near-persons and the merely sentient. They have additional value added by storytelling. These include the value of reexperiencing past events and anticipating future ones (165–6). Varner is skeptical that any animal aside from humans could count as a person (21).

Near-persons are those animals who have autonoetic consciousness but not a biographical sense of self. Autonoetic consciousness involves having a "consciousness of one's own past, present, and future" (160). Animals with autonoetic consciousness have greater moral significance than the merely sentient because their sense of their own past, present, and future adds value to their lives that the merely sentient do not have. In his characteristically rigorous way, Varner takes a deep dive into the science of animal cognition concluding that candidates for near-personhood include great apes, cetaceans, and elephants as well as, quite possibly, scrub jays (217–18). Merely sentient animals are those who are sentient but "live entirely in the present" (22). They have basic interests as well as an interest in the fulfillment of their noncategorical desires that are attached to the present and immediate future.

I pause here to note that I have concerns about Varner's hierarchy of moral significance. I have more to say about hierarchies in Chapter 3, but for now it is worth mentioning that I am unconvinced of the moral significance of a biographical sense of self. I do not see how possession of a biographical sense of self makes a being's life more valuable than the life of a being who lacks such a sense of self. Choosing a biographical sense of self as the determining factor in having the most moral significance looks like another instance of recognizing, as Rosalind Hursthouse put it, "a few psychological capacities selected ad hoc to capture intuitions about which animal should win in cases where interests conflict" (2006, 139). Certainly, Varner's selection of traits is not ad hoc. Rather, he put quite a lot of thought and research into the development of his approach, but Hursthouse's general sentiment applies. Varner starts out trying to determine what gives humans special moral significance, so it is no surprise that he finds something to account for that significance. Yet, I do not see that having a sense of one's life as unfolding over time according to a narrative makes one's life any more valuable than the life of a sentient creature who is embedded in relationships of love and care and who stands to lose everything that matters to her by being deprived of her freedom or her life. Lori Gruen asks whether having grand plans for the future makes a being's death worse than that of one who is not capable of making such grand plans. As Gruen says, if her life goal to write a play is thwarted by premature death and her dog's desire to go on a walk by a river in the afternoon is thwarted by death, both experience a total loss of the valuable experiences they were anticipating (Gruen 1991, 347). It may be, then, that my ability to reason at a high level and conceive of my life as unfolding according to a narrative points to reasons to consider my interests as less morally significant in situations where the animals involved stand to lose the totality of what matters to them (cf. Agar 2001, 97). I can regroup, reconsider my projects, undertake new projects, or try to mitigate the damage done by foregoing my interests in ways animals may not.

This might be as true of pain as it is of death. Pain in a being with less cognitive sophistication might be even worse than it is for a more cognitively complex being precisely because she cannot understand that it will end or what purpose it serves. An animal who has no sense of herself as having a life unfolding over time cannot discount current pain in service of future well-being (Akhtar 2011) as many of us observe as our companion animals resist care at the veterinarian. Moreover, if pain avoidance is your chief interest in life along with very few other interests, then having pain inflicted on you constitutes a significant change in your welfare in comparison with someone whose interests are more numerous and diverse (ibid.). The project of determining whose life matters more and making comparisons between human and animal experience is full of difficulties as is the project of determining specifically what kinds of cognition various living creatures possess (de Waal 2016). In Varner's case, his reliance on a hierarchy of life-forms causes problems for him in grounding protection for merely sentient animals' interests, which, I believe, is not what he wanted given his commitment to taking animals' moral significance seriously.

Varner's hierarchy of interests flips the ones invoked by Singer and Taylor on their heads by putting basic interests at the bottom of the hierarchy. For Varner, our most important interests are our ground projects/categorical desires followed by noncategorical desires and then basic interests on the bottom. Varner sees basic interests as foundational—they must be met if other interests are to be fulfilled—but they are not the most morally significant. He rightly observes that a person could have all of her basic interests satisfied and live a miserable life if, for example, all of her most meaningful projects were thwarted (1988, 96–7). Our ground projects/categorical desires are those interests that give our lives meaning, that "help constitute a *character*" (Williams 1981, 5), and that are the most deeply connected to our sense of a life well-lived of all our interests. My interest in a delicious mug of hot chocolate is not a ground project, but my interest in doing meaningful work that hopefully improves life for animals and vulnerable humans is. Ground projects/categorical desires give us reasons for living. Noncategorical desires are characterized as interests that do not so deeply define our character or give purpose to our lives. I like doing paint-by-numbers paintings, but I would remain content even if I found I could no longer do them. The things that matter to us but that do not give meaning to our lives are our noncategorical desires. For Varner, like Singer, basic interests concern our subsistence needs and nothing more.

We can see now how Varner's hierarchy of life-forms reflects his hierarchy of interests. Persons have all three types of interests—the ground projects/categorical desires are reflected in the biographical sense of self. Near-persons have noncategorical desires that can extend further into the present and past than those of the merely sentient. Moral significance, then, tracks the kinds of interests a being has: the more complex the interests, the more moral significance they will have since they will have all the interests of other beings plus more. For Varner, noncategorical desires (what Taylor would consider the more trivial nonbasic interests) carry some weight in determining conflict resolution depending on the being who possesses them and her cognitive status, but what gives the most status is having a biographical sense of self and categorical desires.

To his hierarchy of life-forms and hierarchy of interests, Varner adds the Principle of Least Necessary Harm to help adjudicate conflicts of interest. This principle stipulates that "other things being equal, it is better to satisfy ground projects that require, as a condition of their satisfaction, the dooming of fewer interests of others" (Varner 1998, 93). This principle helps us decide which of our possible ground projects to fulfill as well as to address conflicts between individuals' ground projects. For the latter, Varner talks about Jack's ground project to beat the world record for serial murder and Jill's ground project of becoming an academic. Assuming Jill's academic interests do not doom others' interests, we can mitigate the conflict of Jack wanting to kill Jill by noting that Jack's ground project will doom his victims' interests whereas Jill's ground project seemingly dooms no one's interests (92–3). The Principle of Least Necessary Harm tells us that Jack's ground project must give way to Jill's. This principle includes language discussing how to manage different, competing, noncategorical desires. For "two noncategorical desires similarly situated in an individual's hierarchy of interests, the satisfaction of the desire that dooms fewer [basic] interests is preferable" (Varner 1998, 95). If I have a noncategorical desire to entertain myself by foxhunting or by watching a movie, the Principle of Least Necessary Harm would direct my energies toward the movie thus saving the interests of the fox(es) I would have killed in my hunting endeavors. I need to come up with a different noncategorical desire to pursue because this one dooms far too many basic interests. The Principle of Least Necessary Harm is important to Varner's system. Without it, his hierarchy of interests would give priority to any ground project regardless of its impact on others' interests and it would be impossible to say how to solve the conflict between Jack and Jill's ground projects or between my desire to go foxhunting and all the creatures who will be harmed in my doing so versus me just watching a movie for entertainment.

This all seems straightforward and promising enough. We should select ground projects and noncategorical desires that doom the fewest interests of others. It certainly seems as though the foxhunting interest, for example, would need to yield to other, less destructive, ways of amusing myself. Despite Varner's long-standing theoretical and personal commitment to improving animals' lives, however, I do not think his system will protect animals' interests much of the time. This is because of his hierarchies and the way he introduces context into his view. Let us consider the latter for a moment.

Consideration of context is vital for accurately understanding and resolving interanimal conflicts of interest. That Varner considers context is certainly a step forward. It is also a much more honest version of utilitarianism than Singer's in that Singer often waves concerns about background conditions off trusting that the utilitarian calculations will somehow nearly always come out in favor of the animals. Unfortunately, Varner uses context in a way that, I believe, results in unjustifiably overriding animals' interests in some situations.

Varner introduces context into moral deliberations through what he calls the "conservative bias or inertia" (56–7). His view requires us to include in our calculations the views and feelings of those who are relying on a particular practice when we consider changing the rules or guidelines around that practice. This is in addition to taking the technical, ecological, cultural, and economic background conditions into consideration. One must, then, take the feelings of farmers into consideration when contemplating making changes to animal agriculture. When it comes to questions of how we treat animals, deeply entrenched social and economic interests count as costs that must be weighed against welfare improvements that various social reforms would have and that technological advancements would make possible. When determining new policies around farming practices, for example, we need to consider "economic interests, cultural traditions and existing consumer preferences" (Varner 2010, 41–2) along with the feelings of those impacted by the proposed changes.[21] This is not to say that an individual could not determine for themselves to live according to moral rules that eschew, for example, eating animal flesh. His view has what he calls a "revolutionary bent" making room for individuals to be forward-thinking in their ethical choices (Varner 2010, 42–4; 2012, 58). He gives the example of John Stuart Mill's advocacy for women's suffrage well ahead of most thinkers in his time and well before women attained the right to vote. This revolutionary bent is, however, at the level of personal morality. Each individual will decide for themselves how capable they are of living in accordance with moral rules that go beyond the common morality. When it comes to systems and social policies or practices, however, the introduction of background conditions in the form of the conservative bias will play a significant role. In anticipation of Chapter 5 on recreational hunting, we will consider what Varner says about foxhunting to highlight my concern about how his view will

[21]Compare this to Tom Regan's view that those who benefit from immoral industries ought not to have their interests taken into consideration when abolishing the practices from which they benefit (Regan 2004, 338–43, 346–7). Note, too, that it is precisely this factoring in of transition costs and feelings that makes Regan skeptical that utilitarian accounts of animal ethics can end intensive agriculture (1980).

ultimately fail to protect animals in many cases where most people concerned with animals' lives would find it fairly straightforward to rule out the activity. To be fair, Varner acknowledges that his view will disappoint many animal rights proponents as his view is more squarely in the "animal welfare camp" (2012, 22).

R. M. Hare, Varner's predecessor in two-level utilitarianism, was fairly optimistic about his view's ability to rule out endeavors where thousands of people get a great deal of pleasure from torturing one unfortunate individual, as in Roman times, or foxhunting. Some might worry that in such cases the aggregate enjoyment would override the animals' interests. Hare thought otherwise, saying:

> For what ought to be done, on any theory including the utilitarian, depends on the alternatives to doing it. It would be absurd to suggest that there is no other way in which the Roman populace could get its pleasures. The right thing to have done from the utilitarian point of view would have been to have chariot races or football games or other less atrocious sports; modern experience shows that they can generate just as much excitement. Mass sadism does occur, perhaps; but it does not have to. It is in accordance with utilitarian critical thinking to recommend the adoption of prima facie principles which forbid its indulgence and encourage less harmful pleasures. If we all had the right intuitions (the ones which a wise critical thinker would seek to inculcate) we would condemn such practices unhesitatingly. (Hare 1981, 142)

This makes for a hopeful case for the foxes. If utilitarianism can condemn "sadist" practices, then clearly foxhunting can go the way of Roman man versus tiger spectacles. We can replace rooster fighting with soccer or NASCAR and the same for so many other sports that depend on animals' suffering to generate human pleasure. This is promising as far as it goes, but Varner seems more conservative than Hare. After noting that Hare thinks we should find a replacement activity that would "generate just as much excitement," Varner says, "This is certainly correct, but a consistent utilitarian must admit that it takes time to accomplish such changes when the targeted activities are deeply entrenched in a culture's traditions, and that various 'transition costs' must be taken into consideration" (Varner 2010, 41). In a footnote, Varner quotes Hare's line about how, "if we had the right intuitions … we would condemn such practices unhesitatingly," and adds that he "tend[s] to think that Hare underestimates the degree to which bull fighting and foxhunting are entrenched in the cultures that celebrate them," (48, fn3).

I find this discussion disquieting. Is Varner suggesting that foxhunting is so deeply entrenched as a national pastime (for the wealthy, to be sure) that when we factor in the transition costs of redirecting people's foxhunting energies to less cruel endeavors we will see that it is in fact too much to ask of people right now?[22]

[22]It may be that the difference between how Hare and Varner see the foxhunting issue relates to how they are counting the transition costs. Hare may think that the transition costs of shifting one's interest

If so, this is an unfortunate result. Moral theories striving to take animals' interests seriously should be able to unequivocally support the abolition of foxhunting as a means of entertainment. Foxhunting was, in fact, banned in the UK through the Hunting Act of 2004, which prohibits hunting with hounds. The law is controversial, however, and opponents consistently seek new angles from which to challenge it (Weaver 2024). Foxhunting is alive and well in the United States, however.[23] This stagnation is precisely what I am endeavoring to avoid when I introduce the robust interests at stake in some human interests into our thinking about interanimal conflicts of interest. I seek to note the entrenchment but not allow it to override animals' interests. Varner does the right thing by noting the possible depth of the foxhunter's interest, but he goes awry in allowing the weight of the interest to potentially override the foxes' interests.

My sense is that the situation for merely sentient animals is complicated on Varner's view because he adds a priority of interests linked to ground projects to the conservative bias. Taken together, these will result in tremendous overriding powers for humans' ground projects and categorical desires. When combined with the Principle of Least Necessary Harm, counterintuitively things go even worse for the merely sentient, as I argue later. In Varner's defense, a utilitarian could not fail to be conservative in this way. Utilitarianism requires a full accounting of the interests on all sides, including transition costs. Varner's approach embraces hierarchies of life-forms and interests that further the problems caused by the conservative bias, however. It is possible to be a utilitarian and not endorse Varner's hierarchies. Nicholas Agar, for example, situates his biocentrism in a utilitarian, consequentialist framework while rejecting the very hierarchies Varner embraces (Agar 2001, 153–73). Some utilitarians, like Peter Railton, take a very different approach to the conservative bias than Varner. Railton highlights the importance of being alienated from one's ground projects if that alienation would lead to better lives for others. Like Varner, he takes the transition costs of sweeping changes into consideration. Unlike Varner, he thinks there are reasons to be wary of the conservatism in taking transition costs into account. He suggests that the disruption to people's lives caused by making changes "may be offset by the opening of more avenues of self-development to a greater number of people" (Railton 1984, 162). The point here is that while Varner is tied to taking background conditions into consideration due to his utilitarian framework, there is no reason he needs to be tied to a hierarchy of life-forms or, as Railton demonstrates, the idea that transition costs are as weighty as Varner thinks they are.

---

from foxhunting to football, for example, amount to very little whereas Varner may think they amount to quite a bit. The disparity between Hare and Varner's assessments of the transition costs points to the empirical difficulties of making such assessments.

[23]See the Master of Foxhounds Association of North America.

On Varner's account, at first, it looks as though the Principle of Least Necessary Harm would prevent humans from engaging in foxhunting. If I could either foxhunt or go to the movies and nothing very important turns on which I do, I ought to go to the movies. That much is clear. Yet, with ground projects, our desires are not so interchangeable because the desires in play are categorical (answering the question Why is life worth living?) rather than noncategorical. A ground project simply is not the same as wanting to pass the time pleasantly. If the desired activity is part of a ground project, the project is not necessarily rejected on his system. Rather, it may be the case that the person must find a way to achieve the fulfillment of the project that dooms fewer basic interests. When Varner discusses the principle giving priority to ground projects over other interests, he says the principle "does not always give humans carte blanche to use animals in any way we like, but it does imply that, where our most important interests are at stake, we can use animals in various ways" (1998, 79). Varner has written in multiple places that a plausible environmental ethic will have to elevate some human interests above animals' interests (Varner 1998, 79; 2003, 416).

Clearly, if there were a virtual reality foxhunt that could give me the experience of foxhunting then the Principle of Least Necessary Harm would recommend that over participation in foxhunting in real life. If, however, the virtual reality hunt just does not cut it for the hunter or if it cannot make up for the losses in other areas—relationships with loved ones, the costs to those who raise the horses and hounds necessary for the pursuit, and so on—then the foxhunt may just be permissible on Varner's account. If foxhunting matters so much to the hunter that nothing else will do and it answers the question of what gives life meaning, then I do not see how Varner's theory has a way to object to the foxhunting other than to say that those participating should minimize the amount of unnecessary harm they cause. Of course, nearly all animal advocates will say that *all* the harm of foxhunting (to the foxes, the dogs, the horses, etc.) is unnecessary. But I do not see how this answer is available to Varner because (1) I have selected foxhunting as one of my ground projects and (2) ground projects generally override the noncategorical and basic interests of the merely sentient. The hunter's position at the top of the moral significance hierarchy coupled with her project's standing at the top of the interests hierarchy will work against any claim that the foxes, dogs, or horses have. Add the conservative bias to this, factoring in the social, emotional, and cultural costs of my giving up foxhunting, and the foxes are in even deeper trouble. While there are restrictions on the kinds of ground projects we can pursue when it comes to conflicts with other persons and their ground projects, these restrictions do not seem to apply with the same stringency when it comes to conflicts between humans and the merely sentient. Persons have different status than the merely sentient, and this translates into protections the latter do not receive. This is further underscored when we factor in that Varner believes merely sentient animals are replaceable. So long as we do not cause them too much suffering and we replace them with new sentient animals who will experience mostly pleasant lives, we are morally doing all that is required for merely sentient animals when we kill them.[24]

Varner's commitment to the replaceability of merely sentient animals helps us understand why the Principle of Least Necessary Harm will not protect them in many cases where animal advocates think, very reasonably, that they ought to be protected. If a being is replaceable, then there is no barrier to killing them. Why are animal activists so certain that animal interests should prevail? The answer will depend on the activist, but generally their claim will be justified by pointing to worries about causing unnecessary suffering, respect for animals' noninstrumental value, and an acknowledgment that animals are creatures with emotional and relational attachments that are thwarted when we use them as means to our ends. The idea that an individual animal is replaceable by another animal is misguided. Most animal advocates (and people with companion animals) will see that clearly. Even though Varner believes that a Principle of Least Necessary Harm will be a good norm for any culture to adopt, he also says that killing the merely sentient for food unnecessarily is morally justifiable due to their replaceability. Varner's view would require more attention to animal welfare than current animal agriculture involves, to be sure, but (1) so-called "humane slaughter" is deeply questionable and (2) raising animals for food who lead pleasant lives until they meet a painless death does not seem possible. Regarding (1) there are multiple discussions of the myth of humane farming and slaughter (see Abbate 2020; Gillespie 2010, 2011; Gruen and Jones 2016, 160–2; Hawthorne 2013; Singer and Mason 2006). Regarding (2), built into the very process of raising animals for human consumption is the necessity to curb their species-typical behaviors, thwart the pursuit of some of their interests, and cause them stress when it comes time to kill them. Gene Baur notes, for example, the emotional impacts on cows and calves when they are separated. Quoting Temple Grandin, he reports that the mother and calf sometimes "bellow themselves hoarse" when they are parted (Baur 2008, 120). A concrete example of where Varner's view leads is his suggestion that one option for "humane sustainability" is a plan that would use breeding methods to develop a strain of blind hens (2012, 277–8). Apparently, blind hens are far less likely to peck one another than sighted hens. Hens confined in battery cages often peck one another, sometimes to death, because of the stress of being confined in such small spaces with other hens (Food Empowerment Project, "Chickens (Hens) Raised for Eggs"; Grandin and Johnson 2009; Varner 2012, 268–9). This is a disturbing solution to the horrific conditions endured by laying hens in industrial agriculture for it fails to address other morally problematic aspects of battery cage use, for

[24]For his arguments showing why merely sentient animals are replaceable but not merely sentient humans, see Varner (2012, chapter 9). See section 9.6 for his discussion of the nonreplaceability of persons. For those interested in Singer's struggles to cope with the problem of marginal cases, Varner's discussion in chapter 9 regarding replaceability and marginal cases will be of particular interest.

example, that blinding chickens does nothing to improve their physical welfare when crammed inside wire cages with five to ten other hens and that in using battery cages we limit the value of a hen to her egg-laying capacity. Varner notes that this is precisely how many animal advocates will feel about the proposed solution, but he thinks that using blind strains of hens would "make significant improvements from an animal welfare perspective" (278) if only people would not be frightened by the science involved.

To summarize, the way Varner's account contextualizes interests is both intriguing and troubling. He says that his theory "situates discussions of animal welfare and animals' rights amid the changing ecological, technological, cultural, and economic background conditions of real-world, evolving human societies" (2010, 46–7). By thinking about the implications of broad social changes to our interactions with nonhuman animals on human interests, he incorporates both the context and robustness of those interests into the discussion of interanimal conflicts. Yet, the ways in which weighing the ecological, technical, cultural, and economic background conditions tips the scales of conflict adjudication in favor of human interests is precisely what I am trying to avoid by bringing up the relevance of context. Background conditions need not work toward giving human interests more weight or providing a justification for moral inertia. Rather, they can help us understand what moral agents are up against and what moral work may need to be done when certain facets of our robust interests are given up. In Varner's system, the context he includes in thinking about changes to systems and behaviors is combined with hierarchies of life-forms and interests to defend the priority of humans' interests in too many situations.

1.4 Mary Anne Warren's Multi-Criterial Approach

Mary Anne Warren's view is the last we will consider in this section devoted to categorization and prioritization of interests approaches. Warren's view is a perfect bridge to the next section on relation-based accounts because her approach to conflict resolution includes discussion of relationality. The views we have considered so far are all "uni-criterial" to use Warren's term. That is, they all identify a single necessary and sufficient condition for possessing moral status—sentience for Singer and Varner, organic life for Taylor (Warren 2003, 440–5). She argues that none of the uni-criterial theories of moral significance are satisfactory. Rather, what is important to moral status is all of these criteria: moral agency, sentience, life, and social and ecological relationships (445–6). Warren combines the uni-criterial conceptions of moral considerability based on a being's intrinsic properties and develops a hierarchy of life-forms: all living things have some moral status, sentient beings have more status than nonsentient beings, and moral agents have more status than the merely sentient (445). What follows from this is that no organism should be harmed without good reason, but nonsentient organisms may be harmed sometimes for reasons that are less compelling than vital human need (e.g., pulling weeds to improve a garden's appearance (ibid.)). Harming sentient organisms requires stronger justification (e.g., self-defense, preservation of human life), and harming moral agents requires the strongest justification of all. Like Varner, Warren takes cognitive capacity to be a justification for thinking that what we owe animals will depend on their species membership since "sentience and other mental abilities come in degree" (447). She adds that not all animals are equal because some are "members of species whose relationships to human beings have often involved friendship and mutual affection" (448). Finally, she observes that "ecological relationships must guide the allotment of time and resources to protection of animals of various species" (ibid.). This is why, she avers, more resources should go to protect endangered California Condors than to ubiquitous white-tailed deer (ibid.).

We can see how this plays out in practice with Warren's discussion of human infants and mice and elephants and foxes. Why do we owe more to human infants than mice? It is not because of moral agency as human infants are not moral agents. According to Warren, we owe more to human infants than to mice because infants are part of our social communities. Why is it more important to protect elephants from poachers than rabbits from foxes? This is due to elephants' "unusual intelligence and sensitivity" and their ecological relationship—their slow reproductive rate makes them especially vulnerable to human predation (446). Noting that this multi-criterial theory is a complex system for understanding moral status, she offers seven Principles of Moral Status to aid with that complexity (446–7, see also 1997, 148–77). I will not go through all seven principles in detail here. It is sufficient to note that principle number five, the "Interspecific Principle," gives higher moral status to "nonhuman members of mixed communities" than their sentience alone would provide for (446).[25] This demonstrates how the combination of intrinsic (i.e., sentience) and relational properties (i.e., membership in a mixed human/nonhuman community) impacts conflict resolution. Thinking through a conflict that involves a domesticated horse and a wolf, for example, the horse will have higher status than the wolf due to her place in a mixed community (assuming that the horse and wolf have similar degrees of sentience).

There are many features of Warren's view that are complex and rich. I want to emphasize three problems here. First, her view maintains a hierarchy of life-forms where moral significance (or status to use her word) increases with a being's degree of cognitive complexity. Warren thinks some sort of hierarchy is necessary because, not being gods, we have "biological needs [and] physical vulnerabilities" that must be attended to (1997, 153–4). She says, "It is not human

[25]In Warren (1997), the Interspecific Principle is number six (switched with the Ecological Principle).

hubris, but human vulnerability and need that compels us sometimes to put the interests of human beings ahead of the interests of other animals" (154). I do not deny that human need and vulnerability will require that we override animals' interests at times. As I argue in Chapter 3, however, I do not accept that a fixed hierarchy of life-forms is the framework from which to make decisions regarding prioritizing interests. I appreciate that Warren's hierarchy has nuance built into it by including relationality into moral status, but as I shall argue in my discussion of ecofeminism, static hierarchies are deeply morally problematic.[26] Second, while I rejoice in Warren's recognition that animals' different relationships with humans can generate differences in how we think about interanimal conflicts of interest, I would like to see more nuance here. For example, when Warren discusses animals in mixed communities, it is always in the context of relationships with *humans* and not the relationality they share with conspecifics or other nonhumans. This is an important lacuna given that it is not at all clear why animals' relationships with other nonhumans should not play some role in how we think about them in cases of conflict.

Finally, third, Warren is too quick to accept that some human interests are so deeply entrenched or important to us that they will override animals' interests. The Anti-cruelty Principle, for example, tells us: "Sentient beings are not to be killed or subjected to pain or suffering, unless there is no other feasible way of furthering goals that are (1) consistent with principles 1–3; and (2) important to human beings, or other entities, who have a stronger moral status than could be based on sentience alone" (1997, 182–3). In discussing recreational hunting, Warren notes that such hunting may be tied to nontrivial interests. She uses this information to justify some recreational hunting if it is "done in ways that are not cruel, that do not damage species or ecosystems, and that do not endanger human beings or animal members of mixed communities" (238). I am not sure there are any hunting conditions in which these stipulations are met, but even if there were, it is Warren's hierarchy of moral status that is enabling the interest in hunting to be fulfilled when of all the recreational activities humans can partake in, recreational hunting involves shooting and killing an animal who is living his life, playing a role in his animal community, and causing harm to no one. The animals are doomed because they are merely sentient, and the humans' hunting interest is robust. As I argue in Chapter 5, there are ways for a moral system to recognize the robustness of some people's interest in recreational hunting without thereby rendering it permissible.

Warren's system is weakened by her hierarchy of sentient beings, her one-dimensional discussion of relationality and being a member of a mixed community, and the way her hierarchy makes even the most unnecessary cause of animal suffering imaginable (hunting for sport) permissible if the interest of the hunter is

[26]Elisa Aaltola believes Warren's approach "suffers from anthropocentrism," and I agree (2005, 35–6).

important enough. Still, her acknowledgment of the role relationality might play in approaching interanimal conflicts of interest adds an interesting element to thinking about such conflicts. Let us turn now to fully relations-based approaches to conflicts of interest and see how they fare.

2 Relations-Based Approaches

In this section, we will consider two relations-based approaches to interanimal relationships. Where Singer charged that anytime we show preference for a human interest by overriding an animals' equally important interest it must be an expression of an unwarranted preference for our own species (speciesism), these views challenge the idea that all such preferences for humans are a pernicious, animal-disregarding manifestation of speciesism. I begin with Nel Nodding's discussion of animals then turn to Mary Midgley's. As Elisa Aaltola succinctly puts it, "Instead of emphasizing more or less objective factors such as rights, interests, or mental capacities, [the relations-based model] underlines the subjective by bringing forth the concepts of kinship and attachment" (2005, 29).

2.1 Nel Noddings's Special Relations Account

In *Caring: A Relational Approach to Ethics and Moral Education*, Noddings lays out the central role relationality plays in human morality. In interhuman morality, we have an obligation to "summon the caring attitude" that is "limited by the possibility of reciprocity" ([1984] 2013, 139). The reciprocity Noddings has in mind is not the quid pro quo of transactional interactions but rather the idea that the caring "must be completed in the other" (142). That is to say, that I can only have an obligation to another human where there is the possibility of the cared-for receiving the care. This may take the form of the cared-for offering "a disclosure of his own subjective experience in response to the one-caring or by a happy and vigorous pursuit of his own projects" (140). Thus, the cared-for need not pay the carer back in kind, but there must be an opportunity for the caring act to be received. As Nodding puts it, "We may live sensitively and reasonably, but obligation can only arise on encounter. Caring, natural or ethical, must be completed in the other" (142). This raises troubling questions regarding obligations to distant others (ground well-trod in the literature following publication of Noddings's book). She does make the point, however, that there may be obligations that arise to "those too far removed for caring" if the "the cry for help may be heard directly in my own circle" (143). That is, so long as the person in my circle asking for my help can be trusted and is accurately relaying the need for help in the distant other, I have an obligation to respond (ibid.). This will become relevant in my critique of Noddings's view.

Where being in relation with other humans is just a fact of human existence—we are born in relation and die in relation—relations with other animals are a choice, according to Noddings. We are in "necessary association (without which we could not be human)" with members of our own species (1991, 418), but this is not so with other animals. Noddings avers that "affection for animals is more individualized" (2013, 139). Noddings offers an anti-cruelty principle in response to other animals' sentience; she notes that we "must not inflict pain without justification" (2013, 140). Relationships with particular animals will add more obligations to that most basic injunction. In discussing her cat Puffy, for example, there is "natural caring" because Puffy is familiar to Noddings. Puffy is responsive to her care and affection in the characteristic ways of a feline (2013, 145). Though Noddings points to the "restricted" nature of Puffy's responses, there is reciprocity in the interactions between the one caring (Noddings) and the cared-for (Puffy) (ibid.). Hence, all of us will have special obligations to the animals with whom we are in relationships of care. These are relationships we have chosen, according to Noddings, thus we cannot judge others for not being in relationship with other animals ([1984] 2013, 148–9). Those of us who make a choice to "enrich and complicate [our] ethical live[s]" by being in relationship with some animals have elected a more complex moral life that we cannot impose on others or judge them for not participating in (ibid.).

What of animals with whom we are not in relation but who nevertheless interact with us? Noddings answers this by pointing to the differences in her obligations to cats and rats. Because she has a relationship with prior or other cats, when the stray cat arrives at her door yowling for food, she has "committed herself to respond." This is because "if I have pleasant memories of caring for cats and having them respond to me, I cannot ethically drive a needy one away from my back door. A chain has been forged. A stranger-cat comes to me formally related to my pet. I have committed myself to respond to this creature" ([1984] 2013, 145). There is, she says, a "very important sense of maintaining internal truth and serenity" (ibid.). When the stray cat comes yowling, she must respond.

This is not so with the rat who comes calling. Noddings feels "no such stirring in connection to rats" (146). She has no affection for rats that generate a relationship to them. She has an ethical responsibility to cats, not rats. It might be the opposite for you. If you have loved and cared for rats as pets, but not cats, then the call for response will be exactly the opposite for you than it is for Noddings. You can ignore the cat but must respond to the rat. It is clear, here, how different this is from a view like the others we have considered in this chapter. Noddings is not talking about what grounds the moral status of cats and rats in terms of their intrinsic properties. Sentience is relevant to a general prohibition on causing unnecessary suffering, but further obligation will depend on whether one is in a caring relationship with a particular animal and what caring responses this implies for their conspecifics. This is important because, where many animal advocates would find some way to handle a rat situation that is as kind as possible (if, say, we need to remove a rat from our home), Noddings would not poison or torture the rat but she would "shoot it cleanly if the opportunity arose" ([1984] 2013, 146).

As Noddings puts it, we humans are apt to make two mistakes when thinking of other animals. The first is to assume human superiority over other animals and reduce them to mere means to our ends. The second is to suppose that all animals induce the same moral obligations that are "familiar to human associations" (1991, 422). Unless we are in special relations with animals, their only claim on us is to not inflict unnecessary suffering. All other obligations are rooted in special relations to us. Though Josephine Donovan accused Noddings of being a speciesist (Donovan 1991), Noddings asserts that her account is not speciesist because there are reasons to have a preference for our own species: "Our species is the group within which we reproduce, live our daily lives, communicate in speech, and build a culture. By virtue of this necessary association (without which we could not be human), members of our species have claims on us that others do not" (1991, 418).

My issue with Noddings's special relations account is that it lacks imagination and engagement with complexity. First, we have opportunities to directly encounter some animals but not others because of factors both entirely within and without human control. I will begin with the latter situation. Unless I go to a zoo, which I ought not to do (Acampora 2008; Deckha 2012; Emmerman 2020), I will not encounter hippos living in the Pacific Northwest of the United States. We do not have hippos in the wild here. Thus, it is entirely appropriate that I do not encounter them or, subsequently, have a relationship with them that would generate obligations in the ways Noddings requires. How are we humans meant to generate caring for wild or otherwise unencounterable animals if, by nature, we are not meant to be in space with them? On Noddings's account, caring could only come if a trusted friend who did have such encounters could relay the hippos' need to me. I do not know how that can work if, as it should be, none of my trusted humans encounter a wild hippo themselves. Perhaps one of my friends will go on a trip and encounter a hippopotamus rehabilitation center and spread the word along to myself and others in our group. Depending on who our friends are, that could be extremely unlikely. This idea that ethical caring can only stem from encounter is counterintuitive in the case of some animals when, by their nature or geography, encountering them is itself unethical or nearly impossible. I do care about hippos despite Noddings's claim that I certainly cannot under the circumstances.

Noddings says that efforts to save other animal species are not acts of care if no relation has been established ([1984] 2013, 147–8). She lists problems associated with professing to care for creatures with whom we are not in relation: (1) we may not know the creature well enough for the care to be completed, (2) we may override what humans need in our desire to help the creature, and (3) we could confuse raw feeling "with the more gentle, considered, committed, and often conflicted state of ethical caring" (148). I agree that the first is a genuine problem. Humans frequently label as "caring" quite maladroit efforts to provide relief to animals about whom we know very little or nothing. Knowledge and perhaps some expertise is necessary to appropriately meet the needs of animal others.[27] I also agree with the third point inasmuch as there does seem to be a difference between having-caring-feelings-for and the kind of complicated, deep, and committed relations involved in caring-for in the profound sense that Noddings defines "ethical caring." The second problem (that we may override humans' needs out of a desire to help an animal), however, is contentious. Part of the matter at hand is determining which human needs and interests must give way in service of animals' needs and interests. If not being in relation with another animal (or any of their kind) means I cannot care for them at all beyond a basic obligation not to cause them unjustifiable suffering, then many of the earth's creatures are doomed.

So many of the animals we *do* encounter regularly are those whom we have domesticated and either live along with as companions or breed and use as tools for human ends. For many such animals the conditions of their confinement are such that encounter by the public is virtually impossible. Industrial animal agriculture is purposefully carried out in windowless warehouse-like farms and similarly enclosed slaughterhouses. Research laboratories are inaccessible to the public unless a whistleblower has made pictures or a narrative of what goes beyond closed doors available to the rest of us.[28] Slaughterhouses are situated off the beaten path and not equipped with windows, and laws are passed to punish those who obtain undercover footage of what goes on inside industrial animal agriculture facilities. This is by design. It is meant to protect these exploitative industries from oversight and interference *and* to make it difficult for us to access our feelings of compassion, empathy, and concern for the animals within (Luke 1995, 2007). Noddings is not without concern for such animals, but her relational account makes it very easy for humans to override these animals' interests and to further distance us from feeling care for them. If encounter is necessary, that just will not happen in these cases. On purpose.

With respect to the liminal and wild animals in our world, Noddings's view again goes wrong. It is not a flaw of the rat that she scurries past me and that it would be, as Noddings notes, difficult to forge a relationship with her ([1984] 2013, 146). That is the nature of being a wild rat (*Rattus rattus*), a liminal animal living life as an undomesticated creature but one in contact with human

[27]In Lori Gruen's articulation of entangled empathy, an ethic of care for our relations with other animals, she emphasizes that understanding and expertise in both species-typical needs and an individual animal's needs is important for caring-for (2015).

[28]The University of Washington built an entire Animal Research and Care Facility underground. People can stroll right over the facility and have absolutely no idea what is happening beneath their feet (Cowan 2014).

individuals and communities.[29] Cats, on the other hand, we have domesticated and are ubiquitous. Thus, I have an opportunity for meaningful encounters with them on a regular basis. I can adopt them as my companions, cuddle them at my friends' homes, have a regular meetup with a cat who scampers outside near my home, and so forth. I do not have those opportunities to connect with the wild rabbits who munch on the weeds and grass on my lawn, however. By nature, they are wary of me, and I am respectful of their need to live their own lives free from intrusions from me into their daily affairs. The idea that the rabbit only receives special obligations from me if I am in a relationship where he and I are responsive to one another in some sort of enriched way misses the point. A good relationship with a wild rabbit is one where I do not have an enriched encounter with him where that means proximity, the cared-for receiving my care in some concrete way, and so on. Still, my own experience tells me that I have feelings for this rabbit—I *care* for him. It may be mere "raw emotion," as Noddings calls it. It is tangibly different from the ethical caring I have with my dog, Paddington, but it is meant to be so by virtue of the kind of being a wild rabbit is. So, I will not take a gun and shoot this rabbit because he munches on my lawn, and I believe it would be wrong to do so whether or not he and I ever reach the kind of caring that involves more direct and deep encounter. To reiterate, that is in part because ethical caring for some animals is exhibited precisely by avoiding deep and direct encounter. When it comes to such animals, keeping to myself other than to express some care in a distant way is exactly what care requires of me most days. Thus, between Noddings's clear endorsement of the priority of human-centered ethical caring and the complications of her relational account for our relationships with animals, I think we can do better.

2.2 Mary Midgley's Special Relations Account

Mary Midgley bases her special relations account on the idea of nearness and kindship (Midgley 1983). Midgley argues that absolute dismissal of animals' interests is not ethically warranted *and* thinking of all preferences for members of our own species as speciesism is also not warranted. According to Midgley, some preference on the basis of species is natural. Where Singer likened speciesism to racism and sexism, Midgley differentiates racism and sexism from speciesism by noting that we cannot know anything about someone's needs from their race or sex (beyond cultural and a few other considerations). You can know the needs of most humans from merely knowing they are a human. This is not so when it comes to

[29]Indeed, matters are more complicated. Some rats are domesticated and kept as pets (*Rattus norvegicus*), but wild rats (*Rattus rattus*) are not domesticated. Noddings is not clear whether the rat scurrying past her is a wild or domesticated rat and, if the latter, whether prior encounter with, say, a hamster would engender relational obligations to them on the grounds of being somewhat similarly situated.

differentiation among species. As she puts it, "A zookeeper who is told to expect an animal, and get a place ready for it, cannot even begin to do this without far more detailed information" (1983, 98–9). Species is highly relevant to understanding what a particular animal's needs are and how we can attend to those needs. As Aaltola says, "To put it simple: we cannot feed rabbits meat or sustain a lion on a diet of parsley, but we can feed all humans the same" (2005, 30). Responding to need does require information about species whereas we can respond to quite a lot of human need, certainly the basic needs, without reference to an individual's race or sex. Midgley might be oversimplifying the case for humans somewhat, but her main point stands. Knowing about species and species-typical needs, behaviors, and activities is crucial for understanding how to treat an individual animal. As a canine, my dog does not need an opportunity to graze for hours in open pasture, but cows and other bovines certainly do. I can meet a humans' basic needs, however, simply by knowing they are a human; race or sex is irrelevant to determining their subsistence requirements.

Midgley notes that some actions may be discriminatory but nonetheless fair. That is, the tendency to take a special interest in our own children or rescue those close to us in an emergency is a form of discrimination in the very literal sense that one is making a deliberate choice, carefully noting distinctions, but it is not thereby prejudiced (102).[30] It is wrong to call a preference for our own species a prejudice, according to Midgley, because showing preference based in nearness and kinship is simply a part of nature (1983, 105). When thinking about interspecies conflicts, she notes, "The notion of simply rejecting all discrimination as *speciesist* looks like a seductively simple guide, an all-purpose formula. I am suggesting that it is not simple, and that we must resist the seduction" (103). This kind of discrimination is just part of being alive for most animals, she argues.

Where one might think such an approach would result in rampant permissibility on the part of humans to override animals' interests, Midgley's does not. She is clear that "the proper way to treat it is to recognize nearness as a perfectly real and important factor in our psychology, and therefore in our morality, but to refuse to treat it as the sole or supreme one. We are subject to other claims. Nearness alone can never have a walkover" (21). Other considerations, such as justice and compassion, are highly relevant to moral life as well, for example (22). She goes on to say:

> In cases of real, sharp, life-or-death competition, we can indeed owe special, overriding duties based on kindship and other forms of social nearness. From a burning building, or even a milder disaster, we are right to rescue first our nearest and dearest. Theorists who deny this, exalting impartiality as the core

[30]Midgley defines discrimination as "the power of distinguishing carefully between different kinds of cases" (26).

> of virtue, are muddled. And this is true of nearness in species as well as of other kinds. But it cannot possibly mean that those further from us are always too far down in the queue to be reached. There are two reasons for this. First, sharp competition is not always present. (In fact, for us in the prosperous West, it is pretty rare.) And second, there are plenty of other claims which can, on occasion, outweigh nearness. (23)

Thus, in rare "real, sharp, life-or-death competition" it can be justifiable for the natural nearness and kinship we feel to take priority. This will not be the case in more quotidian moral dilemmas, and these special obligations generated from nearness and kinship are defeasible by other considerations. Species preference cannot be allowed free reign to trample upon the needs and interests of our fellow creatures. "Absolute dismissal," as Midgley calls it, is impermissible (17). We can recognize our natural preference for those nearest to us, including members of our own species, and take that nearness into consideration in some conflicts, but we can still ask questions about how far this takes us (105). Species is not an "impenetrable social barrier, cutting us off from other creatures in a way which makes them none of our proper concern" (124).

There are legitimate concerns that Midgley's account runs afoul of the naturalistic fallacy (Aaltola 2005). My chief worry about Midgley's account is that I simply do not know what to do with it when it comes to conflicts of interest. She provides an interesting and somewhat compelling case for not labeling all preferences for human interests in conflicts as a pernicious kind of speciesism but walks the fine line of noting that this natural consideration for nearness and kinship does not provide a free pass to override animals' interests in all conflicts. If we stick only to the rare "sharp" and "life-or-death" competitions, then it in fact grants overriding power in very rare cases. One can only write so much in one book and Midgley's is understandably focused on the questions most salient to her, namely how to account for the reality of claims of nearness and kinship without absolutely dismissing animals from moral consideration. Unfortunately, however, that means we get very little to help us in determining what to do when interests inevitably conflict. I am not sure, for example, what Midgley would say about the kinds of cases I consider in Part 2 where nearness and kinship play a crucial role in the interests at stake, but they are not matters of life or death. Midgley's view accomplishes what she set out to do but falls short of answering the questions at the heart of this work. I am not even certain that Midgley's account leaves us particularly well-supported in tackling those questions aside from the important recognition that one can value human connection without thereby allowing it to override animals' interests. That nearness and kinship is one consideration among many is an important contribution to conversations about human-animal interactions. Where I am concerned with how issues of nearness, kinship, and connection factor into interanimal conflicts of interest, however, Midgley focuses chiefly on nearness and kinship as it relates to a general preference for members of our own species.

The special relations accounts introduce relationality into the conversation about conflicts of interest, which enriches the discussion beyond where the categorization and prioritization interests approaches leave off. Still, Noddings's use of relationality is too limited to account for much of human/animal relationality and Midgley's is too underdeveloped to provide much action-guidance. We turn now to contextual approaches to see how to further enrich approaches to interanimal conflicts of interest before turning to relational vegan ecofeminism in Chapter 3.

3 Contextual Approaches

Contextual approaches are another family of approaches that differ significantly from the categorization and prioritization of interests approaches. As was evident in the earlier discussion of Singer, Taylor, and Varner, context does factor into their thinking about conflicts of interest. As utilitarians, Singer and Varner must include context as weighing interests and how to maximize utility requires understanding both what interests are involved in a conflict and to whom they belong. Taylor includes context inasmuch as he recognizes that some interests develop in a context that renders them deeply important to our sense of a flourishing life. These ways of considering context are quite different from a contextualist approach. Contextualist approaches put context at the center of moral deliberation, noting that it is impossible to know what right action is without a quite detailed understanding of the circumstances one confronts. I will consider two contextual approaches in this section. First, Carlo Alvaro's virtue ethics approach requires contextual information in order to determine what virtues apply to a situation and what choices a virtuous person would make as a result (Alvaro 2019, 67). Second, Elisa Aaltola's contextual approach demonstrates how context is necessary in cases where there is conflict between equally important interests.

3.1 Carlo Alvaro's Virtue Approach

In *Ethical Veganism, Virtue Ethics, and the Great Soul* (2019) Carlo Alvaro lays out his defense of veganism on virtue grounds. A virtuous person would be vegan, according to Alvaro. This is what he calls an "inside-out" approach rather than an "outside-in" approach. That is, where Peter Singer and Tom Regan offer principles external to the agent that are meant to direct their action, the virtue approach starts from what kind of person someone ought to be then uses those virtues to ground their actions regarding other animals. Principles act from without whereas virtues act from within.[31] As Alvaro puts it, "One should not be motivated to be vegan by such principles [maximization and abstention]; rather, one should be internally motivated by a virtuous character and by observing the lives of animals and their objective moral characteristics" (xix).

Alvaro sees veganism as a manifestation of four virtues: temperance, compassion, fairness, and greatness of soul (92–103). Veganism demonstrates temperance by "eating what is healthful, what is noble, and what is within one's means" (95). Alvaro discusses the negative health impacts of a meat-based diet in detail but also notes that eating animals is problematic because it is "an expression of excess" (ibid.). Given that many of us can eat healthily on a plant-based diet, it is intemperate to consume animal products. Veganism demonstrates compassion by being "motivated to make a concerted effort to help and to alleviate the pain of others" (99). The compassionate person is not a party to causing unnecessary pain and suffering. Moreover, the compassionate person is empathetic and "also recognizes that animals not only wish to avoid pain, but wish to survive and flourish" (100). Veganism demonstrates fairness because the vegan refuses to be part of a practice that "causes countless animals to suffer and be killed for trivial reasons, such as taste, fashion, and amusement" (102). A just or fair person will realize that using animals in this way is not magnanimous, just, or caring. The person who possesses greatness of soul "possesses great moral qualities such as compassion, temperance, and a sense of justice in the sense of what is right or wrong in a given circumstance" (100). Such a person will want no part of the cruelty, excess, and environmental degradation involved in using animals as tools for humans' purposes.

A virtue approach to animal ethics must be attentive to context, for it is through context that the virtuous person determines right action. In order to know what is brave in a given situation, one must know what the situation is; what constitutes bravery on the battlefield differs from bravery in the classroom. As virtue ethics requires developing the correct character and intellectual traits, the view does not lend itself to rules proscribing behavior, which means Alvaro does not tackle conflicts in the ways we saw with the principle-driven theories earlier in the chapter. He notes that in "tragic dilemmas" (his example is the dilemma at the heart of the film *Sophie's Choice* where a mother must pick which of her children to send to certain death with the Nazis and which to keep with her) we pull together as much of the context as we can and make the decision a "noble" or "honorable" person would make (65–7). If one has a virtuous character, one will act well and engage the relevant facts in a challenging situation (114). In Alvaro's virtue approach to animal ethics, the virtuous person does not draw lines regarding moral status as the utilitarian and deontological approaches do.[32] Rather,

---

[31]Lori Gruen discusses inside-out approaches in Gruen (2011, 42).

[32]Cf. Hursthouse (1991) for a virtue approach to abortion that is centered on character rather than the moral status of the fetus.

> a compassionate individual, for example, is concerned about the well-being of all living things. He respects creatures because all have dignity and deserve moral respect. For a virtuous individual, it is not the case that only certain beings have moral worth while others are absolutely worthless or irrelevant. … A virtuous individual respects insects in that he does not kill them intentionally or take pleasure in torturing or killing them. Since he also respects nature, he will not destroy plants or pollute waters. At the same time, virtue ethics is consistent in its approach because it does not categorically prohibit killing animals who threaten our lives or insects that, for example, might infest our homes. (115)

Having the right character will lead to ethical decision-making and, specifically for Alvaro, to the recognition that veganism is the right response to the question of how a virtuous person would be in relationship with animals.

There is much to consider with respect to Alvaro's virtue approach to animal ethics, but we will focus on just one aspect: how he thinks about the triviality of human interests with respect to dietary choices. Unfortunately, Alvaro makes a similar mistake to Singer in that he trivializes that which I am certain a virtuous individual would in fact find quite complex. For example, Alvaro trivializes human interests tied to tradition. In discussing temperance, he notes that the temperate person would not take on the negative health consequences of consuming animal products "just for taste or tradition" (98, cf. 145). Later, he says killing and eating animals "not out of necessity but rather for trivial reasons is not in accordance with the actions of a great-souled individual" (103). It is unclear why a great-souled individual who has character traits of ethical and intellectual virtues would lump together trivia with tradition when there is a significant difference between those kinds of interests that is highly relevant to understanding the context. If my brother wants to eat a hamburger because that's just what he is interested in eating and, though there are numerous plant-based nutritious options available, he just goes head and satiates his trivial craving for a burger that is very different from him wanting to eat the chicken soup our mother made from our grandmother's recipe and is serving at the Passover seder. How would the person with greatness of soul miss that nuance? How could they leave it out of their moral deliberations?

I am also skeptical of how little context moves Alvaro in his discussion of whether being lost on a deserted island would count as a justifiable time to consume animal flesh. He starts by saying that there are situations in which consuming animals is justifiable for the virtuous person, listing being left on a desert island with only animals to eat among those situations (109). He notes, though, that eating animals in such a case would still be "disgraceful" (109–10). It is justifiable but not thereby a good thing that is happening. So far, I am with him. My account will also make room for the idea that there are situations where compromise of vegan values might be justifiable, but a moral remainder is left behind. I will also argue that moral remainders will sometimes occur when we opt to adhere to veganism but in doing so hurt our loved ones. The idea that you can do what is justifiable but also face remainders makes sense to me, though I would not use the word "disgraceful" to characterize most situations where moral remainders arise. I also agree with Alvaro's efforts to dig deeper into the desert island context where there is no choice but to eat animals. It is, indeed, relevant to the dilemma to ask whether there are no plants on the island and, if so, how the animals survive (109–10). There could be reasonable answers to these questions (perhaps there are fish in the sea but literally nothing living on land) but asking them is certainly relevant to determining whether even lifeboat and desert island scenarios are really the easy, intuition-pumping scenarios their users proclaim them to be. As I noted earlier in this chapter, good ethical deliberation involves rejecting truncated narratives.

Where I part ways with Alvaro is in his discussion of how his approach tackles situations wherein people live in nonarable parts of the planet. In discussing the Inuit, for example, he says they can import plant-based foods and that they live "in communities with stores, schools, and modern buildings. Modern Inuit import food grown elsewhere and buy it in local stores" (111). Not having ever visited the Inuit and seen how they live, I cannot attest to whether Alvaro's description of their current way of life is accurate. Perhaps he has spent extensive time among the Inuit. That said, I do know that whenever I have traveled anywhere that requires the importation of plant-based foods, those food items are extremely expensive. We cannot simply will genuine conflicts away by offering simplistic out-of-pocket solutions. Here, as with grouping tradition with trivial pleasures of the palate, Alvaro is not engaging in context sufficiently deeply. Who buys the food goods imported into Inuit communities? Is it accessible to most community members or just the most economically advantaged? Is access to plant-based foods inclusive of proteins and other nutritional elements necessary for humans to thrive? There are many questions important to context that are left out of Alvaro's discussion. I do not think this is a flaw in the theory itself but rather one in Alvaro's particular way of thinking about matters. There is nothing built into a virtue-based animal ethics that requires simplifying context in this way.

Alvaro's approach offers several important tools for moral reflection as vegans. His emphasis on an inside-out rather than an outside-in approach to obligations to animals is, I think, preferable to the principle-driven accounts. People are more motivated and more equipped to act with integrity when, rather than following abstract rules imposed from the outside, they instead follow their considered and informed internal sense of their own character. As I will discuss in Chapter 3, there is a place for principles to be sure, but surely part of our moral lives should involve the kind of character development and identity as a person of virtue that he discusses. I also appreciate Alvaro's decreased focus on moral status. Though there is some discussion of cognition in his book, he focuses not on why animals matter but how a person of temperance, compassion, fairness, and greatness of soul would be in relationship with animals. As will become clear in Chapter 3, my ecofeminist approach rejects hierarchies of life-forms and too much concentration on moral status.

My view differs from Alvaro's in three important respects. First, he is a theoretical monist, positing one moral theory from which to guide one's moral actions (i.e., virtue theory). My view is theoretically pluralist. Second, my account is explicitly feminist. Though early in his book Alvaro says his work is a combination of feminist and virtue responses, aside from the occasional reference to care and a few citations of feminist theorists, I see scant evidence of a deeply feminist view in his work. Feminist approaches tend to focus significantly on relationships and how they factor into morality as well as the social, economic, political, and systemic realities that shape the moral dilemmas we face and our choices for responding to them. I do not see much of this focus in Alvaro's book. Third, Alvaro does not address relationships of love and care and how they impact questions around humans' relationships with other animals. He also trivializes tradition, grouping it together with other trivial interests. The one place in his book where tradition is raised aside from a one-off mention here and there is where he talks about the objection to his view based on the idea that exploiting other animals is what we humans have always done, so it is what we should continue doing. Alvaro deftly bats this old chestnut of an objection away by noting that we do not or certainly ought not continue traditions when they are immoral and then points to enslaving people as an example (120). Again, I see nothing in his theoretical position that prohibits Alvaro from tackling questions of relationality and cultural and familial traditions as he accounts for context. Unfortunately, he just does not engage with those issues in any focused way (or not at all in some cases).

3.2 Elisa Aaltola's Contextual Approach

Elisa Aaltola offers a contextual approach centered on interanimal conflicts where interests of equal importance are in conflict with one another (2005). Her critique of what she calls the "interests model" (Singer and Taylor's approach to categorizing interests) is similar to mine. Aaltola notes that categorizing interests is much more challenging that it first appears, asking "what sort of interest is the need to engage in a certain cultural tradition?" (20).[33] Life, she notes, is too complex to be reduced to categories (22–3). She further observes that measuring the importance of different interests is quite complicated cross-culturally when the measures themselves might differ (23). Making a hierarchy of interests, she argues,

[33]Cf. Aaltola and Oksanen (2002) for further discussion of whether traditions count as "primary" interests.

might work when it comes to conflicts between interests with clearly different degrees of value (basic vs. nonbasic, for example) but is not useful for conflicts between interests of the same type (24).

Aaltola argues that approaching conflicts of interest involves taking various factors into consideration when deliberating: rights, interests, mental capacities when relevant, and attachment when relevant. She notes, however, that "something more is needed to solve conflicts of equal interests, and that … something more ought to be less abstract and more focused on the practical level" (36–7). Aaltola's approach embraces monism at the theory level, positing just one theory of value, and pluralism of principles (37). This is how she describes the difference between contextualism and pluralist and multi-criterial models:

> [Contextualism] emphasizes not only (1) theory and (2) pluralism of principles, but also (3) the particularities of specific situations. Contextualism differs from pluralism in underlining the meaning of theory, and from the multi-criterial model in giving room for the possibility of unlimited amount [*sic*] of principles; it also differs from both in giving special importance to the context. (37)

The monist theory of value Aaltola relies on is "experientialism" where the focus is on welfare and the capacity to experience (38). When interests conflict, "we ought to seek to best serve the individual welfare of those involved, humans, cows, and giraffes included" (38–9). When conflicts involving equal interests arise, we will rely on the monist "principle of theory" that "includes respect for the welfare of others, and equality between experiencing beings" (39) and "principles of practicality" that focus on the "specifics of welfare, and can give room for various approaches, ranging from utilitarianism to rights theory and virtue ethics" (ibid.). These principles of practicality "articulate how the principles of theory should be understood in a practical context by stipulating exactly what respect for welfare includes" (ibid.). When equal interests conflict, Aaltola employs the three-pronged approach of focusing on the value of welfare (principle of theory), whatever principles of practicality apply in helping us achieve the value of respect for welfare, and context. She considers the concrete example of whether killing an animal is permissible.

In general, it will not be permissible to kill animals because doing so goes against their welfare, their rights, and the principle that we ought not to take another animal's life unless doing so is necessary to meet our "primary" interests (40) where primary interests are understood as those that "are essential to human identity and … promote the quality of life" and where "denying the right to follow them would be a gross neglect of human rights" (Aaltola and Oksanen 2002, 455). Aaltola further notes that, thinking about a cow, not only can we not kill and eat her but we also cannot keep her in dairy production or raise her and keep her confined, so we can turn her skin into leather. Using cows for food and clothing under nonsubsistence conditions does not fulfill our primary interests. Aaltola says it is permissible, however, to kill an elk if we have no other way to nourish ourselves. It might also be permissible to kill an animal if her own welfare requires it (euthanasia). Context will add more nuance: "We can kill a bear in order to protect a child or a dog if the harm is immediate, and when facing a compulsory decision between different animals, we ought to favor the one with more mental ability, with the ability to live longer, with more ties of her own, and so forth" (ibid.). She adds that we have added responsibilities where the animals in question are the result of domestication or where we have impacted their ecosystems. What I take away from this is a fairly straightforward permission to kill animals in cases of self-defense with the addition of context revealing other considerations: we can kill the bear to protect a child. Aaltola's contribution to the discussion of conflict involving equally important interests is to emphasize context's role in such cases. She draws attention to the importance of incorporating "practical considerations" into resolving conflicts of interest (41). This is an important contribution to be sure. So many approaches to interanimal conflicts of interest either ignore context altogether or only focus on limited contextual detail rather than the complete picture.

The view I defend in Chapter 3 is also a contextualized approach, taking seriously the importance of contextual detail to resolve interanimal conflicts of interest. I also share Aaltola's skepticism of hierarchies of life-forms, particularly the emphasis on cognition to differentiate the degrees of value a living being possesses. There are important differences in our approaches, however. First, Aaltola relies on a monist theory of value where I do not. I maintain that animals' value derives from a multitude of considerations. Second, her approach is focused on cases where interests of equal value conflict whereas I concentrate on situations where the interests at stake appear to be of different values—the deer's life is on the line while the recreational hunter wants to participate in the family's long hunting tradition but will certainly survive without doing so. I emphasize the importance of relational moral attention in such cases whereas I do not see much attendance to relationality in Aaltola's approach. I believe there is room in her approach for such considerations, but they do not come to the fore. It would be interesting to see where Aaltola's approach takes us in cases like those that are at the center of this book, how she sees relationality complicating interests, and how her contextualized approach can offer a deep analysis of important, but nevertheless nonbasic, interests.[34]

[34]Aaltola does take up the complicated issue of cultural hunting (Aaltola and Oksanen 2002), providing some insight into how her contextual approach might be used for nonbasic but important interests. Unfortunately, it is not quite detailed enough to gain sufficient insight into the conflicts I discuss in Part 2.

4 Conclusion

In this chapter we have considered multiple approaches to interanimal conflicts of interest: categorization and prioritization, relations-based, and contextual. The categorization and prioritization systems go awry in two ways: (1) Singer, Varner, and Warren all invoke hierarchies of life-forms that are problematic, as I will discuss more in Chapter 3, and (b) they either fail to fully account for the complexity of humans' most important issues (Singer, Taylor, and Warren) or become so mired in that complexity that they are too willing to override animals' most important interests (Varner). Other than Warren, they all fail to adequately address how relationships of love and care will complicate deliberations over whether and how to forego important interests in service of respecting animals' lives. Noddings's special relations account is lacking because she only allows room for obligations to animals with whom we can complete the relationship of care, failing to observe that so many of our entanglements with animals are designed precisely to render it impossible to have such encounters and build such relationships. She also does not attend to the reality that for some animals we humans are in right relationship precisely when we do not encounter them in a way that makes reciprocal care possible. I absolutely should not be in a position to develop a one-caring/cared-for relationship with the wild bears in Washington state. If I am, something has gone tragically wrong for the bears. There is a failure of imagination here about what it means to be in a caring relationship with an other-than-human. Mary Midgley's special relations account is more inclusive of other animals but focuses on why nearness and kinship in humans means showing preference for humans' interests might not be speciesist. This issue will be in the background as we think together about the applications of my theory in Chapters 4–6. I share Midgley's view that relationality, nearness, and kinship are relevant and also not necessarily overriding. Midgley stops there, whereas my project is to see what happens when we take that insight and apply it to real-world cases—not only in terms of nearness and kinship between humans but also nearness and kinship between humans and other animals and between other animals and their fellow other-than-humans. Finally, we looked at two contextual approaches. Alvaro's virtue account offers important considerations about developing character traits that guide who we are and how we will be in relationship with other animals. Unfortunately, Alvaro trivializes important human interests in service of showing how straightforwardly a person of virtue will see that veganism is the right thing to do. I agree with him that a person of true virtue will see the necessity of veganism; however, I do not believe that it is so straightforward in cases of deep relationship and connection. Indeed, I imagine a person of strong virtue will wrestle mightily in cases where their respect for animals conflicts with their desire to respect the traditions of their people and the connection and care they feel for their loved ones. Aaltola's contextual approach seems worthwhile in helping us approach cases where interests of equal value conflict (e.g., my life and the life of the bear who threatens me on a hike) but has little to say about how a contextual approach comes together in cases where interests are not of equal value aside from what she and Oksanen discuss in their piece on bird hunting in Åland, which is certainly worth reading for an interesting case of cross-cultural conflict related to minority hunting practices but does not engage with intracultural conflicts of interest (Aaltola and Oksanen 2002). A contextual approach can offer a way to approach conflicts of interest that takes seriously both the importance of respecting animals and the ways relationships of love and care complicate humans' important interests. The relational vegan ecofeminist approach I put forth in Chapter 3 endeavors to do just that.

3 RELATIONAL VEGAN ECOFEMINISM

1 Introduction

In the previous chapter, I considered several theories aimed at resolving interanimal conflicts of interest and raised concerns about their approaches. I have not exhausted all the theoretical resources the approaches considered in Chapter 2 can offer. No doubt, more could be said about each and how it might be adjusted to better account for the concerns I have raised. Still, I feel sufficiently unhappy with those approaches to warrant thinking about an alternative. Here, I articulate an ecofeminist approach to such conflicts. An ecofeminist approach, I believe, can better lead us out of the tension between acknowledging animals' moral importance by not sacrificing their basic interests in service of humans' less important interests and the reality that some human interests seem unimportant but are, indeed, tied to highly valued ends, relationships of love and care, and so forth.

In this chapter, I will first situate ecofeminism in feminist theory then articulate its primary theoretical commitments. I then provide a deeper description of the central theoretical commitments of vegan ecofeminism and briefly discuss vegan ecofeminists' approach to conflicts of interest in the cross-cultural realm. I end by briefly returning to relational moral attention and its role in addressing moral remainders.

2 Ecofeminist Theory

I begin with the caveat that ecofeminist theory is diverse. There are many versions of ecofeminism with most adhering to very similar principles but differing importantly in their particulars. Ecofeminists focus on a plurality of issues with some theorists and activists focusing more on some than others. It is impossible to give a singular description of ecofeminism due to this rich and important plurality. Here, I offer a version of ecofeminism that is prominent in the academic literature and added to by many activists, that highlights some of the most salient insights in the ecofeminist literature. Keep in mind, too, that ecofeminism goes back a very long way. Long before academics and activists were writing ecofeminist theory, activists, community organizers, and so many others were practicing ecofeminism in their daily lives and advocacy. The struggle against the patriarchal domination of our natural world has long been a part of some people's lives and communities, though too frequently their contributions are overlooked. I endeavor to articulate ecofeminism in a way that honors their work and lives. I begin with what is feminist about ecofeminism.

Feminist theory has expanded in waves where, ideally, the view becomes more expansive and inclusive (Gaard 2002).[1] Articulations of feminism are offered, it becomes clear what and who is missing from those accounts, new thinking is done, and important voices hitherto excluded from the conversation are included with the result that the theory develops. This process can be painful and exhausting for those left on the margins. It is not close to being complete, and much labor is done by those most harmed by exclusions. It is an imperfect process to be sure and one that, I hope, will always achieve greater levels of inclusivity, insight, solidarity, and humility. To wit, ecofeminism developed as a response to feminist views that were either overtly dismissive of nature, reifying the human/nature/culture divide, or simply that left our earth cohabitants out of the conversation altogether. For the ecofeminist, merely grounding a theory in feminism is insufficient; a theory must also include nature and animals (ibid.).

Ecofeminism is feminist in many ways, including that it emphasizes the themes brought forth in feminist work on the ethics of care, which highlight the moral relevancy of issues connected to interpersonal relationships of love and care, context in moral deliberation, and the important role of emotion and affect in morality alongside reason (Donovan 1993; Gaard 2002; Gilligan 1982; Gruen 1991, 1993, 2004; Held 1995; Kheel 1985, 1993; Luke 1995, 2007; Slicer 1991; Walker 1989, 1995). As Carol Gilligan explained the care framework:

> The moral problem arises from conflicting responsibilities rather than competing rights and requires for its resolution a mode of thinking that is contextual and narrative rather than formal and abstract. The conception of morality as concerned with the activity of care centers moral development around the understanding of responsibility and relationships, just as the

[1]The "waves" conception of feminism is useful but also contested (McAfee et al. 2024).

conception of morality as fairness ties moral development to the understanding of rights and rules. (1982, 19)

Care ethics argues for the salience of close, loving attention to the other in order to learn what matters to them, what their needs are, and how their interests can be best understood (Cuomo and Gruen 1998; Donovan 1994, 2007; Gaard 1993; Gruen 2004, 2011, 2015; Luke 2007). In care ethics, relationships "are not an 'add on' feature of human nature; they play an essential role in shaping what it is to be human" (Warren 1990, 143). Care ethics insists on the value of the first-person narrative as a source of information in moral deliberation (Lugones and Spelman 1983; Warren 1990). Feminist theory also devotes considerable attention to the structural mechanisms that reinforce the exploitation and domination of women, seeking to end sexist oppression (Warren 1990, 126). Ecofeminists observed that nature and naturism were either dismissed or ignored in most feminist thinking and sought to articulate "connections between the domination of women and the domination of nature" (ibid.).

Karen Warren helped shape ecofeminism by providing an analysis of the conceptual frameworks that lead to the shared oppression of women and nature. Analyzing the features of an "oppressive conceptual framework" and a "patriarchal oppressive conceptual framework," Warren helps us see clearly the oppressive nature of the "socially constructed lens through which we see ourselves and others" (1990, 127). An oppressive conceptual framework "explains, justifies, or maintains relationships of domination and subordination," and a *patriarchal* oppressive conceptual framework "explains, justifies, and maintains the subordination of women by men" (127–8). Oppressive conceptual frameworks have three features: (1) value dualisms, (2) value hierarchical thinking, and (3) the logic of domination (128). Understanding these three features is crucial to understanding ecofeminism.

Value dualisms are disjunctive pairs seen as oppositional and exclusive. They are "value" dualisms rather than merely disjuncts because higher value is ascribed to one side over the other. Value dualisms ecofeminists have identified include reason/emotion, competition/cooperation, justice/care, human/animal, man/woman, and culture/nature. The left-side disjuncts are perceived as more valuable than the right. The distinction between the disjuncts is not imaginary, of course. There is a real difference between a jungle and a museum. However, the idea that the world can be divvied up into binaries is profoundly problematic. The reason/emotion divide, for example, is deeply questioned in philosophy as well as science. Adams and Gruen note that some people believed ecofeminism was trying to "valorize" the nondominant half of the dualism by arguing that the right disjuncts are just as valuable as the left, but really ecofeminism points to the problematic nature of the dualisms themselves (Adams and Gruen 2014, 30). The value dualisms are not just injurious to moral deliberation itself by oversimplifying our understanding of the world but also provide justification for domination and exploitation by valuing one side of the dualism over the other (Gaard 2002; Gruen 1993; Warren 1990). The value-hierarchical, up-down thinking that places higher value on what is up and lower value on what is down creates fertile ground for oppressive beliefs and actions. It is the second feature of oppressive conceptual frameworks. Greta Gaard argued that we need to examine the dualisms vertically as well as horizontally, that is, we should look carefully at all the right-side disjuncts as a group. When we do so, we are better able to see how oppressive conceptual frameworks link together the vertical disjuncts resulting in linked oppression (i.e., emotion, cooperation, care, animal, woman, nature) (1997).

According to Warren, the logic of domination is what turns benignly noting difference into domination, oppression, and exploitation. For, the logic of domination tells us that if someone/something is superior to someone/something else, then the superior party is justified in subordinating the other (129). This logic of domination justifies oppression. Looking at the human/animal value dualism, we see how this oppressive conceptual framework functions. First, we note the human/animal binary. Then, arguments are given for why humans are superior to animals. Such arguments about what makes humans distinct from other animals (e.g., speech, tool use, and moral agency) are ubiquitous and have been contested for decades as science demonstrates over time that other animals share capacities previously identified as manifesting only in humans.[2] Now we have value-hierarchical thinking in place and add the logic of domination, which says that since humans are superior to animals, humans are morally justified in subordinating animals. As Warren argues, even if we want to talk in terms of superiority, we do not get domination without adding the logic of domination rendering subordination morally permissible (129). One could merely think oneself superior without dominating others. The logic of domination is what directly permits the subordination of that which is deemed inferior. The process can be run for any dualism in the list where the binary is noted, argument (however problematic) is given for the superiority of one disjunct, and the logic of domination is applied. This is how ecofeminism demonstrates how the logic of domination works to create the shared oppression of women, animals, nature, marginalized humans, care, emotion, and so forth. This is also why animalizing humans, as has been done throughout history in the Holocaust, racism, sexism, and the trading of enslaved people, is an effective tool for further marginalizing a group of people to this day (Kim 2015; Ko and Ko 2017). Once compared to an animal, the human is shifted to the animal side of the human/animal disjunct and loses the presumed superiority of membership in the species *Homo sapiens*. The very logic of domination that renders it permissible to breed animals as tools for

---

[2]Many readings in animal ethics present evidence for the failure of these human/animal dividing lines. Science and ethology have demonstrated the misconception humans have about our exceptionalism (Bekoff 2000; deWaal 2016; Gruen 2011; Rollin 2007; Taylor 2009).

human use also justifies the practice of enslaving people, the exploitation of natural resources, the failure to design a community that offers equal access to people with disabilities, and so forth. Thus, ecofeminists have argued forcefully that feminists must be environmentalists and environmentalists must be feminists. As Warren puts it, "Feminism *must* embrace ecological feminism if it is to end the domination of women because the domination of women is tied conceptually and historically to the domination of nature" (143). Feminism has not been sufficiently inclusive of nature and animals. Being feminist is not enough. Similarly, environmentalism must embrace feminism. Without acknowledging the joint oppression of women and nature, environmental ethics and advocacy is incomplete. A proper approach needs to be feminist and includes nature and animals. Carol Adams articulated the connections between women's and animals' oppression in particular in her groundbreaking *The Sexual Politics of Meat* ([1990] 2010), making the strong case that feminism must be inclusive of both women *and* animals.

In addition to identifying the roles of value dualisms, value-hierarchical thinking, and the logic of domination in the joint exploitation of women and nature, ecofeminism has several important theoretical commitments. It is pluralist, contextualized, and often nonhierarchical. I say "often" because some versions of ecofeminism more overtly focus on problems of hierarchy than others and because vegan ecofeminists in particular have been accused of invoking an animal/plant hierarchy, thus being nonhierarchical in name only (McKenna 2023; Plumwood 2012). Ecofeminism's pluralism is evinced in the theory's recognition that moral significance is derived from multiple sources rather than one, essential, feature. Unlike Singer, for example, who grounds animals' moral significance in sentience, ecofeminists note not only animals' sentience but also their cognition, important relationships, status as living beings in their own rights, and so forth. Ecofeminism is a contextual theory in that it takes the particulars of a situation as germane to ethical deliberation. I have more to say about ecofeminism's pluralism, contextualization, and rejection of hierarchy in Section 3. Ecofeminists also move away from the idea that the goal of ethics is to be objective or to deliberate from, as it were, the view from nowhere. This is largely because we reject the idea that there is such a point of view. We all have our own subjectivity and will see the world from the perspective of being that subject. This is not to say that we cannot light upon widely applicable truths of human experience or that ethics reduces to relativism, but that the idea that we can deliberate from a perfectly impartial and unbiased perspective is false. One idea, for example, is that calls for impartiality should be interpreted as requirements to name our biases and attempt to work through them, which will be helped along by using intersubjectivity to ensure others will locate our biases when we cannot to do so alone (Friedman 1989). There is a vast literature on the question of whether objectivity is possible or, if possible, whether it is desirable. Ecofeminists often deny the possibility and absolutely deny the desirability.

One final feature of ecofeminism involves the rejection of "sameness" arguments in considering animals' moral considerability. As Gruen and others have pointed out, traditional animal liberationist theories are focused on arguing that animals are importantly like us in ways that make them similarly morally significant. This focus on similarity or sameness has enabled us to gloss over what is importantly different about animal others and thus leads occasionally to a failure to recognize all that is morally important about them (cf. Curtin 1991, 64). Instead of searching for how other animals are *the same as* us, ecofeminism emphasizes the importance of recognizing difference. We learn what is morally important about them by careful attention to who they are. This study will reveal some features that overlap with human characteristics (e.g., sentience and cognition) but will also reveal ways animals are different and how those differences can guide our moral interactions with them (Gruen 2004, 2012; Warren 1990). We try to understand them for who they are rather than simply seeing ourselves in them. Importantly, we recognize difference to better attend to individuals' needs rather than to establish rankings between beings.

This concludes the brief discussion of ecofeminism's origins and commitments. Pushing feminism that denied or ignored the significance of nature to instead take our relationship with ecological others seriously, ecofeminism highlighted the dual oppression of women and nature. Nature was often defined quite narrowly, including trees, rocks, rivers, and ecosystems but failing to address animals and, in particular, animals domesticated and driven into service as tools for human ends in factory farms, abattoirs, laboratories, zoos, rodeos, and so on. This brings us to animal-inclusive ecofeminism and vegan ecofeminism in particular.

3 Vegan Ecofeminism

Animal-inclusive ecofeminism includes all the features of ecofeminism discussed earlier with the addition of animals as an essential part of ethical life. It recognizes both the moral significance of animals and the complexity of our relationships with them. These relationships can be loving and mutually beneficial (as in some of our relationships with our companion animals) whereas others are horrifically violent and exploitative (as in our raising and slaughtering of animals in horrific conditions, so we can eat their bodies). Animal-inclusive ecofeminism takes seriously that human lives are inextricably tied to animal others and that our relationships with them warrant considerable ethical focus and care. Vegan ecofeminism differs from other types of animal-inclusive ecofeminism by calling specifically for veganism as a response to both animals' moral standing and our objectification and commodification of them as mere tools for human use.

I return now to the pluralist, contextualist, and nonhierarchical features of ecofeminism alluded to earlier, offering more detailed accounts of each. What I say here is in line with many other vegan ecofeminists' interpretations but may not be representative of all vegan ecofeminist views. My vegan ecofeminism is pluralistic in two ways: (1) it takes a pluralist approach to animals' moral significance and (2) it is methodologically pluralist in that I advocate for moving between principles and particulars when undertaking moral deliberation. I begin with pluralism about moral significance.

It is crucial that we avoid myopic conceptions about what makes animals morally significant. Arguably, this is important in considering what makes humans morally important as well, though I leave that aside. In Chapter 2 we saw the dangers of myopic approaches to animals' moral significance in Varner's endorsement of creating blind strains of hens less prone to stress-induced pecking and thus better able to cope with life in a battery cage. Varner's singular focus on reducing suffering for the merely sentient prevents him from seeing the other crucial features of hens' moral significance. A pluralist conception of moral significance asks us to recognize that sentience matters but as only one consideration among many. Many animals are, as Tom Regan put it, subjects-of-a-life. They have a perspective on their own lives that varies from individual to individual—one that includes memories from the past and desires for the future (Regan 2004a). They are also individual creatures with interests in building relationships with others, nurturing their young, and fostering communities of their own according to their species-typical norms. These account for what Lori Gruen has called the "external" reasons we have for recognizing the moral significance of animals (2011, 42), where "external" is meant to indicate reasons that operate from outside of moral agents, pushing us to recognize morally important features of animals, but that do not necessarily connect to any sentiments of compassion, care, empathy, or love that we may also use to understand their moral significance. The traditional animal liberation views have a long-standing history of eschewing mechanisms internal to the agent—compassion, empathy, and care—in favor of abstract principles that can be applied universally. Hens are either sentient, or they are not. They are, so they have moral significance. You can hate hens, experience no empathy for them, and still recognize the significance of their sentience. One merely reasons one's way to the conclusion that, since hens are sentient, they matter morally just as human sentience matters. This, they argue, is far more reliable than internal, affect-based, ways of recognizing moral significance (Singer 1994, 38).

Put another way, animal ethics has a long history of enforcing a reason/emotion divide, in keeping with the themes of most Western ethical approaches rooted in nineteenth-century thinkers (i.e., Bentham, Mill, Kant, etc.). Animal ethics theories that grew out of traditional Western ethical views insist that one key to thinking about our moral obligations to animals is to rely solely on reason, rejecting anything emotional in content. This way, as the point earlier about caring not one whit about chickens illustrates, treating animals as worthy of moral consideration would not be up to the whims of how an individual might feel about them. This focus on reason-only approaches has been the subject of much feminist criticism at the level of normative ethics as well as in the literature on animal ethics. One might question, for example, whether the clean divide between reason and emotion even exists. Beyond that, one might wonder whether, even if it does, ethical deliberation is in fact possible or desirable if focused only on reason with no role for affect. This insistence on reason-only approaches in the animal ethics world trickled down to the animal rights movement. Cleveland Amory, founder of the Fund for Animals (which became part of the Humane Society of the United States eventually), spoke about the animal rights movement as one that consists of more than just "little old ladies in tennis shoes" (Adams and Gruen 2022, 15). A distinct effort was made to remove women from the animal rights story in an attempt to prove the movement was driven by reason, not emotion (Adams and Gruen 2022, 14), an especially obnoxious approach given that women have been leaders of the animal rights movement from its beginnings. Sunaura Taylor discusses the late-nineteenth-century diagnosis of the "zoophilpsychosis" illness, which meant an excessive concern for animals and was mostly attributed to women (2017, 151). The reason/emotion value dualism reigns supreme among much ethical theory and in particular in the history of animal ethics.

Feminist critiques of reason-only approaches abound, some of which I discussed in Chapter 2. Virgina Held noted, "An adequate moral theory should be built on appropriate feelings as well as on appropriate reasoning" (1995, 157).[3] As Gruen helpfully notes, external reasons for thinking animals are morally significant are useful, particularly in situations where we do not have time for serious reflection, where the people involved have not yet found their way to compassion for animals, or for discussions with industry leaders so focused on efficiency and profit that they cannot respond to anything other than dispassionate, abstract argument (2011, 42). Yet, conversations focused solely on these external reasons will feel lacking and will sometimes prove less persuasive than those inclusive of internal reasons for seeing animals as morally significant. As Brian Luke put it, "There is also something artificial about reducing animal liberation to a principle of respect for sentience (or subjecthood), since we do not in fact respond to oppressed animals as *cases* of sentience or subjecthood, but as individuals who are in one way or another communicating their needs to us" (1995, 295).

Internal reasons "allow us to see and act differently because we view such action as consistent with our sense of ourselves, our commitments, projects, and desires" (Gruen 2011, 42). If we do not want to be a party to cruelty, for

[3]Cf. Donovan (1993); Gaard (2002); Gruen (1991, 1993, 2004); Kheel (1985, 1993); Luke (1995, 2007); McKenna (1994); and Slicer (1991), among others, for feminist critiques of moral theories built solely on reason.

example, the problems with industrial animal agriculture will be abundantly clear to us once we inform ourselves of what that industry entails (Hursthouse 2006). Internal reasons allow us to take what we learn about how animals are treated and see how that information attaches to what is already within our hearts and minds. This process requires knowledge about our treatment of animals and openness to experiencing compassion and empathy for them. As Josephine Donovan wrote, "We should not kill, eat, torture, and exploit animals because they do not want to be so treated, and we know that. If we listen, we can hear them" (1993, 185). Seeing animals in their joy and suffering is important to recognizing what matters about them. When we look in their eyes, hear their screams of agony, or are privileged enough to observe their delight we see just how much their lives matter to them and how deeply they feel their despair and joy. Our emotional responses help us access who they are and what matters about them in addition to who we want to be and what practices we wish to support. True, some people do not have emotional responses to animals' suffering. Someone may wish to suggest that those who work in vivisection and factory farms will not feel these kinds of feelings. In fact, there is some evidence to suggest that people whose jobs require causing animals to suffer do have emotional responses but that they must become desensitized in order to continue their work and remain employed (Bauer 2008, 159–60; Gluck 2016; Pachirat 2011). Humans have developed intricate systems to "*forestall* the development of sympathies for exploited animals as well as powerful mechanisms for *overriding* any sympathies that might remain" (Luke 1995, 303). Responding with empathy and compassion to animals is aided by what Gruen calls "empathetic engagement," which "involves both affect and cognition and will necessitate action" (2012, 229–30). This requires understanding the other and how she is both similar and different from us. Rather than putting ourselves in the others' shoes, as so many conceptions of empathy enjoin us to do, Gruen's entangled empathy requires us to do our best to understand "how the one being empathized with experiences the world," to feel as best we can what it is like to be *them* in their shoes (2012, 229). Josephine Donovan writes about sympathy in a very similar way to Gruen's entangled empathy (Donovan 2007, 176–80). Seeing the other and feeling empathy for who she is and what she is experiencing is a tremendously effective way to overcome the mechanisms of forestallment and overriding that some people find stymying their emotional responses to animals. This is hard work. Understanding the other without projecting ourselves into that understanding is a process we are bound to get wrong at times as all good friends, lovers, and parents know. Noting this, Margaret Urban Walker suggests that as we cannot hope to always be correct in the care perspective, we will have to rely on "incomplete versions of care" (Walker 1989, 130). An incomplete version of care is preferable to not endeavoring to care at all. As in so much of life, we learn from our efforts and strive to do better the next time.

Recognizing another's sentience or capacity for self-awareness is one part of moral attention. Trying to understand them, their behaviors, what matters to their species, and what matters to the particular individual before us provides another level of information that is necessary for capturing a being's moral significance. Pluralism of this kind is a commitment in most ecofeminist theory as well as in theories that do not self-identify as ecofeminist (Warren 1997).[4] Recognizing the multiple sources of moral significance points to the second kind of pluralism in my approach—methodological pluralism.

The methodological pluralism of my account endorses moving between guiding principles and attention to particulars as the best way of approaching animal ethics (and perhaps ethics between humans, though I do not defend that here). Put another way, the approach involves both a top-down and bottom-up form of deliberation. Feminism recognizes a tension of sorts between principles and particulars. Sole reliance on abstractly formed, universal, principles is antithetical to the feminist commitment to the inclusion of contextual details in moral deliberation. Yet, solely attending to particulars threatens us with relativism or ad hoc decision-making. A balance must be struck between principles and the facts on the ground. George Elliot expressed this point beautifully in her novel *The Mill on the Floss*, though she limits her discussion to humans where I would expand it to animals:

> All people of broad moral sense have an instinctive repugnance to the men of maxims … [who] are guided in their moral judgement solely by general rules, thinking that these will lead them to justice by a ready-made patent method, without the trouble of exerting patience, discrimination, impartiality, without any care to assure themselves whether they have the insight that comes from a hardly-earned estimate of temptation, or from a life vivid and intense enough to have created a wide fellow-feeling with all that is human. (Elliot 2003 [1860], 518)[5]

Many years after Elliot wrote those words, Virginia Held said that feminist moral inquiry "would be a pluralist ethics, containing some principles at the intermediate level of generality, relevant to given domains, and many particular judgments sensitively arrived at in these various domains" (1995, 161). My view is that there is no way to capture all of what is important in interanimal ethics and interanimal conflicts of interest specifically by attending only to principles. Rigid adherence to abstractly derived principles can block the important moral attention involved

[4]Cf. Karen Warren on pluralism (1990, 139). There are also pluralist positions in environmental ethics. For an interesting back and forth about pluralism versus monism and worries about relativism in environmental ethics see Stone (2003); Callicott (2003); and Light (2003).

[5]My thanks to Jean Roberts for encouraging me to read Elliot, particularly this passage.

in seeing others as individuals, engaging with them empathetically in the way Gruen recommends, and understanding how their interests and needs are deeply embedded in particular social, economic, historical, and oppressive contexts. Unquestioned adherence to general moral principles turns our attention away from the particularity of the animals with whom we are in relationship. There are cows and their needs and ways of being in the world as a bovine and then there is Betsy the cow living her life in a sanctuary and who she is, what she experiences, and how she shows up in the world. What we do as we care for Betsy matters in a principled way to be sure, but it is crucial that we get her particulars straight if we wish to engage in right action and loving attention toward her.

Hence, in my vegan ecofeminist approach, we move between certain guiding principles and particulars in order to give our best moral attention to the situation before us. I see these guiding principles as providing a basic framework with which to approach interanimal conflicts of interest but not as predicting how matters will be resolved in particular cases. Thus, they work differently than the kinds of principles advocated by philosophers who claim that there is an abstractly justified, universally applicable hierarchy of life-forms or interests or those who work from clearly defined, abstract principles to specific cases employing a top-down, one-directional method. In a way, methodological pluralism is a kind of reflective equilibrium between specific cases and abstract principles, though like Held, I distinguish this from Rawlsian reflective equilibrium by noting the inclusion of affect as part of the reflective process (Held 1995, 155).

Pluralist views of this sort can be disconcerting for some. They worry that working without principles that determine in advance the outcome of particular conflicts will result in ad hoc decision-making, where what is right is simply up to the agent and how she feels in a situation. This concern, while common, is misguided. As Held wrote, "While the dangers of ad hoc decisions are real, so are the dangers of distorting actual situations in order to fit them into abstract legalistic categories of general principles. Persons cannot increase the trust between them by misinterpreting each other's problems and pains" (1995, 162).[6] I prefer to face worries about ad hoc decision-making rather than endorse an entirely principle-driven methodology that risks distorting reality. Moreover, claims that principle-driven moral approaches avoid complexity or render ethical life straightforward are dubious at best. Moral life is messy, complicated, and at times gut-wrenchingly difficult. We need a theory that recognizes this and offers a way forward rather than one that appears straightforward but offers clear guidance in only a very few, rather circumscribed, situations.

[6]This topic is well-covered ground in the feminist and ecofeminist literature. For example, see Donovan and Adams's discussion of the apparent relativism involved in an ethics of care (2007, 4). See also Gilligan (1982) and Walker (1989, 130).

What sort of general, guiding principles do I have in mind? My methodology does not posit principles that predetermine the outcome of conflicts between different kinds of beings and different interests. No doubt we will be in situations with animals where we will sometimes need to cause them harm just as we are sometimes in situations with humans where there is no escape from causing someone harm—minimally or maximally. Generally, in interhuman conflicts, we try to minimalize harm, avoid treating one another as having merely instrumental value, and strive for compassion and attentiveness rather than cruelty and disinterest. These same guiding principles apply in the interanimal case as well.

Josephine Donovan and Carol Adams have offered the following core principles for animal ethics:

> It is wrong to harm sentient creatures unless overriding good will result *for them*. It is wrong to kill such animals unless in immediate self-defense or in defense of those for whom one is personally responsible. Moreover, humans have a moral obligation to care for those animals who, for whatever reason, are unable to adequately care for themselves, in accordance with their needs and wishes, as best as the caregivers can ascertain them and within the limits of the caregivers' own capacities. Finally, people have a moral duty to oppose and expose those who are contributing to animal abuse. (2007, 4)

My view is informed by Donovan and Adams, though I alter the details somewhat. For example, the principle of self-defense should include strangers for whom we are not personally responsible but who we can help as when I am hiking, and a party of other hikers is threatened by a bear, and I am in a position to render aid. I interpret the principle of the wrongness of killing animals except "in defense of those for whom one is personally responsible," to include the killing of animals in situations where one must consume them in order to survive. Finally, I add the principle that we should treat interanimal conflicts with the same careful attention we give to interhuman conflicts, where the parties are on equal moral footing. These are the principles I invoke to guide us in moral deliberation over interanimal conflicts of interest.

Concretely, if a family of rats overtakes my home and threatens the well-being of my family then I will need to do something about the situation. This would also be true if a person suffering from drug addiction takes up residence on my front porch, littering it with used needles. Though the addicted person is just as morally valuable as the individuals in my family, I cannot allow her to threaten our well-being. This does not mean, however, that I can leave out poisoned food for her to eat thus abandoning her to a slow and agonizing death. I also cannot put her in the back of my car and toss her wherever I choose or set a trap for her and leave her there to die a protracted death from thirst and starvation. I will need to be thoughtful about what to do, consult with others, try to understand her needs and what is best for her, and undertake the course of action that meets my family's needs while limiting harms to her. I should also recognize the social, economic, and political structures that may have influenced this person ending up on my front porch with nowhere else to go. While consideration of these background conditions does not necessitate that I allow the addict to stay on my porch, it will help me better understand the situation and provide important information about how my options for handling the conflict may be limited by structures beyond my immediate control. Reflection on the background conditions may reveal that this woman would be best taken care of in a treatment facility, but if I live in a city that has cut the budget for such health care or if the woman refuses treatment, then that kind of care may be impossible. My handling of the rats will require the same careful consideration.

We live in a world where billions of animals are exploited in service of human ends. This means that human and animals' interests will be in tension much of the time. Many of our conflicts with animals are "false" in that we bring the animals into existence for the sole purpose of using them for human ends and then try to work out our moral obligations to them (Francione 2004, 132). Living in accordance with a principle requiring that we treat interanimal conflicts with the same attention we give interhuman conflicts will become more feasible over time as the movement for animal liberation gains ground and we reduce the number of morally inappropriate relationships we have with animals in the first place. If we banned factory farming, for example, that would eliminate roughly 9 billion instances of conflict on a yearly basis in the United States alone.

The principles I offer will become clearer when we consider them in conjunction with the contextual and nonhierarchical elements of relational vegan ecofeminism. I turn to discussing these elements now, beginning with contextualization. When we say ecofeminism is contextual, we are referring precisely to this attention to particulars that methodological pluralism requires engaging with. Decontextualizing moral dilemmas is problematic both because doing so strips important details from our deliberations and because it is obnoxious to demand that people make difficult decisions while we simply ignore all the complexity they face.

Relational vegan ecofeminism, like other forms of ecofeminism and feminism, highlights the context that both creates the dilemmas we face and controls what options are available for solving those dilemmas. In part, this entails politicizing the ethics of care (Curtin 1991; Donovan 2007, 187–9; Donovan and Adams 2007, 3). A politicized ethic approaches interanimal conflicts of interest by addressing how power structures play a role in creating our predicaments, shaping our needs, and defining our choices. Thus, vegan ecofeminism pays attention to issues of interlocking oppressions—seeing the ways in which animals' fates continue to be tied to the fates of women and others, how factory farmed animals and factory farm workers are both exploited by modern, industrialized farming, and so forth

(Adams 1990; Donovan 1993; Donovan and Adams 2007; Gaard 1993; Gruen 2011; Kemmerer 2011; Taylor 2017; Warren 1990). We consider the role of capitalism in creating the dilemmas we face as well as the social, economic, political, and other structures relevant to these dilemmas. Contextual analysis also includes local details such as where the dilemma is taking place, the important relationships involved, who the individuals are, and what is morally relevant about their particulars. To deliberate morally on such a view is to include detailed descriptions of what is at stake for the humans and the animals, situating those details in historical, political, and societal context, and asking hard questions about how we found ourselves in the situation of conflict to begin with. It involves being aware of interlocking oppressions, privilege and how it is functioning in our deliberations, and the necessity of cross-cultural understanding and communication.

I have said that in addition to being pluralist and contextualized, vegan ecofeminism is nonhierarchical. Gary Varner said that any viable theory of environmental ethics has to show why certain human interests are more important than animals' interests (Varner 1998, 79). Contra Varner, I maintain that any viable theory of animal ethics striving to take both animals and humans seriously ought to reject preconceived hierarchies that abstractly posit who or what kind of interest matters most prior to the examination of a given conflict. This means that human lives are not prima facie more valuable than animal lives. All sentient creatures enter moral deliberation with the same moral value regardless of their species membership. As Lori Gruen wrote, "By establishing superiority in theory, the groundwork is laid for oppression of the inferior in practice. … Constructing, and then naturalizing, hierarchies has been one of the more insidious justifying mechanisms for the oppression of both women and animals" (1993, 79).[7] Varner defends his hierarchy on the grounds that it is axiological rather than valuational. That is, rather than denying moral considerability to animals, it "gives pride of place to certain interests that only human beings have" (2012, 248). For my part, I am suspicious of a methodology for thinking about interanimal conflicts of interest that starts with the presumption that the only viable way forward for such a methodology is to give pride of place to certain kinds of interests, namely ones only humans have. Though Varner certainly does not hold the view that humans must *always* win in a conflict, he clearly believes a fixed hierarchy is necessary in order to make moral decisions. Like Taylor's biocentric egalitarianism, my ecofeminist approach embraces a methodology that acknowledges differences without ranking them in a static, universally binding way.

One way or another humans and their interests always come out on top in fixed hierarchies. This move is often defended by appeal to the idea that humans' rational

---

[7]For ecofeminist discussions of hierarchy and defenses of nonhierarchical approaches, see Donovan (1993); Gaard (2002); Gruen (1993); Kheel (1985, 1993); Lucas (2005) and Taylor (2017). For a rights-based rejection of hierarchies, see Taylor (1996).

capacities set us apart from other animals. Indeed, these capacities constitute a large part of what it means to be human. We are cognitively capable of choosing our own ends, partaking in moral deliberation, exercising our will, and so forth. It is often thought that these rational capacities are precisely what we value in one another.

I have never quite understood the jump from recognizing that humans have rational agency to the claim that this in turn renders humans *more* morally significant than other sentient animals. Species differences are relevant to understanding needs and capabilities rather than to rankings of moral significance. While I might value other humans for their rational nature (and for their other features as well, I would hope), I do not see that this insight should cross the species boundary and reflect on, say, a cat's value. I can value the cat's loving and loyal treatment of me or the special kind of intelligence he shows when he stalks and pounces on the red dot of a laser pointer. My husband cannot hear as well as our dog, Paddington, but this is not a reason to think Paddington is more morally significant than my husband. That Paddington's hearing is more acute than my husband's helps me understand the needs of each (Paddington might be agitated by a noise my husband cannot hear), but the differences are not relevant to their ranking in terms of moral value. This parallels nicely what many of us think is true in the interhuman realm, namely that differences of cognitive capacity point the way to understanding differences in need but not to differences in moral significance.

I offer the same response to the idea that humans' cognitive capacities generate interests that are more valuable than other, less cognitively enriched interests. I am unconvinced that the kinds of interests humans have belong at the top of a fixed hierarchy. It is true that I have interests in long-term projects that provide direction and meaning to my life and desires that extend into the distant future. True, too, is that I could suffer considerable harm if those projects and desires are thwarted. This does not, however, justify a blanket statement claiming that my interests are more morally significant than those of a creature who does not have life-guiding plans or desires for the far distant future. For, I struggle with how to compare human and nonhuman experiences, and I believe that attempts to do so in a fixed and assured way demonstrate a considerable lack of humility or commitment to epistemic modesty.[8] To his credit, Varner was always open to scientific evidence proving that his hierarchy needed to be adjusted. The issue is that humans' capacity to fully grasp what other animals are capable of, even in the world of ethology, is far less reliable than we like to think (de Waal 2016).

When I ask myself if my life is more valuable than Paddington's life, I return always to the question "More valuable to whom?" My life is quite valuable to me

[8]I understand epistemic modesty in this situation along the lines Bill Talbott suggested. He said that "a moral philosophy is *epistemically modest*, if it acknowledges its fallibility" (2005, 75–6).

as I suspect his is to him. The life of a hen bred and raised only to produce eggs for human consumption is merely of economic value to the farmer who crams her into a battery cage with fifteen other hens, deprives her of light, and exploits her reproductive labor until she is spent. Her life is valuable to her, however. Moreover, the only perspective from which we humans can judge human and animals' comparative moral significance is our own, human, perspective. Given the natural preference one might tend to feel toward one's own way of being in the world and the ways in which humans have come to rely on animals as instruments for our ends, it strikes me as quite possible that we have a problem thinking clearly about these questions. I am not only unconvinced by the arguments offered defending humans' greater moral significance but also suspicious that our largely unquestioned adherence to the belief in human exceptionalism reflects hubris on our part. Ecofeminists are not alone in rejecting the idea that human characteristics render us superior to other animals. Recall that Paul Taylor's biocentric egalitarianism is based on the rejection of human superiority as the most important element in the attitude of respect for nature (1986, 129).

One worry about this nonhierarchical account is that hierarchy is crucial to decision-making. We cannot begin our day without making some sort of hierarchy reflecting our priorities about what is most important and least important. Some may say that any time we decide that one consideration is more important than another we are making a hierarchy. I think of hierarchies as rigid systems of ranking, generated in abstraction, and used to predetermine outcomes. These sorts of hierarchies often result in justifying dominating others. The kind of "hierarchy" that grounds decision-making between competing claims is different and less insidious than the fixed hierarchies I speak of here. Ranking in the moment in response to what is before us and what is most important *today* or *at this precise decision point* is very different from a rigid hierarchy positing that ground projects are more important than noncategorical desires or that having a biographical sense of self makes a being more morally significant than one lacking that sense of self. It is a fluid kind of ranking informed by the specifics of the situation before us. As Rosalind Hursthouse put it, "Virtue ethicists are not going to commit themselves in advance to saying that the cited differences will always guarantee that, in cases of conflict, it is the cats that will go to the wall because of their inferior status" (2006, 139). The same can be said of the relational vegan ecofeminist approach. Here, again, we come up against the worry that this sort of flexibility produces problematic ad hoc decision-making. Yet, this is a process we engage in quite regularly in our interpersonal relationships with high degrees of success. Elizabeth Dodson Gray puts the point nicely:

> The point is that we parents continually find some ground for making our decisions, grounds other than ranking our children in some hierarchy of their worth. What we perceive instead is that our children have differing needs,

> differing strengths, differing weaknesses. And occasions differ too. It is upon the basis of some convergence of all these factors that we make our decisions. (1979, 148)

There are ways to resolve conflicts, as this work will show, that neither rely on fixed hierarchies nor reduce to individuals' passing whims. We do this successfully regularly as people in relationship with others. Whether my son, my dog, my husband, or my dear friend comes first is a decision made in response to the moment with attention to the needs and characteristics of each individual and the options before me. Much of the time, we get these things right. When we do not, we have an opportunity to acknowledge the hurt we caused and undertake the work of repair.

Hierarchies of moral significance are not only problematic because they select and elevate arbitrary features and most often lead to exploitation and marginalization of those who do not share those features. They are dangerous to moral deliberation itself. We are driven to such hierarchies in part because we want to feel justified in pursuing our interests at the expense of others' interests. The hierarchy provides the justification we need to say that we were right and that our choices were morally sanctioned. We are relieved of further moral discomfort. This is misguided. Hierarchies ease our minds with the thought that we are justified. Yet, whether we are ultimately justified in our choices, we cannot escape that these choices frequently generate collateral damage for others. Recognizing the damage, seeing it for what it truly is, and confronting what we might do about it (as Taylor suggests with his Principle of Restitution) is a crucial part of navigating interanimal conflicts of interest. To the extent that fixed hierarchies obscure this reality, they undermine moral deliberation. I have more to say about moral remainders in the final section of this chapter when I discuss relational moral attention as part of relational vegan ecofeminism.

There is another important worry about vegan ecofeminist, nonhierarchical approaches. Erin McKenna has noted that vegan ecofeminists claim to be nonhierarchical but maintain an animal/plant value dualism and, in drawing the line at sentience, simply endorse a hierarchy of a different kind than other theorists (McKenna 2021). Marti Kheel warned against the dangers of replacing one hierarchy with another (Kheel 1985). McKenna's criticism is correct. This may disappoint some readers, but while I will share some thoughts on the matter, I will not resolve it here for I am not yet clear on how best to theorize about nonsentient living things. I acknowledge, though, that living beings must nourish and that humans do not have an obligation to die rather than nourish. That much is obvious to me. We also cannot move about the world, till earth, or flourish in any way without creating damage for some other living beings. What must be determined is whether there is a way to confront that reality without creating a hierarchy. Paul Taylor believed he had done so, though many critics of his work believe otherwise.

Why might vegan ecofeminists seeking a nonhierarchical account draw the line at sentience? One response asks what empathetic engagement would look like with nonsentient living things, wondering if that is even possible? Gruen believes such engagement is impossible as there is no perspective in the other with which to engage; sentient beings can have deep experiences in the nonsentient natural world, but we do not share those experiences with that world (2015, 68–75). I am not sure whether I agree, but it is important to note that where ecofeminists have drawn lines at sentience there is not an "anything goes" ethos. Karen Warren, for example, discussed rock climbing and attending to the rock in a loving rather than domineering way (1990, 134–8). Ecofeminists have long engaged in activism fighting the plundering of earth's resources and the poisoning of the planet's living things. To paraphrase Mary Midgley, no ecofeminist would endorse torching the forest just to watch it burn. So, the hierarchy that remains in vegan ecofeminism is one that embodies deep respect for the nonsentient world, a desire to protect all living things, and a sense that wanton destruction of their lives is wrong. Something curious is going on here morally, with ecofeminism deeply endorsing a nonhierarchical approach but often drawing the moral line at sentience thus seemingly endorsing at least one hierarchy. However, diagnosing and resolving that strangeness will take me too far afield. So, I recognize it as something that requires more thinking and focus and move forward acknowledging all the while that to call a view nonhierarchical that draws the line of equal moral significance at sentience is in tension with itself.

We now see clearly how vegan ecofeminism endorses the rejection of animal flesh foods. As ecofeminism is pluralist about why animals are morally significant, there is a long list of morally salient considerations that would preclude using animals as tools for human consumption—they are sentient, they are often beings with memories and plans for the future, they have value well beyond being useful to humans, they can lead flourishing lives of their own according to their species-typical ways of being, and they have meaningful relationships with their conspecifics and others. Vegan ecofeminists oppose the consumption of animal flesh on feminist grounds, noting the deep connections between the domination and exploitation of women and the domination and exploitation of animals. Vegan ecofeminists further note that our food system involves the extensive exploitation of marginalized human laborers as well as contributes significantly to environmental destruction at both the local and global levels. Veganism is a response to all the animals pressed into service on humans' behalf and also to the humans who are maimed, injured, and who die right alongside them particularly in industrial agriculture and slaughtering facilities (Dreier 2025; Fitzgerald 2010; Hribal 2003; Pachirat 2011; Schlosser 2001; Torres 2007). Vegan ecofeminists put out a call for veganism as a stand against climate change and environmental racism. Veganism, we say, is one important way to resist the violence, suffering, exploitation, and domination of animals, humans, and the planet (Curtin 1992,

132–3; Emmerman 2024; Kheel 2004, 334; Ko and Ko 2017; Taylor 2017). As Marti Kheel noted, the overwhelmingly problematic confluence of patriarchal structures that intersect in identifying and producing animals as a source of food "invite[s] vegetarianism as a response" (2004, 334). Thus, we advocate for veganism.

In the ongoing evolution of ecofeminist theory, however, it became apparent that the call to veganism appeared to be in strong tension with vegan ecofeminism's rejection of universalizable moral edicts and moral absolutes. Activists and theorists began to worry that ecofeminist vegan advocacy was reifying colonialist, imperialist, and racist positions antithetical to ecofeminist values. Cathryn Bailey sums up the criticism nicely:

> In their zeal to extend sympathy for animals, white privileged women have at times been insensitive to the different meanings that both animals and food have for women of color and for women globally. This absolutist position, that it is morally wrong for feminists to eat meat, has met particularly harsh criticism for its insensitivity to women's real lives. (2007a, 50)

What would ecofeminism say to those living in nonarable climates, to families in refugee camps, or to people in industrialized nations who lack access to fruits and vegetables because of systemic racism and food apartheid?[9] How can a theory that takes context seriously take an apparently absolutist position against the consumption of animal flesh?

"Contextual moral vegetarianism" (CMV) is vegan ecofeminism's reply to these questions.[10] Deanne Curtin explained CMV this way:

> I do not see the commitment to vegetarianism as a decontextualized, purely rational, duty, but as a situated, feminist response to the contemporary moral landscape. The approach I propose is contextual, though not relativistic. That is, it sees vegetarianism as one situated response to a complex set of neocolonial, ecological, and feminist issues. Although it is contextualist, it is not relativist since it resolutely opposes neocolonialism, naturism, speciesism, and sexism. Finally, it is moral in the sense that, while its situatedness may include health issues, for example, it is to be understood primarily as a moral response, a way of *being* ethically in the contemporary world. (2004, 273)

---

[9]I follow Food Empowerment Project in using the language of "food apartheid" rather than "food deserts." Deserts are naturally occurring phenomena whereas lack of access to healthy foods is the direct result of racist policies and practices (Food Empowerment Project, "Food Deserts*").

[10]The "vegetarianism" here is best understood as veganism. CMV as a term was coined before "veganism" was widely used.

Hence, CMV is a stance that takes people's situatedness seriously and recognizes that vegetarianism is an appropriate ethical response in many but not all contexts. Marti Kheel expanded on this idea by noting that while she will not "'defend' vegetarianism as a universal norm to be imposed on all people as a moral imperative," she asks, "What are the factors that support meat eating as a dietary norm?" and "What factors might invite vegetarianism as a response?" (Kheel 2004, 327). Both Curtin and Kheel see veganism as a political act of resistance against patriarchal norms.

Much has been written on CMV in the years since it was first articulated.[11] Those discussions largely take place in the intercultural context—thinking about the complexity of claims that calls for vegetarianism is culturally insensitive (Gaard 2002; Kheel 2004; Twine 2022), and, more recently, noting that while concerns about vegan scholarship and activism being imperialist are crucial to heed, it is important to recognize that it is industrialized animal agriculture that is being exported to developing nations at an alarming rate rather than veganism (Twine 2022). These are vital discussions worthy of time and attention. I am more concerned here that CMV theory has generally ignored the very important *intracultural* context where similar concerns can arise. Issues of gender, race, class, ethnicity, and tradition play out locally as well as globally. Vegans throughout the world feel the pull of these issues as they join loved ones at the table. Veganism is "not itself immune from becoming entangled with exclusionary notions of the human, be they along lines of race or class" (Twine 2014, 197). This realization has come as a shock to some, white, vegan activists and scholars and some reject its truth. Twine is right to acknowledge the ways that vegan scholarship and activism have and continue to operate on limited and essentialist conceptions of what it means to be human. At the same time, I share Twine's frustration that some calls to label vegan advocacy as colonialist or insensitive to cross-cultural consideration themselves miss that industrialized nations are exporting capitalist practices and industrial animal agriculture far more than veganism and that culture itself tends to be conceived of anthropocentrically (ibid., cf. Afshari 2026). For example, Twine observes that defending bullfighting on the grounds that it is important culturally evinces a "speciesist term and frame," because culture is itself an anthropocentric concept (205, cf. Kim 2015).

Vegan ecofeminists have incorporated CMV into their work in different ways. As Twine notes, some have responded with a call for semi-vegetarianism, others advocate for a "near universalist" stance supporting veganism, others have a slightly less universalist stance that demonstrates more comfort with seeing values such as opposition to cruelty as universalist, while others have focused on opposing carnism as a compulsory norm (ibid.). My position is closest to the

---

[11]For examples see: Curtin (1991, 1992, 2004); Gaard (2002); Gruen (2022); Kheel (2004, 2008); and Twine (2022).

third option. I have some comfort with universalist values such as a prohibition on wanton cruelty and a proscription to demonstrate care, love, and respect in our dealings with animal others. At the same time, I do not know what it can mean to assert that someone in a refugee camp, for instance, or malnourished from the ravaging impacts of war ought to be vegan. I similarly do not understand what it would mean to assert that such a person should keep her promises. The context does not seem amenable to these kinds of moral edicts. The cases I consider in Part 2 are ones in which people generally do have choices and some element of control over their actions, but I never lose sight of the commitment to CMV and to understanding that part of contextualizing is understanding the potential limits—logistical, systemic, familial, economic, relational, and others—of both what options we have and whether we can avail ourselves of them without incurring too many costs for ourselves or others.

There are two criticisms of CMV to discuss before moving on. The first, as expressed by Gary Francione, is that CMV is not sufficiently absolutist. The second, expressed by Erin McKenna and Val Plumwood, is that it is overly absolutist. Francione argues that by allowing for the permissibility of flesh eating in some circumstances, CMV theorists like Curtin reify a human/animal hierarchy and treat animals as things. Where the rights view rejects the idea of animals as tools for human use, Francione argues, CMV renders treating animals as tools permissible. Failing to advocate for veganism as an absolute requirement leaves animals vulnerable to suffering and death, something that would not be permissible if ecofeminists were to defend animals' moral rights. Francione claims that the ethic of care ecofeminists advocate for relative to humans contains moral absolutes (enslaving people is always wrong, for example) but that the ethic of care is different in the case of animals because CMV does not rule out exploitation of animals by issuing an absolutist prohibition on their use for human ends. He reads ecofeminism as speciesist because of this difference and argues that ecofeminism does not protect animals because it is insufficiently absolutist (Francione 1996).

This argument is misguided on many fronts. First, Francione is asking for absolutism that works in theory only. Again, what does it even mean to tell a person in a refugee camp relying on food provided by an aid agency that she must be vegan? What does that mean for a person living in a part of the planet where the ground is inarable? I suppose it can feel morally righteous to issue edicts for veganism meant to apply at all times and in all places. Perhaps one receives credit for one's consistent defense of animals, but in practice I genuinely cannot understand what possible good those edicts do in some cases. Vegan ecofeminists who advocate for some version of CMV understand this and are responsive to reality. We oppose issuing absolutist moral commands without recognition of how people are actually situated. Second, perhaps it is a failure of creativity, but I truly cannot imagine a scenario where conditions are such that enslaving people is the only possible option for an individual's survival. If such a situation were to occur, we would be so far into the nonideal as to render universalized moral principles ill-suited to the task of determining right action in a formulaic way. The issue is not that the vegan ecofeminist conception of the ethics of care makes a distinction between the moral value of humans and animals. The issue is that we make a distinction between what is reality and how things look from the armchair abstractly contemplating what we all ought to do.[12] Some people really do live in climates inhospitable to growing plant foods and where it is logistically or economically unfeasible to import such foods. Others live in urban areas where access to fresh foods is severely limited due to food apartheid. Since ethics is guided by a long-standing "ought implies can" rule, I fail to see the usefulness or compassion in claiming that all people in all places at all times ought to be vegan when they cannot. Moreover, the vegan activist movement as well as academic work on veganism has been subject to deserved criticism for making statements about what others ought to do from the standpoint of white, affluent people (Adams and Gruen 2014, 33–5; Harper 2010; Ko and Ko 2017; Ornelas 2012). Vegan ecofeminism needs to take these claims seriously and demonstrate considerable humility in how we theorize and talk about what moral demands exist.

So much for the worry that CMV is insufficiently absolutist. What of the concern that it is *overly* absolutist? Some arguments challenging the absolutism of vegan ecofeminist claims are grounded in concerns about the particular nutritional needs of women and children (George 1994). I find those arguments less than compelling in the face of nutritional science. Plumwood and McKenna's positions, however, go much deeper and challenge the very root of vegan ecofeminist beliefs. Plumwood distinguished between ontological veganism and ecological animalism. The former refers to universal calls for veganism whereas the latter advocates for a "context-sensitive semi-vegetarian position, which advocates great reductions in first world-meat-eating and opposes reductive and disrespectful conceptions and treatments of animals, especially in factory farming" (2012, 78). Plumwood's ecological animalism is an animal-inclusive ecofeminism, encompassing deep respect for animals, noting their "life stories of attachment, struggle, and tragedy not unlike our own" (80). She argues that ontological veganism supported by numerous vegan ecofeminists is problematically ethnocentric, anti-ecological, and misguided in terms of who counts as food (2012). The latter issue around who counts as edible is of great importance to Plumwood as well as to McKenna who shares Plumwood's views on this issue.

[12]Marti Kheel asked what would happen "if we refrain from the urge to make an ethic of care emulate the purported rigor of a theory of justice and rights" and focus instead on the "more important questions" relating to care and connection (2004, 337). Francione's critique is rooted in the idea that justice approaches are more rigorous than ecofeminist approaches, but I join Kheel in being disinterested in trying to emulate a form of "rigor" that I think ultimately does not focus on the right questions or the reality of lived experience.

The issue they have with vegan ecofeminism is that its calls for veganism are grounded at least partially in the idea that animals do not belong in the category of the edible. Just as there is a denial of humans as part of the food chain, Plumwood and McKenna see vegan ecofeminists as moving animals out of the realm of the edible (McKenna 2021, 2023; Plumwood 2012). They identify this as a central part of Carol Adams's vegan ecofeminism, Lori Gruen's, and others who argue that animals should not be seen as edible. To do so is to objectify and commodify their bodies, to treat them as instruments for human ends, and to ignore their wishes, interests, and needs. Vegan ecofeminists like Adams and Gruen, they argue, see all forms of animal agriculture as morally problematic because they are based on the idea of animals as edible and instruments for human needs. Plumwood sees this move as anti-ecological and supportive of the human/nature dualism for it removes humans from the natural world. Moreover, it is false to claim that humans and animals are not edible. As she put it, "But humans *are* food, food for sharks, lions, tigers, bears, and crocodiles, food for crows, snakes, vultures, pigs, rats, and goannas, and for a huge variety of smaller creatures and micro-organisms" (2012, 80). Plumwood herself experienced the edibility of humans when she became prey for a crocodile while canoeing in Australia's Kakadu National Park (1996). Removing humans from the realm of the edible sets us aside from the rest of nature. Removing other animals from the realm of the edible is an attempt to extend that category of inedibility to them (82). McKenna avers that "not seeing humans as food is another form of human exceptionalism" (2023, 29, 37).

Both McKenna and Plumwood maintain the wrongness of industrialized animal agriculture and believe veganism is a correct response to such abject cruelty and lack of respect for animal others (McKenna 2021, 55–56; 2023; Plumwood 1996, 89). They object to the vegan ecofeminist move that rejects ontologizing animals as edible, however, thereby refusing to issue a mandate for veganism. A call for veganism is not the only dietary response to the logic of domination (McKenna 2023, 20). Here the idea is that one can ontologize animals (and humans) properly as edible but not endorse their exploitation in mass animal agriculture. Plumwood, for example, calls animal flesh resulting from industrialized animal agriculture "meat" but being seen as edible need not involve animals being "ontologised reductively as meat" (89). We should all be recognized as "food and more than food" (ibid.). Claiming that ontological veganism assumes "an insensitive and ecologically destructive economic context," Plumwood argues that not all animal food is "meat" in the exploitative and instrumentalist way she defines that term. Though ecological animalism is opposed to industrialized animal agriculture, it allows for animal consumption where the consumptive practice is not indicative of domination or alienation (90). McKenna, too, believes that ontological veganism offers a false dilemma between no use of animals at all and instrumentalizing forms of use (2023). Both call for a reduction in consumption of animal flesh, an opposition to meat, and an openness to animal food that does not manifest an instrumentalist approach, viewing animals as food and more. McKenna's pragmatist ecofeminism notes that "while there are clearly many unethical ways to engage in relationships with other animal and plant beings, there isn't just one way to engage such relationships ethically" (2023). Rejecting an absolutist stance, she points to Maasai people as a potential example of "reverence and use" as well as grassfed beef (2021, 57–8). Both Plumwood and McKenna are examples of animal-inclusive ecofeminists who do not endorse an absolute vegan mandate.

I see two related issues in Plumwood's and McKenna's objections to ontological and ecofeminist veganism: (1) the claim that just as humans are not edible, other animals also do not belong in the category of the edible is anti-ecological and potentially underscores human exceptionalism, and (2) the claim that the absolutist mandate for veganism is wrong because it is too broad a claim, painting all forms of animal consumption with the same brush. I take the point of the first objection. We cannot deny that humans are, in fact, edible and that animal others are as well. This is one reason we use shark cages when diving with great white sharks and sing loud songs to ward off bears and cougars while we hike. We know we are edible, and we seek to avoid becoming someone's dinner. Vegan ecofeminists, me included, could take more care in how we theorize about the issue of edibility. Perhaps we have not been clear enough in noting that humans and animal others are, of course, edible but we reject the objectification, commodification, and exploitation that go along with much animal consumption. For my part, I aver that animals, while literally edible, ought not to be reduced to instruments for human purposes—defined only as what they are to us humans (farm animals, lab animals, zoo animals, etc.). When we view someone as edible, we often do not merely mean that the being or plant in question can be eaten (as opposed to a desk or a pen) but that we view them as reducible to edibility. I wonder if McKenna and Plumwood think vegan ecofeminists make a simple category mistake by saying animals do not belong in the category of the edible. Clearly, that sort of category mistake defies all we know about ecology and the food chain. What most of us mean when we say animals do not belong in the category of the edible is that animals should not be seen merely as edible and objectified and instrumentalized toward that end. Acknowledging that all living beings are "food and more than food" puts us in the same camp as McKenna and Plumwood as far as it goes. Where the difference in views truly lies is in vegan ecofeminists' insistence that veganism is the correct response to animals' moral considerability whereas McKenna and Plumwood make more space for the idea that when practices show reverence for animals, they could be a permissible form of animal consumption. I am not alone in struggling with that idea for a variety of reasons including that whether a practice truly shows "reverence" for animals is difficult to determine.

Regarding the second objection, that vegan ecofeminism is overly absolutist and thus ethnocentric and wrongly views all animal consumption as an expression of an instrumentalist and reductionist view of animals, I respond differently. First,

I believe that CMV avoids much of the worry about ethnocentric and colonialist concerns regarding vegan ecofeminism by recognizing the ways in which context limits and shapes people's options. CMV, particularly Curtin's version, recognizes too that cultural beliefs about whether animals are sacred or whether there is human-animal reciprocity in a spiritual or literal sense differ. Vegan ecofeminism ought not to assume that all expressions of animal consumption reflect a coarse kind of objectification and commodification, but that is exactly what CMV avoids. It is a response to precisely that worry. At the same time, as others have argued, it is problematic to recognize cultural viewpoints as nonexploitative when we do not fully understand the views or when those views reflect problematic ideas regarding class, gender, race, and species (Gaard 2001; Kim 2015; Twine 2014). To give a concrete cross-cultural example, the argument in the Pacific Northwest regarding the Makah tribe's interest in reinstating cultural whaling often relied on essentializing presentations of Makah beliefs and a failure to address the ways in which whale hunting was rooted in several misogynistic practices as well as inequity between classes. To gloss over all that important detail in the name of multiculturalism is to ignore ethically relevant details.

Though the call to reinstate cultural whaling was popular among some men in the Makah community, for example, efforts led by women elders in the tribe to counter that call were ignored or silenced (Fisher 2011; Gaard 2001; Kim 2015). Information regarding the commercial whaling industry's role in backing the Makah tribe in the hope that opening the door to cultural whaling would ease restrictions on commercial whaling was also obscured (Hawkins 2001). This is not to defend the actions of primarily white activists whose activism was terribly racist and not at all reflective of respect and understanding for the Makah. It is simply to note that a contextual analysis of animal food production, hunting, and so forth needs to take the *entire* picture into account. I believe that CMV at its best does this as does many vegan ecofeminist's commitment to amplifying the voices of resistance within a culture rather than leading activism on their behalf or simply leading it in their place. Following Gaard, I focus on the significant violence against animals within my own milieu because there are sufficient issues there to keep me busy for a lifetime and more. Recognizing my status as an outsider to other cultures and traditions, I prefer to focus my attention on what is happening closer to home (Gaard 2001).[13] In doing so, I show a deference for concerns about ethnocentricity and epistemic humility about what I can know, in depth, about other cultural practices and the spiritual, economic, and political beliefs that form their foundation.

One potential concern about my response is that thinking everyone should be vegan while making room for exceptions creates a moral underclass (George,

---

[13]Richard Twine argues that Gaard is too careful about non-native ecofeminists and our role in cross-cultural conflicts (2014, 201).

1994, 407). By granting exceptions to an absolute moral rule, the objection goes, those who are excepted take on an inferior status. This objection is misguided in two ways. First, vegan ecofeminists are not declaring by fiat what all people must do. Again, CMV is a way of acknowledging precisely the reality that absolutist claims are problematic. As Rosalind Hursthouse (a virtue theorist, not an ecofeminist) said, what good, exactly, is the instruction to avoid all medications tested on animals if you are sick and your only option is such a medication (2006). The absolutist claim fails to be action guiding unless one thinks she should die rather than take a life-saving medication tested on animals. This does not render the person who takes such medications a member of an ethical underclass. They are simply a person who is living in a context where a principled stance against biomedical research on animals can only be carried so far by individual action. One has to bring quite a bit of judgment and harshness to a situation to adopt the position that such a person is excused but thereby less-than.

Seeing moral decision-making as deeply contextual, vegan ecofeminism has room to allow us to say that we mourn animals' deaths, take seriously their roles in their relationships and ecosystems within which they live and acknowledge the loss their deaths create. We can mourn that human lives are perpetuated using them as a means. This may be "anti-ecological" as Plumwood suggests, but I am not so sure. When I see a crow sweep down and grab a mouse to eat, I recognize it both as natural *and* sad. That mouse was alive and now he is not. His mouse family may miss him. He may have been very excited to nibble on some delicious spring grasses he will now never taste again. I understand the crow, too, needs to eat and feed her hatchlings. Is it anti-ecological to feel this sadness? I do not think so. The sadness stems from the empathy of knowing someone just became someone else's meal and that that someone is now gone even if this is the right order of things. It would be anti-ecological to yell at the crow or fault her predation but mourning that the world is organized in such a way that all our lives depend on the lives of others is compatible with respect for the ecological order of things. Aldo Leopold once wrote, "One of the penalties of an ecological education is that one lives alone in a world of wounds" (1966, 197). I sometimes feel this is an apt description of what it is like to open one's heart to other animals. I feel for both the crow and the mouse, just as I feel for both the human and the seal they kill to feed their family in the arctic north. I do not think of either of them as members of a moral underclass, however.

Vegan ecofeminists call for veganism as a response to both the moral significance of animals and the context within which we live. It is true that many of us believe that veganism is an appropriate response to animals' moral significance and that veganism is called for wherever it can be practiced. If one looks at the theory carefully, however, noting the inclusion of CMV, it should be clear that vegan ecofeminists do not maintain that those who cannot eat only plant-based foods are less-than or morally inferior to those who can. Vegan animal rights activism has at times crossed this line and has been rightfully charged with racism and elitism by calling for universal veganism with no regard for the differences in access to vegan foods (including simply fresh fruits and vegetables) in industrialized nations, let alone in nonarable climates and so forth. As Marti Kheel wrote, her call to veganism is an "invitational approach" rather than one issuing a universal norm. She went on to say that "although ecofeminist philosophy may not support the case for vegetarianism as a universal norm, it may, nonetheless, help to dislodge the conceptual substructures that support the practice of meat eating" (327–9). Now, she also speaks of planting the seeds that "invite a vegetarian ideal" (ibid.), which can understandably raise concerns about those who do not meet that ideal being subpar. As Kheel wrote, though, ideals "may be viewed as an invitation; and invitations cannot always be honored and may be declined" (335). Kheel asks us to recognize there are contexts where veganism may not be possible *and* to avoid letting that recognition turn us from examining "the cultural associations that exist between meat eating and gender, status, and class" (ibid.). Once, an undergraduate student asked me why vegans come across as directive and superior. I answered the only way I knew how, which was to point out (1) that people often perceive as directive and superior that which challenges their behaviors and (2) that vegans should avoid being superior jerks. The more professional way to put the second point would be to note that veganism should at all times be seen as aspirational (Gruen and Jones 2016) and that no one, vegans included, has a morally pure way of life. Acknowledging this helps us avoid labeling all who cannot practice veganism as members of an ethical underclass. Like so many of us, they might just be doing their best to commit as little violence as possible in this complicated life of ours.

Vegan ecofeminism as I conceive of it is a contextualized, pluralist, and nonhierarchical approach that moves between guiding principles and the particulars of individual situations. My approach is best situated within CMV as it strongly emphasizes that consumption of animal flesh is a practice rooted in different climates, situations, and conditions. What "meat eating" means or signifies can be different across different populations worldwide and across different situations (i.e., a refugee camp versus a neighborhood barbecue). I hope to have shown that vegan ecofeminism and CMV are neither insufficiently nor overly absolutist and that the call to avoid consumption of animal products is one given with humility that comes from recognizing the multiplicity of ways people and practices manifest in the world and compassion for those who are unable to heed it. Vegan ecofeminism resolutely opposes the exploitation and domination of animals in industrial animal agriculture. I also oppose the exploitation and domination of animals in "humane farming" operations, which are, in fact, far from humane (Gillespie 2010, 2011; Gruen and Jones 2016, 160–2; Hawthorne 2013; Stanescu 2014). Where it is possible to eat nutritiously and live a flourishing life on a vegan diet our respect for animals' individual lives and our commitment to compassion and care call for veganism as a response.

Hopefully, a picture is emerging about how vegan ecofeminism can approach interanimal conflicts of interest. Instead of relying on an assessment of what sorts of beings and interests are involved and then turning to a fixed hierarchy for an answer, the approach I advance involves rejection of hierarchies. In lieu of hierarchy, conflicts are adjudicated based on a deep contextual analysis, with recognition for the moral value of all lives involved. We cannot resolve a conflict by noting that one party is a turkey and the other a human. Instead of a hierarchy of interests based on a distinction between basic and nonbasic interests, I jettison reliance on that distinction in a way that predicts outcomes in conflicts of interest. The basic/nonbasic interests distinction should be added to the heap of other normative dualisms feminists have identified as injurious to moral deliberation. As with most dualisms, the binary has some truth to it. In as much as we need words to differentiate between our subsistence needs and all of our other interests, I do not strongly object to the words "basic" and "nonbasic" to describe interests. We can recognize, for example, that there is a difference between my subsistence needs and my interest in attending a Bruce Springsteen concert. I part ways with the distinction, however, once we use it to draw normative conclusions about interanimal conflicts of interest. The issue is not that the words "basic and nonbasic interests" fail to capture *anything*. Rather, the issue is that the basic/nonbasic interests distinction encourages truncated narratives by stripping interests of their contextualized richness (political, social, relational, and cultural). It pushes us toward rigidly hierarchical thinking, obscures moral remainders that result from conflict adjudication, and, in doing so, feeds a false security that our moral engagement ends along with our interest-weighing endeavors.

I am not suggesting that whether an interest is basic or nonbasic is irrelevant to moral deliberation. My point, rather, is that we cannot rely on the distinction to predict outcomes or help us determine priority before obtaining more details about the conflict in question, the interests at issue, and the particular interest bearers. Focusing on categorizing interests also obscures understanding of how the interest is informed by particular socioeconomic or cultural context or how it grows out of a history of exploitation and abuse that justified using others in morally questionable ways. As Kheel (1993) argued, "If we do not understand the world view that produced the dilemma that we are asked to consider, we have no way of evaluating the situation except on its own terms" (255). The use of the basic/nonbasic interests distinction contributes to masking the importance of asking questions regarding the worldview responsible for the dilemmas we face.

One final criticism of reliance on the basic/nonbasic interests distinction is that it engenders moral errors in both our dealings with people and in our thinking about conflicts by disengaging from context. These moral errors include, but may not be limited to, mistaken assessments of people's characters and failing to acknowledge and attend to moral remainders. More on the latter in this chapter's next section. An example will illuminate what I am pointing to with respect to character assessment. We might rightly note that wearing fur is not a basic interest for a New York socialite. Knowing what is entailed for the animals in making the fur coat we may thereby conclude that she ought not to wear it or support the fur industry. That all seems right as far as it goes. However, that the coat is unnecessary for this woman does not close the morally relevant features of our discussions with her. We might chastise her and accuse her of all kinds of moral callousness for failing to see that her need for a mink coat is nonbasic. Alternatively, we might contextualize her interest somewhat, noticing that women are put under significant pressures to look particular ways. Rather than go the route of chastisement and character attack, we might instead offer information to aid the woman in understanding how the objectification of women interlocks with the objectification of animals. As Kheel wrote, we should understand "the cultural context that leads a woman to see glamour where others see death. She is the product of a society that robs women of their own self-image and then sells it back to them in distorted form" (1993, 259). This is not a defense of fur wearing by wealthy, urban dwellers in temperate climates. It is a recognition that we open ourselves to moral error when we use basic/nonbasic distinction to drive our moral thinking and assessments of others. In Chapters 4–6 it will become even more evident why the distinction is problematic. For all these reasons, I set it aside.

One important element of conflicts that must be assessed is whether they are, indeed, conflicts at all. The tendency in patriarchal conceptual frameworks is to think always in terms of conflict and competition where one party's interests must be overridden in service of the other's. "Conflict is taken for granted; it is assumed that one part of nature must always win, while another must always lose" (Kheel 1985, 137). Since humans are part of the natural world and many of our decisions impact us as much as they impact other beings, some so-called conflicts are actually false dilemmas. Stepping away from industrialized animal agriculture, for example, would in fact help humans as much as it would help other animals for several reasons, among them that industrial animal agriculture is a leading contributor to global climate change, which is killing more and more humans every year. Paul Taylor enjoined us to turn situations of conflict into situations of mutual accommodation whenever possible, noting that this is sometimes possible when humans adjust their interests and plans (1986, 297). As Josephine Donovan put it, "In most cases, either/or dilemmas in real life can be turned into both/ands. In most cases, dead-end situations such as those posed in lifeboat hypotheticals can be prevented" (1993, 184).

Once real conflict is identified, the approach encourages a full contextual analysis of the situation. I demonstrate in detail what this looks like in practice in

Part 2 of the book. As noted in the introduction, most vegan ecofeminist discussion of interanimal conflicts of interest centers on cross-cultural conflict where one group of people engages in a practice harmful to animals and another group, from outside that community, objects to that practice. There are many examples of cross-cultural conflicts one could point to, for example, the Taiji dolphin hunts in Japan, dog eating in Asia, protests in France voicing opposition to the slaughtering methods involved in production of Halal and Kosher meats, and opposition to cultural whaling. What these conflicts have in common besides the harm of some set of animals is the presence of outsider critics, often in a position of privilege compared to those engaging in the practice, voicing loud opposition and concern for the animals' well-being. This activism is sometimes undertaken by those who themselves consume animal flesh, by those who have ulterior, racist motives as in the case of some of the French activism against Halal and Kosher slaughter (given a famous face in the form of Brigitte Bardot) (Vanderhoof 2021), and a disregard for understanding the full context in which the practices and people are situated. There is excellent ecofeminist work offering an approach to such conflicts that rejects racist and imperialist norms but also casts off the idea that animals' interests are not relevant in the face of cultural and ethnic traditions (Gaard 2001; Hawkins 2001; Kim 2015). Claire Kim's work in *Dangerous Crossings: Race, Species, and Nature in a Multicultural Age*, in particular, is an exemplar of deep contextual analysis, thoughtful consideration of the racist, misogynistic, and otherwise problematic aspects of some activism in the cross-cultural setting, but also the importance of not losing sight of the animals in the midst of these complications. In Chapters 4–6 I demonstrate how such a careful contextual analysis is important in resolving interanimal conflicts of interest within one's own families and communities rather than cross-culturally.

In many ways, my approach is similar to those advanced by Gaard and Kim. I, too, insist on contextualizing conflicts and operating without a hierarchy of life-forms. My approach also highlights the importance of care in theorizing or undertaking activism against practices engaged in by marginalized groups and individuals. At the same time, like Gaard and Kim, I maintain an allegiance to animals. I reject discussions that, in service of cultural sensitivity, leave out the speciesist element of instrumentalizing animals for human purposes. This is a tight line to walk and the role of outsiders in cross-cultural conflicts of these kinds needs to be questioned and carefully considered. In the intracultural conflicts I consider in this book, the problem of outsider activism and critique is less of an issue, but the general guidance to keep alert to how race, class, religion, and so forth complicate interanimal conflicts of interest is crucial. To Gaard and Kim's approaches, I add a focus on the role of relational moral attention as a significant feature of interanimal conflicts of interest. I turn to this now, in the final section of this chapter.

4 Relational Moral Attention

As I noted earlier in the chapter, recognition of moral remainders has an important role in my approach to interanimal conflicts of interest. I am not suggesting that there are *always* moral remainders. If I make a promise to a friend and keep that promise then, at least on the face of it, I will not have generated any moral remainders.[14] Mercifully, there are some moral interactions from which we can emerge with clean hands. In interanimal conflicts, however, I suspect moral remainders will be the norm rather than the exception. Rosalind Hursthouse notes that it is likely impossible to live with the respect for nature Paul Taylor suggests because "we have already made such a mess of things that there is no virtuous way of sorting them out by human means" (2007, 169). We are embedded in exploitative systems over which we have very limited (or no) direct control. As a result, there may not be good ways to extricate ourselves from interanimal conflicts without causing some, perhaps significant, harms. Moreover, given that attending to animals' interests in a robust way remains on the fringes of common morality, it will be difficult to attend to animals without generating some problems in the interhuman realm, in particular with loved ones and other community members.

Any view discussing interanimal conflicts of interest must take these realities seriously and address the issue of remainders head on. Sharon Bishop has a thorough discussion of how principle-based theories fail to handle feelings of remorse and guilt. She notes that on such views:

> so long as agents believe they are acting rightly, they can be confident that any guilt or remorse they feel should be dismissed as irrational. Where they believe that they have done as they should, they will regard any guilt they happen to experience as something to be gotten over privately or perhaps with a friend or analyst, but they will not think that reparative acts or forgiveness are appropriate. (1987, 10)

I seek to move away from the sort of view Bishop describes to one that can more easily recognize remainders and the appropriateness of acts of forgiveness and repair. Though opting for one path over the other may have been the best we could do, we notice that damage was done when we made our choice, and we struggle for how to account for and attend to that damage. Lived experience tells us that, in many cases, we do not merely maximize the good, respect rational agency, or show loving attention and move on worry free. We know this is not merely squeamishness or sentimentality; we can feel it.

[14]I say "on the face of it" because if I keep the promise by robbing a bank to loan her the $50, I promised her, then for sure there are remainders. So much depends on the details.

This idea that we often will not emerge from resolving interanimal conflicts of interest with clean moral hands may lead some to wonder if I am suggesting that we are all just miserable sinners. This is the question Thomas Nagel asked in *The View from Nowhere* when he discussed the problem of overdemandingness relative to interhuman morality (1986, 189–207). Stephen Gardiner talks of "marring evil" and "blighting evil" where marring evil occurs when a moral agent chooses the lesser of two evils, but we still think of her action in an overall negative light. "Blighting evils" occur when it is impossible to redeem oneself from a marring evil insofar as there is no way to "outweigh" or "expunge" the evil that occurred through other, good actions (2010, 466). I certainly do not think all interanimal conflict resolution generates blighting evils for the humans involved. The picture I am piecing together in this work is aimed at demonstrating how we must do the work to address moral remainders and that, in doing so, intracultural and interanimal conflicts of interests can shift in their seeming intransigence. Until we make serious changes in our relationships with animals, however, we may well find ourselves in situations where something like marring evils occurs. Our lives may be "tarnished," as Gardiner says, because as individuals we may not be empowered to change the options available to us and thus will generate harms no matter what we do. As I often tell my students, in a world replete with systemic injustice and oppression, we are limited in what individuals can do. The television show *The Good Place* is one of the best and funniest depictions of this tragedy. Something is rotten in the structures of the world, which is why the character Chidi Anagonye, an ethics professor, thinks he must be a terrible person because of the almond milk he took in his coffee to avoid consuming dairy on ethical grounds. The almond milk was trucked in! He knew that was bad for the environment! In the face of these structures and conceptual frameworks that hem us in, we do our best as individuals and then, as I tell my students, we turn our rage and despair outward and shake our fists at those structures, thinking about how to tear them down bit by bit.

5 Conclusion

As I articulate it, relational vegan ecofeminism is pluralist, contextualized, and nonhierarchical. It puts considerable emphasis on recognizing the multitude of ways animals matter, the interlocking nature of oppression and domination, and the idea that veganism is an appropriate response in the face of all we humans do to cause misery and suffering to animal others. I emphasize, too, the necessity to think relationally. This is important for two reasons. First, when we think relationally and in particular in terms of relational moral repair, we better understand the conflicts we face. Where opportunities for repair are nonexistent or profoundly nonideal, we take that information into consideration as we deliberate about our options. If it is impossible to undertake repair with animals in a given scenario, that should influence our considerations. If it is impossible to undertake repair with beloved humans that, too, should influence our considerations. Second, thinking in terms of relational moral attention offers us a way forward from the seeming intractability of some of the conflicts vegans face. My personal experience mirrors that of so many vegans I have spoken with; choosing to remain stalwart in one's commitments to animals can put considerable pressure on our relationships, generating harms of many kinds as we turn away from important familial or cultural practices and traditions. This felt experience can dissuade some from taking on veganism at all or, even for the most committed vegan, wedge us between the proverbial rock and a hard place. Thinking in terms of relational moral attention can help unwedge us both by providing a fuller understanding of the dilemmas we face and by offering relational moral work as a way forward. Unwedged, we can approach ourselves and others with compassion and care and encourage them to do the same for us. This brings us to Part 2 of this book where I examine three particular cases of interanimal and intracultural conflicts—traditional foods, recreational hunting, and vegan parenting—demonstrating how relational vegan ecofeminism works in practice. Each chapter highlights how contextualizing conflicts properly aids us in moral deliberation. It complicates matters too, to be sure. All that context can overwhelm. At the same time, the context is there whether we acknowledge it or not. Ignoring it only strips important information from our moral deliberations in ways harmful to both deliberation and outcomes. In these chapters I also articulate specifically how relational moral attention is crucial to resolving conflicts in ways that enable us to respect animals while addressing disappointing people.

PART TWO

APPLYING RELATIONAL VEGAN ECOFEMINISM

4 ANIMALS, FOOD, AND CULTURAL TRADITIONS: A FULLY CONTEXTUALIZED BOWL OF CHICKEN SOUP

1 Introduction

In the United States alone, upward of 10 billion animals yearly are raised and slaughtered for human consumption. Some of these animals are consumed casually and unreflectively as a matter of convenience or habit. Others become the centerpieces of familial, cultural, and religious gatherings where their importance and meaning go unquestioned. Depending on where vegans live, it can be comparatively simple to avoid fast-food restaurants, steak houses, and casual lunchtime sandwich meats, but foods enmeshed in important traditions and practices, lovingly prepared by people with whom we are in relationship, pose a far greater challenge. We find ourselves torn between our commitment to animals and our relationships with the most important people in our lives who we know take issue with our refusal of these identity-forming traditional foods. Our presence at the table but rejection of the food placed upon it is often taken personally and deemed hurtful, casting a pall over an otherwise amicable gathering. We cannot seem to do right, for in honoring our commitment to opposing animals' suffering we seem to cause a different kind of suffering for people we love.

The proliferation of websites and cookbooks offering vegan recipes for traditional foods of various ethnicities and cultures underscores both how widespread veganism is becoming and how important it is to vegans to reinterpret traditional recipes so that the foods that were central to their identity prior to becoming vegan can remain an important part of their lives.[1] This is not only a

[1]Examples include veganmexicanfood.com, veganlaofood.com, veganfilipinofood.com, veganchinese-food.com, vegansoulfood.org, veganindianfood.org (all put together by Food Empowerment Project),

matter of remaining connected to important parts of ourselves, of course, but also reflects the desire many vegans have to remain connected to their loved ones and communities through foodways that are culturally and traditionally important to them.

The interest in participating in cultural and traditional foodways is, therefore, often tied to relationships of love and care. We grow up watching the adults in our lives cooking, we learn the ways "our people" prepare, flavor, and serve certain foods, and we understand that we can anticipate which foods will appear at the table as we transition through annual seasons and celebrations. Vegans keenly feel the tension that arises when their commitments to animals conflict with food-based traditions and the treasured family members and friends who prepare them. Vegans' loved ones often feel uncomfortable, sad, or offended by their vegan beloved's refusal to partake of the foods that contribute to their sense of group identity. At the table, it can feel virtually impossible to defend animals without disappointing people. In this chapter, I take up this dilemma and aim to demonstrate how thinking contextually and relationally can aid us in navigating a solution where one need neither renege on one's commitments to animals nor leave loved ones perpetually hurt and disappointed.

I center the discussion on the example of my grandmother's chicken soup because I am an Ashkenazi Jew who has faced this very dilemma, though I recognize that Judaism and Jewish people come in many forms that might not resemble my own experiences. There are innumerable other examples from other ethnic and religious communities spanning the globe. Readers can insert their own culturally important foods or traditional animal-based practices. In doing so, they will feel the full force of the conflict as well as the need for a theory to help us work through these kinds of interanimal and intracultural conflicts of interest.

In what follows I will describe what has gone wrong in previous discussions of vegetarianism/veganism and the interest in food by animal ethicists. I subsequently turn to what ecofeminists have said about contextualizing discussions about food choices and food-based practices, focusing on contextual moral vegetarianism. I will then offer a fully contextualized account of my interest in my grandmother's chicken soup followed by a discussion of how the work of relational moral attention can help us move forward in these cases of conflict. I conclude by articulating complications with my account and offering potential solutions.

---

the-jewish-vegan.com, veganricha.com, Bryant Terry's work on Afro-veganism (Bryant-terry.com), and many more.

2 Traditional Animal Ethicists on Food

We can understand the importance of providing the full story of some of our food-based interests by noting the way others writing on animal ethics overlook, ignore, or dismiss important aspects of those interests. Reading through traditional approaches to the conflicts that arise between doing right by animals and making food choices, one gets the impression that resolution should come easily. Recall that, as discussed in Chapter 2, when we consider the diet of people in industrialized countries Peter Singer encourages us to notice that the animals' interests weigh more heavily than the humans'. We cannot put our "trivial" interest in the pleasures of the palate ahead of the interest in not suffering (Singer 1989, 79–80). He argues that equal consideration of interests requires that humans' nonbasic interests must yield to animals' basic interests when those interests conflict. Assuming other food is available, and I am not starving, I cannot eat my grandmother's chicken soup. My nonbasic interest in eating delicious soup pales in comparison with the chicken's basic interest in not suffering horrifically in factory farming conditions. Singer does not contemplate that my interest in the soup might go beyond its deliciousness. I should tell my grandmother "No thank you" when she offers me the soup.

There is immediate, action-guiding appeal to Singer's approach. It enables us to sift the so-called easy cases from the hard ones by noting that the human interests at stake relate to nonbasic, trivial, or minor pursuits. As activists, we can get some traction wielding a tool this blunt; it enables us to point to a picture of a chicken in miserable conditions, then point to a bowl of soup, and ask why someone would think that the interest in eating something delicious would outweigh the wretched life the chicken lives. Though I never did give in and eat my grandmother's soup, it would be unfair to describe my behavior had I done so as a failure to accurately categorize and prioritize conflicting interests as basic and nonbasic. Had I eaten the soup I would have done so because of the moral significance of my relationships. My interest in the soup may not be basic, but it is far from trivial. In facing my grandmother's soup, I face a significant dilemma. If the interest were as trivial as Singer suggests, I would not feel the nagging sense that I cannot get out of the conflict with clean hands. If the interest were trivial, I would avoid the soup and proceed with my day without a second thought as I do in most cases when offered food made from animals' flesh.

At first glance, Tom Regan appears to bring more nuance to his discussion of the interest in food than does Singer. In a paper criticizing Singer's utilitarian approach for failing to ground an obligation to be vegetarian, Regan points out that Singer trivializes the interest in food. He notes that many "thoughtful people" he knows do not, in fact, consider food trivial—they put considerable effort into finding and preparing delicious food, for example (Regan 1980, 309).[2] This

---

[2]Regan believes Singer's utilitarianism does not ground an obligation to be vegetarian because if you factor in that food is a major rather than a trivial interest, and add that to the interests of all involved in

indicates Regan's understanding that food can play a significant role in people's lives, not merely as nourishment but also as a means of expression and as a source of pleasure. Three years later, in *The Case for Animal Rights*, Regan highlighted people's interests in culinary prowess and the importance of tastiness yet again and called eating animal flesh a "habit" that would require "pains of withdrawal and the loss of convenience" to surrender (Regan 2004a, 333). Regan at least acknowledges that food can play an important role in people's lives.

Yet, when he turns to considering what he calls the "taste and culinary challenge" to vegetarianism, Regan also trivializes the interest in food by failing to recognize the ways food ties to ethnic, religious, and cultural identity as well as important relationships of love and care. Regan rightly notes that for many people food is far more important than Singer suggests. He is also right that some subset of people find food important because of issues of taste and the opportunity to cultivate culinary skills. I agree with him that these descriptions of the interest in food as a justification for carnism are easily done away with when weighed against the suffering animals endure in the food system as well as the violation of their rights. He correctly notes that many nonanimal foods taste delicious and that one can hone one's culinary skills without cooking meat (335). Where he errs is in stopping his reflections on the interest in food at the taste and culinary challenge, something he continues to do decades later in *Empty Cages*. For example, here is Regan talking about the animal rights position against turning animals into food:

> To eat in ways that show respect for animals, though it is unusual at this point in American history and while it may cause some inconvenience now and again, is no great hardship. … there is an incredibly delicious, colorful, and nutritious animal-free cuisine out there to be discovered, a menu of possibilities that includes foods from every place and ethnicity in the world. … I said this before, but let me say it again: It is the great new food we gain, not the customary old food we lose, that is the real vegan surprise. (2004b, 106)

Insofar as this describes what is going on in much day-to-day eating in industrialized nations, Regan's observations are spot on. Many people who transition to veganism find their repertoire of foods and recipes expanding, not retracting, in the absence of animal flesh foods. Unfortunately, his account fails to capture what is at stake for other, less day-to-day kinds of eating, nor does it account for the experiences of marginalized populations and people living in diaspora where the symbolism

animal agriculture (veterinarians, farm workers, manufacturers of caging, farm equipment, etc.), it is not at all clear that utility is maximized by going vegetarian. Singer does not actually do the utilitarian math and, according to Regan, his confidence that the math will result in a vegetarian obligation is unearned (1980).

of particular foods takes on an especially important meaning. When foods are important to people in these ways, hardship and even "great hardship" can result from rejecting those foods. We need to be honest about this and welcome a discussion about just how challenging this can be as well as how one might go about resolving the resulting conflicts.

As we saw in Chapter 2, Gary Varner offers a theoretical approach that is honest in these ways. In *Personhood, Ethics, and Animal Cognition*, Varner offers a Harean two-level utilitarian account of "humane sustainability" or "thinking about sustainability with the well-being of the affected animals as a primary focus" (256). Though Varner does not offer much direct discussion of veganism, he lays out a "nuanced and contextualized" utilitarian approach to issues related to animals in the food system (283). Recall that two-level Harean accounts have what Varner calls a "conservative bias or inertia" precisely because adopting new practices and norms involves a transition cost that must be taken into account in a utilitarian approach. The transition costs he points to are often economic or logistical in nature, but he observes that cultural entrenchments are a factor:

> Similarly, some visions of humane sustainability can be read as challenges to deeply entrenched cultural traditions and economic interests, and people who strive to live up to these ideals in the present can be understood as attempting to reeducate the public by example. Thus, from a Harean perspective, self-styled "animal activists" can be understood as living lifestyles that would be unethical to force upon society at large at present, but which might become feasible as social norms in future generations. (270)

The "animal activists" Varner refers to are holding themselves to moral standards that require more of them than common morality, something he notes is supererogatory (2012, 51–3). On the Harean two-level system, people who take on this added moral burden in their actions are potentially "shifting the goal posts of common morality" and thus changing the background conditions over time, making it possible for common morality to embrace those standards at some point in the future. Varner does not point to veganism in particular here, but it is hard to tell what else he would be referring to when he talks about the lifestyles of animal activists. For, of all the changes animal activists make to their lives, transitioning to veganism is among the most significant and widespread. When he does mention vegetarianism, he notes that "traditional foods and etiquette surrounding meals are central to all cultures, and for this reason dietary choices can set off discussion—sometimes very heated discussion, as many a college student has learned upon returning home a newly converted vegetarian" (271). He notes further that precisely because of the centrality of meals and traditional foods to culture, a decision to adopt vegetarianism can "exercise a subtle but significant influence on background cultural traditions and consumer preferences by critical reflection on accepted practices" (ibid.).[3]

For our purposes it is important to note that, unlike Singer and Regan, Varner directly engages the contextual details that can render entrenched food-related behaviors and practices difficult to shift. Though he focuses most on economic and logistical context, he recognizes that culture and tradition also contribute to the complexity of our interest in food. Varner concludes his book by saying: "In my estimation, Harean two-level utilitarianism mirrors the complexities, uncertainties, and hazards of the moral life as we actually encounter them better than any alternative theory" (283), and he points out that his theory will not "produce simple, clear-cut, once-and-for-all answers on such complicated issues" (ibid.).

This almost sounds like ecofeminism in its resistance to a set of one-size-fits-all moral guidelines and its insistence on the importance of context. Though he does not address the relational factors that complicate our connections to particular foods and food-based traditions, I believe his theory could accommodate those insights were he attuned to them. Still, there are numerous reasons Varner's view is inconsistent with an ecofeminist approach—his adherence to a reason-only approach, his commitment to a hierarchy of life-forms, his very limited conception of what counts as context, to name just a few—but it is closer to taking contextual complexities seriously than either Regan or Singer.[4] At the same time, Varner's lack of attunement to the role of relationality in life, and the moral life in particular, renders him unable to see that those very relationships can provide the way forward out of the kinds of entrenchments he gets bogged down in. As I will argue later in the chapter, I have more hope that we need not throw our hands up and conclude that the cultural entrenchment of animal-based traditions is of such an intractable nature that anyone who adopts vegan practices is doing something we cannot ask of others. Through courageous action, mutual understanding, and relational moral attention, we can seek to move the process along and facilitate a better solution to the dilemma right now rather than waiting for the goal posts of morality to complete their terribly slow movement toward compassion and peace for animals.

One step in that direction is to offer a more fully contextualized account of the interest in food that takes seriously the issues of identity, relationality, and care

---

[3]Part of R. M. Hare's reasoning for his "demi-vegetarianism" was that it had "propaganda value" when discussing it at other's homes (1999, 238, 242).

[4]A contextualized ethic can be very different from the kind of contextualization ecofeminists and care ethicists articulate. Margaret Urban Walker talks about utilitarianism as a contextualized ethic but notes that the utilitarian approach to context is very different from that found in an ethic of care. For utilitarians, human relationships are simply part of the "math problem" of moral decision-making whereas an ethic of care takes these relationships to be in and of themselves a central piece of moral decision-making and as having something to teach us about what it means to be a moral agent (Walker 1989, 126–7).

that complicate our interest in traditional foods. I take up this issue later in the chapter, focusing on the example of my grandmother's chicken soup. First, I will return briefly to contextual moral vegetarianism, discussed at length in Chapter 3. In the rest of the chapter, I expand ecofeminism's analysis of CMV by articulating an approach to intracultural conflicts around food, particularly those connected to relationships of love and care. I begin by offering a fully contextualized account of my grandmother's chicken soup. Again, I invite readers to consider their own culturally important foods or animal-based practices and how these considerations play a role for them and their loved ones.

Many, though as I made clear in Chapter 3 not all, animal-inclusive ecofeminists call for veganism as a way to be in right relationship with other animals. This is well-covered territory in the ecofeminist literature and in Chapter 3, so I will only briefly touch on ecofeminist reasons to eschew animal products in our diets.[5] As ecofeminism is pluralist about why animals are morally significant, there is a long list of morally salient considerations that would preclude using animals as tools for human consumption. This list includes animals' sentience, their bodily integrity, and their important relationships with one another, among others. Vegan ecofeminists oppose the consumption of animal flesh on feminist grounds, noting the deep connections between the domination and exploitation of women and the domination and exploitation of animals. Ecofeminists note that our food system involves the extensive exploitation of marginalized human laborers as well as contributes significantly to environmental destruction at both the local and global levels. Thus, many ecofeminists advocate for veganism.

3 A Fully Contextualized Bowl of Chicken Soup

A reminder: My aim in this project is to put forth an account that views human interests in all their robustness while also recognizing strong obligations to animals. By acknowledging how relationships of love and care can complicate our interests and attending to those interests in a contextualized way, this approach brings forward important values that are connected to some of our seemingly less important interests. I bring them forward not to serve as a free pass for humans to override animals' interests but as moral features that should not be ignored. I also offer a way to address them through dialogue and the work of relational moral attention. There is a plurality of reasons that I should forego my grandmother's chicken soup out of concern for the chickens, but there is work left to do with my grandmother (and perhaps my family generally) to properly attend to the moral

[5]For a detailed discussion of feminist veganism, see Emmerman (2024).

damage I may have caused in the relationship by refusing her soup. As I argue later in the chapter, there is also relational work my family must undertake in service of our relationship.

Contextualizing begins with recognizing the interests at stake for the chicken, which include interests in avoiding a life of pain and suffering as well as a premature and painful death, being able to live their life with all the chickeny pleasures associated with being a chicken, living according to the normal biological rhythms of their reproductive lives, and having the ability to live in relationship with other chickens with whom they have established bonds.[6] I am certain there is even more at stake for the chickens and that those who spend their lives caring for chickens would be best equipped to fill in the gaps. Readers unfamiliar with how chickens are treated in the food system are invited to learn more and then ask themselves what interests are being violated. This will be easier to accomplish by also learning about chickens' joys and pleasures, none of which are available when they are raised for food. It is perhaps easiest to learn the more positive aspects of chickens' lives by learning about those freed from the food system or those who were never involved in the food system at all. I now turn to a full account of my interest in my grandmother's chicken soup.

In my family and cultural heritage, the giving and receiving of the matriarch's chicken soup is a culturally integral way of giving and receiving love. My grandmother and I have a close relationship, and I know that by refusing her soup I will deeply hurt her feelings. In refusing my grandmother's soup I will ostracize myself from the rest of my family because they will take my behavior as an affront to my grandmother and to themselves (for, clearly, I object to them eating the soup as well).[7] I may, indeed, be seen as guilty of moral failure despite my efforts to minimize suffering.[8]

Fully contextualizing my interest in the chicken soup also entails understanding how cultural foodways contribute to both broad cultural identity and the narrower scope of family identity. As Bailey puts it, "It is critical to reiterate that ethnic foodways are not merely ornamental; rather, the reproduction of ethnic identity is, in part, dependent upon their maintenance. Here, as in other contexts, one creates one's own identity and those of one's children, through foodways" (2007a: 47). In her work on veganism and maintaining Japanese identity, Mei Horiuchi asks how we can "imagine a decolonial Japanese veganism while maintaining our cultural authenticity" (2017, 3). Margaret Robinson tackles similar themes in her work on veganism and Mi'Kmaq culture (2013).

[6]See Jones (2004), Davis (2012), and Marino (2017) for more about the complex social lives of chickens.
[7]Cf. Twine's discussion of the vegan killjoy (2014) and Adams (2009).
[8]Cf. Bishop (1987) and Walker (1989, 1995) for discussions of how in meeting our moral obligations in one area we might act wrongly in others.

In her sociological study of families and meals, Marjorie DeVault makes the important observation that mealtimes are integral to constructing a group of people as a family (1991, 39). As she argues, "'Family' is not a naturally occurring collection of individuals; its reality is constructed from day to day through activities like eating together." Thus, "producing meals—at least in today's U.S. society—has increasingly become work aimed at maintaining the kind of group life we think of as constituting family," (ibid.). Hence, it is not merely that meals are an important means through which cultural identity is reproduced. Importantly, meals play a crucial role in establishing the family *as a family*. Having meals together regularly is something that sets family apart from other social and community groups.

> The meal is part of the ongoing process that constitutes the life of the household. Whatever its particular features, a "family" has a problematic existence: it is a socially constructed group, continually brought into being through the activities of individuals. Repeated activities—and especially routines and rituals like those of family mealtimes—sustain the reality of a family. (54)

Thinking of the role meals, particularly ritual meals, play in maintaining the family as a group helps us see just how much is at stake when I refuse the bowl of my Grandmother's Rosh Hashannah chicken soup. This refusal can be perceived as a strong threat to the cohesion of a group that requires for its maintenance an adherence to ritual and routine meals. Indeed, the reason we have all gathered on Rosh Hashannah—the reason *this group* has gathered and not some other group—is that we establish ourselves as a family in part by coming together on important holidays and eating the ritual and traditional foods we all recognize as part of our family's and culture's traditions. Moreover, when we factor in DeVault's insight that meals are planned "points of intersection" aimed at bringing together family members whose paths "do not necessarily cross" we can see just how much is at stake at the family table (78). This partly explains why it is so significant to others when I refuse the chicken soup. Refusing the soup is rejecting a main element of a meal that is central to identifying my family as a familial social unit and to the togetherness that is sought from this planned intersection of disparate people. In families and cultures that have experienced marginalization, genocide, and diaspora, maintenance of ritual, routine, and family connection takes on a heightened meaning.

A full ecofeminist telling of the chicken soup interest will also examine the role gender plays in the interest.[9] In thinking through the chicken soup, we must understand that when my grandmother was born a woman's main source of worth in a family involved what she could produce in the home. Had my grandmother

[9]Adams ([1990] 2010), Kheel (2004), and Gruen (1993) examine the role of gender in meat-based cultural practices.

been able to become a professor, we might not be in a situation where eschewing her soup is so impactful to our relationship. As it is, her cooking is, profoundly problematically, one of the only status-conferring activities available to her.

Gender also plays a role when, following DeVault, we think of meal preparation as work. DeVault's discussion of the work involved in meal preparation is meticulous and detailed. In the United States and many other countries, this work is gendered as it is typically done by women. DeVault says that in doing this work the one preparing the meals "is constructing her own place within the family, as one who provides for the needs of others" (48). The amount of planning, preparation, thought, energy, and so on that my grandmother put into meals was tremendous. Not only was she left with no choice but to do that work by the patriarchal systems in which we live, but also her toil was largely invisible.[10] She was expected to do this work without complaint, largely without recognition, and nearly always without the help of male members of the family. Moreover, as Julie Rubio notes, this "kinwork" includes "balancing multiple values," among them "strengthening family" and "passing on traditions" (Rubio 2014, 45). Meal preparation is full of meanings beyond the foods themselves—nourishment is one among many of the values being balanced and passing along long-held traditions and food preparation skills constitute part of the labor. My rejection of the soup is, therefore, complicated both by the limitations placed on my grandmother by patriarchal norms regarding her gender and the fact that in rejecting her soup I am also rejecting her labor understood as far more than the preparation of particular foods for us all to enjoy.[11]

Attending to the role gender plays also involves attending to the gender of the person who maintains a commitment to veganism in the face of familial discord. Eschewing animal flesh at the table may be more challenging for men than for women because of cultural associations between vegetarianism and femininity. Men who make public commitments to vegetarianism sometimes face charges of femininity that are deeply linked to heterosexism and homophobia (Bailey 2007a, 44–5). Adams points out that vegetarian men are often called "fruits" or "wimps"

[10]In the Jewish culture in which I was raised, women's contribution to ritual meals involved planning, shopping for, and preparing the meal as well as laying the table. Women were also the ones who lit the candles. Beyond that, women were never granted a leadership role in running the more text-based or intellectual parts of the meal. For example, at Passover seder, the seder itself was always led by the men. Women prepared everything and ensured everyone's needs were met while men sat at the head of the table and ran the evening. Rejecting my grandmother's soup takes on a particularly problematic hue when seen in this light.

[11]In her discussion of meal preparation, DeVault details the many steps and processes that are part of meal preparation: "Doing a meal," then, requires more than just cooking; it takes thoughtful foresight, simultaneous attention to several different aspects of the project, and a continuing openness to ongoing events and interaction. These kinds of effort must be considered part of the work of feeding a family, but they are seldom identified as work; they remain invisible even as they are done. (55)

(Adams 2009, 50) and that there is a tendency, especially among teens, to call male vegetarians "gay" and think of female vegetarians as lesbians (86).[12] For some men, rejecting animal flesh foods is seen as a form of resistance against patriarchal norms enforcing a "real men eat meat" belief system (Curtin 1992, 132–3; cf. Kheel, 2008, 242–4). Dangers of the same sort loom for those identifying as gender expansive or transgender. This is important context for considering intracultural conflicts regarding food. These issues also arise in Chapter 5 when I discuss conflicts around recreational hunting.

Another important contextual feature to note is that family members may feel resentment about vegans questioning well-established norms in ways that make them feel guilty for their eating practices.[13] This often lurks under the surface in these intracultural conflicts and a failure to address it can lead to fractured relationships of love and care.[14] I am certain numerous members of my family felt, and perhaps continue to feel, resentment toward me.

Some of this resentment may be deserved. As a young convert to vegetarianism, I admit, I would moo at the table while my family ate their brisket. Deane Curtin reminds us that veganism is a moral direction rather than a moral state (Curtin 1992, 131), and Gruen and Jones discuss veganism as an "aspiration" rather than as the achievement of moral purity (Gruen and Jones 2016). If vegans in general were less smug about their moral superiority and better equipped to understand that—as vegan food justice activist lauren Ornelas often reminds people—even veganism is not cruelty-free, these issues of resentment might dissipate somewhat.

Still, some resentment is misplaced, and it is not necessarily the case that all feelings of resentment must be addressed by the vegan as vital moral relational work. In *Living Among Meat Eaters*, Carol Adams provides a theory of what is happening when meat eaters voice resistance and resentment about vegetarians' food choices. Adams argues that the issue is not interpersonal or relational but a matter of the meat eaters being "blocked vegetarians" (14–15). That is, carnist loved ones understand very well the plurality of reasons in favor of vegetarianism, but they keep consuming animal flesh—unlike the vegan they are blocked.[15] Dominant culture in the United States facilitates that blockage, further complicating relations between vegans and carnists. Adams details the coercive and manipulative tactics family members often employ to persuade vegan loved

[12]For an interesting discussion of meat and masculinity in the military context see Kildal, Lilleby, and Syse (2017).

[13]Grant and MacKenzie-Dale's discussion of the TV characters Lisa Simpson and Darlene Connor as vegan-feminist killjoys helps highlight the interpersonal phenomenon here (Grant and MacKenzie-Dale 2016).

[14]See Lori Gruen's discussion of resentment and when it is and is not legitimate in the intercultural conflict setting (Gruen 2001).

[15]Barbara McDonald refers to the "repression of knowledge" phase in the progression of people learning about veganism and changing their lifestyles (2000, 5).

ones to rejoin the carnist fold.[16] She argues that looking at this issue as purely a matter of interpersonal dynamics is a mistake. Family members have a strong desire to maintain traditions and norms and are therefore deeply invested in not questioning the oppressive systems undergirding those traditions (160). The vegan's presence at the table "strains" the "relaxation and exhilaration" of the event, with family members wondering "what is this individual going to take away from us?" (ibid.).

I agree with Adams that our interactions with meat eaters are shaped by the phenomenon of the blocked vegetarian. I agree, too, that thinking of conflicts around traditional foods only through the lens of relationality is a mistake. Adams provides invaluable guidance for navigating the world as a vegan without taking personally the resentment, anger, frustration, fear, and confusion carnists hurl at us at the table (i.e., them being disappointing people when we defend animals). When relatives employ shame and guilt to get their vegan loved one to eat the chicken soup or "Aunt Edna's casserole," as Adams puts it, Adams cautions against feeling responsible for their feelings (143) and offers many useful responses the vegan can deploy. At the same time, the dynamic is also, often, relational. It is a complex dynamic that is fed by both cultural issues around the creation of blocked vegetarians, as Adams argues, and moral issues related to love and care, as I am arguing. The defending animals/disappointing people problem requires both understandings as we think about how to navigate conflicts and will require multiple approaches for achieving resolution. Sometimes, Adams's insightful suggestions will suffice. Other times, the more robust and reparative response I articulate later in the chapter, which can include many of Adams's techniques, may be necessary. The closer and more important the relationship is in which the dynamic is taking place, the more likely it is that increased relational moral attention will be necessary.

As I argued in the introduction, this is more than simply an issue of hurt feelings; it is a moral issue. The foods we eat when gathered around the table shape our relationships to each other. Those shapes constitute part of the stable foundation for the relationships. When we change our responses to the foods, we change those shapes and in turn we destabilize the relationships' foundations.[17] Adams is right that this is partly due to the cultural forces creating blocked vegetarians for which

[16]Barbara McDonald notes that in conversations within families with a newly vegan member, "conversations with others were one-sided, heated, or fraught with the intention to persuade" (12). I don't know of any vegan who has not had this very unpleasant experience at the table with family or even with strangers.

[17]This may sound dramatic, but those of us who have turned our backs on the foods that contribute to cultural or religious identity know the depth of the problem here. In some cases, family gatherings fracture and relationships are compromised. See Jonathan Safran Foer's discussion of table fellowship for more on the importance of gathering around food to families and communities (Safran Foer 2007).

vegans are not responsible. However, to the extent that refusing traditional foods alters the previously accepted terms of our relationships and changes the relational narrative, the entirety of our loved one's responses cannot always be explained by the blocked vegetarian model. Sometimes they are responding to the deep relational rumblings they feel when the accepted terms and narrative are suddenly shifted and that points to the necessity for relational moral attention.

Another set of concerns that are also relevant to fully contextualizing cases of intracultural conflicts are worries about animal activism and vegetarian commitments having an imperialist, elitist, or classist bent. For some families, the introduction of values that center on the needs of nonhuman animals can be experienced as elitist. My refusal to eat animal flesh may have been seen as an expression of elitism or privilege by my family who, until the 1970s, were working class. My grandmother-in-law, a Holocaust survivor who experienced starvation in addition to many other untold horrors, viewed my veganism as privileged pickiness.[18]

Writing about veganism in the South African context, Yandisa Ngqangashe discusses the way meat-eating reflects upward social mobility there with meat being associated with affluence (2019, 150). Ngqangashe talks about "aspirational associations" with meat-eating that "can result in people being reluctant to consider reverting to diets that remind them of their poorer years" (ibid.).[19] In Mexico, too, particularly in marginalized contexts, eating animal flesh is also seen as a symbol of economic status (Iván Sandoval Cervantes, personal communication, November 25, 2025). In some cultures and families, then, electing to eschew meat-eating is perceived as a distasteful exercise of privilege. In some contexts, it also comes across to loved ones as a capitulation to imperialism or neocolonialism. As Jane Meyerding noted many years ago, traditional foods can take on more importance for members of marginalized communities (15). This context is important to considering the best way to respond to the defending animals/disappointing people dilemma as it manifests around the family table.

This is the full telling of my interest in a bowl of my grandmother's chicken soup. It is certainly a tasty soup that pleases the palate, but stopping the analysis there is a deep mistake. Accounts of interanimal conflicts of interest that fail to include the whole ethical narrative of the interests at stake also fail to provide adequate theoretical support for those facing the conflict (Gaard 2001). Labeling my interest in the chicken soup "trivial" is not remotely helpful. Where do we go from here?

---

[18]See Bailey (2007a, 51–5) for a discussion of feminist vegetarianism and elitism.

[19]For a stimulating examination of the intersection of food, identity, culture, and colonialism in the Peruvian context see García (2013).

4 What Is a Vegan to Do *Now*?

I cannot imagine I am unique among philosophers in having had friends remark on how skilled I am at making clear just how complicated a situation is, parsing all relevant distinctions and so forth, and then having far less directiveness to offer regarding how to exit ourselves from the highly complex situation I have just described. My capacity to describe the very specific nature of the mud we are stuck in is far greater than my capacity to describe the path out of the mud. I know university students of mine often feel this way following an ecofeminist analysis of particular moral dilemmas. They have an intricate view of the ethical landscape, the ethical contents and contexts, as Greta Gaard calls them (2001), but wonder at how we will make our way out of the ethical quagmire. This is partly due to the highly contextualized nature of the theory, the lack of a single guiding principle, the rejection of hierarchies, and the radical acceptance required to face the reality that the human condition involves a lack of clarity we find deeply uncomfortable. The answer I always give about how we will find our way out is that we *will* find our way, but it will not be through fixed rules and principles. It will involve a pluralist ethical strategy and a firm commitment to identifying moral remainders and opportunities for relational moral attention. It also involves accepting as messy and complex that which we wish with all our hearts would be clean and simple.

I begin with the observation that in most cases, the right thing to do in situations involving traditional foods and familial or community attachments will be to prioritize obligations to the animals over relational obligations. I articulate why this is the case later with the caveat that I say *in most cases* precisely because of all the complexity I have offered earlier. As a general guideline, I believe that we can in fact defend animals in ways that recognize we have disappointed humans and, through relational moral attention, mitigate those moral costs to loved ones. Hence, for many (possibly most) vegans or vegetarians, the right thing to do is to not partake of the chicken soup and instead undertake the work of relational moral attention as articulated in the section following this one. It is reasonable to ask why wouldn't you just eat the bowl of chicken soup and ease all of these relational concerns? If the relational considerations truly are so deeply felt and morally salient, simply eat your grandmother's chicken soup or your father's famous barbeque ribs the few times you see them and go back to your daily veganism at all other times. Why wouldn't those heavily weighted considerations of love, care, tradition, and connection override moral considerations about animals in these specific and limited instances?

There are many reasons a person committed to animals might feel this is not a dilemma easily resolved by relenting and eating the animal flesh put before them. A person could have many reasons for feeling it is not obvious that they should eat the soup (or whatever particular traditional food they face) in these kinds of cases. These reasons might include (but are not limited to): a belief that raising, slaughtering, and eating animals violates their most basic interests and rights; a belief that animals matter for a variety of morally important reasons including that they are sentient, possess rights, have relationships that matter to them, and are not mere means to human ends; a belief that breeding, raising, and slaughtering animals for human consumption reflects an anthroparchal worldview centered on domination and othering that is morally unacceptable; a commitment to embodying the virtues of compassion, temperance, and fairness that is unattainable when being a party to cruelty;[20] a belief that the practices that uphold slaughtering animals for food also uphold the marginalization and oppression of women, BIPOC, people with disabilities, and so forth; environmental commitments that recognize that mass production of animal flesh is destroying the planet and local ecosystems and a desire not to be a party to that kind of destruction; and finally a recognition that one way or another we are in relationship with other animals and we want that to be in right relationship rather than one rooted in cruelty, commodification, exploitation, domination, and violence.

For a person with any of these beliefs singularly or taken together, it most likely will not be an easy decision about what to do in situations where family food traditions violate any one of these deeply held commitments. There are perhaps people for whom the choice will be easy—there are a variety of views that would defend not just the permissibility but also potentially the obligation to eat the animal flesh in these cases (Hare; Rubio). It's been my experience, however, that most animal advocates do not find these kinds of conflicts so easily resolved because both horns of the dilemma tug on issues that are central to their identities: they love their families and identify strongly with their cultural traditions while also caring deeply for animals, the environment, and everyone deeply impacted by systemic injustice in the food system. These individuals are not confused, failing to see the virtue of flexibility, or entrenched in a sense of vegan moral superiority. Rather, they are feeling the tension that arises when living in the nonideal where any decision is going to cause some sort of moral damage to oneself, others, or both. For those who feel it is straightforward you would eat the chicken soup in such cases without guilt or regret, this chapter may not feel particularly compelling. So much for why one would struggle with the decision.

A more specific and I think more formidable concern combines a consequentialist worry with an observation about proximity. For some time, there has been a robust discussion among consequentialists about whether we do, indeed, have an obligation to be vegetarians given that in complex capitalist systems like ours it is likely our individual choice not to eat animal flesh at any given moment has no impact at all on the food system writ large (Almassi

[20]For virtue approaches to vegetarianism and veganism see Hursthouse (2006) and Alvaro (2019a, 2019b).

2011). What is most relevant for our purposes here is that the consequentialist worry does get some teeth when it is combined with a relational observation about the proximity of my loved ones. The objection rests on two undeniable observations that are forceful when combined: *(1) the chicken has already been raised, slaughtered, and purchased at the time the bowl of chicken soup is presented to me. My decision to forego the soup will have no impact at all on the chicken used to make this soup. And (2) these loved ones are right here, right before me with all their relational entanglements, cultural expectations, and traditions. While my decision has no tangible impact on the chicken whose body became this batch of soup, it has considerable negative impact on my loved ones.* Given 1 and 2 are true, the objection goes, why wouldn't the relational considerations override in this case?

Let's start with the obvious: It is undeniably true that a decision to refuse the chicken soup will have no impact on the chicken being consumed at this moment. My choice to reject the soup cannot be defended on the grounds that it makes any kind of difference for this unfortunate chicken. That makes this case very different from one Yandisa Ngqangashe (2019, 153) discusses where a vegan Xhosa bride is confronted with her fiancé's family's adherence to practicing a cultural tradition of slaughtering an animal during a wedding ceremony. There, the vegan's choice about whether to adhere to the tradition will have consequences for an animal. Still, granting that in my case I cannot impact the chicken's life with my decision does not mean there are no compelling reasons to reject the animal flesh-based traditional foods. To begin with, one's sense of moral integrity may preclude one from partaking of such foods. If I view myself as kind, compassionate, and caring toward animals, eating the soup is at odds with that important moral self-conception. If I identify as a feminist opposed to violence and domination, eating the soup is at odds with that important self-conception. In short, I cannot be who I am ethically if I eat animal flesh food because doing so is in violation of what I take to be central to living the right kind of life and to my moral conception of myself.

Moreover, as was discussed in Chapter 3, many vegans differ from nonvegans in having a fundamentally different view of what counts as in the category of the edible. I do not view animals' bodies as edible. It may be difficult for nonvegans to feel the force of this reason but imagine the following scenario. Bashi lives in the United States and visits new friends for dinner. Bashi is unaware they have an unusual conception of what counts as edible and serve her roasted German Shepherd Dog. Now, who and what counts as edible varies geographically and culturally, of course, but in the United States it is a dominant norm that dogs are not in the category of the edible. Confronted with the roasted German Shepherd, Bashi is uncomfortable for a variety of reasons—she wrestles with questions about what it means to be a good guest, wonders whether her hosts have violated some norm of good hosting, and so on but she also is confronted on her plate with something she categorically does not regard as food.[21] It's as if someone roasted a shoe and put that in front of her with a hearty "bon appetit!." This is how some vegans feel when confronted with animal flesh. We have reconceptualized what "edible" means and do not include animals in that category. To eat one, even out of love and care for family and tradition, would not be possible because animals are not food.

Hence, a vegan might reject traditional flesh-based foods out of a sense of moral integrity or because they do not consider animals edible. Someone could still ask here why those reasons would override commitments to one's loved ones given that to feel the force of this dilemma at all one has to feel very strong ties of love and care. One response is to assert that the obligations to the chickens have lexical priority over obligations of love and care.[22] Lexical priority grants precedence to one principle over others, showing which priority is most important in conflicts. If principles defending chickens' well-being have lexical priority—perhaps because one thinks principles of justice take precedence over principles of care—that would account for why, even in the face of all the relational considerations, obligations to the chicken would take precedence. While appealing to the lexical priority of obligations rooted in justice would provide a decisive response to this question, it is not consistent with my feminist ethics to do so. I am not interested in endorsing a static hierarchy of moral considerations. As Virginia Held notes, the perspectives of justice and care can and do conflict (2006, 97), but "the claims of caring relationships are at least no less fundamental" than the claims of justice (102). Context will help us best assess which should prevail in conflicts where we cannot meet the demands of both. I do not sanction a moral method that relies on asserting that considerations of justice are always primary to considerations of care, though certainly there will be circumstances in which they are.

Additionally, I am uncomfortable framing our moral relationships with animals as merely a matter of justice. There is a plurality of moral considerations relevant to thinking about animals. These include considerations of justice to be sure but also considerations of care, empathy, love, a desire to be in right relationship with other living beings, and a deeply held rejection of the anthroparchal systems of oppression that result in speciesism, carnism, sexism, racism, ablism, homophobia, transphobia, and the like. When I stare at the bowl of chicken soup, I see a whole lot more than the injustices committed against that chicken and her conspecifics.

If the answer to why concerns for animals' well-being and retaining one's moral self-conception can override relational considerations is not the lexical priority of principles of justice, then what might the reason(s) be? It is permissible (perhaps even ideal in some settings) to reject the soup, thus causing relational moral distress (and in some cases harm) for a variety of reasons. First, it is simply not

---

[21]Cf. the anecdote Melanie Joy uses at the beginning of her book about carnism (2010, 11–12).

[22]My thanks to Peter Vallentyne for raising this issue.

the case that we must alienate ourselves from firmly and genuinely held ethical commitments to prove to our loved ones that we value them. For those who do not share the animal advocate's commitment to our other-than-human fellow creatures, this is perhaps easier to see by appealing to a case involving racism rather than speciesism. Imagine your family has long-held white supremacist values manifesting, in part, in racist jokes at the holiday table. Through educating yourself, listening to Black peers and colleagues, and thorough consideration of who you want to be in the world, you've come to reject the white supremacist values of your youth. There you sit at the holiday table listening to the latest in racist jokes from your family. You love them and they love you. You understand they will be hurt and feel judged if you do not participate in their racist merrymaking. Yet, you cannot do it. You cannot think the thoughts necessary to make the jokes, you cannot form the words, and you cannot endure the idea of uttering them. You therefore decline to participate. It is just as true in this case as it is in the case of the chicken soup that your refusal to participate has minimal directly perceptible consequences for the cause of racial justice. There are no people of color in the room. No one outside your family will know you participated, and so forth. Still, it must be clear to most readers that it cannot be the case that you have to join in the racism out of love and care for your family. To stew in racism, stoke its fires, embrace or enact its ugliness fundamentally goes against who you are as a moral being. No amount of love and care for others should force you to alienate yourself so thoroughly from your moral commitments—moral commitments, moreover, that move the world more consistently toward a more just and equitable life for everyone.[23] The same applies for the anti-speciesist.

Second, in the kinds of dilemmas under consideration in this chapter, the relational obligations run in multiple directions. Vegans are not solely responsible for the relational harm that comes about when traditional foods and food-based practices involve animal flesh they no longer consume. Loved ones who refuse to adjust practices, alter recipes, or make accommodations for their vegan loved ones demonstrate a failure of love and care. Relationships are entities that are under the stewardship of their members. They will flourish or fail depending on the decisions and actions of those who are parties to them. The very difficult position the vegan finds herself in at the holiday table can be made better but only through both her actions and those of her loved ones. In such a situation, it is not reasonable to say that a vegan must eat traditional foods in order to avoid harming her relationships. When put in a position where that is her only option, the relationship itself is ethically marred because of failures of love and care that are the result of others'

[23]It is arguably the case that those who have moral commitments that make life worse for others do need to alienate themselves from those positions out of love and care for others. I won't argue for this here.

choices. She need not alienate herself from her moral integrity because others either will not or cannot demonstrate care.

Third, the kinds of dilemmas under consideration in this chapter are unlike some ethical quandaries that involve the awful realization that no matter what one does one's hands are forever dirtied. Here there are opportunities for relational moral attention as laid out in the following section. This work will be challenging and may face limitations. What those challenges are and what limitations we will encounter will differ from family to family, case to case, and even meal to meal. Despite these challenges and limitations, it is moral work that we can do, and it can heal the relational harms that result from rejecting deeply held traditional and familial culinary practices. There are also other activities I can partake in that will demonstrate love and care for my family without necessitating a betrayal of my values. These activities can count as forms of relational moral attention as well as ensure ongoing relationship building. I can play a game I intensely dislike but that they love, ensure my presence at important life events and rituals, take an interest in what interests them, and so forth.

This brings us to a final and crucial point, namely that whether or to what degree relational moral attention is possible as a factor in adjudicating conflicts of interest. Knowing the interests involved is vital, of course. So is understanding the possibilities for moral attention. While there are numerous ways to show care for loved ones, demonstrating a commitment to animals is more limited in modes of expression. We can write letters and attend protests, but rejecting actions that reduce animals to objects of consumption remains one of the most direct and important methods of expressing one's opposition to animal exploitation. Moreover, moral attention for the chicken who became our family's soup is impossible.[24] That chicken has died. Billions of her fellow chickens share her fate. Where my family and I can do the work of relational moral attention to mitigate the relational difficulties that would arise should I forego the chicken soup, there is very little I or they can do that would mitigate the moral harms to the chicken. Now, again, a consequentialist might want to say that this is a silly point because the chicken is already dead so eat her or do not eat her but either way it makes no difference for that chicken (or perhaps even the billions of other chickens like her). For the diehard consequentialist vegan that might feel true. For those of us whose ethics are rooted in other ways of seeing the moral life, however, that reasoning is usually uncompelling. For, when I face this conflict, I see that even though my actions right at this moment will not change things for this chicken,

[24]Attentive readers will observe that I have removed the word "relational" from relational moral attention here. That is because whether there is a relationship with the chicken who became soup is a question depending on particulars. If one raised the chicken oneself, then clearly there is relational moral attention involved. Otherwise, while we certainly are "in relationship" with animals we eat, use, and experiment on that is a conception of relation that is far more attenuated.

I (1) do not know for sure what impact my refusing to eat this chicken soup might have on the future. There is a chance, for example, that as a result of my refusal someone else at the table might change their stance on eating animal flesh or my family will stop eating chicken soup altogether. (2) Given that opportunities for relational moral attention abound with my family, there is no reason I should have to compromise my moral integrity and sense of self, and (3) I know with certainty that opportunities for reparative work with animals are few and far between. I take all of this information about the possibilities for effective relational moral attention into consideration when I decide how to resolve the conflict about eating my grandmother's soup. If, for example, my grandmother is extremely unwell and I know relational moral attention will be impossible due to her imminent death, that difficulty with undertaking relational moral attention would factor into my thinking as well. Though here, too, whether or not one ultimately eats the soup in this, very sad, scenario will depend largely on the particulars of their context.

This accounts for why it is permissible to opt for foregoing traditional foods in service of defending animals. In situations where opportunities for relational moral attention abound, food is plentiful, other points of relational connection are available, one's identity is not so marginalized as to render further attention or discord unsafe, and one is situated high enough in the family hierarchy so as not to fear losing too much by adhering to one's principled stance it is optimal to reject the flesh-based foods. In the case of traditional foods and animal-based practices, there will be many situations where disappointing people we love while defending animals will be the right thing to do. As relational moral attention plays a significant role in why that is the case, I turn now to articulating what that looks like in these kinds of intracultural and interspecies conflicts.

5 Relational Moral Attention

Recall the discussion in Chapter 3 where I emphasized that relational moral repair will not be required or necessary in all situations and that both care and relational moral attention are about particular individuals with distinct relationships. Therefore, the nature of this approach precludes offering one standard for how to address the issue of relational moral attention. There are no one-size-fits-all answers here, which is a strength rather than a weakness in the account. Later in the chapter, I offer suggestions for how relational moral attention might work.

First, I should realize that while centering a family's gatherings around chicken soup seems random and silly, something much more complex is going on. Of course, my grandmother could prove her culinary worth through making lentil soup instead of chicken soup, but this is where the Ashkenazi Jewish culture enters the picture and complicates matters. The Soup has always been *chicken* soup.

Tradition is partly a reliance on a nonquestioning stance about norms.[25] We derive comfort, mutual understanding, and predictability from doing what has always been done. This insight must be operative in my understanding of the moral remainders with my grandmother.

In my case, I suspect the path to moral repair starts with communication with my grandmother. As Walker puts it, "We might just try turning to each other; talking and listening and imagining possibilities together" (Walker 1995, 143). My grandmother and I need to discuss something more dialogically productive than my pointing out to her that this or that interest is basic or trivial, for example. With my grandmother and situation, we could go the route of considering the values we share and how these shared values can partially explain my choice. We both value being thoughtful and kind. We both avoid being callous or cruel. We both think the family cat deserves empathy, consideration, and love. I can talk with my grandmother about these shared values and help her see that my choice to reject her soup is in part a manifestation of the very values we share. Certainly, on the face of it, we have different values about what the world should be like for chickens. Still, we do agree about the cat, and we can use that agreement as a foundation of mutual understanding.[26] This conversation is not the time for a discussion of the inconsistency involved in recognizing the moral value of our cat but not the chicken. Pragmatically, engaging in conversations about animal ethics with loved ones can be counterproductive and energy depleting for the vegan. In fact, in her advice to vegans Adams repeatedly cautions against engaging in these kinds of arguments (2009).[27] In the moment when I pick my care for animals over eating the chicken soup, the issue is about the moral strain I have placed on my relationship with my grandmother and not one of persuading her to believe that chickens matter. Animal advocacy tends to focus on the moral education of individuals, but that approach is limited. "Simply imparting 'better ethics' to people ignores how everyday life is caught up in relational complexity" (Twine 2016, 262). In pointing to our mutual respect for the family cat, I seek to bridge what seems like a large chasm between us by noting that we both care about animals and that my choices reflect a different manifestation of those values.[28] This process is, to borrow Walker's language again, one that is "deployed in shared processes of discovery, expression, interpretation, and adjustment between two persons," (Walker 1995, 140). This is a strategy a family friend and his wife use in explaining their veganism

---

[25]I owe this point to a participant in the Wesleyan University "Sex, Gender, Species" conference.

[26]Adams discusses the importance of finding commonalities in her strategies for vegans (2009, 72–3). Aaltola and Oksanen make a similar point in the cross-cultural setting (2002).

[27]Barbara McDonald's research demonstrates that in the context of changing people's views of veganism dialogue was not an effective teaching tool (2000, 14).

[28]Adams points to the helpfulness of drawing connections between one's veganism and loved one's values. Language, she suggests, includes "You are the one who taught me to care and I have extended this sense of caring to other animals and the environment. Thank you for teaching me this!" (2009, 143).

to their Jain family members. Jain practices are rooted in a commitment to ahimsa (reverence for all life-forms and adherence to nonviolence in thought, word, and action). Dairy is a part of their traditional foods, and their rejection of those foods can cause some tension. This tension is partially managed by appeal to shared values—they can ground their veganism in the practice of ahimsa, something that resonates from the Jain perspective thus rendering their choices easier to understand as part of the family's moral and religious commitments (Tejas Mehta, personal communication, November 18, 2025).[29]

Of course, a dialogical process may not succeed. Arguments at the holiday table have shown us all that dialogue has its limits. Still, dialogue is the most reasonable chance we have for beginning the work of relational moral attention. Traditional methods of conflict resolution relying on agreement about abstract principles tend to miss the importance of individuals' stories being heard and how these narratives can lead to mutual understanding and healing (Lugones and Spelman 1983).

Even if my grandmother and I could agree on an abstract principle about causing the least necessary harm to animals, that agreement would neither foster an understanding of why my refusal of her soup is so hurtful nor illuminate how to move forward in our relationship. Even when difficult, dialogue will reveal these crucial features. It is better to take our chances with difficult discussions that at least hold out the promise of successfully understanding one another than rely on appeal to abstract principles so that the particulars of our stories become obscured.

Another element of relational moral attention is to both give my relatives' resistance the most charitable interpretation (at least initially) and to recognize that adjusting to my veganism requires work of them. In her research on the "face-saving" strategies employed by vegans and vegetarians, Jessica Greenebaum notes that some vegans "interpret the omnivore's hostile reaction as a combination of denial, ignorance, and guilt" (2012, 315). Having been on the receiving end of much hostility as a vegan, I can empathize with this interpretation. The contextual issues I've raised in this chapter, however, illuminate the importance of openness to a more charitable interpretation. Hostility can be the outward manifestation of various internal states of discomfort including fear of being rejected and feeling unappreciated. When working through issues with loved ones, it is important that vegans attempt to push past our less charitable interpretations in favor of more fully understanding what is going on with them.

Along those lines, our loved ones might be under the impression that our veganism will create more work for them and that this is work they are ill-equipped

[29]Our friend notes, however, that grounding their veganism in the shared focus on ahimsa is easier with younger relatives or family living in the United States. When they return to India and see older relatives it is more complicated because they "do not see dairy consumption as being a harmful thing at all" (pers. comm.). There are often differences in how members of varying generations respond to their loved ones' veganism.

to undertake given a lack of knowledge about vegan cooking. In the case of my grandmother's chicken soup, for example, I must recognize that she likely feels my rejection of her soup as a call for her to provide an alternative option. That may not be what I had in mind, but as a grandmother who wishes to provide nourishment and be a good host she may well interpret the situation in that way. My commitment to veganism seemingly puts an added burden on her both in terms of the work of providing an alternative and in developing the skills needed to do so.[30]

One possibility for assuaging those concerns is to bring one's own food. Adams considers the vegan bringing her own food to gatherings as an act of self-care that also demonstrates the plentifulness of vegan food and the vegan's ease with her own choices (2009, 26). This approach has many benefits in that it ensures the vegan will have something to eat, helps loved ones see and taste what vegan food can offer, and alleviates the burdens on hosts of providing vegan food. It can be taken on as one of the many skills of social negotiation that vegans need to hone as they go about their lives (Twine 2014) and can be considered as a potentially reparative gesture as it spares loved ones from additional labor on one's behalf.

Whether or not one ought to bring one's own food to familial and communal gatherings is a question of context, however. Bringing one's own food might be an act of repair in some settings and an act of hostility or cultural ineptitude in others depending on cultural norms and traditions. For example, while I could have made my own soup to bring to my grandmother's house, I was thirteen when I became a vegetarian and my grandmother would never have accepted that as a solution. Children providing their own food was antithetical to her understanding of the right ordering of things. Understanding what we, as vegans, can do in the form of relational moral attention requires understanding the particulars of the context we are in as we face the defending animals/disappointing people dilemma with traditional foods.

It is reasonable to ask if loved ones and family members have any obligation to engage in relational moral attention or if the weight of this moral work falls solely on the vegan. Loved ones have a significant role in the relational process, and the vegan certainly does not carry the weight on their own. Given relationships involve multiple parties working toward care, compassion, and love it is overly burdensome to claim that the person concerned with animal welfare has the obligation to shoulder the burden of the social nature of food and food-based traditions all on their own. Mutual regard and respect are a central part of caring relationships. With this in mind, I might suggest to my grandmother that the best

[30]Barbara McDonald discusses the "instrumental learning" that goes into adapting to veganism (2000, 21). She has in mind the kind of learning new vegans must do (cooking, ordering food out, and understanding ingredient labels), but the issue of instrumental learning is just as relevant for loved ones seeking to accommodate and show care for the vegans in their lives.

way we can demonstrate this mutual regard is for me to respect the importance of her cooking and for her to recognize that, because of our relationship, she should not put me in a position where I have to reject her cooking time and time again.[31] Something disrespectful happens when a grandmother consistently puts chicken soup in front of her vegan granddaughter. I might also say something loving that recognizes how difficult it is for my grandmother when I refuse her soup but then offer her suggestions about what I currently enjoy eating (Adams 2009, 143–4). Perhaps we can work together to make a soup I can eat and then, over time, we can replace the chicken soup with the alternative. My grandmother and other loved ones need to do work on their end to be open and receptive to these efforts and to refrain from taking an oppositional stance toward my veganism and the values it expresses. Note that I am making a limited point here about loved ones being open and receptive to vegan values. I do not mean to suggest that caring relationships require that we remain open and receptive to just any value expressed by someone we love. Some values are harmful, hate-filled, unjust—of the kind no one should welcome. Though loved ones may disagree with veganism or fail to understand it being felt as a moral imperative, there is nothing intrinsically harmful, hate-filled, or unjust about it. Therefore, there is no reason loved ones cannot work to embrace the vegan in their lives.

Another area where carnist loved ones can participate in relational moral attention is in challenging their perception that their vegan loved one's choices are an expression of a negative judgment about them. The vegan's choice to avoid animal flesh foods is just that, their choice. Any interpretation of that choice as a judgment on others' behaviors or a desire to convert others to veganism is a projection of the carnist's feelings about their own choices. "They use your vegetarianism to judge themselves" (Adams 2009, 63). It is crucial that loved ones get this projection under control rather than tagging their vegan loved one as judgmental. Part of their side of relational moral attention is coming to peace with their own decisions and leaving their vegan loved one to the peace of theirs. Doing so will help restore the relationship to one centered on love, care, and mutual respect.[32]

Loved ones must also make efforts to cease the endless joke-making about veganism that is so common when someone in their family embraces vegan values. This may seem like a small gesture, but it goes a long way toward demonstrating care and respect. I have been vegan for over thirty years, for example, and my veganism remains a joke among some family members. They say things like "We're

[31] A participant at the Wesleyan University "Sex, Gender, Species" Conference raised this important point.
[32] It is certainly possible that some vegans are overtly judgmental of their carnist loved ones. It is also possible that some make judgments but leave them unexpressed out of respect for their loved ones. It is difficult to describe, but I often feel deep sadness about the animal my loved ones are consuming without necessarily feeling judgmental toward them. I wish things were different, but I do not sit in active judgment of their behaviors when we interact. I imagine I am not alone in this.

on our way to your house from the airport. Stopping to get a burger first, though, because we won't get any at your house!" or "Don't show Karen that rack of lamb in the oven!." Whatever the reason for these quips, family members and friends need to avoid making the heartfelt and identity-forming values of their vegan loved one a source of jokes and backhanded hostility. We know you have a rack of lamb in the oven, and we don't need to know if you are going to stop for a burger before visiting us. These kinds of comments demonstrate a fundamental lack of respect and care and set the vegan up as "other." They are contrary to right relationship.

Finally, loved ones participate in relational moral attention by demonstrating loving curiosity. Instead of setting themselves in opposition to our veganism, they ought to cultivate a spirit of wonder about it. This can involve asking sincere questions about veganism and why it is important to us, expressing curiosity about what our new favorite foods are or where we like to go out to eat, and genuinely asking us what it feels like to be vegan in a place where carnism is the norm. Loving curiosity involves avoiding invasive questions or demanding answers at inopportune times. It is best left for times when we are not amid a meal where animal protein is present for those are times no one wants to hear one's reasons for veganism. Loving curiosity can assuage the ways in which we feel obscure to one another, as Walker puts it (1995,143), and open doors to mutual understanding and even respect. Once that door is open and relational moral attention is underway, we might all make room for the possibility that traditions can change and cultures can evolve. Might we gain something by changing traditions? Perhaps life is enhanced rather than impoverished by doing so?[33] While often painful, change can be for the better.

We might, for example, consider shifting our traditions to reinforce solidarity between our community and other human and other-than-human communities. Jews have survived pogroms and genocides and continue to face anti-Semitism. Given this history, it shouldn't be a tremendous leap to express care for other animals and other marginalized groups most impacted by animal agriculture (e.g., undocumented laborers and low-income and communities of color). I can inform my family about movements within the Jewish community that view vegetarianism or veganism as part of a Jewish response to the interlocking oppressions of humans and nonhuman animals that intersect in animal agriculture. Shifting our traditions could enhance our ties to other marginalized groups as well as solidify other values within our own families—values around repairing the world.

Doing so could expand our ideas around who constitutes part of the Jewish community. While chicken soup is central to my family's identity as Ashkenazi

[33]See Safran Foer's discussion of how Thanksgiving dinner might be enhanced without the traditional roasted turkey (Safran Foer 2007, 249–57). For more on the possibility of shifting traditions see Twine (2016) and Ciochetti (2012).

Jews, focusing on this ignores the multiethnic nature of the broader Jewish community. There is no single answer to the question of what makes food Jewish (Sameth 2011, 229). Jewish grandmothers the world over prepare different foods for their grandchildren. Broadening our conception of what it means to be Jewish might help my family connect to other Jewish people throughout the world who view their culinary identities quite differently than we do. We may grow by avoiding the essentialism implicit in my family's insistence that Jews eat chicken soup.[34]

Conflicts between defending animals and disappointing people are felt so deeply in part because animal advocates are torn between their sincere convictions and internal moral commitments to live more compassionate lives and the traditions, people, and activities central to their identity and most important relationships. To date, guidance from animal ethicists has been slim and largely unhelpful. While that guidance has certainly helped animal advocates solidify their moral positions, it has offered no real reprieve from the felt experience of various parts of our identity being pulled in different directions. I believe this is because of a failure to think relationally about interests and these kinds of conflicts. As a result of this failure, contemplating how thinking relationally can help us find our way through these difficulties is unhelpfully obscured.

6 Complications

I have suggested that appealing to shared values, engaging in relational moral attention, and actively pursuing avenues of reconciliation rooted in respect, care, love, and curiosity are the way forward when one opts (or one's vegan loved one opts) to defend animals in a way that disappoints their people. There are several complications and questions that may be raised about this approach. I take these up here, beginning with worries about the complexity of appealing to shared values.

Appeals to shared values are not quite as simple as they may initially appear. On the face of it, we might think it would be uncomplicated for a family grounded in the same ethnic, cultural, or religious tradition to identify values shared by all involved. This is not always the situation, however. In the case of the chicken soup, for example, there may be numerous obstacles to identifying shared values. To begin with, as is true of other cultural and religious groups, Jews are not a homogeneous group (though within a family one might expect some

[34]My family may not care what Ethiopian Jewish grandmothers feed their families. They care that in our family we eat chicken soup, and the chicken soup is what my grandmother fed my mother and so on all the way back to the shtetls of Poland and Ukraine. Therefore, my appeal to the multicultural nature of Judaism may require time to take root.

homogeneity). As a people, we differ considerably in our interpretation of our religious texts, for example.[35]

This complication is evident in the debate over the aftermath of the AgriProcessors/Rubashkin kosher slaughterhouse debacle. In 2004 and 2008 undercover footage of AgriProcessors showed egregious abuse at the plant (Preston 2008). In May 2008, AgriProcessors was the target of what was then the largest single-site immigration raid in US history. Three hundred eighty-nine employees were arrested, and the plant was charged with more than 9,000 counts of child labor violations (Shapiro 2008).

The ensuing debate among Jews illustrates the challenge of finding shared values even within one's own community. Some Conservative and Reform Jewish communities responded to the AgriProcessors revelations by calling for an expanded conception of *kashrut* (the rules dictating what foods adhere to Jewish law) that included increased animal welfare and social justice considerations (Freedman 2007; Preston 2008).[36] Some Orthodox rabbis rejected this interpretation of Jewish law, maintaining that adding ethical considerations to kosher criteria moves the conception of kosher too far from religious concerns (Shafran 2012; Vitello 2008). Reading accounts of this debate, one quickly gets the impression that finding shared values within the broader Jewish community may be impossible.

There is no denying that intracultural relational moral attention is complicated by the plurality of values that exist within a community. But significant challenges are present in most cases where such attention is necessary and yet we persevere. In the example of my grandmother's chicken soup, there is still room for common ground. For, whatever our beliefs around what counts as kosher, we do share a general vision for kindness and compassion. We also share the Jewish value of *tikkun olam* (repairing the world). Relational moral attention with my grandmother and extended family might involve appealing to the overarching value in Judaism of repairing the world and how I see both my choice to respect chickens and my recognition of the distress that choice causes them as part of that effort. They, in turn, can see my decision as an instantiation of *tikkun olam* and therefore approach it with more respect.

I can also remind my family that Jews understand strong stances. Safran Foer tells the story of his grandmother, who was on the brink of death from starvation during the Holocaust, refusing the one piece of food offered to her—an unkosher piece of pork (Safran Foer 2007, 16–17). Later, when Safran Foer articulates why he does not serve factory farmed meat at his table, he returns to

[35]This issue is articulated nicely in Talia Raphaely and Asher Meyerson's discussion of "Ben" whose veganism is based on his interpretation of Jewish values but who finds other Jews in his community either ignorant of those values or unable to see how they would lead to veganism (2019).

[36]This movement is known as Hekhsher Tzedek.

his grandmother's story noting "to feed the food it [the factory farm] produces to my family, to support it with my money—would make me less myself, less my grandmother's grandson, less my father's son" (Safran Foer 2007, 267). Despite the noise generated by the plurality of values within our own cultures, there are places of mutual understanding and agreement. In Jewish culture, we understand drawing lines around food and adhering to them even in the face of potentially grave consequences. I truly would be less my grandmother's grandchild and less my parents' child if I ate the chicken soup. Drawing attention to that fact could open the door to relational repair.

A second consideration about my approach focuses on why one would have to present an argument for the permissibility of rejecting traditional foods in these kinds of cases at all. Isn't it obvious that rejecting the food is permissible? The answer here is no. In conversations with students and participants at conferences where I have presented this work, the question of whether it is permissible to reject the soup comes up regularly because of my emphasis on the moral importance of relationships of love and care. I took up this issue earlier when I discussed why it is permissible to forego traditional foods on vegan grounds. Here, I focus more specifically on the view, articulated by some, that eating animal flesh foods is obligatory in certain settings.

Julie Hanlon Rubio has argued that there are contexts where eating flesh foods might not be merely permissible but also obligatory (Rubio 2014 and personal correspondence). Working in the Catholic cooperation with evil framework, Rubio argues that relationships, hospitality, and social connections can, and possibly should, take precedence in cases where partaking of animal flesh is tied to the fundamental human goods of family and community (52). As she puts it,

> By viewing eating as a social practice, it becomes clear that feeding people and partaking in their hospitality are fundamental to human community. While those who have adopted vegetarianism or an absolute stance against eating factory-farmed meat legitimately hope for another world, the Catholic moral tradition at its best makes room for this complexity and allows for limited cooperation with evil while constantly calling for greater cooperation with good. A flexitarian stance is an ethical option that allows people to balance conflicting goods as they begin to imagine a different world. (52–3)

Rubio's discussion moves between treating serving or eating the flesh-based food as a "can" and as a "should," so it is reasonable to wonder whether she thinks eating my grandmother's Rosh Hashannah chicken soup is permissible or obligatory. Rubio notes that "while the overall argument is more of a 'could,' I was imagining situations where 'should' would emerge from moral discernment" (personal correspondence). Rubio herself finds it difficult to "cooperate" with evil in this way but is "still convinced enough of the difficulty of purity and inevitability of conflicting goods to stand by the possibility of 'should'" (ibid.). I gather, then, that Rubio's position is that eating flesh foods in certain social contexts is certainly permissible and sometimes obligatory when the eating of those foods is linked to the fundamental social goods of family and community relationships or when one is a guest in someone's home and "one's host would otherwise be deeply offended" (47).[37] As she puts it, "Respect for animals can conflict with respect for family and friends. In cases like these, prudential judgment is required to discern rightly one's duties. At times, it seems that serving and eating meat may constitute a necessary and permissible form of material cooperation with evil" (46). She notes that "buying and serving factory-farmed meat might be permissible when important to one's primary obligations to family and community" (ibid.). This is something my friend Iván Sandoval Cervantes, a vegan anthropologist, encounters when doing fieldwork in economically marginalized parts of Mexico. The families sacrifice to provide him with meat-based dishes. In that context his rejection of the food can be seen as disrespectful of their sacrifice (personal communication, November 25, 2025).

Contra the consequentialists who argue that it is likely permissible to eat animal flesh when alone and the animal is already slaughtered, butchered, and cooked (e.g., your roommate's Kung Pao chicken leftovers) (Fischer 2020), Rubio argues that, as a matter of virtue, for those who care about animals, foregoing flesh foods in private is obligatory (47). For Rubio's virtue approach (where virtue is understood in the Catholic rather than Aristotelian sense), the obligation is most strict in private where the goods of family and community are not at stake. Flexibility is introduced only in the social context.

I am sympathetic to Rubio's careful consideration of the complexity of our competing values and appreciate her discussion of how women tend to be most burdened with sustaining families and cultures through food (44). I agree with her about the centrality of eating as a social endeavor and of its significant contribution to sustaining culture (ibid.). She is right when she notes that "a person's choice about what to eat is not simply an individual choice because eating is a social practice embedded in families, communities, and cultures" (45). Finally, she is right that the social and communal nature of eating puts the person who not only values animals but also loves her family "under duress" (45–6). I disagree, however, that eating flesh-based traditional foods with loved ones is obligatory. It is possible I see the source of the tension and conflict in these kinds of cases differently than Rubio. Her focus is on the complexities generated by social context whereas I see the conflict as social to be sure but specifically I see it as relational. Social context,

[37]Here she has in mind several different scenarios, including students doing homestays abroad with economically disadvantaged families (personal correspondence). See also Steven Fesmire's discussions about the problems of moral absolutism (2024, 44–9, 88–93) and his claim that eating animal flesh in cross-cultural settings is obligatory out of conscientious regard for hosts (2015, 141).

with its lack of individual specificity and its group nature, can be entrenched and very slow to shift. Relationality, on the other hand, can present more opportunities for reconciliation and joint effort because it is rooted in specific relations of care—this grandmother and granddaughter, this uncle and nephew, this young person and this community elder, or even this family of ten. As I have argued, it is possible to mitigate the relational harms generated by a vegan's rejection of their family's or community's food traditions through the work of relational moral attention. Moreover, as I argued earlier, the relational obligations run bidirectionally, which means that loved ones must show care for their vegan beloveds by shifting habits and traditions and demonstrating respect and curiosity. The duress the vegan experiences should be attended to by everyone involved, not viewed as an individual problem for her to resolve by forcing her to "cooperate with evil." It is everyone's job to work toward "greater cooperation with good" where "good" is understood as both the end of animal suffering in the food system and the goods of family and community.

To summarize what I've said thus far, I believe it is permissible, indeed ideal, to refuse to eat animal flesh foods in the context of deeply held traditions related to relations of love and care. It is my hope that most vegans will refuse such foods. I have also argued that it is not obligatory to eat those foods. For several reasons, I have not offered an argument that it is *obligatory for all vegans to reject the foods.* To begin with, I recognize that the issues of moral integrity, conceptions of the edible, and understanding of veganism as a rejection of the interlocking systems of oppression rooted in an oppressive conceptual framework are reasons internal to me (and many others, I think) that may not translate to others.[38] I hope these reasons do translate to some, particularly after reading this book, but it is no doubt true that other vegans operate with different conceptions of personal morality and therefore may not find the reasons I have articulated compelling.

Along these lines, Bob Fischer has argued that obligations to be vegan do not stem from act-consequentialist (maximizing the good in every individual action) or rights-based reasons but instead can be seen as a "duty to signal." On his view, there are reasons to think there is a duty to demonstrate to others (to signal) that you are willing to make sacrifices for animals, but he argues that this duty is not strict. Fischer notes there are situations where signaling by eschewing animal flesh might not be required, among them in cases of cultural traditions.[39] In

[38]My thanks to Bob Fischer for raising this point.

[39]This is where Fischer mentions the roommate's leftover Kung Pao chicken, noting that there are no negative effects of that act on yourself, animals, the environment, or others. Moreover, there are potential negative impacts of buying a vegan alternative that, for example, involved killing field animals during harvesting of the vegetables. Therefore, there is no duty to signal by adhering to one's vegan principles. Instead, you might eat the Kung Pao leftovers and explain your reasons for doing so to your roommate (2020, 165). As I noted earlier, this is different from Rubio's virtue account where the obligation to eschew meat is strongest in private.

these situations, one should make clear one's general opposition to consumption of animal flesh on moral grounds while clarifying one's reason for making the exception in this case. Concretely, that would mean me eating my grandmother's soup and saying something to the group along the lines of "I oppose the systems of oppression that see sentient creatures as tools for human consumption, but I also love you and see how important it is to grandma that I eat her soup, so I will do that now while avoiding animal flesh in my daily life." Here, the sacrifice on behalf of animals one is demonstrating is one's willingness to endure the hardship of being transparent with loved ones.

There are reasons to be skeptical about this approach. Briefly, insofar as one's veganism is a "signal," it is not merely a signal to others but also to oneself about where one draws moral lines. I am less concerned about a slippery slope here (e.g., that if you eat the chicken soup on Rosh Hashannah you'll devolve into eating McNuggets unreflectively on the way to work on a random Tuesday) than I am about signaling to ourselves who we are, what our aims are, and who we want to be in the world. My veganism is not merely a signal to *others* that actions on behalf of animals are important but also an important signal to myself about who I am. Moreover, I would think signaling in these kinds of cultural and familial spaces would be of more importance than other instances of signaling precisely because you demonstrate a willingness to "sacrifice" for animals that is so strong you are refraining from eating them even when arguably your action changes nothing and you have isolated yourself from your loved ones. I put sacrifice in quotes because many vegans do not view veganism as a sacrifice, though it is often perceived as one by nonvegans. Finally, there are difficulties with the kinds of exception-explaining utterances Fischer advocates for. I suspect many families would completely tune out the explanation as merely more pontificating from a self-righteous vegan. Worse, they would rush like sharks to the chum at the opportunity to point to hypocrisy and contort that into a reason they have no obligation to avoid animal flesh.

Nevertheless, Fischer makes the compelling point that there are times when strict adherence to veganism signals something problematic to others—something more like what a morally superior set of jerks vegans are—and that in these cases flexibility could be the better side of valor. Better to eat the soup and explain why you are making the exception than to harm the cause of animals *and* harm your relationships by generating an audible groan at the table as everyone thinks about what a killjoy you are. Though I generally think Fischer's confidence in the efficacy of signaling verbally if not with action is flawed, I take his point that there may be situations in which the context is such that a vegan could opt for this strategy. I do not wish to rule this out as an option, though I imagine its applications are quite limited.

Another reason I will not assert that it is obligatory to reject animal-based traditional foods that are tied to highly valued relationships is that I see veganism as a practice embodying a commitment to compassion and justice rather than as a destination of moral purity. Gruen and Jones refer to this view of veganism as "aspirational" and contrast it with "identity veganism" where the latter asserts veganism as the only ethical way to live (2016, 156). In a capitalist economic system with industrialized agriculture, extensive biomedical research on animals, and so forth it is impossible for vegans to avoid being a party to violence. As Gruen and Jones beautifully put it:

> We can rail against the massive violence that is done to the huge number of living beings who did nothing to deserve their tragic fates, but neither our political commitments nor our moral outrage place us above the violent fray. All aspects of consumption in late capitalism involve harming others, human and nonhuman. (157)

They note that this is not to be misinterpreted as an argument for "compassionate carnivorism" or "humane meat." Rather, it is a call to recognize veganism as aspirational—a crucial step on the path to compassionate consumption and living but not a fast track to the pinnacle of moral purity as some vegans would have it.

I should have some humility about the fact that, for example, I call out the chicken soup as morally unacceptable while eating vegetables cultivated and harvested by migrant laborers who are denied basic human rights (Food Empowerment Project, "Produce Workers"). Now, I do what I can about the latter issue by supporting organizations that work to end injustice across the food system, learning to grow my own vegetables, and so forth, but my hands are most certainly not clean despite thirty years of veganism.[40]

When we view veganism as aspirational in the way Gruen and Jones suggest, we can see why it might be a mistake to claim it is obligatory for all people in all situations to reject cultural and traditional foods tied to relationships of love and care. Vegans make moral compromises all the time in service of highly valued ends (and some not so highly valued ends), though we often do not discuss it. I have written about the dilemma of feeding my premature son when he was in neonatal intensive care and there were no completely vegan infant formulas (Emmerman 2022), but compromises arise even in less dire situations including taking medications that have been tested on animals to relieve a headache, eating vegetables that involve the death of field animals for their cultivation (Fischer and Lamey 2018), buying vegan shoes we can afford but that do not meet our values regarding labor conditions, and so on. In light of these kinds of compromises, it feels disingenuous to declare by fiat that no one who cares about animals can ever eat an animal-based traditional food under circumstances where rejecting that food significantly strains relationships of love and care and where their rejection

---

[40]It is also true that numerous field animals die in plant agriculture, though determining precise numbers is difficult (Fischer and Lamey 2018).

comes too late to save the animals' life. Recall that contextual moral veganism sees veganism as a response to a particular context. In industrialized, affluent nations it is a response to the systems of domination and oppression that exploit animals, humans, and the natural environment. It is also, however, a response that plays out in more local contexts—your grandmother's kitchen, your ethnic community's potluck, and your religion's traditions around major life events. That context is relevant to how one lives one's veganism.

Another potential reason one might think it is obligatory to reject flesh foods even in the contexts under consideration here is that our choices have an impact on others and could move the cause of animals forward by spreading veganism. This is often referred to as "social contagion" or as a form of role modeling, and one might think it is a reason to argue that strict adherence to veganism in these cases is required. These considerations are similar to Fischer's notion of "signaling." We never know who might be bent or moved by our vegan ways.[41] Ben Almassi notes that "role-modeling effects of our individual dietary and consumer ethical choices may justify these choices even when the direct act-consequentialist case seems quite thin" (2011, 404–5). Indeed, he argues that even in light of worries about causal impotence, an act consequentialist might have reasons to make morally motivated dietary and consumer choices. Still, Almassi notes that role modeling can backfire, and acts can be both negatively and positively contagious (405). Confronted with the apparent moral perfectionism of a vegan, for example, some people are apt to baulk and decide that kind of life is beyond their reach. I join Gruen and Jones in noting that worries about "backfire role-modeling" and negative social contagion are best met by ensuring one's attitude toward one's veganism is aspirational rather than self-righteous (167, n. 17). These considerations are crucial, though, in assessing the context of one's situation. If it seems like the social contagion has a chance to work toward the good and that the likelihood of moral backfire is low, that is important information and would provide excellent reasons to think the vegan might want to adhere strictly to her values in that moment.

While I have not argued that it is *obligatory* for vegans to forego traditional flesh-based foods in situations where they are tied to highly valued relationships of love and care and where the animal's life can no longer be saved, for many reasons that is ideally what most vegans will do. These reasons include those I mentioned earlier regarding moral integrity and no longer viewing animals as edible, but there are other reasons as well. First, it is helpful to maintain a consistent ethics for others. As Almassi puts it, "A clear policy of vegetarianism may be easier to communicate successfully than a complex vegetarian/omnivorous situational ethics easily misunderstood by onlookers, as omnivorism, risking unintended reverse role-modeling" (407). Put another way, the kind of nuance involved in

[41]This is what Varner has in mind when he notes that people adopting veganism as part of their personal morality, managing hard conversations at the dinner table, can shift "the goalposts of morality."

Fischer-style verbal signaling or making exceptions in proscribed circumstances is often lost on others or misinterpreted in ways that negatively impact the fight for justice, something Fischer recognizes when he notes that "some signaling strategies are 'self-undermining' and sometimes perceived as hypocritical" (2020, 166n6).

Moreover, maintaining a consistent ethic is important for ourselves even among those who do not share my sense of moral integrity and conception of the edible that render exception-making impossible for me. For, as Gruen and Jones note, private actions (or the kinds of public actions I have been talking about here) might increase the chance you eat more animal flesh in the future (168). Actions, even those undertaken in private, are important for "stabilizing" "[one's] ability to act on one's aspiration" to avoid contributing to suffering and oppression (ibid.). Finally, as I have argued in this chapter, there is moral work we can all do to ease the relational pressures that arise when our commitment to end animal suffering conflicts with the interest in partaking of important food-based cultural and familial traditions. In doing that work we can, over time, shift those traditions to minimally be more inclusive of veganism or, ideally, to embrace vegan alternatives entirely. This work may be slow and sometimes painful, but it is worthwhile.

To summarize, the approach I offer here maintains that there is a way forward in intracultural conflicts around traditional foods that does not involve overriding animals' interests despite the robustness of the interest in those foods. The ethical ideal is for vegans and their families to recognize the relational moral elements of these conflicts and undertake the work of relational moral attention. I maintain that this is the path most vegans should take, rather than eating the food to placate their loved ones. I recognize, however, there may be contexts where the details are such that a person might choose to eat the food. My fervent hope is that these cases will be rare and only arise after considerable, honest, reflection on the part of the vegan that the situation truly cannot be resolved in a different way. In this way, I hold out the approach I have articulated here as an ideal but not as a universal, absolutist position that all intracultural conflicts of the kind under discussion can or must be resolved according to this ideal. Marti Kheel articulated this well when she said:

> Although my personal hope is that ecofeminists will view veganism as an integral part of the ecofeminist "gathering" or "quilt," I do not attempt to impose this position as a universal *injunction*. My avoidance of universal claims does not detract from my heartfelt adherence to veganism as an ethical ideal, or from my desire that others share it. Nor does it diminish my wish to convince others of the ethical and health benefits of a vegan diet. (2008, 235)

In a similar vein, I hope that most vegans and their families will chose to (and be able to) resolve conflicts around culturally important foods tied to relationships of love and care in the manner I have laid out here. I do not, however, defend a universal injunction that they do so.

It would be more satisfying to a theorist like Francione and many animal activists if my approach produced moral absolutes. Indeed, it would also be more satisfying to the parts of me that desperately want to see the end of animal exploitation. Moral injunctions insensitive to context, however, can be unhelpful at best and extremely harmful at worst. Moreover, as Kheel argued, care approaches need not be invested in establishing themselves as just as rigorous as justice approaches (2008, 337). She asks, "What if we ask the more important questions: What is it that nourishes care and connection and what causes it to fail? And how are caring relationships forged?" (ibid.). I believe that undertaking the work of relational moral attention will nearly always best nourish care and connection for animals and humans in cases of intracultural conflicts around traditional foods.

Before concluding, I want to say a word about the role "cultured" or "in vitro" meat (animal flesh grown in a lab from cells rather than on a farm in the form of a living being) could play in changing the nature of conflicts around commitments to animals and traditional foods. Some might wonder if these dilemmas will simply disappear if the proliferation of in vitro meat comes to pass. For some contemplating the competing values I have discussed here, the option of in vitro meat would appear to offer the perfect solution. Make your holiday soup from lab-grown chicken flesh and no one gets hurt. In vitro meat is not going to offer the way out of these dilemmas, however. First, issues of squeamishness regarding meat grown in laboratories are significant (Alvaro 2019a, 2019b; Lee 2018). I suspect that in vitro meat will not be a widespread option for quite some time. Should it become widely available, affordable, and appealing to the public many vegans will object to consuming it. Vegans might object to in vitro meat on the grounds that it still involves animals to procure the cells used in labs, thus perpetuating animal exploitation (Alvaro 2019a, 2019b). More importantly, some vegans will object because cultured meat also perpetuates the conceptualization of animals as edible and underscores the separation of humans from nature through the use of technology (Alvaro 2019a, 2019b; Lee 2018). Consuming animal flesh grown in laboratories would, therefore, be unacceptable to some vegans on virtue and ecofeminist grounds. I do not rule out the possibility that the proliferation of in vitro meat options could shift the conversation around cultural and traditional foods over time, but it will be a complicated issue for many vegans.

7 Conclusion

While focused on the ethnic, religious, and cultural practices of my own family and community, the approach I offer here provides a road map for others facing similar conflicts. Given the ubiquity of animal use and abuse, most people who take on ethical veganism will face tension between their commitment to animals and the identity- and relationship-based practices of their community. The particulars and central cultural norms of each situation will differ. Still, individuals facing these kinds of dilemmas can undertake the work of understanding the various ethical nuances of the practices and traditions in question and engaging in relational moral attention when they (or their loved ones) turn their backs on those practices and traditions. I leave it to members of other cultural and ethnic groups to offer an analysis of how the work I propose here would manifest in their communities.

Focusing on relational moral attention generates numerous possibilities for growth and reconciliation. If I merely sat at the table declaring that we are murdering chickens because we like soup and I will not participate in that, all this richness would have been lost resulting in weakened bonds of love and care. When faced with the tension between recognizing robust obligations to animals and the realization that some human nonbasic interests are tied to highly valued ends, there is a way forward that need not involve abandoning animals. By fully contextualizing interests and attending to their relational elements we can honor animals' importance while recognizing and repairing the losses incurred in our relationships when we do so.

5 THE BUCK (KILLING) STOPS HERE: CONTEXTUALIZING RECREATIONAL HUNTING

1 Introduction

Every five years, the US Fish and Wildlife Service (FWS) conducts a national survey of fishing, hunting, and wildlife-associated recreation in the United States. According to the most current survey taken in 2022, 9 percent of the US male population aged sixteen and older, 2 percent of the female population, and 4 percent of "other genders" "enjoyed hunting in 2022" (US Fish & Wildlife Service 2022). The numbers for fishing and angling are higher with 22 percent of all males sixteen and older and 10 percent of all females sixteen and older having fished in 2022 (ibid.). Though there appears to be an uptick in the percentage of people fishing and hunting (particularly among females) in the United States in 2022, in general there has been a consistent decline in those numbers at least with respect to American males.[1] Given that the general trend is toward a decline of hunters in

---

Jon Littlefield criticizes those who write about hunting without having interviewed hunters, relying instead on secondary data (2006, 9). He makes a valid point, and I have certainly run afoul of his criticism here as I have relied entirely on secondary data for this chapter. I understand and, to some extent, share Littlefield's worry. At the same time, we are not all trained for fieldwork, nor are we all embodied in ways that make in-person interactions with certain groups of people feasible for us—scholars must always rely on colleagues with expertise we lack ourselves. In part out of deference to Littlefield's concerns, I have endeavored to provide a compassionate and multifaceted portrayal of hunters' relational issues here based on the data available to me.

[1]The 2011 report noted that of people sixteen years of age and older 11 percent of men in the United States hunted and 1 percent of females (US Fish & Wildlife Service 2011). In 2016 for people sixteen and older, those numbers were 8 percent of males and 1 percent of females (US Fish & Wildlife Service 2022). In their definition of hunters, the reports do not specify whether they are tracking recreational hunting, subsistence hunting, or both. The 2022 report notes that "the participation rate in hunting increased until it reached incomes of $200,000 or more. The participation rate was highest among those with incomes of $150,000 to $199,999 at 9 percent" (US Fish & Wildlife Service 2022, 25). It stands

the United States, one might wonder why it is necessary to devote a chapter of this book to thinking through the conflicts of interest posed by recreational hunting.

There are several reasons: first, though the numbers of humans hunting have diminished, the numbers of animals killed by hunters have not. It is challenging to find data tracking the number of animals killed yearly by hunters in the United States, but estimates put it in the millions. Hunting is, therefore, highly relevant from the standpoint of anyone who cares about the well-being and bodily integrity of our fellow creatures. Second, recreational hunting provides an excellent case study for the kinds of moral dilemmas at the heart of this book. As will become clear, recreational hunting is a deeply relational endeavor—passing from parents to children to grandchildren across the generations. As a recreational activity, it determines seasonal activities, travel, gatherings, and traditions. For those who come from hunting families, hunting is one of the definitive identity markers in their community. In short, recreational hunting is profoundly connected to relationships of love and care, so much so that a fifth-generation hunter newly attuned to obligations to animals will find himself confronted with a plurality of conflicts between his interests, values, relationships, and traditions.[2] Third, that recreational hunting is so deeply connected to relationships of love and care has been largely ignored by ethicists writing on the topic, including ecofeminists committed to a deeply contextualized understanding of moral life.

In this chapter, I will examine the conflict between obligations to animals and recreational hunting traditions, answering the question of what an ecofeminist, contextualized approach can say about the conflict between the fifth-generation hunter's interest in hunting with his father and brothers and his desire to respect animals as morally important beings with lives of their own. I will show that a contextualized, ecofeminist approach can help shed light on this conflict and ways to move forward. Ecofeminist theory has highlighted the deeply patriarchal nature of hunting in the United States and has shed light on the connections between hunting, violence, and domination. But ecofeminists have not discussed the relational elements of hunting. A fully contextualized view of hunting will show that while, yes, hunting is rooted in patriarchal conceptions of power and violence, it is also rooted in connection, care, and identity.[3] Hunting is multifaceted. If we

---

to reason that most people at that level of income in the United States are not subsistence hunting if we understand that to mean hunting to provide food for oneself or one's family that otherwise would not be accessible. It is possible the increased number of people hunting in the United States between 2016 and 2022 is attributable to the effects of the COVID-19 pandemic. Hunting licenses experienced a "Covid bump" during the pandemic years (Moritz 2021). Gun sales in the United States have been increasing since 2015 and increased considerably between 2019 and 2021 (Tobin-Taylor 2023, 65).

[2]I refer frequently to the "fifth-generation hunter." There is nothing special about fifth-generation hunters in particular. I am referring to anyone with a long familial background with hunting.

[3]I recognize that some who hunt may reject the idea that hunting is related to connection and care; they may profess to be in it for the bloodsport alone. Thanks to Monica Aufrecht for highlighting this for me.

ignore its complexity, we fail to provide any way forward for the person who seeks to extricate themselves from hunting as an activity.

I begin with a bit of framing to clarify what I mean by recreational hunting. In Section 2, I discuss what traditional animal ethicists have said about recreational hunting and briefly explain why their approaches are inadequate. In Section 3, I discuss ecofeminist writings about recreational hunting and argue that ecofeminism needs a more carefully contextualized approach. In Section 4, I provide a fully contextualized analysis of recreational hunting—one that offers a better standpoint from which to understand and respond to the conflict faced by those who question continuing with hunting activities. Finally, I offer a way forward out of the conflict and consider complications. To be very clear from the outset, this chapter is not a defense of recreational hunting, nor is it a plea to adopt a kinder, gentler view of those who hunt for pleasure. Like many other animal ethicists, I believe hunting for sport or pleasure is morally unacceptable. My aim in this chapter is not to defend those who pursue this activity but rather to recognize that hunting in the United States is sometimes a nuanced affair—one that we cannot seek to end if we diminish the important ties hunters feel between hunting, identity, and relationships of love and care.

As I define it, recreational hunting is hunting undertaken for sport or recreation regardless of whether the flesh of the animal is consumed. That you consume an animal after killing her does not make it subsistence hunting. Recreational hunting can involve canned hunts (where animals are corralled and confined to provide more shooting opportunities for hunters), trophy hunting (where hunters pursue particular animals in order to display their bodies), list hunts (where hunters collect the heads of dead animals according to lists they want to check off), as well as the more standard and familiar kinds of hunting that involve stalking and killing prey in the wild. Most of my research on recreational hunting did not discuss the demographics or traditions of canned or trophy hunting, thus this chapter focuses mainly on the more familiar and popular form of hunting where people hunt and kill animals living in situ.

I do not include indigenous or genuine subsistence hunting under the banner of recreational hunting. I exclude indigenous hunting from my definition of recreational hunting and from discussion in this chapter for several reasons. First, some indigenous hunting may very well be undertaken for the purposes of recreation, but I lack the requisite knowledge to parse those distinctions. Moreover, how relationality factors into indigenous hunting likely varies considerably depending on the specifics of a given community. I leave it to scholars from within those communities or writers with deep familiarity with specific indigenous hunting traditions and practices to take up the questions I ask here in those settings.[4] I exclude genuine subsistence hunting because it raises additional

[4]Ecofeminist theorizing about cultural whaling would be a helpful addition to the conversation about indigenous hunting practices. My thanks to Amy Reed-Sandoval for highlighting these connections.

ethical questions that are beyond the scope of this project. For those living under subsistence conditions without access to plant-based options, for example, it can be argued that acquiring animal flesh through hunting is morally preferable to acquiring it via industrial animal agriculture at the local shop. It has also been made clear to me in discussions with others who grew up around subsistence hunters (I did not) that the subsistence and recreational hunting communities are sometimes different in both ethos and practices.[5] My exclusion of subsistence hunting from this discussion should not be taken as either an endorsement or a rejection; the exclusion is rooted in the need for a different sort of contextual discussion regarding subsistence versus recreational hunting. That said, I recognize that it can be challenging to distinguish instances of subsistence hunting from instances of recreational hunting. I leave it to those who hunt to undertake the self-reflection necessary to truthfully and accurately categorize the nature of their hunting pursuits. Moving forward, for the sake of brevity, I will simply refer to recreational hunting as "hunting."[6]

According to the 2022 US FWS survey, 14.4 million Americans over the age of sixteen hunt. Seventy-seven percent of hunters are male (thus the use of he/him pronouns for hunters in this chapter). Seventy-seven percent of hunters in the United States are white (USFWS 2022, 25).[7] Consequently, when I refer to recreational hunting, I mean hunting primarily engaged in by white men. This includes big game hunting (by far the most popular kind of hunting in the United States) as well as less popular types of hunting for migratory birds (e.g., ducks, doves, and geese) and smaller game (e.g., squirrels, rabbits, quail, and grouse).[8]

2 Traditional Animal Ethicists on Recreational Hunting

In the environmental ethics literature, discussions about hunting have historically centered on questions related to wildlife management and the morality of preserving species at the expense of individuals. Environmental ethicists often prioritize species preservation over individual welfare. As a result, it is not difficult to find environmental ethics literature defending hunting on conservation

[5]Monica Aufrecht and Rachel Fredericks were particularly generous in sharing their insights.

[6]While I do not discuss fishing in this chapter most of what is said about hunting applies equally to fishing.

[7]This is down from 97 percent in 2016 (USFWS 2016, 31–32).

[8]In the 2022 report, for example, 11.5 million hunters reported big game hunting, 5.3 million reported small game hunting, 2.8 million reported hunting migratory birds, and 2.3 million reported hunting other animals ("other animals" includes "groundhogs, feral pigs, raccoons, foxes, and coyotes") (FWS 2022, 20).

grounds. Relatedly, environmental ethicists sometimes defend hunting as a means of population control as well whether that is because burgeoning populations of wild animals threaten local flora or fauna or because wild animals are suffering starvation and disease from overpopulation. Because hunting in the United States has been deeply connected to wildlife management for decades (fees from hunting licenses are often what provide financial support for state wildlife management agencies, for example), it is virtually impossible to separate recreational hunting practices from wildlife management hunting practices. Whether hunting does, indeed, achieve conservation goals and whether those goals are achievable in ways that do not involve hunting is highly contested and beyond the scope of this chapter.

Unlike the environmental ethics literature, animal ethicists have traditionally argued against the moral permissibility of hunting. Working within a rights framework, Tom Regan categorically opposes hunting as a violation of animals' rights. For Regan, hunting reduces animals to having merely instrumental value in service of human interests rather than respecting their inherent value as individual subjects of a life (Regan 2004a, 356). Though Regan notes that hunting and trapping might be permissible in cases where animals pose an "innocent threat" to humans (e.g., if rabid foxes in the woods are biting children), these instances are rare (353). No justifications for hunting, including population control for conservation purposes, are defensible from the rights standpoint. Regan briefly recognizes that hunting can be tied to an interest in social relationships and camaraderie but quickly dismisses that consideration and suggests hunters find different outdoor activities to enjoy that do not involve killing animals. While I agree with Regan's position that hunting is morally unjustifiable, his approach demonstrates what is problematic about a method that focuses solely on arguing for the impermissibility of an act without careful consideration of how people experience the moral constraint. Moral theorists need to have more to say to people about how to navigate these moral constraints in the face of other, deeply felt, moral obligations and relationships with moral valences.

For an animal ethicist, Singer spends surprisingly little time discussing the morality of hunting, which renders his position less clear that Regan's. He generally opposes recreational hunting with very few exceptions for cases where perhaps suffering in nature is excessive. In *Animal Liberation*, Singer notes that he is opposed to harvesting overpopulated animals through hunting and suggests reducing fertility and other, nonlethal, means of population control (1990, 234). Years later, in a lecture given at Williams College, Singer said that while he will not defend hunting, it might be morally preferable to other kinds of deaths wild animals might experience in cases of serious overpopulation where fertility cannot be controlled (Singer 2008). Unlike Regan, Singer does not address the potential robustness of the interest in hunting at all.

Paul Taylor is a rare example of an environmental ethicist who thinks about hunting from the standpoint of individual animals rather than ecosystemic stability. Taylor opposes hunting on the grounds that it serves a nonbasic interest *and* is intrinsically incompatible with the attitude of respect for nature. As discussed in Chapter 2, when Taylor says a practice is "intrinsically incompatible with the attitude of respect for nature," he means that the activity is inherently exploitative and someone who has respect for nature would not engage in that activity. At its root, Taylor's opposition to hunting centers on his belief that it treats wild animals as mere means for human ends (Taylor 1986, 273–4). Rather than treating animals as valuable in their own right, hunters reduce animals to things "that can be manipulated and used to bring about human pleasure" (ibid.). That this is in service of nonbasic interests means that animals' most basic interests are being assigned lower value than humans' nonbasic interests, "which no one who had the attitude of respect for nature (as well as the attitude of respect for persons) would find acceptable" (275).

Taylor's objections to hunting, interestingly, go beyond the worry that hunting reduces animals to having merely instrumental value. He notes that hunting breaks the Rule of Fidelity, which prohibits breaking a trust wild animals place in us (179). He calls hunting, fishing, and trapping "the clearest and commonest examples of transgressions of the rule" (ibid.). Deception, Taylor notes, is the essence of hunting. "Much of the excitement and enjoyment of hunting as a sport is the challenge of one's skills in getting animals to be trusting and unsuspecting. The cleverer the deception, the better the skill of the hunter" (181). These forms of deception integral to hunting include the use of camouflage meant to conceal hunters' positions, the use of food bait to lure animals out of their hidden positions, luring males in rut, and faking species-specific vocalizations. While deception may be permissible in cases where it serves animals' well-being (e.g., when restitution for wrongs requires handling wild animals who can only be approached using deceptive techniques), hunting involves deceiving animals in a way that indicates a failure to appreciate the animals' inherent worth as individuals.[9]

Like Singer, Taylor does not address the relational elements of hunting activities. Though in his work on interspecies conflicts of interest Taylor at times recognizes that an interest might be nonbasic but nevertheless tied to highly valued ends, he does not explore the possibility that an interest could be inherently exploitative of animals and also tied to highly valued ends. He simply asserts that such interests would be rejected out of hand by someone who has adopted the attitude of respect for nature. As discussed in Chapter 2, this is a significant flaw in Taylor's otherwise quite impressively nuanced treatment of conflicts of interest. It is certainly likely

[9]In addition to breaking the Rule of Fidelity, Taylor argues that hunting also breaks the Rule of Nonmaleficence and the Rule of Noninterference (Taylor 1986, 183).

that someone with a true attitude of respect for nature would acknowledge that hunting for sport runs counter to that attitude, but there remains more to be said. How is that person meant to act when the realization of hunting's incompatibility with respect for nature conflicts with the most meaningful relationships in his life? Taylor offers no guidance.

Of the traditional animal ethicists who offer extended reflections on conflicts of interest, Gary Varner stands out for considering the robustness of the hunting interest for some people. Like Taylor, Varner thinks hunters should find other, less harm-inducing, pastimes. Unlike Taylor, Varner does not imply that this would be a trivial undertaking due to the nonbasic nature of the hunting interest. Instead, Varner notes that hunting can be deeply rooted in tradition and other values. On his account, the culturally entrenched nature of the hunting interest might mean the practice can continue for some time (Varner 2010, 41–2). This is primarily because, as we have seen, Varner's two-level Harean account includes a "conservative bias or inertia" that introduces context into moral deliberations by noting that transition costs and the entrenched nature of some cultural traditions must be taken into consideration when we determine what moral rules should guide common morality (2012, 56–7). Though Varner does not mention the relational elements of hunting, his inclusion of the cultural costs of shifting traditions puts his approach in a different category from Regan, Singer, and Taylor's on the question of hunting. Whereas the latter philosophers either ignore or dismiss out of hand the idea that there may be important values tied to the hunting interest, Varner brings those issues to the fore. Unfortunately, as we saw earlier, what Varner does with that recognition of robustness renders his view less protective of animals than many animal advocates would like. Though he includes a principle of least necessary harm for evaluating different interests a person could satisfy, the combination of Varner's hierarchy of life-forms, his hierarchy of interests, and the conservative bias would make it very difficult to justify telling the fifth-generation hunter that he needs to give up his interest in hunting.

Regan, Singer, Taylor, and Varner all make a strong case for opposition to hunting. Unfortunately, none of these philosophers working within traditional animal ethical theory adequately addresses the conflict of interest faced by hunters who start to turn toward defending animals' moral standing and away from their exploitative practices. Regan, Singer, and Taylor robustly defend animals' interests while offering no guidance whatsoever for someone faced with such a moral quandary. Varner defends animals' interests but risks giving hunters a pass to continue their killing considering the profound challenges they face in shifting deeply entrenched traditions. None of these positions is sufficiently nuanced to defend animals while offering guidance for how to do so knowing we will disappoint people we love.

3 Ecofeminists on Recreational Hunting

While there may be some ecofeminists working in environmental ethics who defend hunting in some circumstances, most ecofeminist *animal* theorists strongly oppose recreational hunting. There are numerous reasons to reject hunting on ecofeminist grounds. First, ecofeminism opposes recreational hunting out of recognition for the moral status of animals as sentient beings with their own lives and experiences. Gratuitously slaughtering creatures with lives and relationships of their own in service of sport is paradigmatic of the sort of devaluing of animal lives ecofeminists abhor. Additionally, ecofeminists object to hunting because the practice is rooted in patriarchal systems of violence, hierarchy, and domination that ecofeminists oppose. Arguably, one of ecofeminist theory's most significant contributions to discussions about the morality of hunting has been to push past establishing that hunting violates animals' moral considerability to highlight the ways hunting perpetuates deeply problematic conceptual frameworks that support domination and exploitation. Hunting is problematic because of the animals, to be sure, but also because of its perpetuation of anthroparchal systems of oppression.

Marti Kheel and Brian Luke wrote extensively about hunting from the ecofeminist perspective. Both noted the deep connections between hunting and the dynamics of power and control that oppress both women and animals (Kheel 1995, 1996, 2008; Luke 1997, 1998). As Luke put it, "The erotic nature of hunting animals allows sport hunting to participate in a relation of reciprocal communication and support with the predatory heterosexuality prominent in Western patriarchal society" (Luke 1998, 628). He noted the use of imagery in men's magazines that sexualizes women and positions them as prey as well as the tendency to position hunted/fished animals in a sexualized, feminized way (644). Talking about a particularly poignant example of one such instance in a magazine, Luke says, "*Sports Illustrated* blends the iconographies of pornography, hunting, and racial conquest, using each to reinforce the others and in so doing promoting a unified white male identity of sexualized dominance over all disempowered others" (649–50).

While many hunters cite a desire for a deeper connection with nature as the motivation for their hunting, ecofeminists have long pointed to the perversity of expressing a desire for connection through violence and killing. Moreover, hunting in the United States has long been viewed as a desirable and important mechanism for developing male character (Kheel 1995, 1996; Leopold 1966; Loftin 1984; Luke 1997; Marks 1991). Note that hunting has not been deemed necessary for the development of desirable female character traits. As Kheel put it, "Hunting was a patrilineal, cross-generational inheritance, to be passed on from fathers to sons" (2008, 70). In her discussion of the quintessential American hunter, Theodore Roosevelt, and environmental ethicist/naturalist, Aldo Leopold, Kheel noted that both men conceived of hunting "as a cross-generational legacy to be 'conserved' for future generations of boys" (2008, 11). In reading Stuart Marks's arduously detailed ethnography of hunting in a rural South Carolina community, the sense that a boy learns to be a man through hunting pervades the comments made by members of the community he studied. From father to son to grandson, lessons of appropriate male character and conduct are passed along through the practice of hunting. The violence, death, and domination at the foundation of a practice that involves killing other living beings for sport remain largely unquestioned. This is partly why ecofeminists see hunting as a paradigmatic of anthroparchal systems of domination.

There are numerous important links between hunting and misogyny.[10] Though Marks does not specifically call out the misogyny on display in his interviews with hunters, it is a noticeable theme in his book. For example, in discussing how judges evaluate dogs during bench shows, one hunter says, "The feet, legs, back, just like you'd be looking at a woman. You look for a dog with shape" (Marks 1991, 106).[11] In Marks's field notes about a deer hunting trip he went on for his research, he notes that the hunters spent some time sharing vulgar and sexualized stories about a young girl (118). Luke echoes this point about the connection between hunting and misogynistic activities and narratives:

> The casual hunter not heavily invested in trophy collecting may see the hunting trip primarily as a vacation, a chance to get away from the restrictions of work and family life for a while to unwind with the guys and blow off steam in masculine fashion—nominally by shooting at animals but perhaps also by drinking, gambling, passing around pornography, frequenting the local strip clubs that cater to hunters, and so forth. (1998, 650–2)

There are numerous instances in Marks's book where hunters discuss theirs and others' wives, highlighting what a drag it is when the ladies tag along on their outings. They discuss how gender equity is a bad thing, why they refuse to hunt

---

[10] There are also well-documented links between intimate partner violence (IPV) and gun violence. "A victim or survivor of IPV is five times more likely to die when an abusive partner has access to a gun" (Tobin-Tyler 2023, 65). It stands to reason that, since hunters typically own guns, *if they are also abusive* their partners are at considerably higher risk of death than they would be had there been no firearms in the home. IPV that involves guns disproportionately impacts women, in particular women who are members of marginalized communities (ibid.). Carol Adams writes about hunting, guns, and domestic partner violence. On the basis of the connections between firearm ownership and domestic partner violence, she argues that environmental philosophy advocating for hunting needs to be reconsidered (Adams 1994).

[11] Interestingly, the misogyny also involves disvaluing female animals. Marks notes that when breed quality improves for hunting dogs, the male gets the credit rather than the female. Since male dogs can provide "almost unlimited stud service," whereas females can only produce a few litters a year, the dogs (males) get more credit and value (Marks 1991, 119).

with men who bring their wives along, and marriage causing disruption to men's hunting commitments. As Marks puts it, "Membership and participation in hunting clubs provide some men a haven from their wives, children, and job-related responsibilities" (79). He goes on to note: "Half of my sample agreed with the statement that women would find hunting difficult to understand. Men blamed women themselves for their lack of participation in the field" (ibid.).[12] This last observation is particularly troubling since it is the men themselves who opt not to socialize or mentor their daughters and wives into their hunting world.

Even the language hunters use to discuss their prey is steeped in misogynistic imagery and language. Discussing why it is easier to kill bucks when they are in rut (i.e., during breeding season), one hunter remarks on the cross-species stupidity that he sees as afflicting males of many species. Here is a sampling of his insights:

> "When a deer goes into rut, he's foolish. He's just like a man or a male dog chasing after a female in heat" (Marks 1991, 156).
>
> "And people are the same way. People do funny things, you know. If you're out there with a good-looking woman and some dude comes up and tries to take her away from you, you're gonna fight. You're gonna protect her. And you act a little bit more foolish than if you were just out with Jo Snow down the street and you didn't care if you lost her or not" (ibid.).

Noting that bucks sometimes use does as the deer equivalent of a human shield during hunting season, this hunter normalizes that behavior in decidedly sexist terms: "He's using her. I've used my wife several times. Every man does that" (ibid.).

The violent taking of innocent animal life and the connections between hunting, misogyny, and violence against women are all significant reasons many ecofeminists object to hunting. Those who defend hunting, including environmental philosophers, rarely engage with the latter considerations, preferring instead to focus on questions of moral considerability and wildlife management. This is deeply problematic. We cannot responsibly theorize about hunting without taking these deeply problematic anthroparchal elements into consideration. Ecofeminists have been vital to bringing these historically ignored moral considerations related to hunting to the fore.

I agree with what ecofeminists have said about hunting and its expression of violence, domination, and hierarchy. My project is meant not as a rebuke to what has been written previously but rather as an opportunity to move the ecofeminist project forward. Ecofeminism is, after all, "theory in process" (Adams 1991, 138).

---

[12]Some men in Marks's sample do express an interest in taking their wives hunting but often follow that up with lamentations about their wives looking into an animal's eyes and then asking their husbands how they can shoot them. The idea that women are too emotional and caring for hunting permeates the hunters' discussion of women.

Later, I make the case that ecofeminists have left out an important part of the contextual picture of *recreational* hunting and that these lacunae must be filled in.[13]

In looking at ecofeminist writings on hunting, I notice that the contextual picture being drawn ignores the relational elements of hunting. In particular, ecofeminist accounts have failed to engage with the fact that recreational hunting is often tied to deeply important, cross-generational, relationships and important familial and community traditions and values. This is happening even though ecofeminism is a deeply contextualized ethic with roots in feminist care ethics, a theoretical framework that ascribes moral value to relationships of love and care. A whole part of the picture is being left out. Why?

I suspect there are numerous reasons ecofeminists have neglected the human-to-human relational context of hunting. First, ecofeminism's contribution to the hunting discussion has been unique and important—no one else was drawing out the anthroparchal elements of hunting or focusing on the problematic expression of domination manifested in hunting. Bringing these crucial elements to the fore was a vital and substantial contribution to the literature. Second, I suspect that, like me, some ecofeminists did not grow up within a hunting culture where, even if one's own family did not hunt, the flow of the calendar matched the hunting seasons.[14] One might not easily see the important relational values attached to some hunting without access to those who hunt. Third, many of the most prominent examples of hunters, from Ted Nugent to the Trump brothers, are egregiously and gratuitously violent and misogynistic in their public discussions of hunting. Listening to Ted Nugent talking about hunting makes it nearly impossible for anyone who cares about animals to attend to the possible relational elements of hunting. Fourth, hunting is so deeply offensive to those of us who take animals seriously that it is challenging to want to delve into what is really going on with hunters. We just desperately need and want them to stop hunting. Finally, the kind of nuanced conversation I want to have about hunting is difficult. Nuance can generate misunderstandings and misreadings. A constant worry for me is that,

[13]Adams goes on to note that she offers her critiques "sympathetically" (1991, 138), as I do here. Past ecofeminist discussions of hunting often theorized about the "relational hunt," one in which the relationship between hunter and hunted is understood as reciprocal. Working within the contextualized nature of ecofeminism, these theorists were wondering whether there might be important moral differences between such a relational hunt and one more clearly manifesting male dominance. As Adams argued, however, this was a contextual account that was leaving out important context. For example, even in situations where hunting is seen as reciprocal, the animals killed are still ontologized as edible (137–8). Something was going awry with the ecofeminist contextualization of the relational hunt. Adams pushed the ecofeminist project forward by noting morally relevant details that had been left out of the contextualized account of relational hunting.

[14]Both Pluhar and Littlefield's discussions of hunting mention school being closed on the first day of deer hunting season (Littlefield 2010; Pluhar 1991). Interestingly, Marti Kheel and a group of fellow animal rights activists attended hunter safety classes, so they could apply for the lottery to kill mountain lions and then, if they won, take the place of someone who would actually hunt and kill mountain lions (Kheel 1995, 91n13).

taken out of context, some of what I write here could be misconstrued to offer a defense of practices that exploit and harm animals.

There are perhaps other reasons ecofeminists have not engaged with the relational elements of hunting. Whatever the reason, this is a lapse that requires attention. If we focus only on hunting as a manifestation of violence, domination, and hierarchy, we fail to provide the full moral picture. It is problematic theoretically to deliberate with a partial understanding of hunting. It is also pragmatically flawed. We will never change the hearts and minds of hunters, never provide proper counsel to those who seek to quit hunting, if we persist in describing hunters as if they have no heart. As John Littlefield has argued, ecofeminism's conception of masculinity relative to hunters is incorrectly monolithic. The masculinity expressed by hunters is far more complex than ecofeminism has allowed—in particular with respect to relationships of love and care (Littlefield 2010). In the following section I offer a contextualized account of hunting, demonstrating that it can be tied to important relationships, traditions, and community interests.

4 Contextualizing Hunting

In his introduction to the 2016 US FWS Hunting and Fishing Survey, Principal Deputy Director George J. Sheehan wrote:

> Over my nearly 40 years of hunting and fishing, I have been able to pursue a wide variety of fish and game in states across the nation. I've developed deep and enduring friendships through hunting and fishing and marked the progress of my kids to adulthood with every passing season we spent together in the field and on the water. … I will carry these memories with me forever, and I'm far from alone. Millions of Americans have grown up hunting, fishing, and spending time outdoors with their parents and grandparents, in turn passing those skills on to their children and grandchildren. (Sheehan 2016, vi)

These reflections on the role hunting plays in Sheehan's connections to others as well as the cross-generational relationships forged through hunting reflect the deep relational ties binding hunters together—bonds of love, friendship, and community. Hunting can also be bound to important traditions and community interests. While it is true that hunting involves the slaughter of innocent animals for human recreation, it is equally true that for many hunters the activity involves opportunities to bond with loved ones, establish connections in the community, enjoy camaraderie and friendship, hone technical skills, and pass along values and skills from one generation to the next. Animal advocates have generally been interested in only one element of relationship in hunting, namely the one between the hunter and the animal he seeks to kill. However, relationality manifests in hunting through multiple dimensions—relationships with other humans, with the land, with other animals, including the hunted of course, but also horses and dogs who assist in the hunters' endeavors.[15] Fully contextualizing hunting requires attending to these aspects and others I will explore in this section.

In Marks's ethnography of southern hunters in a rural South Carolina community, themes of relationality and connection through hunting consistently percolate to the fore. As Marks puts it,

> For many Southern men living in or close to rural landscapes, hunting is a passion. It is something that comes with the air and the land and with the people who live there. Hunting is woven into the very fabric of personal and social history. Through participation, these men celebrate their relations with others, differentiate between themselves and animals, and observe their connections with the land. (1991, 5)

Throughout Marks's book, his interviews with hunters reveal the way hunting is deeply connected to important relationships. Marks's study takes us from antebellum hunting practices through to the twentieth century; it encompasses various forms of hunting from deer to foxes to quail to raccoon. The constant throughout both time and form of hunting are the hunters' connections to loved ones. Hunters speak of learning at their fathers' knees, of practicing hunting with their brothers and friends, and of hunting with their most trusted and valued friends as adults. One hunter discusses the reliability of hunting-based friendships, noting that he can always count on his hunting friends to help him when needed (Marks 1991, 221). Hunting is about grandfathers, fathers, and sons (as well as grandmothers, mothers, and daughters) and connections to other relationships of trust and care.

This is why Littlefield challenges ecofeminism's monolithic conception of hunters' masculinity. From the ecofeminist description, one gets a view of hunters focused on those elements of masculinity most commonly associated with problematic patriarchal conceptual frameworks, in particular violence, domination, and hierarchical thinking. In Littlefield's research on hunters, which included field research spending time with those who hunt, he points to a very different side of the masculinity evinced by hunters. As he and Julie Ozanne wrote, "We find that some hunters privilege distinctly non-traditional masculine values of love of nature and family, which suggests that masculinity is more ambiguous, dynamic, and malleable than is seen from this traditional perspective" (Littlefield and Ozanne 2011, 337). The hunters from Littlefield's study often invoke

[15]How willingly these animals "assist" in hunting is open for questioning.

camaraderie and relationships with others in discussing hunting. Talking about a kind of hunter Littlefield calls "efficient traditionalists," he notes:

> With their valuing of family and tradition, efficient traditionalist hunters construct narratives that privilege hunting skills and close relationships with family and friends around the activity of hunting, typically resulting in close bonds between males who share significant history together and subscribe to similar, often rural values. (2010, 105)[16]

Littlefield concedes that the efficient traditionalist hunter is easily criticized from the ecofeminist perspective. He might emphasize bonding with men in particular, privilege the group over individual animals, dominate nature, and so forth, but much of his interest in hunting has to do with bonding with others (ibid.). In discussing Andrew, one of his study participants, Littlefield describes his "caring ethos," noting that Andrew will only kill animals who will be consumed and that, "rather than being characterized by being bloodthirsty and violent," Andrew's hunting is best understood as "caring for family, for friends, and for those less fortunate" (107). I part ways with Littlefield when he describes Andrew's hunting ethics as a "caring ethos" as it is far-fetched to describe slaughtering innocent wild animals as an act of care, but in reading both Littlefield's and Marks's studies of hunters I can easily see that their hunting often connects to relationships of care with both loved ones and the broader community.

Littlefield's taxonomy of hunters includes those he terms the "compassionate transcendentals" for whom hunting is sewn into the fabric of their lives. Unlike most other kinds of hunters, for compassionate transcendentals hunting "is less an activity and more a lifestyle" (2006, 136). He describes them as manifesting a masculinity "deeply embedded in the emotional connections they have both with equipment and with family and friends" (2010, 112). These social connections are so deeply important to this group of hunters that their hunting narratives "are less characterized by competition than by cooperation and solidarity and convey an expression of masculinity that is comfortable showing aspects of the stereotypical feminine" (ibid.). Social connections forged through hunting remain central to these hunters' conceptions of what is important about engaging in the hunting activity. In summarizing the diverse expression of masculinities he found among hunters, Littlefield focuses again and again on connection—social connection, connection with nature, and connection to family values (113).

---

[16]Littlefield distinguishes the efficient traditionalist hunter from the "rational gearhead hunter" (most interested in mastery of technology and skill development), the "eco-buddy" hunter (who values immersion in nature more than domination over nature), and the "compassionate transcendental" hunter (who values a deep connection with both the natural and social worlds) (2010).

In their study of how hunters are socialized into hunting practices, Littlefield and Ozanne note four stages: pre-hunter, neophyte, apprentice, and competent hunter. They point out, "At each level, these stages are marked by different skills, rites, values, and social support" (2011, 340). I have certainly been guilty of imagining only adult, fully grown hunters as if they pop into existence from nowhere. Littlefield and Ozanne's work, along with Marks', demonstrates how untrue this is.[17] Youth from hunting families start young. In their pre-hunter years, they help in family activities related to hunting (e.g., preparing for the hunt, tagging along with their fathers on hunting outings, and helping to carry unloaded firearms) (340–2). After demonstrating the development of important hunting skills and values, pre-hunters move to the neophyte stage. The rites of passage associated with this level of hunting socialization include being trusted with a loaded weapon and making their first kill. Though the children often describe mixed feelings over their first kill, they are highly praised by their fathers and other male adults as well as given lessons in hunting etiquette (343). The apprentice hunter demonstrates good safety skills, increased independence, and more hunting with their peers rather than their mentors (344). The classmates or friends with whom they hunt are people "with whom relationships are characterized by high levels of trust and identity exploration" (344). This camaraderie can not only include companionship but also peer pressure and egging one another on. In the final stage of hunting socialization, competent hunters demonstrate mastery of skills and participate in a wide array of hunting experiences. They cleave to a well-defined set of core hunting values. Often at this stage hunters are less concerned with making a kill and place more value on patience (346). Throughout this socialization process, relationships are central for skill mentorship and teaching hunting values.

In discussing the patrilineal nature of sport hunting, Kheel emphasizes how hunting has often been viewed as a way of developing male character (2008, 70). From Theodore Roosevelt to Aldo Leopold to the hunters in Marks's study, hunting is seen as playing a vital role in boys' moral development. Leopold wrote of the cultural values in hunting (1989, 177). He also highly valued the "ethical restraint" called for in sportsmanship. This ethical restraint is demonstrated when hunters refrain from killing or opt not to use technologically advanced weaponry in order to "augment the role of skill and shrink the role of gadgets in the pursuit of wild things" (178). Failing to follow the ethical code of hunting degrades one's ethical status for Leopold. Similarly, Robert Loftin's defense of hunting makes references to "the edifying effects of hunting on the character of the hunter" (1984, 246). Indeed, hunters' ethical codes are so robust and well-defined that Brian Luke was able to use that code to argue that the very reasons hunters have for following the code show they ought not to be hunting at all (Luke 1997).

---

[17]Marks also has a detailed account of how hunters learn to hunt (1991, 72).

I mention this for two reasons. First, because it is worth noting that hunters often have an ethical code regarding what is and is not respectful treatment of the natural world. Hunting opponents object to the scope and employment of this code, but it nevertheless exists and plays a central role in forming hunters' identities. Second, because the cross-generational way this code is passed from experienced hunter to young child points to how deeply hunting is related not only to relationships of love and care but also to how hunters perceive one another. In a hunting family, someone might find that hunting is the primary way they can demonstrate they have learned the lessons of their fathers and grandfathers.

Hunting is an activity through which families pass along deeply held values regarding nature, sportsmanship, and skill. One result of this is that, in hunting communities, whether and how one hunts becomes a litmus test for what sort of person someone is (Marks 1991, 204). The hunters Marks studied often discuss assessing others' characters through the lens of hunting. Are you the kind of hunter (called a "slob") who would break the laws limiting the amount of game you can "take" and trespassing on others' land to increase your haul, or are you a real "sportsman" who demonstrates the values of adherence to the hunting code and foregoing more kills in service of those values (265)? Whether you fall into the category of slob or sportsman will heavily influence how others in the community see you both within hunting activities and beyond them. As Marks notes, hunting can be the activity through which new community members are assessed and sorted:

> Hunting is part of a man's commitment to locale and supports his other obligations to family, church, work, and friends. Like marriage, hunting is a way of integrating a newcomer into a rural community. It allows residents the opportunity to assess the stranger's behavior and to assign him to a known category of persons. In some circles, getting into the right group is important for sustaining one's reputation and source of livelihood. Therefore, if the stranger is not a hunter, it is unlikely that he will acquire the standing necessary to accomplish other things within the community. (6)[18]

It appears hunting matters not only for character assessment but also, by extension, for social standing and access to community goods. In hunting communities, then, much hinges on whether and how one hunts. Given this, I can only imagine how lonely and terrifying it might be for a fifth-generation hunter still living in such a community to begin to contemplate stepping away from hunting. One risks losing

[18]Marks notes that deer hunting, in particular, is an expensive activity but that hunting can be "an important investment because it provides a man with the opportunity to establish social bonds within the larger community of his own choosing" (165).

not only the respect of one's loved ones but of the entire social system within which one lives. This is a vital piece of the contextualized hunting picture.

In addition to relationships, values, and character, hunting is also about deeply held traditions. As Dena Jolma noted in her discussion of hunters who quit, "Hunting survives in America because for some it remains a family tradition, passed down from one generation to the next. Adults rarely take up hunting on their own—a mere 5% of hunters participate for the first time after their early 20's" (1992, 40). Family schedules and comings and goings are shaped around the hunting seasons; rituals follow a predictable yearly course. The idea of hunting as a tradition transcends the familial realm into the community and even, sometimes, the nation. In her discussion of national identity and English foxhunting, Sarah Egan notes that when Parliament was considering banning foxhunting, many English people objected on the grounds that it is a central English tradition. The depth of this tradition, they argued, is visible in the landscape (e.g., the iconic hedgerows dotting the English countryside) and in the art in pubs and country inns (Egan 2014). One parliamentarian had this to say about banning foxhunting:

> I support hunting and oppose this Bill as I believe that hunting is part of our national tradition expressed in literature, in poetry, in painting and in music through popular songs … we should not forget that tradition is to a nation what a soul is to an individual. We should tamper with it only if there is an overwhelming case for doing so. (Egan 2014, 76)

Interestingly, just as the pro-hunting coalition made the case that foxhunting is a tradition central to England's national identity, others claimed that love of animals is a key component of England's national identity and tradition (77).[19] This raises the very important question of what traditions get selected and held up as "central to identity." Why would foxhunting be more central to Englishness than, say, love of animals? A similar question arises in discussions of indigenous cultural whaling. Why focus on the long-standing practice of whale slaughter when, for example, there are numerous other culturally important practices that are far less violent (Gaard 2001; Hawkins 2001)? It is often traditions involving violence and domination that are held up as central rather than those involving artistry or care, a charge Marti Kheel leveled against Deep Ecologists who focused on indigenous hunting traditions rather than, say, artistry (1995, 101). Hunting encompasses

[19]Parallel conversations about national identity and bullfighting are taking place in Spain where the Spanish parliament continues to defend the activity as a vital part of Spanish culture despite increasing public anti-bullfighting outcry (Horta 2018; María et al. 2017). In the sixteenth century, Pope Pius issued a papal bull banning bullfighting (Alvaro 2020, 488). For an interesting discussion of the hypocrisy involved in some corners of the anti-bullfighting movement, see Bailey (2007b).

interests rooted in familial, community, and national traditions *in addition to* ties to traditions that are open to moral questioning.

Any fully contextualized account of hunting would also be incomplete without discussing hunters' relationships with other animals and the land. Clearly, hunters are in a relationship with the animals who constitute their prey. From the ecofeminist standpoint, this relationship is hierarchical and built on a foundation of domination. Not surprisingly, hunters view their relationship with their prey differently. Sometimes hunters are described as being in caring relationships with the animals they track and kill (Littlefield 2010, 107). The general idea here seems to be that, through culling, hunters help improve life for the population of animals they hunt.[20] Certainly, there are ways to express care for wild animals that do not involve killing them. I do not want to dwell on this point but just mention that how one conceives of the hunter/hunted relationship depends largely on how one views animals to begin with.

In addition to being in relationships with the animals they hunt, hunters form strong relationship with the animals they use in hunting. In North America, these animals are most likely dogs and sometimes horses. Here is Aldo Leopold writing lovingly about his hunting dog:

> My dog, by the way, thinks I have much to learn about partridges and, being a professional naturalist, I agree. He persists in tutoring me with the calm patience of a professor of logic, in the art of drawing deductions from an educated nose. I delight in seeing him deduce a conclusion, in the form of a point, from data that are obvious to him, but speculative to my unaided eye. Perhaps he hopes his dull pupil will one day learn to smell. (1966, 63–4).

Leopold's dog figures prominently in *A Sand County Almanac*. His description of the dog's role in grouse hunting shows deep respect for canine abilities (55). Lamenting the toll mechanization and advanced technology has taken on hunting, Leopold notes with glee that "the gadgeteer has reached the end of his tether in dogdom" (182). For some hunters in Marks's study, understanding animal pain was rendered accessible to them through the suffering of their own dogs (78), demonstrating that through caring for their dogs they came to understand other animals' pain more completely. Several hunters in his study reference their love of hearing the dogs in the hunt with one hunter going so far as to say he goes

---

[20] A quail hunter in Marks's study said, "I shoot the same covey of quail that I've shot for thirty years, and there's a companionship even with the quail itself, and we're very careful not to shoot down a covey of quail too much" (184). On the one hand, there does appear to be some form of care here on the part of the hunter. Still, it is unclear if they do not shoot down the covey out of care for the birds or because they want to ensure a sufficient number of birds to hunt in next year's season.

hunting to hear the dogs and watch them run, indifferent to whether he makes a kill (205–6).

For others, however, dogs are expendable hunting tools. Used extensively in buck hunting, dogs are often lost, killed, or traded (137). Some kill dogs who snap (245) while others reject dogs who do not perform in the field (92). For those engaged in foxhunting, for example, fox hounds who do not perform correctly—either due to incompetence or overcompetence—are killed. Marks adds, "Otherwise, owners risk having aspersions cast on their own reputations" (99). Apparently, these dogs have merely instrumental value to their humans, for otherwise surely a dog who shows flaws in the field could remain in the family as a beloved companion. The standards for fox hounds in field trials are high and the consequence of not meeting them is, as we've just seen, quite serious. Here is one of Marks's study participants relaying the reasons a dog might be eliminated from field trials:

> A hound is eliminated for anything that's a fault to an ideal champion. Loading, that's probably the most prevalent. Loafing, not going hunting, quitting, laying around, standing around the road, trotting up and down the road after trucks, showing no inclination to hunt a fox. (110)[21]

In other words, dogs are eliminated for being dogs and exercising their agency. This speaks to the point that hunting certainly involves power and domination, only in this case it is power and domination over the hounds rather than hunters' prey. In their discussion of foxhunting, Palmer and O'Gorman push on this point, arguing that in foxhunting the real power dynamic is between humans and horses and humans and dogs much more than between humans and foxes. The foxes remain beyond human control most of their lives whereas the horses and dogs are totally in human control down to their genetics. The fox, they note, has more opportunities for resistance (2003, 290). Though Palmer and O'Gorman were writing mostly about foxhunting in England, their point is relevant to both foxhunting and other types of hunting in the North American context where it is also the case that wild animals have more opportunities to exercise agency and express resistance than the domesticated animals used in hunting. The relationship between hunters and dogs (as well as horses) is complicated to be sure. At times, those relationships appear rooted in love and care. At others, the precarious position the animals occupy highlights the domination and exploitation undergirding the relationship. Whether the relationships are rooted in love or exploitation, it is unwise to ignore the interspecies relational complexity of hunters' interest in hunting.

---

[21]I have tried to find a definition of "loading" in this context but cannot find anything definitive. People seem to refer mostly to either the loading of a dog into their crate/vehicle or loading as the time between noticing a stimulus and responding.

In addition to relationships with loved ones and other animals, hunters often highlight feeling deeply connected to the land.[22] Hunters' relationship with the land is often left out of discussions about hunting but warrants attention. There is certainly an element of domination in some hunters' attitude toward the land. In those cases, they veer away from what Karen Warren called a relationship of "loving attention" and instead lean toward one marked by conquering (1990). Reading hunters' comments in Marks's and Littlefield's work as well as on various online message boards, however, I sometimes felt envious of the knowledgeable and attentive relationship these men had with the land. It struck me that hunters spend far more of their time outdoors reading the landscape than I do; that they know the ways of local flora and fauna with a level of detail that my own outdoor pursuits will likely never achieve. This feeling, bordering on envy, is strongest when I read Leopold. He lived with the land the way one lives with a beloved—understanding its moods and movements, tracking its progress, rejoicing in its successes, and mourning its failures.[23] Of course, Leopold was a trained naturalist, so it is perhaps overdetermined that he would have a deep and abiding love and knowledge for the land. It is striking, though, how many hunters without Leopold's extensive training exhibit a similar attitude.[24]

Many of the hunters in Marks's study exhibit strong attachments to the land. Hunters live in relationship with the land they hunt. By necessity they must understand its contours. They spend considerable amounts of time walking, during which they observe changes in flora and fauna. When asked whether land plays any role in his tradition of hunting, one of Marks's respondents replied: "I think so. I think the love of the land carries over into hunting. You just like to be out walking through the woods and fields and that feeling that a person has when he likes the land, and he likes outings and closeness to the land" (182). This description of a "closeness" with the land shows up in many hunters' descriptions of their endeavors. Relationality and hunting cross the sentience, as well as the species, divide.

Land plays an important role in hunters' lives for many reasons. In addition to a genuine love of the outdoors, land ownership and access is deeply connected to social standing and class (Marks 1991). Issues of class are perhaps more obvious in the English foxhunting setting, where depictions of the hunt often include images

---

[22]In talking about hunters' relationships and identity, Marks says, "The act of hunting is a representation of a 'self' in relationship with some group, a community of others, perhaps predecessors, and to the means, the land, and the techniques of making this behavior possible" (269).

[23]Leopold's attitude toward the land is on display not only in "The Land Ethic," of course, but also in much of *A Sand County Almanac*. I join Marti Kheel in having concerns about some of Leopold's framework, but I remain always touched and impressed by the eloquence and detail with which he describes landscapes and ecological systems.

[24]Leopold expresses disdain for outdoor recreationalists, including hunters, who swarm and damage the outdoors in their pursuit of woodsy pleasures (Leopold 1966, 166).

of toffs gathered on large estates, riding to hounds across the local aristocrats' fields.[25] However, class plays a significant role in relationships with the land in the North American setting as well. Whether one has access to land determines where and who a hunter can hunt. Among deer hunters, there is tension between "club hunters" who belong to clubs on private land and those who hunt state land. Club hunters sometimes resent those who hunt on state-managed lands due to the large numbers in their groups, their disregard for local boundaries, and the constantly changing makeup of their hunting groups (Marks 1991, 149). Club hunters have reliable access to land and, therefore, to animals to kill. This sets them apart from those who must rely on overcrowded state lands for their hunting. In rural communities, rabbit and squirrel hunting require either owning land or having relationships with landowners (218). Poachers are reviled among many hunters because of their failure to respect land boundaries. Access to land for hunting has long been a gatekeeping mechanism through which members of the landed classes can maintain rights and privileges inaccessible to those who do not own land.

Relatedly, which game a hunter pursues "is a marker, a visible bit of social differentiation" (4). Who one predates upon reveals much about one's economic and social status. Nearly two-thirds of Marks's respondents agreed with the statement "that the rank of the game pursued reflected the social standing of those in pursuit" (81). Such markers may be subtle to the outside observer but are nevertheless deeply entrenched. In the South, for example, raccoon hunting is considered the province of those with lower economic status (231–62). This is partly because, unlike foxhunting, which is a daytime pursuit, raccoon hunting happens at night when "displays of emotion, color, and power" have "minimal effect" due to lack of visibility (ibid.). Hence, raccoon hunting became popular with those more focused on sustenance than spectacle. These class differentiations are also exhibited in deer, quail, squirrel, and rabbit hunting. Prey is a signifier of class and social standing—an indication of one's access to land and one's reasons for hunting. The raccoon hunter and the society fox hunter are from two very different economic and social worlds. They know this and so do the other hunters around them.[26] Hunting, therefore, contributes to a hunter's sense of social identity, of knowing who their people are and how they are different from others.

Similarly, whether, where, and who one hunts is influenced by race. The 2016 FWS survey shows that 97 percent of hunters in the United States are white (35). Certainly, in the United States, whether one hunts can be an identifier of race. It is not surprising that hunting is pursued predominantly by white men in the

---

[25]Interestingly, in Marks's study of foxhunting in the southern United States it is clear that initially foxhunting was associated with lower economic status and is now being claimed and differentiated by those with more economic privilege (Chapter 5). In the UK context, Richard Ryder questions the prevailing idea that foxhunting has a long aristocratic history (2005).

[26]This made it very difficult for former enslaved people in the postbellum South to feed themselves and their families (Marks 1991, 271).

United States. In the antebellum American South, enslaved people were used as beaters and drivers by wealthy landowners (19). After Reconstruction, the number of Black hunters dropped in part because access to the tools of hunting became more complicated for them. White former slaveowners grew uncomfortable with the idea of their former slaves taking up arms against them. Talking about the state of race and hunting in the 1980s, Marks notes:

> In light of the region's past history of racial repression, it is not surprising that comparatively few [B]lacks hunt. Moreover, [B]lacks are not likely to congregate in large armed groups and engage in quasi-military activities, as many whites do. Such overt militant displays by [B]lacks are likely to provoke countermeasures by whites seeking to sustain [B]lack subservience and dependency. Reconstruction and its aftermath brought new levels of racism and violence against [B]lacks, and this has affected hunting as well as other walks of life. Hunting and hunting rights were particularly important in establishing new social lines between [B]lacks and whites. (67–8)

Adding what Marks notes here to the anti-Black racism and violence still occurring in the United States, it is not hard to imagine one possible explanation for why so few Black people hunt and how hunting can become part of some hunters' manifestation of white privilege and sense of racial identity.[27] Of course, a contextualized ecofeminist account will not condone this, but leaving it out of the understanding of the complexity of the hunting interest is not advisable. If we want to ask hunters to reconsider their hunting practices and embrace a different outlet for their hunting-based interests, we need to fully understand the deep extent to which hunting attaches to hunters' sense of identity and group membership.

Marks's respondents recognized race and class as "important factors in determining who hunted what" (82). In the hunting community he studied, it was well-established that white people hunted deer and birds whereas Black hunters more commonly hunted raccoon and rabbit. This marks an important intersection between race and class—deer hunting requires more expensive equipment than raccoon and rabbit hunting, which makes it less accessible to those living with the impacts of systemic economic oppression. Moreover, how easily one can integrate into a hunting group, and therefore which animals a hunter can pursue, is also influenced by race. One Black respondent who did try deer hunting noted not wanting to go inside the white hunter's house for a pre-hunt breakfast because he

---

[27]It is certainly possible, of course, that some hunters in the United States use hunting as an excuse for building an arsenal of weapons that they can then use to defend their rights to have guns. Perhaps this group of hunters is more concerned with maintaining a "well-regulated militia," as discussed in the Second Amendment to the US Constitution, than they are about hunting itself. I thank Rachel Fredericks for raising this point.

thought having a Black man in the house would discomfit the hunter's wife (Marks 1991, 220). For some of Marks's Black respondents, one gets the impression that raccoon and rabbit hunting is a way of manifesting inclusivity and control as well as of passing down important survival skills from one generation to another. Whether white or Black, race and class will influence how the hunting interest links to self-conception and identity for hunters.[28]

It should now be clear that a fully contextualized understanding of hunting reveals multiple ways hunting can be tied to highly valued interests and relationships. Hunting relationships are cross-generational, familial, and communal. In hunting communities, whether and how one hunts is an important metric for assessing one's character. Not hunting can result in being excluded from the goods of society. Hunting is tied to hunters' conception of masculinity and the performance of a male identity. It is connected to important interspecies relationships and deep connection to the land. Where and who one hunts is a signifier of class and, often, race. Hunters' sense of self and location in familial and social settings are tied to their hunting activities. Reading accounts of hunting written by and about hunters, it is virtually impossible not to be struck by how complicated, how heart-wrenching, how frightening it might be for a hunter to want to step back from hunting out of respect for animals' lives. Indeed, I often wondered how unsafe it might be in some settings given the extent to which hunting and patriarchal conceptions of masculinity are interwoven. Walking away from hunting, one risks being feminized in ways that could result in diminished safety in the family and larger community.

While the ecofeminist picture of hunting is accurate as far as it goes, it leaves out these crucial elements. It risks essentializing the hunting interest as merely an expression of domination and violence. No doubt domination and violence are part of hunting. I would not wish to suggest otherwise. Nor would I wish to give the impression that I think misogyny and racism do not also play a part in some hunters' hunting activities and narratives. Reading Marks's respondents commentaries about women and the transcript of their chats while hunting makes clear that these are all terribly problematic aspects of hunting. The fully contextualized picture of hunting reveals, however, that love, care, respect for elders, connection to others (be they other humans, animals, or the land), and self-understanding are also significant elements of hunting. Littlefield's suggestion that the masculinity expressed in hunting is not the monolithic pernicious patriarchal one suggested in the ecofeminist literature but rather a deeply nuanced one worthy of examination is important. In short, hunting is about so much more than killing animals. Those of us who are horrified by the violence and death manifested in

[28]Marks's study included participants of the local Lumbee Indian community. I have left out discussion of the Lumbee because their hunting is likely better understood as indigenous rather than recreational in many cases.

hunting must also address the love and care. We must acknowledge that asking someone to give up hunting constitutes a request to turn their back on their families, friends, community, their standing in their social world, and quite possibly their sense of self. To ignore these elements is to imperil the moral analysis of hunting and to risk failing to reach those who might otherwise be persuaded to put down their guns in favor of cameras and walking sticks.

Once again, we have arrived at the impasse where respect for animals and an interest tied to highly valued ends seem irreconcilable. The hunting interest is nonbasic, to be sure, but once contextualized we see it as a complex interest tied to highly valued ends related to relationships (human and interspecies), community, social standing, and identity. Is it too much to ask of people that they forego hunting? How should we proceed in thinking about hunting given what is revealed by contextualizing the interest? I take up these questions later in this chapter.

5 Quitting Hunting, Repair, and Avowal

One option when faced with this impasse would be to resolve the dilemma by supporting the permissibility of hunting in cases where the interest is not merely a manifestation of dominance over animals but a reflection of genuinely deep attachment to other humans, the land, or the community. If a hunter risks losing much that is important to him when he quits hunting, perhaps we ought to let it go in these cases. This is not the way forward, however. Genuine respect for animals entails setting aside those interests that involve harming them except when doing so is in their best interests. Hunting for sport, and even for connection, involves gratuitous death and harm for animal others. It is a practice that needs to end.

There is some overlap between what I said in the food chapter about the way forward and what I say later about hunting. There are, however, some significant differences between the two cases that are worth exploring. First, there could be more potential for damaged relationships when quitting hunting than with eschewing traditional foods. For hunting families and communities, hunting just *is* the activity, whereas in the food case the activity is a gathering with food consumption as a part of the whole. As I discussed in Chapter 4, food is a tremendous part of familial and cultural traditions, but though I refuse the chicken soup I remain at the table equipped to partake in other parts of the traditional meal. Not so for the hunter who, in refraining from going hunting, loses out on the entire activity.[29] There is a chance someone might not even notice if I do not have my grandmother's soup, but if a fifth-generation hunter fails to join the family for

[29]This might not be the case in all situations. A person could go out hunting with their family but just carry gear or shoot but purposefully miss the animal. Perhaps they will be labeled as a "bad shot," but

the first day of hunting season, his absence will certainly be noted and questioned. As one member of a fishing family put it, "It was a sad day in my father's life when he invited me to join him on a fishing trip and I declined" (Amato and Partridge 1989, 178). Additionally, that I remain at the holiday table increases opportunities for reparative gestures and discussions. For the hunter who can no longer participate in the hunt, the opportunities for such gestures and discussions may be fewer and farther between.[30]

Second, I have not seen much evidence that participation in food-related traditions plays the same role hunting does on the community level. With hunting serving as a litmus test for character and trustworthiness in some communities, there are added complexities to refraining from hunting out of respect for animals. This is not to deny that there could be analogous issues in some cultural groups regarding adopting veganism, but the issue of character and community standing does not seem to percolate to the fore in discussions of traditional foods in the way it does in studies of hunters. The person who walks away from hunting out of respect for animals risks losing community standing and a social position in a way I do not when I turn down chicken soup in the privacy of my grandmother's dining room.[31]

Finally, there is more community support around those who adopt veganism than there is around hunters who quit out of respect for animals. There are Jewish vegan groups, websites, and newsletters and similar resources for many other cultural and ethnic identities. By definition, hunters who quit cannot hunt. A Latinx person who embraces veganism is still Latinx with all the many facets of belief and identity that entails. That is also true for a Jewish person who adopts veganism and a Ghanaian and so on. A hunter who leaves off killing animals is no longer a hunter.

Despite these differences between rejecting traditional foods and quitting hunting, starting with contextualization is as crucial for the latter as the former case. A nuanced approach to attending to the complex set of values at stake for many hunters begins with contextualization at both the general and individual levels. By general level, I mean something like the analysis I offered earlier noting the multifaceted nature of the hunting interest and identifying highly valued ends tied to the activity. At the individual level, a person can examine his own particular hunting context noting the relationships, values, and norms that are tied to his hunting interest. Hence, this contextualization work is as important for

---

they will still be a "hunter" (Rachel Fredericks, personal communication, January 18, 2022). Whether these options are available or attractive will depend on the individual's context.

[30] My thanks to Jeremy Mazner for bringing this issue to my attention.

[31] This does raise the issue of some communities where eating is more public or where, perhaps, what one eats becomes a conversation among extended relatives or community members beyond the immediate circle. Still, though the defender of animals may be judged for hurting their mothers/grandmothers, they won't necessarily be stamped as fundamentally untrustworthy in the way an ex-hunter might.

activists and ethicists arguing against hunting as it is for the hunters themselves who are contemplating quitting but feeling a deep resistance to doing so due to the significant role hunting plays in their lives. I will return to activists and scholars at the end of this section. For now, let's think about what individual hunters contemplating quitting out of respect for animals, their family, and community members might need to think about and do.

Because the challenges presented by quitting hunting might be more complex than those involved in turning away from traditional foods, would-be former hunters may need to do more work to identify shared values and locate new ways to explore and express those values. Recognizing that his refusal to hunt will deeply impact loved ones, the hunter seeking to walk away should think carefully about what values he still shares with his hunting family and community and how he can instantiate those values without hunting. It will be important to emphasize to loved ones that, for example, long walks in the woods without a gun are a way of honoring the values he shares with the rest of the group.[32] This is a way for the person who turns away from hunting to practice relational moral attention—he can demonstrate and reassure those around him that he still holds and cherishes many of the same values at the foundation of his family and community.

As with the food case, the hunter who questions the morality of hunting out of respect for animals should focus less on the moral standing of animals and arguing to persuade others and more on acknowledging what could and will be lost by his decision to quit hunting. He can then emphasize that, *together*, the family or group will find and reclaim those values in other ways. This is not to say that discussion of animals' moral standing should never take place. Nor do I mean to suggest that advocating for others to quit hunting is wrong. Rather, the argument about animals' moral standing is both tactically and ethically ill-advised in the early stages of these difficult discussions. Tactically it is ill-advised because few people can listen to the moral arguments about animals when they are emotionally troubled by what they perceive as losing a loved one or having a loved one turn their back on important family traditions. In many cases, the discussion about animals will just have to wait until a time when loved ones are more equipped to hear it out and give it the attention it deserves. It is an ethical mistake to focus at first on differences about animals' moral standing because that isn't the central *relational* ethical issue. After all, what complicates turning away from hunting is in large part the closely held and cherished relationships hunters have. As I argued earlier, those relationships have moral valences. In these complex cases where turning away from an activity out of respect for animals risks rupturing important

---

[32]Interestingly, several hunters in Marks's study mention hunting without a gun (178). They do not explain why they still consider this hunting or why they would not call it "hiking" or "taking a walk in nature." But, if hunting without a gun is something the family can understand and if the would-be former hunter is comfortable with it, this is certainly an option that can be explored.

relationships of love and care, it is ethically primary to address the relational issues before trying to convince anyone that they, too, should see animals as individuals worthy of respect and bodily integrity.

When the time is right to have the difficult conversation about animals' moral standing and respect for living beings, something like Kim's process of mutual avowal is a promising way forward. There will be social justice struggles that come up within families that are related to religion, race, gender, and so forth. In as much as conflict around quitting hunting hits upon these issues, Kim's social justice-focused mutual avowal will be important. It will also be true that a modified mutual avowal process will be vital to relational moral attention. The most pressing issues may not be related to acknowledging social justice struggles but center instead on "open and active acknowledgment" of the values espoused by one's family and community and the ways turning from those values toward unfamiliar or seemingly hostile values impact our loved ones. The hunting family may have strong values about caring for the land and the creatures dwelling therein, seeing hunting as a manifestation of that care. Though it is a confusion to think hunting manifests care, acknowledging the values central to the hunting family is important. It both demonstrates a willingness to understand and creates opportunities to discover better ways to instantiate those values in the world than hunting. As Kim emphasizes, mutual avowal makes room for critique. The would-be former hunter can openly discuss his feelings about animals and why hunting is morally impermissible. He can challenge and question the defenses of hunting proffered by his family and friends. Doing so through the lens of critique and avowal rather than disavowal, "an act of dis-association and rejection," as Kim puts it (181), will better serve the interests of relationality and repair.

Family members have obligations here as well, of course. They ought to come to the discussion able to hear and accept their loved one's reasons for quitting hunting. Ideally, they would express genuine curiosity and interest in their reasons for quitting and demonstrate respect for their position. In other words, they should embrace their half of the process of mutual avowal. They should also be open to thinking creatively about new and exciting ways to express shared values and shift traditions. If the family has always taken a yearly trip to hunt, for example, they might consider adding a nonhunting family gathering to the annual calendar. They should consider carefully whether inviting the former hunter on hunting outings with the understanding he is not expected to make any kills is a reasonable invitation to make. Inviting someone who has espoused compassion and empathy for animals on a hunt where animals will be slaughtered in real time before their eyes has a different moral valence than inviting a vegan to a meal where animal products will be served. While the latter can be deeply uncomfortable for ethical vegans, the harm done to the animals is in the past—attending the dinner does not put the animal advocate in a position where they must witness (or try to prevent) immediate suffering.

In the hunting case, there will likely be an important role for family members to express acceptance and support, if not understanding, of the former hunter to the broader community. This would be a form of mutual avowal translated to the level of avowing *on behalf of* their loved one to the community at large. In a situation where someone risks losing their social standing by embracing animals and refraining from hunting as a result of that embrace, loving and caring family members will be crucial to ensuring the former hunter can maintain access to the goods of the community.

All of what I've laid out here are crucial parts of relational moral repair that are important for mitigating the impact of a loved one turning their back on an activity that serves as the expression of deeply held values. The former hunter will likely feel torn between obligations to animals and obligations to his family and community. This process of contextualization and relational moral attention is central to addressing the ethical tug-of-war happening between two deeply important sets of obligations.

There is also work to do for activists and advocates seeking to put an end to hunting. Disrupting hunts as a means of decreasing the number of animals killed is certainly an important avenue for protecting animals' lives. When it comes to trying to change hunters' hearts and minds, however, we need to come from a place of understanding. Having the fully contextualized understanding of how hunting ties to important relationships and values is crucial. Treating all hunters as though they are blood thirsty and disconnected from nature is tactically unhelpful and morally confused. One strategy for activists would be to start from a place of curiosity in order to explore the hunter's values. We might ask, "What is important to you about hunting?," "What other ways do you express those values in your life?," "What nonhunting traditions are important to you, your family, and your community?," or "What will you need to grieve if you give up hunting?." In this way, we can demonstrate our understanding that hunting is a complex interest and then work together with the hunter to explore what values are at stake and how they might be an avenue for pursuing other activities. Note, this conversation does not begin with a discussion about animals' moral considerability. That discussion will be important but less so initially as meeting someone where they are requires knowing where they are and that requires curiosity and attentive listening.

Since hunting is an interest so deeply tied to family and the broader community, activists might consider offering inroads to other communities. They might provide resources for contacting local hiking, bird watching, and wildlife photography groups. This would be like the kinds of work many organizations do when they offer mentorship to those interested in transitioning to veganism. We activists would do well to remember that in pushing someone to give up hunting, we risk isolating him from long-standing community relationships. We should do what we can to ameliorate that isolation by facilitating connections to other communities and groups. I know from being an activist and advocate myself that these suggestions may constitute a bitter pill. It is terribly challenging to channel patience and understanding when someone's idea of a delightful way to spend the day involves slaughtering innocent animals who are just living their lives. However, it is a mistake to think of this approach as requiring too much compassion or patience for those who perpetrate violence against animals for sport. To begin with, activism should start with a correct picture of the issue at hand. Though hunting involves slaughtering innocent animals for sport, it also includes relationality, love, care, and for some a genuine love of the outdoors. While this may not be true for the Ted Nugents of the world, it certainly is true for some hunters. Fully contextualizing the hunting interest encourages a complete understanding of the hunting issue. This is important for successful activism, but it is also important ethically. We make a moral error when we only partially contextualize hunters' interests and, in doing so, offer only partially useful ethical guidance. Arguing that hunters need to quit hunting on moral grounds is one, significant, piece of the moral guidance a contextualized ethic like ecofeminism can provide. Adding an understanding of how hunting is rooted in anthroparchal conceptions of hierarchy, violence, and domination is another. But we can also contribute to ethical conversations about hunting by noting the ways hunting is tied to deeply important relationships of love and care and by offering ethical guidance for how to manage the experience of feeling pulled, on the one hand, by ethical obligations to animals and, on the other, by ethical obligations to loved ones.

6 Complications

Just as in the case of traditional family or ethnic foods, there are several complications that can arise when confronting the challenge of balancing commitments to animals and a long-standing familial interest in hunting. As in the food example, hunters seeking to quit out of respect for animals will encounter the limits of what open dialogue can accomplish. In the hunting example, too, someone might object that the would-be former hunter seems to bear too much responsibility for relational moral attention. Along those lines, one might object that there are obligations on all sides and that family and community members need to step up and consider alternatives to hunting out of love and respect for their loved ones. The replies to these concerns offered in the food practices chapter apply equally here. Contextualizing the hunting interest and giving it a full analysis can point the way toward crucial relational moral work when defending animals involves disappointing people, but certainly there are limits to what dialogue can accomplish. In those cases, much will depend on the particulars. Are the relationships in question worth maintaining? Is there a different way to approach the dialogue? Can the parties agree to disagree while also finding a path forward to staying in close relationship with one another? No doubt there will be situations in which there is no way forward, where the bonds of relationality will be strained to an untenable degree and where parting ways is regrettably the only remaining viable option.

It is also certainly true that the would-be former hunter has considerable responsibility for undertaking the work of relational moral attention on this approach. This is a strength of the view rather than a liability. Oftentimes, what makes these situations feel so grimly unresolvable is the failure to notice that our interests are tied to important relationships of love and care and that these connections are an asset to change rather than an obstacle. In some cases, the latter will certainly be true. However, in others the connections point to relational work that can be done to alleviate the relational tension and, therefore, enable all parties to find a mutually acceptable path forward. Those of us who feel passionately about defending animals may find that the reparative relational work suggested here is time and effort well spent; that the moral and emotional importance of the relational elements of our interests warrants the time and attention to seeing to it that those elements are maintained even while the interest itself is given up. I also emphasized quite a bit the ways in which family and community members have obligations in the hunting case. The burdens of attending to relational interests are shared on all sides.

A potential complication raised by the hunting case that does not percolate to the surface quite as much in the food case is the problem of moderated interests. When we point to alternative practices hunters could engage in to satisfy their hunting interest without killing animals—activities like hiking, wildlife photography, and bird watching—we are asking hunters to moderate or alter their interest. This raises the question of whether the moderated interest (i.e., wildlife photography) is really the same interest and, if not, what that means for my discussion of the hunting dilemma. If the moderated interest is substantively different from the original interest, can one say that interest is still being met? Does it matter if it is not? These are the questions I take up in what follows.

For nonhunters, it is difficult to imagine why wildlife photography could not serve as a sufficiently similar interest to hunting. Wildlife photography involves stalking, long periods of time outdoors, a cultivated knowledge of the landscape and animals, significant development of skills, an ethical code, and immersion in gear and technology.[33] Even the "rational gearheads" of Littlefield's work, whose engagement in hunting focuses strongly on gear and technology, could be satisfied

[33]The North American Nature Photography Association, for example, includes an ethics committee and publishes several position statements, including one entitled "Ethical Field Practices" http://www.nanpa.org/advocacy/ethics/ (accessed November 15, 2021). My thanks to Daniel Emmerman for answering my questions about wildlife photography ethics.

with the breadth and complexity of photographic technology. Why not just swap a gun for a camera and call it good? Why not, indeed.

Some pro-hunting writers argue against this kind of moderation of the hunting interest. Making an atavistic argument in favor of hunting, Ann Causey argues for the centrality of the kill. Marti Kheel discusses Ortega y Gasset's rejection of wildlife photography as an alternative to hunting, noting his position that "wildlife photography is to hunting what Platonic love is to the real thing" (Kheel 1995, 91). Luke points out that, faced with the conflict between the predatory instinct and the disposition against killing, "hunters reject the obvious resolution of this conflict—for example, such nonlethal stalking practices as wildlife photography—insisting in various ways that the intent to kill is essential to the hunt" (1997, 35). Luke notes that Ortega y Gasset thought killing is an ineluctable and important part of human life and that to turn from hunting to wildlife photography would mark a "fall ... into a new immorality, into the worst of all, which is a matter of not knowing those very conditions without which things cannot be" (Ortega y Gasset quoted in Luke 1997, 40).

Discussing this issue, pro-hunting philosopher Theodore Vitali claimed:

> May not hunting with a camera or shooting animals with paint pellets accomplish the same ends without the loss of life? I don't think so. The hunting act is a killing act. It is, even in sport hunting, a primal act in which the hunter places him/herself in the mode of a predator who pits all of his/her skills against the animal's highly developed instincts for survival. ... The act of predation is the act of killing and, for the human predator, it is the intended and decisive act of killing. (1990, 78)

He went on to say that wildlife photographers have as their aim an aesthetic or artistic pursuit and that this is essentially different from the aim of a predator, which is to affect the game "definitively and irrevocably" (ibid.).[34]

These hunting advocates raise an issue that concerned Varner in his thinking about balancing human and nonhuman interests. He considers the problem of moderated interests, wondering whether a "moderated interest is really the same interest" (1998, 86). This matters to Varner because in evaluating the costs of moderating interests to accommodate moral insights, the costs of that moderation must be included in the utilitarian calculus. If the moderated interest is in fact not the same interest as the original, then the costs associated with moderation may be quite high indeed. In such cases, the moral calculations might show that, at least until conditions change, moderating the interest is supererogatory but not required. Neither Singer nor Taylor worries much about this issue. On both their

[34]For an accessible and helpful discussion of Causey and Vitali's positions and how they differ from one another, see Pluhar (1991).

views, human interests would need to be moderated to accommodate animals' interests, but this is taken as a given without further discussion.

I appreciate Varner's worry. When it comes to hunting, it may be that the costs of moderating the interest are high in part because the moderated interest is not the same as the original. It can be important to recognize when interest modification generates completely different interests rather than merely adjusted interests. Unlike Varner, I do not think these sorts of transition costs need stymy moral progress. Recognizing the moderated interest for what it is helps us understand resistance to giving up highly valued interests and can point the way toward moral work that mitigates the costs involved in transitions. In the case of hunting, it can be difficult to know whether the moderated interest will be a completely different interest. Clearly, for Ortega y Gasset, it would be, though that will not be the case for all who hunt.

Not every hunter thinks moderating the hunting interests generates a significant loss of what is important to hunters. In his piece "Why I Quit Hunting," Roy Dallas Gragg discusses returning to the forest with a camera instead of a gun (1986, 35). Gragg was raised in a rural hunting family and as a child was subjected to ridicule by his family for expressions of empathy for the animals slaughtered, castrated, dehorned, and killed on his family's property. Interestingly, Gragg notes that early in his life hunting did not trouble him whereas these other activities did. After studying ecology and animals, Gragg quit hunting by the time he was thirty. He notes that "tradition is perhaps the worst enemy of the animals" (ibid.) and turned away from those traditions eventually becoming an anti-hunting advocate.

Marks relays a conversation he had with a long-term hunter who turned away from killing and toward photography. Asked about changes to hunting in his lifetime, this respondent replied, "Yeah, vastly. I've noticed the last fifteen or twenty years I don't care as much about killing as I did, and I very frequently go hunting now without a gun. I just go with somebody and carry a camera" (178). This language of "hunting" with a camera comes up frequently enough in Marks's study that it caught my eye. Contra Ortega y Gasset, Causey, and Vitali, some hunters do not take killing to be the central feature of their hunting interest. If you can hunt with a camera, then perhaps the primary value of hunting with a gun was not the kill but rather the enjoyment of the outdoors, company with others, and the demonstration of skill necessary to capture wildlife. These are all values that are maintained when hunting with a gun shifts to hunting with a camera. Though Leopold was an avid defender of hunting, even he suggests at one point that hunters pivoting to photography might diminish the extensive damage done to nature by the proliferation of mechanized hunting (1989, 173). He also discusses wildlife research as an outdoor sport that retains the cultural values of hunting (184).

Whether the hunting interest is the same as the moderated interest will depend on individual interpretation. If one has an atavistic understanding of hunting where the interest is inextricably linked to predation and killing, then it is likely the moderated interest will be considered inadequate to supplant hunting. I suspect, though, that most hunters who consider quitting out of respect for animals either never had or are moving away from the atavistic conception of hunting. It is difficult to imagine someone who believes killing is central to the manifestation of the human identity deciding that they will no longer hunt out of respect for animals' lives and interests. Practically speaking, it is unlikely that the analysis I offer here needs to satisfy that group.[35]

Ethically, though, there are reasons to embrace the hardships engendered by modifying interests. Peter Railton argued insightfully that alienation from one's ground projects (which we can understand as highly valued interests that make life worth living) may be a good thing because people should bring their ground projects up for review or their autonomy is compromised (1984, 147). If we all just keep doing what we have always done without reflecting on how facts on the ground have changed or how our choices impact others, we risk diminishing our capacity as moral agents. It is our job to reflect on our ground projects and at times make the painful realization that alienating ourselves from those projects is called for. I would add, though, that in cases where the moderated interest is experienced as a loss, this needs to be acknowledged even if it is distasteful to those of us who find the original interest abhorrent.

Someone might wish to argue that there is a double loss when the hunting interest is moderated. The hunter loses the art of the kill and compromises his relationships and connections to others. It may be that the loss of community and loved ones renders the moderated interest a different interest all together rather than simply the lack of a kill. I am sympathetic to this worry, but it should be recognized that we do not get to persist in doing what we have always done simply because we have always done it and nearly everyone we know and love has always done it. We should evaluate our ground projects to see if they hold up to moral scrutiny. If they do not, adjustments must be made. This is what the fifth-generation hunter does when he acts on the recognition that hunting for sport is incompatible with his respect for animals.[36] The reflective process will be "alienating or even disorienting," as Railton notes (147). The purpose of this project is to call forward some of the reasons for that alienation and disorientation and then offer suggestions for moving forward. The alienation for hunters who quit is not merely alienation from their understanding of themselves but also from their most beloved relations and important community members and traditions.

---

[35]Atavistic defenses of hunting are suspect on numerous grounds, not least of which is that many human beings live flourishing lives without feeling the need to kill anyone.

[36]There could be numerous moral reasons a hunter might quit on moral grounds. For example, he may realize that hunting involves him in cruelty and that this goes against his sense of himself as a kind, rather than cruel, person. I am using the language of "respect for animals" broadly and include concerns that are rooted in virtue theory as well as other moral reasons one might have for eschewing hunting.

This is no small thing, as Varner reminds us when he talks about the "conservative bias or inertia" built into the Harean two-level theory he embraces.

Perhaps it is simply too much to ask that someone take on extensive alienation of this kind until, through collective action and the long process of change, traditions and mindsets alter sufficiently to diminish the costs involved. I am skeptical of the suggestion that we need to become mired in this kind of inertia. To begin with, it is unclear how the process of collective action and long-term change can come about without individuals who are willing to do the work I lay out in this chapter. It is through this work of relational moral attention including mutual avowal and contextualization that we can gradually shift the facts on the ground so that it becomes easier for future animal defenders to stand against animal exploitation. This has certainly been the case with veganism. Having gone vegan in 1990 when few people even knew what the word meant, I have witnessed firsthand how much has changed over the years. While still difficult, in many places going vegan is a very different, more socially acceptable (or at least not wholly alien), undertaking now than it was twenty or thirty years ago. That is thanks in large part to those of us who endured the hardships of early adoption of that ethical stance.

Moreover, the desire to step back from hunting out of respect for animals comes from within an individual. It is not a response to an abstract moral principle generated from the outside and then imposed upon someone. As Gruen has noted, alienation is reduced when "the force and authority of the ethical demand [is located] within the agent" rather than appearing as "external constraints on behavior" (2004, 285). It may be a lot to ask, but it is what we ask of ourselves in recognition of our own values and understanding of what is important to us. When the fifth-generation hunter faces the challenges of turning his back on hunting, he does so due to a manifestation of his own moral integrity. The resulting tension is not because respect for animals demands too much but because there has been nearly no guidance offered by the mainstream animal rights movement or by moral philosophers for how to think about the interests that exploit animals and their connections to relationships of love and care. The relational moral attention outlined here—including the work necessary for *all* parties (both the would-be former hunter and his community alike)—is vitally important for working through the tension generated by disappointing people while defending animals. Going against tradition is extremely challenging, but when we think relationally rather than individually, it becomes easier to see a path forward.

Finally, quitting hunting is not without precedent. These days, hunters quit for a variety of reasons. Most frequently, they cite concerns about the increasing costs of equipment and licenses. Some hunters quit because they are affronted by the crowds or the environmental damage to the landscape. Others quit because they age out of it or no longer have the hours to devote to such a time-consuming activity.[37] This is sometimes due to physical limitations brought on by aging, but

[37]In her analysis of the US Fish and Wildlife national survey of hunting conducted at the time of her article, Jolma notes the data showed that "almost one-third of those who have hunted haven't done

often it is not. Talking about Thoreau's eventual separation from hunting, Jolma notes that the taking of fish or game that was once essential to him overtime became entirely dispensable (Jolma 1992, 40). Marks also discusses how, as hunters age, their focus moves away from killing and toward the more relational elements of the hunt (225–6). Luke considers another phenomenon related to maturity, noting the not infrequent transformation that happens to hunters as they spend more time around animals and, in doing so, discover they can no longer tolerate killing them for sport (1997, 44).

The USFWS reports on hunting show a continuing downward trend in the number of hunters in the United States. Pro-hunting organizations strategize to increase their numbers. Therefore, despite hunting being tied to highly value ends, hunters are quitting. My forays into the online discussion boards did not reveal anyone who quit because of a concern for animals' welfare, but there are those who do quit on that score (Gragg 1986). Whatever their reasons for quitting, clearly hunters do and are quitting in large numbers. Why would it be asking too much of hunters to quit out of respect for animals if they are already quitting because of the maddening hoards? Hunters quit hunting and their families and communities have already had to find ways to adapt traditions accordingly.

Once again, a contextual and relational examination of the hunting interest reveals morally relevant and action-guiding information. While it is true that hunting can be tied to important relationships of love and care as well as broader community relationships and one's standing in those communities, it is also part of the hunting context that people stop hunting. Surely, this fact is highly relevant to considering the way forward when one's hunting interest conflicts with one's respect for animals. The fact that there is precedent in the community for stepping back from hunting—precedent for rethinking traditions—offers hope for a way forward from the impasse.

One can object that while there is precedent for quitting hunting generally, quitting specifically out of empathy and care for animals will likely generate much more difficulty than doing so for logistical or financial reasons. This might be the case for several reasons. First, there is likely less precedent for quitting hunting for reasons rooted in empathy for animals than for financial, logistical, or maturation reasons. Second, quitting for the animals will be felt as more of a rejection of family and community values than quitting for other reasons—one could still believe in the activity of hunting while recognizing there is no longer sufficient time to enjoy its pleasures. Third, people may be geographically located in places hostile to animal rights or animal rights adjacent values. In such places, noting

so in more than five years," and "18% of American men over the age of 16 have hunted, but only about 8% hunt each year" (39). The 2016 USFWS report does not seem to include this data but given the persistent decline in the number of hunters there are clearly many people quitting hunting on a regular basis.

hunting licenses have become prohibitively expensive will go over differently than invoking animals' moral status. Finally, it may be more dangerous for a would-be former hunter to invoke empathy for animals than other reasons for quitting because animal-directed empathy is often feminized. Narrow conceptions of masculinity and associations of empathy for animals with femininity could render exposing oneself as friendly to animals profoundly unsafe. Risks might increase exponentially if empathy is combined with gender expansiveness or not conforming to cisgendered heteronormativity in other ways. Thus, it will be more socially acceptable (and safer) in some circles to eschew hunting on financial or logistical grounds than animal welfare grounds. Thinking through the objection, a lack of data means we cannot say how true is it that there is less precedent for quitting hunting out of respect for animals than for other reasons. Anecdotally, it seems reasonable to make room for the possibility that it is true. This is particularly the case if those who quit out of empathy for animals are unwilling to say so to others out of fear of derision, opting instead to invoke financial or schedule constraints as a shield.

Where does this leave us? We return to the importance of context and a recognition that this process will likely be neither smooth nor simple. In families where there is precedent for people quitting hunting, there may be some room for using that precedent to help forge a path forward. In other families that precedent may be no help at all. In circumstances of the latter variety, more weight will fall on the work of relational moral attention. In contexts where there is extreme disregard for those who advocate for respect for animals or where it is unsafe to reveal one's empathy for animals, I see only two options. First, if maintaining important relationships still feels valuable, then some lack of transparency may be in order. One may opt to point to nonanimal-related reasons for quitting, for example. This is a form of duplicity to be sure, but where one's loved ones are unable to safely accept who you are, duplicity may be called for. Only individuals can say whether the costs for them of that duplicity are personally worth it. Second, for some, the inability to safely articulate one's true reasons for quitting hunting may result in the decision to separate from their family or community. Though my project is to seek to reconcile the tension between respecting animals and honoring relationships of love and care, such a reconciliation may not be possible. Sometimes repair and mutual avowal are impossible. Sometimes they are insufficient. In such cases, we are left with grieving what has been lost while celebrating the satisfaction and relief that comes from living with integrity according to our values. Little has been said publicly about this sort of grief. Vegans and animal advocates generally may feel as though we need to put a positive spin on life. As ambassadors for a moral outlook that many find overly demanding, we strive to present the best elements of veganism and tend to keep the costs to ourselves out of fear that addressing them will dissuade others from embracing veganism and other animal-prioritizing actions.

7 Conclusion

The hunting example lays bare the truth that defending animals often involves disappointing people. It also highlights the profoundly complex nature of some interests that are both exploitative of animals and tied to highly valued ends. Traditional animal ethicists have historically argued for the impermissibility of hunting while failing to provide analysis or guidance for what to do when hunting is a central part of familial and community relationships and traditions. Varner did recognize the possibility that giving up hunting could be challenging but then suggested that those challenges might make it the case that it is simply too much to ask of hunters to break with tradition. To do so would be supererogatory but not required. Despite commitments to contextualized moral accounts, ecofeminists have not engaged with the relational complexities of hunting. Focusing instead on highlighting the anthroparchal elements of hunting, ecofeminists did not turn their gaze toward other highly relevant contextual details of the hunting interest. This is understandable given the significant and unique contribution ecofeminist analysis has made to the discourse on hunting. I hope I have demonstrated how the ecofeminist project can be expanded to offer even more to conversations about hunting.

Fully contextualizing the hunting interest reveals that hunting is often tightly woven with important relationships of love and care as well as community connections. It reveals that while ecofeminists have been correct to highlight the problematic patriarchal foundations of hunting, our understanding of masculinity and hunting has been incomplete. Littlefield reminds us that it is a mistake to operate with a narrow conception of the masculinity evinced in hunting. For, men who hunt often exhibit strong elements of connection, care, and relationship with one another. When we notice and reveal the deep complexity of the hunting interest for some people, we then have the tools we need to understand how to begin the work of stepping away from hunting. It is not enough for the would-be former hunter to assert his newly acquired appreciation for animals' moral standing. If he wishes to remain in relationship with his hunting family, he must see the relational elements, address the ways in which his change of heart impacts others, and work with them to cocreate new traditions and ways of being together. Similarly, a would-be former hunter's loved ones must demonstrate an openness to the work of mutual avowal, of hearing and holding space for their loved one's new values. They should demonstrate their willingness to partner in finding novel ways to manifest the values the family shares and help advocate for their loved one with the broader community.

The anti-hunting animal advocacy community has obligations as well. We need to find the patience to see hunters in all their humanity and not simply as murderers of the creatures we care for so much. When talking with hunters, we need to take seriously the ways in which quitting hunting might put them at risk of destroying highly valued relationships and, potentially, at risk for their safety and security (either physical or financial if the community turns their back on them). We can offer hunters inroads to other communities that would offer camaraderie and connection. We can advocate for the animals while also addressing the realities for hunters. This is not to say it will be easy or pleasant. Nor is it to say that conversations of this kind will always be welcomed or encouraged by hunters. We should be realistic about what is possible. What is possible may shift over time, however, if animal advocates operate with a more nuanced understanding of hunting, one that recognizes the full picture.

It may not always be possible to reconcile empathy for animals with one's relationships with other humans. There are times when defending animals will result in fractured or weakened relationships. My hope, though, is that in taking a contextual, relational approach to hunting we open possibilities for reconciliation and mutual understanding rendered invisible by decontextualized or only partially contextualized accounts.

6 NO ZOO FOR YOU! VEGAN FAMILIES IN A SPECIESIST WORLD

1 Introduction

Several philosophers have taken up the issue of raising vegan children (Alvaro 2019; Fischer and Fredericks 2024; Hunt 2019a, 2019b; Millburn 2021, 2022; George 1994; Sherratt 2007). There is also popular literature on the "how-tos" of raising vegan children (Lindstrom 2018; Pavlina 2003) in addition to lively conversation on the topic in online forums. Much of the philosophical discussion centers on whether, by raising vegan children, we cause harm to their physical or social well-being. Alvaro, Hunt, and Millburn have an exchange regarding whether compromise is permissible when parents disagree about whether to raise their children vegan. Fischer and Fredericks make the argument that whether parents are vegan or not, there is a defeasible obligation to raise all children on a vegan diet.[1] Mainstream discussion centers on the logistics of raising vegan children (e.g., how to manage birthday parties, school lunches, etc.). In this chapter, I take up the relational moral dilemmas that arise when we raise children with vegan values that run counter to both dominant social and familial/cultural norms.

I use "vegan" here to mean ethical veganism and its associated values. In its fullest description, ethical veganism incorporates many value commitments into life that go well beyond what vegans eat (Hawthorne 2016). In addition to keeping to a strictly plant-based diet, ethical vegans do not wear animal products, support recreational activities that involve animals (e.g., zoos, aquariums, and wildlife "parks"), or use products tested on animals. Thus, when the ethical vegan parent receives the school email announcing their child's class trip to the zoo, they will face a plurality of competing values not faced by the parent who is vegan only for

[1] Fischer and Fredericks's piece is limited to discussion of what dietary choices parents should make for their children. They do not address other aspects of vegan commitments such as avoiding other forms of animal products or recreation exploitative of animals.

health reasons. Moreover, a health-centered vegan may have flexibility regarding periodic compromises of their child's veganism that are not so easily accepted by the ethical vegan parent. For example, some health-centered vegans might cook animal flesh for omnivorous friends with a strong preference for animal protein whereas an ethical vegan most likely will not (Amato and Partridge 1989, 199). When I refer to "vegan parenting" I am limiting discussion to parents who raise ethical vegan children as a parenting choice. I leave aside discussion of vegan young people who are "independent vegetarians/vegans" by their own choice and who are raised in a nonvegetarian family (Hussar and Harris 2010) or who were raised in a vegan family but not as vegans themselves until they chose those values independently. Independent young vegans present a different set of ethical questions that are worth exploring but beyond the scope of this chapter.

Navigating the pull of cultural, traditional, and familial norms and relationships with the commitment to raising one's children with a vegan ethic surfaces important moral questions: Is it permissible for parents to potentially risk their children's social well-being in service of their moral commitments? Do we wrong our children when we raise them with values that run counter to those of our extended families? Do we wrong our family members whose relational intimacy with our children might be diminished by a lack of shared values and practices? Is it incumbent on parents who raise vegan children to be open to some compromises of their vegan values? Note that these questions center on the potential ethical harms of vegan parenting related to relationships of love and care and social well-being generally. There has also been considerable discussion of the potential physical and health harms of raising vegan children both in philosophical writing (Fischer and Fredericks 2024; Gaard and Gruen 1995; Hunt 2019b; George 1994; Sherratt 2007; Singer and Mason 2006, to name just a few) and in the media. I will not discuss heath issues here for several reasons. First, there is ample literature showing that well-managed vegan eating can meet the nutritional needs of growing children and adolescents. What controversy there is on that issue is well-traveled terrain and easily accessible for interested readers. Second, given the nutritional information commonly available regarding the considerable health risks involved with the Standard American Diet, I feel comfortable assuming that veganism poses no more risk to young people and very likely is much healthier for them. For the purposes of this chapter, I will assume that physical health and well-being are managed properly for young people on a vegan diet thus focusing instead on the far less discussed moral implications of vegan parenting.

Another assumption underlying this chapter is that it is permissible for parents to undertake some shaping of their children's values where those values do not cause unnecessary harm to the child or others. This chapter will not get very far if it is true that parents have no rights whatsoever to shape their children's values. Moreover, since it is certainly not possible to raise children in a value-neutral way, it would be an odd thing indeed (disingenuous, too) to raise one's children entirely with values one does not hold. It may actually be impossible. Additionally, it would be unreasonable to require parents to raise their children to adhere strictly to all the dominant norms of their community if the parents do not share those norms. Such a requirement would inhibit freedom across multiple dimensions and cause significant harm to one's autonomy (freedom of religion for religious minorities comes immediately to mind). Shaping values is, at least to some extent, a duty parents have in order to raise morally functional members of a society (Brighouse and Swift 2014, 151). I suppose someone could argue that parents ought not to shape their children with the values they have, but they would then need to explain how unquestioning adherence to status quo norms of one's society and community is not a form of shaping values, albeit a less noticeable one that is more commonly accepted.[2] Certainly, in most democratic societies, we do act as if parents have a right to shape their children's values (at least to some extent). We will proceed accordingly in order to examine what follows about vegan parenting in particular.

Thinking through the relational and social moral conflicts that arise in vegan parenting is made more complex by the multiplicity of contexts in which vegan parenting takes place. Some of the conflicts and relational complications I discuss may not resonate with some vegan young people or their parents. For example, some vegan parents and children may have highly receptive and welcoming extended family (Amato and Partridge 1989, 181). Children also differ in how they interpret and respond to social interactions and being the only vegan in a group (233). There are also regional differences in the availability of vegan foods, which influences how difficult it is to accommodate veganism and find culturally relevant vegan alternatives. It may also be easier to be vegan in some geographic regions than it is in others (ibid.). Some vegans live in low-income and communities of color where they do not have access to healthy foods and meat/dairy alternatives due to food apartheid (Food Empowerment Project, "Food Deserts*"). Finally, how one experiences life as a vegan in a speciesist world can depend on one's identity in terms of economic position, race, gender, and intersecting identities. For example, the intersection of veganism and being queer made my son's journey through a vegan childhood and adolescence far more complicated than I believe it would have been had he been cisgender and heterosexual. As a result of this contextual complexity, some themes of this chapter may resonate with readers more than others. Perhaps some readers have never had to navigate the conflicting moral demands of veganism and relationships of love and care as they manifest in vegan parenting. I have yet to meet that person but knowing they might be out there gives me hope.

Assuming they are loved and cared for, vegan children, like most children, can lead happy and enriched lives full of all the joys and wonders childhood has to

[2]For a rich and detailed discussion of shaping children's values, see Brighouse and Swift (2014).

offer. However, being raised vegan can also complicate a child's life in several ways. Navigating food-centric familial and community events is difficult in a carnist culture. Many schools include trips to zoos, aquariums, farms, petting zoos, and so forth in their curriculum. As young people transition to middle and high school, they will face decisions about dissection and other animal-based science education. Vegan young people whose extended families are carnist will face many of the same issues discussed in Chapter 4 but with the added complication that, as children, they are more vulnerable than adults and also often confronted with epistemic injustice (Mohr Lone 2021).

The kinds of questions raised by vegan parenting are not unique. Many parents raising their children with a minority value system or religious perspective will face some version of the moral issues I raise in this chapter. However, for many children raised on a vegan ethic, they are the only vegan young person in nearly every setting in which they find themselves, which it not often the case for children from ethnic or religious minorities where there tend to be other family and community members in the child's life who share that identity. A child might be the only Jewish person in their class at school but then go to Hebrew School in the afternoons and be surrounded by other Jewish students and teachers. This is not always or even often the case for vegan children. Thus, vegan parents face a unique ethical challenge for vegan parenting because the tension between ethical veganism and cultural/familial practices is particularly acute; the risk of social, familial, and community isolation is high.

In what follows, I begin with a discussion of why some parents feel compelled to raise vegan children. I then explore the potential complications vegan children face in relationships with extended family members and the broader community. In Section 5, I discuss the question of whether vegan parents should be open to some compromise when it comes to the food and activities in which their children engage. I end with an exploration of how relational moral attention might work in the realm of vegan parenting and what structural changes might be necessary to reduce the frequency with which vegan parents and their vegan children face conflicts between defending animals and disappointing people.

2 Why Raise Vegan Children?

> If we are not given the option to live without violence, then we are given the choice to center our meals around harvest or slaughter, husbandry or war. We have chosen slaughter. We have chosen war. That's the truest version of our story of eating animals.
>
> Can we tell a new story?—Jonathan Safran Foer (244)

Mainstream understandings of why vegans are vegan tend to be quite shallow and easily summed up by the idea that vegans just love animals so much that we will not support their use for human purposes. In a way, that is a reasonable summation of some ethical vegans' approaches to their veganism. It obscures, however, several deep ethical convictions held by many ethical vegans. It is important to fully articulate the plurality of reasons ethical vegans may wish to raise vegan children because in doing so we get a better understanding of what motivates some vegan parents. This in turn helps us understand why they may or may not be open to compromises that would seemingly cost them very little but simplify their children's lives and improve relationships of love and care with family, friends, and the community at large. As with any other value system, individuals' reasons for holding those values will vary. In this section, I offer several reasons a vegan parent might have for raising vegan children. I do not pretend to offer a comprehensive list, nor do I think all vegan parents have this set of reasons for their decision to raise vegan children. Whatever their reasons, in reply to Safran Foer's question "Can we tell a new story?," vegan parents respond with a hopeful and enthusiastic "Yes!."

Part of telling that new story, one of harvest instead of slaughter, is refusing to take part in the horrific violence perpetrated daily on sentient and loving animals by the intensive animal agriculture industry. It also involves raising a new generation of humans who understand that choosing harvest over slaughter is an option, a generation who understands that violence toward other animals is a choice, a generation who does not accept as given that humans must be in relationship with animals through domination, objectification, and consumption. Hence for ethical vegans, vegan parenting is a way to orient their children away from the unnecessary and acute animal suffering involved in producing flesh-based foods, incarcerating animals in captive environments for entertainment, and so forth (Alvaro 2019, 657–8; 2020; Safran Foer 2009).

In addition to concerns about the violence toward animals and acute suffering that pervades their lives in the food system, vegan parents object to the normalization of keeping animals in zoos, aquariums, wildlife parks, and the captive breeding those systems require.[3] Rather than seeing trips to these places as awe-inspiring opportunities for children to see and potentially interact with the charismatic megafauna and other creatures who inhabit earth, the vegan parent sees such outings as supporting institutions that exploit and harm animals and perpetuate the idea of human superiority (Jamieson 2002a, 2002b). We might also see the environmental education at zoos, focused on the importance of conservation as being perverse. To begin with, this education is offered on placards mere steps away from where you can buy your child a hot dog for lunch

[3]See Emmerman (2020) for a full discussion of moral arguments against zoos.

made by an industry that is a leader in destroying the very environment the zoo encourages us to respect. Moreover, we might note that frequently the corporate donors to zoos are themselves involved in the degradation and destruction of our natural environment for the sake of profit. Much the same reasoning about zoos can be applied to aquariums, and even worse can be said of the animal exploitation and abuse that occurs in unaccredited, roadside zoos and "wildlife park" attractions.

Vegan parents are often concerned about environmental degradation generally and how a vegan diet is important to mitigating global climate change in particular (Alvaro 2019, 657–8; 2020). Understanding animal agriculture's impact on the natural world, opening oneself up to learning the environmental cost of eating animal-based foods, can be enough to convince someone to pursue a vegan way of life even if one is not moved by the suffering of other animals. Given that the negative consequences of global climate change are increasing in both frequency and forcefulness, some vegan parents feel a moral obligation to raise children who do not participate in animal agriculture, a main source of greenhouse gasses, deforestation, and environmental destruction (Adams and Gruen 2022; MacDonald 2022; Twine 2021, 2024).

Another concern for vegan parents is involving their children in supporting an industry that has a calamitous record of human rights violations in terms of both worker and environmental rights. Even if one cared not at all about animal suffering or even the natural world writ large, the sheer scale of human suffering involved in industrial animal agriculture is enough to turn one away from a hot dog at a barbecue. Some vegan parents might object to their children eating food that comes at the cost of humans' limbs, mental well-being, and worker and children's rights (Dreier 2025; Food Empowerment Project "Slaughterhouse Workers"; Pachirat 2011; Schlosser 2001; Thompson 2012). Slaughterhouse workers have one of the most dangerous jobs in the United States and are rarely supported when injured, sometimes catastrophically, on the job. Animal agriculture is also deeply implicated in environmental racism—positioning farms and their pollutants near low-income communities and communities of color (Food Empowerment Project, "Environmental Racism"; Riley 2022). Thus, those farthest from health care equity must bear the brunt of the health impacts generated by animal agriculture. These impacts include asthma, impaired lung function, physical and mental health issues, and increased risk of exposure to zoonotic illness (Beard et al. 2024; Fox 2024). Some vegan parents do not want themselves or their children to contribute to this level of human suffering through their dietary choices.

In addition to these worries about the concrete effects of animal agriculture on animals, humans, and the environment, some vegan parents worry about the moral impacts of carnism and anthroparchy on their children (Amato and Partridge 1989, 237). Parents have an interest in their children's character development. They have an interest in what sorts of people their children grow up to be, at least in the sense of understanding both the various joys and the various harms a human can cause or participate in over the course of their lives. Vegan parents want their children to be empathetic and to possess an expansive conception of to whom empathy is exercised. Vegan parents want their children to be well-informed and understand relationships between humans and other animals. As William Sarfo Ankomah writes, "Introducing children to animal-welfare and liberation education at home may produce well-informed and educated citizens who in turn will become more responsible for the welfare of other beings as a whole and on a global scale" (2020, 314). In short, whereas other parents might be chiefly interested in how their children treat their family's (or others') companion animals, vegan parents are interested in how their children treat and think about an expanded circle of living creatures with care, compassion, and justice.

In Chapter 4, I discussed veganism itself as an act of resistance against the status quo of exploitation, domination, and consumption. Vegan parenting can be seen as another iteration of that resistance. It can be a form of resistance against the exploitative norms of one's society, against capitalism, against cruelty, and against the expectation that we all just turn our eyes away and ignore what happens in bringing food to our plates, clothes and shoes to our stores, and entertainment to our communities and televisions. Resistance through everyday lifestyle rather than only through more direct political methods is common among vegans, particularly those who become vegan in their teenage years (Cherry 2015). Raising vegan children can also be a form of what Cherry calls a "lifestyle movement," a way to resist through daily choice and action rather than through direct activism. In addition to vegan parenting as a form of resistance against the structures of animal oppression such as the animal industrial complex, I maintain that vegan parenting is also a form of resistance against deceiving children, against the separation of children from their childhood connections to animals over time, and against the ways school and other institutions push young people into an anthroparchal worldview.

In *Our Children and Other Animals*, Matthew Cole and Kate Stewart carefully consider the ways children's relationships with other animals are shaped and influenced throughout the course of their lives through various institutions and family practices. They examine the ways anthroparchy manifests in so much of children's lives. One part of anthroparchy that vegan parents might seek to resist is the endemic deception of children about humans' relationships with other animals, for example, through public education. Cole and Stewart discuss the Farmland game, for example. This video game, developed by the European Commission and translated into twenty-three European languages, introduces students to farms raising animals for consumption. The game includes many buildings associated with raising animals on farms—the farm itself, the transporter truck, livestock buildings, and supermarkets but the slaughterhouse remains inaccessible and unlabeled. "In Farmland, the abattoir is literally unmentionable" (125).

Among other things, the inaccessibility of the slaughterhouse in the game is a form of deception. It leaves out the central mechanism through which the animals in the game transform from sentient creatures living their lives to slabs of flesh wrapped in plastic in the butchery department of the grocery store. Farmland is just one example of many of how children are consistently deceived about where their food comes from and how humans relate to animals as commodities. Certainly, the idea of commodification and exploitation is beyond the ken of young children, but the deception of young children regarding where their animal-based foods come from does not merely involve omitting information. The deception involves a kind of programming about where the food *does* come from—a programming that has no basis in reality.[4] Vegan parents resist this form of deception, preferring instead to focus on friendship, care, and respect for animal others until children are old enough to learn the facts of animal agriculture.

The deception children experience is impactful on them. Jonathan Safran Foer shares his first experience with finding out that his food was once a living creature. A babysitter was taking care of Foer and his brother and explained why she wasn't eating the chicken dish the kids were eating. She explained that she doesn't like to hurt anything. Confused, the children asked her for more details, and she complied. Foer narrates what happened next: "My brother and I looked at each other, our mouths full of hurt chickens, and had a simultaneous *how-in-the-world-could-I-have-never-thought-of-that-before-and-why-on-earth-didn't-someone-tell-me?* moments. I put down my fork" (6). A version of this story has taken place at innumerable dining tables. Vegan parents prefer not to be a part of the kind of deception that generates moments like these. We prefer not to take our children to the zoo to demonstrate the wonder of the various creatures on this planet all the while ignoring their incarceration. We resist with everything we have the kind of cognitive dissonance involved in eating a hot dog while looking at those animals in their enclosures.

Some might wish to point out that raising children usually involves some sort of deception. We can't opt out of ever deceiving our children because children will ask questions about what they cannot understand or about issues where access to the truth would precipitate a harmful loss of innocence and sense of safety. I agree. There are, of course, truths of life that are too much for children to know about depending on their age and developmental stage. As a philosopher who has spent over a decade doing philosophy with young children, however, I can say with some authority that children think about and can manage far more depth about the

[4]I see the long-term implications of this deception regularly in my undergraduate teaching. I am often the first person to tell students that cows do not lactate all day every day without being kept on hormones or consistently pregnant and having their calves taken away. The looks of betrayal and confusion on my students' faces are telling. When I ask them, "Have you ever heard of or encountered any other mammal who lactates constantly?" their betrayed faces shift somewhat—sometimes into anger, deeper confusion, or worry.

world than adults believe. This is not to say that one would sit a five-year-old down in front of a documentary depicting the inside of factory farms. It might, however, be possible to sit with a five-year-old who has asked why we don't eat meat and say, just as I did with my five-year-old vegan, that eating meat involves killing animals and we don't believe that we should kill anyone unnecessarily. Those animals have their own lives to lead and are not ours to hurt. Between deception and unvarnished disclosure lies a great deal of open area replete with options for truthful discussion.

Parents raising vegan children may also see that choice as an act of resistance against a system that threatens children's connections to animals. For many children, interspecies relationships play a central role in their lives. Most obviously, these relationships are forged with companion animals, but they also manifest in relationships with liminal animals (the ducks at the pond, squirrels in the tree, crows in the backyard, etc.). Children who grow up around farmed animals may also experience important interspecies relationships, particularly those participating in 4–H-style programs where young people raise an animal from birth and eventually bring them to market.[5] Additionally, as Cole and Stewart discuss, even the ways we dress our children create an affinity between them and other animals. They are dressed in clothing representing adorable animals, sometimes the clothing even gives them animal-like features such as bear ears (2016). We also provide our children with stuffed animals to care for and provide comfort in times of distress. As Donaldson and Kymlicka put it, "Given [the] overwhelming evidence for the reality that children inhabit, mentally and physically, an interspecies social world, the puzzle becomes how this interspecies fellowship becomes broken" (2019, 285). For some adult vegans, these early childhood connections to animals were forcibly interrupted by the "tricking, prodding, coercing, and confusing" our parents inflicted on us when we were young (ibid., 286). We remember being told we were "too sensitive" or that we "didn't understand how things work" or any number of other dismissive remarks aimed at shifting us away from our compassion and empathy for animals and toward the more socially acceptable cultural norm of animals being ours to use, eat, and experiment on (Gaard 1993, 120). Some vegan parenting can be understood as a rejection of the forces at work in that kind of trickery and, yes, gaslighting. It manifests a desire to keep our children's connection to other animals, to promote compassion and care, and to avoid reaffirming the kind of hierarchical thinking that undergirds the treatment of animals in our world.

Another part of resisting the separation of children from their connections to animals is instantiating vegan parenting as a rejection of the ways schools and other

[5]Though there is discussion about the potentially devastating effects of young people raising an animal from birth and then having to turn them over for slaughter as well as the need for further research into that potential harm (Donaldson and Kymlicka 2019, 286).

institutions push young people into a hierarchical and exploitative worldview. For some vegan parents this constitutes a concern chiefly centered on humans' treatment of other animals. For others with a more intersectional or holistic understanding of how systems of oppression work, this can constitute a concern not only for animals but also for the ways thinking about animals in a hierarchical way can be connected to other forms of marginalization and oppression in society. Donaldson and Kymlicka note that we've long understood the impacts of extreme acts of animal cruelty on children, but less is known about the "effects on children of being indoctrinated into 'normal' acts of animal exploitation" (286). They go on to note that what research has been done suggests that "inculcating attitudes of human superiority over other animals worsens, rather than alleviates, negative attitudes towards minorities, immigrants, and other 'out' groups" (ibid.). Steeping children in the idea of human exceptionalism and superiority, it seems, can aggravate attitudes toward other marginalized people. Some vegan parents opt for vegan parenting at least in part to stymie institutional efforts to root children in a conception of hierarchical thinking that ends poorly for animals and other humans farthest from equity, compassion, and justice overall.[6]

The influence of schools and other institutions on young people is tremendous. I remember entering my son's elementary school cafeteria and seeing enormous posters all over the walls advertising dairy and, in particular, the Washington State dairy industry. The message to drink their milk was everywhere students looked. Schools are also places where students are encouraged to patronize the zoo, perform animal dissection, and drop eggs from high towers in physics classes. As Cole and Stewart note, "Education practices and discourses as a whole serve to objectify the nonhuman animals represented by identifying animals as little more than machines for the generation of 'useful' body parts (whether food or experimental tools)" (128). This objectification of animals through educational practices normalizes relationships of hierarchy and subjugation between humans and other animals. Some vegan parenting can be seen as a rejection of that normalization and in turn an attempt to apply some counterforce to the overwhelming pressure applied by structural systems to produce adults who unquestioningly consume and use animals as mere means to human ends.

Moreover, the prevalence of the message that "real men eat meat" along with gendered ideas of men needing more meat than women or children creates an environment where, as LuAnne Roth puts it, "meat manifests as a symbol of male dominance, a celebration of patriarchy itself" (2005, 187). Vegan parents may see raising vegan children as an act of resistance against traditional and narrow conceptions of masculinity as well as against the forces of education and social structures that push young people into a patriarchal conceptual framework.

[6]Cf. Fischer and Fredericks (2024, 5–9).

Raising vegan children can also assuage worries parents may have about involving their children in practices that cause harm and death to others. Some vegan parents might even worry that, in feeding children animal flesh foods and bringing them to animal-based entertainments such as zoos and aquariums, they make their children complicit in the suffering endured by those animals. I do not share the worry that young children will become complicit in the suffering involved in animal agriculture, zoos, and animal-based entertainment. As Josh Millburn avers, parents are responsible for the moral harms of their child's diet when they are providing the food and, I would add, responsible for moral harms of their child going to the zoo or other institutions (Millburn 2022, 287). Still, since feeding flesh foods to our children, taking them to the zoo, the rodeo, and so on involve making them participants in a harmful chain of events, some parents may see raising their children as vegans as a way to avoid that involvement. This is not an attempt to keep our children from ever being involved in participating in harm of any kind (that is not a realistic goal for any kind of parenting) but rather a desire to avert their participation in completely avoidable practices that generate so much suffering for both humans and nonhuman animals.

Finally, a reason vegan parents might opt for raising vegan children is their interest in having children who share their values. In *Family Values: The Ethics of Parent-Child Relationships*, Harry Brighouse and Adam Swift note the centrality of shared values to fostering the goods of a parent/child relationship:

> Parenting is about having a relationship of the right kind with one's child. Because people's values are central to who they are, because successful parenting requires parents to share themselves with their children, and because value sharing implies at least some degree of value shaping, value shaping is an inherent part of that kind of relationship. (153)

The goods of a parent/child relationship do not justify overriding children's autonomy, according to Brighouse and Swift. Indeed, a key part of parenting on their view is shaping values without inhibiting children's capacity for autonomy and agency (2006, 104; 2014, 168). Assuming parents successfully balance the desire to share values with their children and the responsibility to raise young people who can make their own choices for themselves, then sharing values (by to some degree shaping values) will be an important part of creating the goods of the parent/child relationship. For Brighouse and Swift, shared values are an important part of having the kind of relational intimacy central to the parent/child relationship (155). I find this issue of sharing ourselves with our children compelling. The kind of subterfuge necessary to hide one's central values and moral commitments from one's children would in itself be sufficient to negatively impact the parent/child relationship. Even if subterfuge were somehow unnecessary, however, it would still be the case that a parent concealing the foundational moral beliefs of their lives from their children would involve restricting access to who that parent is as a person. This would certainly undermine the parent/child relationship.

Here one might note that this is a reason to think it necessary to be open with one's children about one's central moral values but not a reason to raise one's child to live according to the same behaviors reflective of those values. More concretely, someone might argue that a vegan parent can talk about his veganism with his children, explain his values, and create intimacy in that way without raising his children to themselves be vegan. This would be true if the issue were merely one of sharing oneself with one's children. Generating that sort of intimacy is part of the goods of the parent/child relationship, but raising children who share those values deepens and strengthens the relationship (Brighouse and Swift 2006, 104). While I can imagine the possibility of raising one's children with slightly different values from oneself, it is difficult to see how one would maintain one's moral integrity while raising one's child to do the opposite of what you see as morally important let alone how one would foster a deep and shared connection when something so central to a parent's identity and way of understanding the world is not shared.

Like the parent who enjoys theater and begins taking their child to plays and musicals at a young age or the parent whose passion for skiing translates into early ski lessons and ski outings, the vegan parent wishes to share what is important to them with their children and to be able to participate in the same kinds of events and occasions (again in a way that is consistent with cultivating their child's autonomy). When our children are old enough to choose for themselves, we of course must let them decide their own path to pursue. The child raised to ski may discover in adolescence that they far prefer cycling to skiing. As parents we must encourage and support that kind of differentiation. The same is true for the vegan parent whose child grows up to embrace going to the zoo or omnivorism. Until the point in our children's lives where they begin to make those kinds of decisions for themselves, however, parents often choose to raise their children in ways that reflect their own values so that these values can be shared, enriching the relationship for all involved.

Frustratingly, the idea of raising children with shared values with their parents goes almost entirely unquestioned when the values selected reflect those dominant in the surrounding culture. My husband and I certainly received far more questioning about our decision to raise our child as a vegan than we did about our decision to teach him to ride a bike or have him go on bike rides with his cycling enthusiast father. In both cases we were shaping values in part in service of creating shared values.

In addition to vegan parents raising vegan children, there may also be nonvegan adults who raise vegan children for moral rather than health reasons. Jeremy Fischer and Rachel Fredericks have argued, for example, that children's caregivers have a moral obligation to raise vegan children whether or not they are vegan themselves (2024). They ground this obligation in children's interests, namely their interests in moral development, the development of their autonomy, and their interest in physical health (2–10). Fischer and Fredericks note that the obligation to raise vegan children is defeasible in some cases (in particular when cultural considerations arise), but that generally "caregivers have a moral duty to raise children on a maximally plant-based diet" (2). Among the many issues Fischer and Fredericks discuss is the importance of prevention over cessation when it comes to plant-based eating (7). It is easier to move from veganism to carnism than it is to move from carnism to veganism. Quitting carnism, as so many adults who attempt to do so attest, is profoundly challenging in the world as it is currently arranged. If parents or caregivers believe it is morally obligatory to raise vegan children for the reasons Fisher and Fredericks give, environmental concerns, and so on, then they have a reason to raise the young people in their care as vegans even if they themselves are not.

Having articulated many of the reasons parents and caregivers might choose to raise vegan children, I hope it is clear that the pull of raising vegan young people can be quite strong. Raising children to be adept and courageous moral thinkers is a central part of parenting. For those whose moral visions stretch to the farther reaches of the animal kingdom and to seeing the ways marginalized human and animals' fates are tied together, raising vegan children may be considered the only option for achieving that parenting goal.

Before turning to a discussion of the potential relational costs vegan children may encounter as a result of being raised vegan, I want to address the question of whether raising children involves forcing or indoctrinating young people in an alarming way. This is a consideration raised often by carnists to their vegan parenting friends and relatives, and it comes up in the literature on raising vegan children as well. Parents may have good reasons to want to raise vegan children, but if doing so constitutes a morally problematic kind of indoctrination, one that perhaps curbs the development of a child's capacity for autonomy, then that would indeed be problematic.

3 The Question of Indoctrination and Worries about Autonomy

In his book *Raising Vegan Kids*, Eric Lindstrom refers to the following dialogue in Richard Watts's comic strip, *Vegan Sidekick*:

First Panel:
Person one: "I don't make my child eat meat."
Person two: "Forcing your way of life on your children is extreme"
Second panel:

Person one:	"I make my child eat meat."
Person two:	"Forcing your way of life on your children is awesome" (Lindstrom, 100)

One would be hard-pressed to find a vegan parent raising vegan children who has not encountered some version of this very conversation. The notion of raising children as vegans in line with parents' values prompts charges of foisting beliefs on children or indoctrinating them into a belief system. The two charges (forcing and indoctrinating) often elide into one another. Most times I have heard this charge it has been a rather shallow assertion offered without consideration. I have left these interactions wondering about what, specifically, the harm is that concerns people. I have also wondered how they are thinking about the issue of "forcing" or indeed if they have thought about it at all.

To begin unpacking the question of indoctrination or forcing a vegan way of life on children it is necessary to differentiate forcing from indoctrinating. When searching for a definition of "indoctrinate" in the *Oxford English Dictionary*, I was surprised by the benign nature of the concept: "to imbue with learning," "to instruct *in* a subject, principle, etc.," "to imbue *with* a doctrine, idea, or opinion," "to bring *into* a knowledge of something," "to teach, inculcate (a subject, etc.) *rare*" (OED). This concept of indoctrination—one that is nonthreatening and focused on instruction—cannot be what people worry about with respect to vegan parenting. If we look to "indoctrination," however, the *OED* offers a link to the definition of "brainwashing." Brainwashing sounds more like what worries people about vegan parenting—"the systematic and often forcible elimination of a person's mind of all established ideas, esp. political ones, so that another set of ideas may take their place … Also *attributive* and in weakened sense: the action of pressurizing or persuading a person into a belief considered undesirable" (*OED*). Let us assume for the sake of argument that the charge that vegan parenting is indoctrination of children packs in this idea of brainwashing such that raising children in a vegan way of life is not merely bringing them "into a knowledge of something" but exerting an inappropriate amount of pressure to form children's beliefs.

The issue of forcing someone is a bit more nuanced. In the most quotidian sense, parents "force" children all the time. The toddler who does not want to put on their shoes but wants to play at the park is "forced" to don their sneakers. The adolescent who would prefer not to do their chemistry homework is "forced" to do so by their parent who withholds screen time until the assignment is completed. We also all force ourselves in this mundane way: getting out of bed in the morning when it feels impossible, going to the grocery store when we are exhausted, grading the papers we assigned to our students. This is forcing of the most mundane kind. It is the application of subtle pressure of some kind to ensure an action is undertaken. No one is hurt. Critics of vegan parenting on the grounds that it forces a way of life on a young person must be using "forces" in a different way. The idea here must be that the parent applies not a subtle pressure but a strong one, the kind of pressure that can cause harm or override another's capacity for agency or autonomy development. Whatever term is employed, there is a belief out there that raising vegan children is a problematic form of forcing beliefs on young people in a way that is perceived as very different from other kinds of beliefs parents "indoctrinate" their children into such as the belief that playing organized sports is important or that going to the zoo is a benign form of entertainment.

Certainly, there are ways of raising children with a problematic form of pressure in belief formation. Speaking about families who raise their children with specific religious values, Brighouse and Swift note that whether that form of child-rearing is conducive to the development of autonomy will depend on the particulars. They emphasize that it is crucial for parents to avoid emotional costs when a child exercises their autonomy to make a decision that goes against the family's values. If, for example, one is raising one's child in a strict kosher lifestyle according to the rules of Judaism and the child knowingly eats a pork sandwich at a friend's house, inflicting emotional consequences on the child (e.g., withholding love, expressing extreme anger, no longer trusting the child, etc.) could very well diminish that child's ability to exercise autonomy in the future (173).

One might also significantly impact one's child's autonomy development by raising them in a monolithic environment without exposure to other ways of thinking and being (172). One way we can avoid indoctrination in the most problematic sense is to ensure young people are exposed to a "diverse environment" (ibid.). Thankfully for vegan parents, unless we are living in a completely vegan community, we cannot help but raise our children in a diverse environment. In a carnist and anthroparchal world, exposure to eating animal flesh is constant; exposure to different attitudes about animal captivity and entertainment is a certainty. Due to the very common aggression carnists and speciesists turn on vegans, vegan youngsters will be all too aware that there are other ways of seeing the world, other beliefs about the comparative value of humans and other animals.

Brighouse and Swift also note that the sharing of values ought to be bidirectional where the child's values and interests should influence what constitutes the shared values/interests of the family (2014, 156). This, too, will help prevent the kind of harmful indoctrination critics of vegan parenting profess concern about. Unidirectional sharing of values and interests will erode the parent-child relationship, and refusing to engage with a child's ideas, questions, and developing values will erode their sense of autonomy and agency. All parenting (not merely vegan parenting) should involve evaluation for how much room is being made for children to influence the family. This will mean that parents may have to spend their time in ways they had not anticipated. It will mean that parents have to entertain ideas they find challenging or that they would rather not think about.

This is all in service of both relational health and developing young people's autonomy.[7]

Fischer and Fredericks also offer ideas for how plant-based caregiving can avoid negatively impacting young people's autonomy development. They suggest we might "emphasize to kids that they need not *identify* as veg*ns or adhere to veg*n *moral doctrines*," and that caregivers could communicate that "they practice plant-based caregiving to protect the kids' interests—or perhaps to form relational bonds by cooking plant-based foods together (alongside, say, playing sports together)" (13–14).[8] They offer this in response to objections from those concerned with imposing something like a Rawlsian comprehensive doctrine on children (Fischer and Fredericks, personal communication, December 9, 2024). Fischer and Fredericks are not themselves concerned about this worry, noting that they are merely making the point that even if one *is* concerned about vegan children's autonomy development due to veganism representing a doctrine, one can protect a vegan child's autonomy by simply not appealing to that doctrine to ground their veganism. Those worried about that issue can raise vegan children who do not identify as vegans in the doctrinal sense, though Fischer and Fredericks believe this is not ultimately what caregivers should do given the myriad reasons inviting veganism as a way of life (ibid.).

I hope I have sufficiently demonstrated that there are ways to raise children with shared values without parents overriding their interest in developing autonomy. I now want to turn to the important point, made by others as well, that if there is a concern about forcing beliefs on young people it rarely arises with respect to parenting that reflects accepted social and moral norms. Dominant social views are foisted on children from the very beginning of their lives without concern. Cole and Stewart articulate this point well:

> A common objection to discourses for social changes, especially insofar as they aim to shape and re-shape children's thoughts and actions, is that they are merely indoctrinating propaganda. The argument goes that they therefore run counter to the dominant cultural value of freedom of choice, in the context of a democratic consumer society. ... However, vegan cultural interventions, as with cognate interventions into other forms of oppression and violence, are highly conspicuous only because they run against the grain of the taken-for-granted indoctrination that continues remorselessly throughout children's

---

[7]Brighouse and Swift also emphasize the importance of being able to sustain a relationship with one's child even without the important shared values (2014, 157). When children grow up and break with their parents' values, that ought not to significantly impact the relationship. There should be sufficient common ground to sustain a relationship into adulthood and beyond.
[8]"Veg*n" is short for vegan/vegetarian.

upbringing. … Children have scant opportunity to engage in "choice" about how they relate to animals. (153)

In "Forcing Kids to be Vegan? Parents Answer," Emily Barwick quotes Raffaela, a vegan parent living in Lisbon, Portugal:

> Accusing parents of forcing their beliefs on children doesn't make much sense to me, because all parents—vegan or not—will use their beliefs as guidance to raise their children. That is kind of a normal process. But, in case of veganism [*sic*], we are not using our beliefs. We are using our knowledge. These are two very different things and this knowledge is so valuable for them, that it would be very stupid of us not to see it. (Barwick 2016)[9]

Her observation that vegan parents are not merely acting according to belief but as a result of knowledge—knowledge of animal agriculture's impact on human and nonhumans' well-being, its damage to the environment, and the reality of animals' suffering in captive environments like zoos and laboratories—is a keen one. Unlike many beliefs parents expose their children to, veganism is grounded not in faith or opinion but in facts. The idea that vegans are somehow foisting beliefs on their children in ways other parents do not is misguided. Fischer and Fredericks note, for example, that most parents do not allow their children to smoke tobacco, and most do teach their children about respect. Neither of these choices is considered illiberal or in tension with children's interests in shaping their own beliefs (26).

One frustration I feel with the charge that vegan parents are foisting their beliefs on their children in a problematic way is that, arguably, vegan parents are more open with their children about their beliefs and what grounds them than parents choosing more mainstream approaches to interactions with animals. In part because we are such a small minority, vegan parents have almost no choice but to explain our thinking to our children, to call attention to why we eat the way we do and will not go to the zoo with our friends. Most of my friends who parent their children according to carnist norms do very little explaining of their food choices. Food appears, is eaten and enjoyed, and that is the end. The same goes for outings to the zoo or animal parks—animals were seen, enjoyment ensued, and everyone went home no questions asked. It seems to me that explaining the values guiding your family's choices, talking them through with your children, and thinking together in an age-appropriate way about what grounds those values are far less likely to manifest foisting or indoctrination than never even noticing that

[9]See also Horta (2018, 3–5) for a description of the epistemic injustice toward vegans on the issue of having knowledge about the world. Horta notes that vegans' claims about animals or nutrition are often not taken seriously by nonvegans.

there are questions to be asked about the values underlying the choices a family makes every single day.

There are certainly forms of parenting that involve indoctrination. We have all seen some of the results of those forms of parenting in media coverage of cults and the like. Vegan parenting, however, is not intrinsically that form of parenting. Moreover, unlike parenting that reinforces dominant norms of human exceptionalism, vegan parenting underscores compassion, care, thoughtfulness, curiosity, and integrity by reinforcing relationality with other animals and noting the impact of humans' dietary and entertainment choices on everyone.

One might object, however, that the problem is not that veganism merely introduces some values into children's lives, it is that those values are unusual. Amy Sherratt raises this concern in her defense of vegetarian parenting (Sheratt 2007). Sherratt notes that the position may not be that parents ought not to make choices on behalf of their children as that is clearly false but that parents ought not to make *unusual* decisions on behalf of their children (427–8). The idea here is:

> We are obliged to make certain choices for our children—but should not foist our more idiosyncratic ideas upon them. Instead, we should dress our children in the same sort of clothes as their peers, give them the same sort of toys, and feed them the same sort of food. Then, at least, they will have a sort of "neutral base" to start from when they come to make their own decisions. (428)

In her response to this objection, Sherratt is defending the choice to raise one's children as vegetarians rather than vegans, but her argument applies here. She notes that there are clear cases where it is appropriate to make unconventional choices for our children as when we raise a multilingual child or an anti-racist in a racist society (ibid.). There are also any number of idiosyncratic choices parents make for their children that are entirely appropriate. My father, for example, is an avid scuba diver and expert scuba instructor. In our youth, my brother and I spent an exceptional amount of time in swimming pools and open water areas with our father while he taught people to dive. While our childhood was unusual due to our father's distinctive devotion to scuba diving, no harm was done. Indeed, there were significant benefits for us.

Being vegan and parenting vegan children are indeed unusual decisions statistically speaking. The values that give rise directly to veganism are not widely shared, and the commitment to facing the realities of humans' impact on other animals and humans through our exploitation of animals is rarer still.[10] The unusual nature of the beliefs involved in veganism is not harmful, however, in the

---

[10]I say "the values that give rise directly to veganism" because there are many values underlying veganism that are widely shared but do not necessarily translate to veganism for many people (e.g., compassion, respect, care, pacifism, etc.).

same way my father's keen interest in the world underwater was not harmful and in the same way the parent who raises their child to be fluent in Amharic in an English-speaking country is not harmful. It cannot be the case that all unusual or idiosyncratic beliefs and choices are off the table once we become parents.

The objection to vegan parenting on the grounds that it foists unusual values on children is not reasonable because unusual beliefs in and of themselves are not problematic. They need to be harmful in some significant way in order to be problematic, a standard, I might add, that applies equally to widely and moderately held beliefs. In the next section of this chapter, I will consider the potential relational harms of parenting vegan children, but concerns about such potential harms are different in tone and tenor from concerns about foisting or indoctrination, so I do not address them here.

A key point to keep in mind is that while there is nothing necessarily harmful or indoctrinating about raising vegan children there may be something harmful and indoctrinating about raising children according to dominant norms of anthroparchy and carnism (Donaldson and Kymlicka 2019; Fischer and Fredericks 2024). Fischer and Fredericks argue that carnist caregiving can harm children's physical health as well as the development of their morality and autonomy. Carnist caregiving impedes autonomy, they aver, by laying fertile ground for cognitive dissonance and irrational beliefs. In their words:

> In carnist societies like the contemporary U.S., plant-based caregiving likely promotes kids' autonomy development, whereas carnist caregiving likely impedes it. For, such societies exhibit widespread anti-vegan bias, ignorance and mistaken assumptions about various diets' costs and benefits, and incoherent attitudes regarding animals and diet. These are obstacles to autonomous belief and preference formation, especially when they result from manipulative carnist public relations campaigns and policies designed for others' benefit, as they often do. Perhaps counter-intuitively, plant-based caregiving in such societies *expands* the options effectively available to children by helping them overcome these obstacles. Thus, promoting autonomy in carnist societies calls for plant-based caregiving. (6)

If, for example, we accept the science demonstrating that industrial animal agriculture has a deleterious and catastrophic role in global climate change, carnist caregiving may impede autonomous decision-making for young people as they grow older by not merely failing to provide important information but by also actively providing misinformation, limiting options, and ridiculing beliefs and lifestyles that in fact minimize humans' negative impact on human, animal, and planetary welfare.

Donaldson and Kymlicka's worry is related but slightly different. They make the broader point that, by rupturing children's interspecies relationality, parenting according to societal norms of human supremacism is "one of the most consequential—and, we would argue, damaging—features of contemporary practices of childhood socialization and education. It is traumatic for many children, it exacerbates inter-group prejudice, and it is catastrophic for animals" (287). Unquestioning adherence to the norms of human supremacism and carnism can harm children. Doing so involves fracturing the kinship and connection many young children feel with other animals, reifying a supremacist attitude that extends to animals and often to other out-groups as well, and actively teaching children lies and propaganda regarding how animals are treated and how that treatment negatively impacts the animals as well as the humans who work with them and the environment in which we live.

For the most part, the charge that parents raising vegan children are indoctrinating their vulnerable charges centers on concerns that vegan parenting involves a problematic form of indoctrination. The idea is that vegan parenting overrides young people's autonomy or autonomy development in a harmful way. I hope to have shown that this charge is unwarranted on the grounds that vegan parenting is entirely conducive to autonomy development and, in the same ways, may be even more conducive than mainstream parenting mimicking anthroparchal and carnist norms. In raising young people, however, cultivating agency and autonomy are two values among many. Most parents are also concerned with introducing and cultivating other values in our children—care, compassion, respect, response to others' needs, kindness, and so forth. Vegan parents often have additional values they are concerned to impart to their children: rejecting human supremacism, widening the circle of care to include all living beings, having a sense of the impact of Western-style consumer habits on the world, a deep care for and commitment to all of nature.

Like other forms of value sharing between parents and their children, unless veganism is being forced through coercive measures, emotional abuse, or physical abuse, then it is a morally permissible way of life in which to raise children. Vegan parents, as well as all other parents, must of course wrestle with issues around their children's choices as they grow up and develop their own sense of self. Teens may, for example, choose to go to the zoo with friends or eat a burger at their extended family's barbeque. Again, as with all parenting around shared values, vegan parents and caregivers will need to have autonomy-respecting responses to these shifts as their children reach various developmental stages. In this respect neither vegan parents nor vegan children are any worse off or challenged than any other parent or child.

Having worked through questions around indoctrination, autonomy development, and whether imparting unusual values to young people is problematic, I turn now to questions about the impact of being raised vegan on a child's social life and relationships with their extended family and community.

4 Potential Relational Costs to Children Raised Vegan

4.1 Social Harms in Schools and Extrafamilial Settings

We now arrive at the most pressing ethical questions about raising vegan children. One might worry whether by raising a child as a vegan we risk their social well-being in service of our moral commitments and desire to share our values. In particular, we may worry that we wrong our children socially and relationally when we raise them with values that run counter to those of our communities and extended families. This worry is not without some foundation. Indeed, it is my own experience parenting a vegan-since-birth child (now adult) that led me to these ethical concerns. The social world for children can be a place of play and joy but also one of heartbreaking cruelty. Where some families respond with love and open-mindedness about vegan children joining their ranks, others respond with resentment, fear, and antagonism. In the literature on vegan parenting, there is a tendency to minimize or simply will these potential relational costs away or, worse, to ignore them to avoid dissuading parents from committing to vegan parenting. As in Chapter 4 where I discussed conflicts around familial food traditions and veganism, here I will provide a contextualized and careful discussion of the potential relational costs to children of being raised vegan. That careful discussion will lead to a relational account of how to mitigate these potential relational costs with particular attention to the question of compromise and the necessity for relational moral attention. I say "potential" relational costs to children raised vegan because it is possible that some vegan children will never face the issues I articulate later in the chapter. I imagine, however, that most readers—whether vegan or not—will recognize the relational complexities articulated in what follows either because they were on the receiving end of others' rejection or cruelty or because they were on the giving end.

I begin with the potential social harms of a vegan childhood in extrafamilial settings and turn later to the potential harms to familial and community relationships. Vegan children can be victims of bullying and what Bouke de Vries calls "social cruelties" (De Vries 2020, 323).[11] Since vegan children do not eat the same diet as carnist children and further may not participate in the same entertainments or pass times as other children (e.g., visiting the zoo or aquarium, stepping on insects, running into a flock of birds to scare them and make them fly away, etc.) they are noticeably different from their peers. One-third of the parents

---

[11]De Vries's essay is about parenting and geographical relocations, not vegetarianism or veganism but the language of "social cruelty" works well in this context.

participating in Amato and Partridge's study of vegetarian children reported that "their children experience social difficulties because of their meatless diets" (232). Note that these are vegetarian children who, compared to vegan children, are considerably less different from their peers. Articles and book chapters have been written to help vegan young people cope with bullying (Borgoyn 2017; Pavlina 2003; Reilly 2025). Oscar Horta uses the term "vegaphobia" to refer to "a bias against veganism," which takes various forms including "mean jokes about veganism, eating meat in front of vegans just to offend or ridicule them" and other forms of harassment (Horta 2018, 3).[12] While it may sound far-fetched to say that carnists eat meat in front of vegans solely to upset or ridicule them, I cannot count the number of times this has happened to me in decades as a vegan and I witnessed it happen to my son as well. We know the goal is solely to upset or ridicule us because carnists who engage in this behavior often relish telling vegans that this is precisely what they are doing.

Marcus William Hunt makes the blunt point that "to raise one's child on a vegan diet is therefore to raise a 'vegan,' and to saddle them with whatever baggage, positive or negative, that comes with this identity in their social milieu" (275). He goes on to say that the unwanted social interactions that can come with being vegan (the unrelenting questioning from friends, family, peers, and strangers) are potentially more difficult for children than for adults (275–6). Given that young people are still developing emotionally and learning social skills, this assertion is plausible. After discussing evidence of the social hardships of being vegan, Hunt says, "It seems reasonable to believe from this evidence that in many social settings the vegan child is *ceteris paribus* [all other things being equal] more likely to face bullying or other negative social interactions than the non-vegan child" (276). Hunt leaves out discussion of the ways that intersecting identities can complicate life for vegan children. Like others, some vegan children are people of color, some are Jewish, some are Muslim, some are gender diverse, and some live with disabilities or neurodivergence. More research should be done on how intersecting identities impact vegan young people and also whether vegan young people are in fact worse off from a social standpoint than their nonvegan peers who are members of marginalized groups. In any case, Hunt's point that vegan children are subjected to considerable social cruelty is worth taking seriously even if it turns out to be the case that vegan children are just as badly off as their nonvegan but nevertheless "different" peers.

Carlo Alvaro disagrees with Hunt's depiction of the hardships of vegan childhood. He makes several points in response to the notion that vegan children

[12]Marcus William Hunt cites a study where vegans were evaluated more harshly by omnivores than LGBTQ and Black people, adding that only drug addicts were evaluated more negatively than vegans (2019b, 276). If this study is accurate then we certainly are sending vegan young people into an extremely hostile world.

are left out of cultural festivals, birthday parties, and other social events. Alvaro's claims are as follows:

1. Given the variety of diets people have, it is unlikely that the vegan child is the only person needing an accommodation at an event involving eating;
2. "Birds of a feather flock together"—it's likely vegan parents will socialize with other vegan people/families;
3. Religious holidays are about celebrating holidays together and not about food;
4. Children do not attend social events to eat, they attend to socialize (2019, 654–7).

Alvaro's responses to Hunt's concerns about the negative social consequences for vegan children are paradigmatic of the kind of willful dismissal that can happen in the literature on this topic. I would love to agree with Alvaro, but experience tells me otherwise. He is correct that there is a plurality of dietary restrictions afoot in the world, but the difference between the child with celiac who cannot eat gluten for medical reasons and the vegan child is that the latter is vegan by choice—in this case their parents'. Some vegans find those with medical dietary restrictions are treated better in social situations than those with ethical dietary restrictions (Edwards 2013, 119). Focusing on the health benefits of veganism over ethical considerations is one face-saving technique that is offered as a way for vegans to manage social situations (Greenebaum 2012). I cannot count the number of times someone has said some version of "you *can* eat it; you *choose* not to" when I have turned down an offer of food on vegan grounds. Not being alone in needing a dietary accommodation very rarely shielded my son from unwanted attention about his veganism.[13] Moreover, that there are children who cannot consume dairy or gluten does not protect the vegan child from ridicule when their parents will not let them attend the field trip to the zoo or the community's annual Thanksgiving turkey hunt.

Regarding #2, this just is not true for some vegan families. Depending on where you live, what people you encounter in life, and so forth, you may very well not have a social circle with much vegan representation. I am an ecofeminist vegan scholar, and I have struggled to put together a local social group of vegans. Moreover, even if we are lucky enough to surround ourselves with people who share our vegan values, that will not protect our children from social cruelties

[13]Alvaro suggests that "there is no reason why a child who chooses to avoid eating animal flesh for ethical reasons should identify himself or herself as a vegan"; they can instead say they avoid animal flesh due to allergies or religious beliefs (2019, 654). I suspect whether a child is interested in or capable of demurring in these ways will be up to the disposition of the individual child. We ought not to assume that lying or obfuscating is simply what a child would or should do when asked about their eating practices.

when they are at school, camp, or other venues populated with people from outside that social group. Based on my arguments about the centrality of food to cultural and community traditions, it will not come as a surprise that I find #3 to be false. Certainly, holiday gatherings are about spending time together, but that time is often centered on sharing culturally or familially meaningful foods. Finally, with respect to #4 and whether for children social events are about socializing and not food, this will largely depend on the individual child. To generalize about how children approach socializing and food in this way when considering the social well-being of young vegan people is dangerous. I am sympathetic to Alvaro in that I agree that Hunt's arguments against vegan parenting are not compelling, and I am grateful for the many points he articulates about why that is so. These claims about the realities for vegan children, however, are a problematic denial of the lived experience of some set of those children. Before turning to the more compelling parts of Alvaro's argument, I want to add a few more potential social consequences for children raised vegan.

First, as Safran Foer notes, vegan young people may be perceived as less socially sensitive or aware than their carnist peers (2007, 32), which can make life more challenging for them. He highlights the irony of this reality when he says, "The utterly insensitive omnivore—'I'm easy; I'll eat anything'—can appear more socially sensitive than the individual who tries to eat in a way that is good for society" (ibid.). Simply by virtue of living according to values that express compassion and care for others, the vegan can seem less socially aware or attuned to social norms. In her phenomenological account of living as a vegetarian child in a carnist community, Sachi Edwards discusses the veg*n child as an outsider, navigating complex social situations and food access on their own (Edwards 2013, 114). Once vegan children begin school, summer camps, extracurricular activities, and so forth they are indeed on their own to navigate the often challenging logistical and relational dynamics of their veganism. Parents can send snacks, talk with their teachers/counselors/group leaders, and plan for logistical issues as much as possible but in the end when we are not with them, our children must fend for themselves in a world often hostile to veganism. This is true of other childhood issues as well, of course. If our child has amblyopia and must wear an eye patch all day, they are also left navigating the social consequences of difference and whatever physical limitations occur as a result of the patching. This is true for many other aspects of youth (orthodonture, injuries, physical differences, acne, etc.). Veganism may present more of a challenge than these other challenges of youth because veganism is chosen rather than the result of biology or bad luck.[14] Finally, as discussed in Chapter 4 carnists sometimes view vegans as killjoys

[14]Of course, the vegan child before a certain age does not *choose* their veganism, but that is not how it is perceived by other young people. For example, my child was often encouraged just to eat whatever nonvegan food was there since he wasn't allergic and thus technically had a choice.

(Twine 2014). Even when vegans refrain from expounding on any vegan beliefs at all, nonvegans say and do things indicating they experience the vegan as a killjoy who challenges their unquestioned norms and ruins their fun. Being pegged as the killjoy at meals and decisions about buying tickets to concerts at the zoo, and so forth is difficult enough for adults who choose to be vegan. For young people, it can be frighteningly lonely and socially ostracizing. Vegaphobia can have a deep impact on young people raised as vegans.

In their research on what they call "independent vegetarians," Karen Hussar and Paul L. Harris make the interesting observation that while independent vegetarian young people give moral reasons for eating the way they do, their carnist peers do not. The latter cite nonmoral reasons for their food choices (e.g., personal considerations around taste) (2010, 633–9). Though Hussar and Harris do not make this assertion, I wonder if one reason children raised veg*n can be the subject of so much social cruelty is that their carnist peers do not understand or see the issue of how we treat animals as moral at all. When the vegan child introduces morality into the discussion, say when asked why they will not go to the zoo or eat the "chicken fingers," perhaps their peers are confused by the moral content of that response having never thought about our relationships with animals as a moral issue at all when it comes to food and entertainment.

I have laid out quite a sad story about the potential social cruelties associated with a vegan-by-parental-choice childhood. I by no means wish to suggest that all vegan children experience all or even some of these cruelties. It is important, however, to note that there is the potential for significant social issues for young people raised vegan and that those issues cannot always be solved by bringing vegan cupcakes for the class or vegan pizza to a birthday party as so much of the literature on vegan parenting suggests. Logistical support is of course vital for vegan parenting, and that support can translate at times into social support. It does not, however, help with social stigma in many cases or the feeling of being an outsider or being labeled a killjoy. One might conclude from this discussion that it is morally wrong to raise one's child as a vegan due to the potential social consequences for them. This is the conclusion Hunt defends (2019b). Hunt's argument is two-pronged, citing concerns about both physical and social well-being. Since we are setting aside the former for the purposes of this chapter, I will just note that the latter concerns are similar to what I have articulated earlier regarding the possible social impacts on young people for being raised vegan. He does note that the social impacts are contingent, not necessary, harms of childhood veganism (275). In other words, there is nothing about the social cruelties others enact on vegan young people that make them a necessary part of life. The world could just as easily have been organized in a way such that veganism was the norm or at least less of a social attractive nuisance. This observation softens his conclusion to the notion that "raising *some* children on a vegan diet bears a risk of harm to their well-being" and that "*some* parents have pro tanto moral reason to not raise their child on a vegan diet" (279). Hunt, however, goes on to say that most parents should not believe themselves to be a special case capable of thwarting all the potential risks that await their children (ibid.). For Hunt, in most cases there are moral reasons not to raise vegan children due to harms to their well-being.

This is the wrong conclusion to draw. Again, setting the nutritional concerns aside, there is a good case to be made that it is morally permissible to raise vegan children despite concerns about their social well-being. I noted earlier that Alvaro is too quick to dismiss concerns about potential social harms to vegan children, but that he makes convincing arguments against Hunt's conclusion that we ought not to "saddle" our children with veganism. Alvaro avers, for example, that even where there are challenges one does not generally give up an important position because of practical concerns:

> It is peculiar to suggest that vegan parents should give up their deepest moral convictions and choose not to raise their children on a vegan diet just to avoid uncomfortable questions or avoid bringing snacks to birthday parties. It is like saying that there is a pro tanto moral reason for Jain parents who live in the US to not raise their child as a Jain because Christianity is the prevalent religion and children may be questioned and ridiculed by others. A moral conviction such as ethical veganism should not be bargained with or given up for practical reasons. (654)

Hunt does, indeed, linger rather a long time on the logistical considerations involved in vegan parenting (e.g., the extra labor of bringing vegan-appropriate foods to social gatherings). Here, though, Alvaro is also getting at the broader point about social harms and it is fair to note that there are numerous minority lifestyles, some chosen and some not, that one would not shy away from because they pose some potential social harm for one's children.

Fischer and Fredericks also reject the idea that concerns about social well-being render vegan parenting a morally questionable choice. They note that the desire for caregivers to spare their young charges from social burdens does not result in the caregivers supporting smoking or young people sexually objectifying themselves to fit in (25–6). Recall that they argue for the strong conclusion that it is not merely morally justified to raise vegan children but morally required. Hence, this observation about not supporting young people in smoking is important for their view not only because of concerns about social harms resulting from being different but also because like smoking they take raising carnist children to be harmful and therefore immoral. I am sympathetic to their view that vegan caregiving is a moral requirement but will not defend it here. Instead, I want to just observe that it is true that we do not generally support our children in avoiding social pressures by doing the wrong thing. Ethical vegans believe that supporting animal agriculture and animal-based entertainment and recreation is morally wrong. Just as we do not raise our children to shoplift lest they suffer socially with their shoplifting-enthusiast friends, we do not raise them to be carnists and speciesists.

In this way, veganism is like other family values centered on ideas of what it means to be a compassionate, caring, respectful, and ethical person. It is true that veganism is a minority view of what that all means but so were many other stances at various times in human history (abolitionism, environmentalism, concern for women's rights, etc.).[15] Insofar as a values system bends toward justice, care, and compassion I do not see how it can be wrong to introduce to young people on the grounds it can make life more challenging for them.

Alvaro states that "a vegan diet in no way harm's a child's social life" (2019, 659). This just seems false to me based on experience with my own child and the reports of other vegan parents online and in books. What is lacking in Alvaro's account is attention to relationality and care. While conclusions like Hunt's are too strong, we cannot simply will away the potential social harms veganism may bring to our children. There is a middle ground between concluding that vegan parenting is immoral based on social harms and concluding that no harms occur. They do occur and the question we are interested in concerns what vegan parents owe our children in light of that fact.

The answer is that we owe them any kind of appropriate protection and mitigation we can provide, an empathetic presence, and an ability to be flexible when they make mistakes or deliberately make choices to engage in behaviors that do not reflect the family's vegan values. This may sound facile, but when taken seriously there is nothing simplistic about it. It is just true that in raising vegan children, vegan parents must take on the additional labor of providing logistical support around food. By this I mean alternatives for animal-based foods for school, social events, and so forth. It is the same labor required of parents raising their children with religiously determined minority diets. We must hone the ability to think ahead, predict potential areas of exclusion or lack of nourishing options, and plan accordingly. We must make the phone calls to other parents offering to bring food and so forth. In short, we must do all the things suggested for logistical support in the literature about vegan parenting. In doing so, we mitigate some of the social isolation and feeling of exclusion but only some. Thus, the requirement to be an empathetic presence, which I take up later in the section on relational moral repair.

Another answer to the question of how to mitigate the potential social harms of veganism on our children lies not with parents but with social structures and communities. Fischer and Fredericks point to the duty governments and other structural organizations have to support vegan caregivers by providing plant-based

---

[15]Sadly, many of these views remain minority positions and, indeed, as I write are being attacked by the US federal government.

foods in settings like school cafeterias, hospitals, and community events (24). They further note the necessity to stop the campaigns showing how happy cows are asking to be eaten, for example (ibid.). Oscar Horta makes the point that governments ought not to force citizens to engage in animal exploitation.[16] We might also question, as Horta does, the practice of the government subsidizing and supporting animal-exploiting industries, thus making it more challenging for schools and other institutions serving children to make alternative, vegan-friendly, decisions (2018). In situations where parents have the bandwidth to advocate on behalf of structural changes, they should do so.

Teachers and other individuals working with young people can support vegan youth and their families by normalizing vegan values. Rare is the young person who can tell the difference between a vegan cupcake and a nonvegan one. Why not suggest that everyone bring vegan desserts to class for birthdays when doing so is logistically and financially feasible? When a vegan family voices discomfort with a field trip to the zoo, rather than responding with a request to let the child fit in with the other children by attending, why not have a conversation with the family and understand better their objections. This is what happened with my son's kindergarten teacher after I pushed back on her request that I just let him be one of the gang. Eventually we reached a compromise where my son went to the zoo with his class but only after I did a community of inquiry-style discussion with the children about the zoo and how we might ask questions about it. I also came along as a chaperone and was allowed to bring another animal studies colleague with me. That was a generous solution and perhaps one unavailable to parents without a PhD in philosophy and experience running philosophical sessions with young people. With that in mind, teachers and schools could rethink their relationships with zoos and other industries that exploit animals, instead teaching what actual conservation and stewardship of animal others looks like.

If the structures and systems our children encounter in the world were open to some adjustment, the burden of mitigating social cruelties for our vegan children would not fall on children and parents alone. Educational institutions should rethink their relationships with zoos and aquariums on both moral and educational grounds. Governments and school systems should ask important questions about the availability of plant-based foods in their programs. Communities should welcome expanding options at public events—barbeques, national holiday celebrations, concerts, sporting events, and so forth. In a world where veganism is less marginalized in general, vegan children will experience fewer instances of social cruelty or unwelcome attention.

In this section I have concentrated on vegan children's social well-being in the public arena (schools) and parts of the private arena (birthday parties

[16]He cites the example of the Faroe Islands where "failing to report a whale sighting is illegal and heavily punished, as the whaling industry is very important in this country" (2018, 17).

and community events). I have noted that some scholars theorizing about vegan parenting err by believing the social harms of a vegan upbringing are so overwhelming as to make them unethical to foist on our children. Others err in defending vegan parenting against worries about social harms by insisting those harms either do not exist or, if they do, are completely manageable through logistical actions like providing vegan alternatives for our children. I hope I have shown that neither of these responses is warranted. We can mitigate the potential social harms to vegan children's well-being by thinking relationally and structurally. In doing so, we neither need to give up sharing vegan values with our children nor ignore the very real hardships they might face as young vegans in a carnist and speciesist world.[17] In the next section, I focus on the private arena by highlighting the potential harms to relational well-being for vegan children that can occur specifically in familial relationships. I conclude the chapter with a discussion of the potential for compromise and how relational moral attention can help us approach the moral questions that arise in raising vegan children.

4.2 Harms to Familial Relationships and Connections

In Chapter 4, I focused on the general kinds of moral dilemmas faced primarily by adult vegans when their values regarding animals conflict with familial and communal traditions and norms involving consuming animal flesh. Many of those considerations apply here, though I will not repeat them. Instead, I will add to what was said there by focusing on what is at stake for vegan children in their relationships with carnist/speciesist family members and cultural or religious traditions.[18] This is important because these morally salient issues are left out of much of the discussion about raising vegan children. Amato and Partridge note that people transitioning to vegetarianism usually anticipate logistical issues (food shopping, learning new recipes, etc.) but not the impact on relationships (175). I believe this is true of some of us who opt to raise our children to share our vegan values. We may know challenges lie ahead but fail to fully appreciate the potential impact of that decision on our children's relationships with other family members.

Impacts on vegan children's familial relationships can originate in differences about food values as well as differences over familial and cultural traditions centered on animal-based ritual, entertainment, or recreation (e.g., ritualized animal slaughter, hunting, bullfighting, attending the rodeo, a visit to Sea World

[17] There are of course pockets of the world that are not carnist or at least not to the same extent as many industrialized nations. Vegans in those areas may face fewer or different hardships.

[18] When I refer to "carnist/speciesist family members" I mean grandparents, aunts, uncles, cousins, and so forth. I do not have in mind parental relationships where one parent is vegan and the other is not or sibling relationships where, for whatever reason, one sibling is raised vegan while the other is not.

or the zoo, fishing, clamming, etc.). The impacts may occur due to the parents' refusing to allow their child to participate in an activity or meal/portion of a meal when the children are young or when the young person themself refuses to participate. Nonparticipation in cultural and familial traditions can result in anger, hurt, frustration, bullying, and teasing by extended family members (Roth 2005, 192). On the child's side, even without expressions of hurt and aggression from family, nonparticipation can result in feeling less a part of the group, less deeply connected, and even less liked. Feeling like an outsider with one's own family at a young age can be deeply sad, frightening even (Edwards 113). This is further compounded when a young person has an intersecting identity that also renders them "on the outside" as when they are the only out LGBTQ+ person, neurodivergent person, or person with a disability in the family. I have some insight into what a gender queer vegan child can experience when present at a family's carnist and heteronormative gatherings. Bearing their sense of isolation and rejection is hard on a parent's heart, though not as hard as it must be for the child themselves to feel that way.

Vegetarians, as LuAnne Roth notes, can be seen as "downright un-family like" (187). This is one thing when one has all the coping and communications skills of a mature adult but quite another when one is a young child or adolescent. Roth goes on to ask the question of whether refusing traditional foods affects the ability to belong to a family:

> Because the sharing of food enables the family to maintain communitas, does *refusing* to eat some symbolically laden food item affect one's ability to belong to that family? It would appear that this very question is a part of what is negotiated via these conflicts and is the root of why, in some cases, the change is taken to be a threat to family foodways and hence a threat to familial identity itself. (188)

Feeling "un-family like" can be a badge of honor for some of us as we age, but it is rarely so for the very young.[19] With young children and early adolescents the situation is likely quite different as belonging is central to identity formation and a sense of safety, particularly when one's social world is largely focused on family relationships.

Families may struggle more to accept veganism because it is a choice rather than an unfortunate biological fact like food allergies. In discussing adults who transition

---

[19]Amato and Partridge quote a study participant who says, "I do not accept dinner invitations with family members, especially holiday dinners where a dead bird will occupy the center of the table. I feel no remorse or apology for this. My family doesn't like it, but I don't particularly like to have violence on the table" (192). This is the sort of position that can feel quite powerful when one has chosen vegan values and is old enough to understand how to navigate healthy boundaries.

to veganism, Roth notes that such a transition might disrupt the family's sense of homeostasis (Roth, 193). This same issue is often at stake upon the introduction of a young vegan into the family mix. Though the family may have adjusted with some effort to adult vegans, a vegan child may prove even more challenging. Family may struggle because veganism is seen as indicative of a rupture with other long-held family values (Roth, 142). Often, infants enter families with much anticipation and love, with a sense of a fresh start and opportunity to forge new connections. These hopes and expectations may become frayed or completely unravel when family members hear the news of the baby's veganism. Grandparents sometimes see new grandchildren as an opportunity to bring themselves to a loved one in a way they expect will be welcomed and cherished. They may believe that they have more of a chance to share themselves with this child than they had with their own children given the burdens of raising children, financial hardships, relational strains, and so forth. Again, these hopes can be dashed by the news that the baby's parents will raise a vegan child. Grandparents and other important family members may worry they will never share values with their new family member, that eventually that child will grow into an adolescent who sees them as immoral for their carnist and speciesist values. In an ideal world, these burdens would not be children's to bear but adults vary in their emotional intelligence and maturity as well as their ability to tolerate difference or discomfort. In some families, sadly, vegan children will feel the repercussions of the family members' dashed hopes.

Family members might also struggle with a vegan child in the family for some of the same reasons they struggle with vegan adults. They might feel annoyance at the inconvenience of accommodating the dietary and recreational needs of a vegan young person. We know from anecdotal evidence and research that important holidays can be a particularly difficult time for vegans and their carnist families (Amato and Partridge, 192–3; Lindstrom 2018, 45). We know, too, that traditions rooted in food and long-standing practices present significant challenges for vegans and their carnist families.[20] All of these challenges and the emotions that reverberate through the family as a result may be felt by the vegan child, only they do not necessarily have the skills or maturity to organize those reverberations in the right way, leaving them to wonder whether they are responsible for all the dissonance they feel around them.

In her discussion of adult vegetarians, Edwards notes the issue of how being unable to share in a meal with others can make one question how to make connections. In her study, some participants worried about "how their personal food choices would impact their ability to build new relationships, sustain current relationships, and adequately share meals with, host, or be hosted by, non-vegetarians" (2013, 123). She notes, further, that some of the participants

[20]See Chapter 4.

experience what are supposed to be "joyous" occasions instead as "moments that accentuate how different their relationship with food is from those who are not vegetarian" (ibid.). Roth observes that, in disrupting long-held family values and traditions, the vegetarian's values can be seen as representing a "radical, subversive ideology to their families" (194). This is in part why family members sometimes push back with such force against the vegetarian in their midst; they resist with everything they have the winds of change that are blowing through their dining rooms (ibid.).

It is naïve to think that being a child will protect someone from experiencing the blowback from these feelings and beliefs. Some children will not experience a negative impact from the way their extended families respond to their veganism, but certainly some do. Building relationships with important family members with whom you do not share values around food and activities is difficult enough as an adult, but for children who came into the world without any of the common ground we adults often share with our families it is daunting. Moreover, as Hunt rightly notes, when you are young and family members tell you there is something weird or wrong with your practices, unpleasant feelings can result (Hunt 2019b, 277). After a certain age, when children understand their veganism as a moral stance, it might be disorienting for them to view others in their lives as committing moral wrongdoing (ibid.).

Part of what is coming to light here is the difference between how those who transition to veganism are situated compared to those who are vegan since birth or very early in childhood. I noticed this in my own case. I transitioned to veganism at sixteen, and it certainly was disruptive to my family. There was much consternation over refusing to eat the traditional foods we all once shared and how my values conflicted with everyone else's. I did not, however, feel on the outside of the family any more than I already did. My veganism did not impact my relationship-*building* because those relationships were already built. It impacted my *existing* relationships to be sure, but that impact was somewhat mitigated by the fact that I had once been fully (mostly?) one of them. Alternatively, my son was vegan from birth, and I have seen the ways that impacted him in building some family relationships. In some sense, he was always on the outside, never quite at one with everyone else. He never ate the chicken soup or tried the gefilte fish (or communed as many Jews under eighty-years-old do about how disgusting it is). He came into the world a brand-new entity as all infants do, but he also came into it with some separation. Efforts were made to bridge that separation—foods were prepared that he could share, other grounds for commonality were sought, and mutual affection and care went a long way toward bringing him into the fold. It would be wrong, though, to say that this went without a hitch or that his ability to forge relationships with important family members was not hampered by him starting life in such a different place ethically than everyone else inhabited. In their research, Amato and Partridge observe that children raised as vegetarians generally do well, that "children are resilient and adapt to a vegetarian diet and lifestyle without major problems" (238). This claim is based, however, on the reports of their parents reflecting on their children now that they are adults. I wonder if the claims would be so positive if the children-now-adults were speaking for themselves.

Of course, some families and communities are welcoming to vegan children, make space for difference, and even celebrate the opportunity to learn something new and engage in novel ways (Amato and Partridge 1989, 193). Moreover, vegan children can live happy and joyous childhoods even if their extended family is occasionally unkind or rude about their veganism. There are many opportunities for vegan children to connect with their families over other interests. What I highlight here, however, is that the literature on vegan parenting often glosses over the relational complexities we introduce into our children's lives by raising them vegan and the ethical implications of those complexities. Do we wrong our children when we raise them with values (in this case vegan values) that run counter to those of our extended families? Is it ethically permissible for parents to potentially risk their children's familial well-being in service of their own moral commitments? I answer these questions in the following sections, paying particular attention to questions of compromise and the importance of relational moral attention.

5 Compromise

Considering the potential for relational harm to children raised as vegans, one might reasonably ask whether there is room for some compromise in vegan values in service of avoiding those relational harms. For example, perhaps we should expect vegan caregivers to make exceptions for culturally and familially important foods and food traditions. Perhaps vegan parents should let their children go fishing with their grandparents who are avid anglers or to the rodeo with their bull-riding uncles.

There is a small philosophical literature on whether vegan parents should compromise (Alvaro 2020; Hunt 2019a; Millburn 2021, 2022). This literature, however, is focused on what should happen when parents disagree with one another rather than relational considerations with other loved ones. These discussions center on what two people should do when one believes in raising their child vegan and the other does not. This is an interesting question, to be sure, but what interests us here is whether there should be compromise in service of helping one's child(ren) build and maintain relationships of love and care with extended family members and important friends.[21] It is worth keeping in mind that there may be

[21]With "important friends" I have in mind the parents' important friends who often function as chosen family for themselves and their children.

different moral considerations involved in compromising around food versus around activities (I will return to this later). I begin here by laying out the reasons for and against compromise in the literature on disagreements between parents regarding whether to raise their children as vegans. This will help us get a general sense of how to think about compromise beyond the intraparent relationship.

William Marcus Hunt argues that compromise is permissible and indeed crucial in relationships between parents who disagree regarding whether to raise vegan children (Hunt 2019a). He begins by differentiating compromise from consensus and capitulation. In consensus, the parties in conflict "reach an agreement over which commitments are best/true," whereas in capitulation, "one party unilaterally decides to abandon any instantiation of their commitments in a shared policy" (2–3). Unlike consensus and capitulation, compromise involves agreeing to a state of affairs where both parties agree "to do something other than what they believed themselves to have the most reason to do *ex ante* to the compromise" (2). In a compromise, then, all parties cede some ground in service of coming to an agreement workable for all. Hunt notes that the coparenting relationship particularly calls for compromise because, at least in most cases, each coparent "bears a morally symmetrical relation to the same child" (4). This point will emerge again in this section when we think about cases of compromise with loved ones where the relation to the same child is morally asymmetrical (e.g., the child's parents as compared to the child's grandparents—the parent's moral responsibility to and for the child is greater than that of the grandparent in most cases). Hunt's argument is that in order to respect the parental authority of both parents, compromise is necessary (9). He believes that veganism lends itself to compromise because it offers opportunities for "intermediate policies" (15). There are situations where no scale of intermediate policies is available. Hunt gives the example of raising children in two religions. He says you can expose children to two religions, but "raising a child as both a Hindu and a Muslim doesn't seem possible" (ibid.). Whether or not that example is apt, it does seem like Hunt is on to something with the idea that veganism does offer opportunities for intermediate policies depending on how one defines veganism. As Hunt puts it,

> We can see that the child who eats a diet that is plant-based save for three servings of fish a week is in an important respect an intermediate case between the child whose diets is entirely plant-based and the child who eats veal every day, and likewise the [Mormon] child who sometimes drinks hot tea but is frequently told stories acclaiming Joseph Smith is an intermediate case between the child who is told these stories and not given hot tea and the child who has never heard of Joseph Smith and drinks hot tea all day. (16)

Whether the child who eats fish thrice weekly is still a vegan, however, will depend on one's conception of veganism. Narrowly construed, veganism does not allow for eating animal flesh whether monthly, weekly, or yearly. If one thinks of veganism differently, then there could be intermediate policies that are acceptable opportunities for compromise.[22]

Josh Millburn argues against compromise between vegan coparents. Following Regan's position that animal rights are a matter of justice, Millburn notes that "a failure to respect the demands of justice must be looked upon harshly. Any compromise on justice will be a tragedy, to be undertaken only in the most regrettable circumstances" (2022, 284). Hence, if one thinks of animal rights as a question of justice, compromise is impossible except in extreme cases. He notes that vegans who think of animal rights as a matter of justice "should be very reluctant to enter into a co-parenting relationship with someone unprepared to raise children as vegans" (291). This is a helpful point in the realm of vegan coparenting since who you coparent with will certainly determine to some extent what disagreements in values arise. It is not possible, however, to make a preemptive strike like that in the case of relationships with your child's future grandparents, aunts, uncles, and other family or friends. Perhaps strictly speaking it is *possible* in some cases to do just that; one could break up a loving relationship where two vegans agree to raise vegan children, but one set of grandparents will be horrible about it on the grounds that that grandparent relationship will be too difficult to manage. This seems onerous, however, and requires foresight regarding how people will behave that is often unavailable to us.

Millburn settles on a "minimal compromise" position where one might make compromises in cases of "unusual eating" (2021, 2022). Millburn is referring to animal flesh sourced from roadkill, in vitro meat, or animal products that will be tossed out if no one else eats them (e.g., the sandwiches left over from the philosophy department's monthly meeting). In these cases, he notes, "animal rights and veganism come apart" (2021, 381). He adds, "It is legitimate to compromise over feeding children the bodies of non-sentient animals, the products of cellular agriculture, and non-vegan food that would otherwise go to waste" (ibid.). For Millburn, these are instances where justice for animals is not an issue and compromise is possible.

These cases will, of course, be extremely limited. At the moment, in vitro meat is not a widespread option though that might change in the future, as Millburn notes (388). Moreover, one would have to have access to the foods appropriate for one's culture and familial practices that can be sourced in these ways. Unless my friend Iván's father can find the dehydrated cod necessary for the traditional Easter meal

[22]Though Fischer and Fredericks argue for the obligation to raise vegan children, they note that it is within parental rights to make compromises to vegan caregiving in compelling circumstances as when important cultural or aesthetic values are at stake (29–30). I agree that parents do have the right to make such compromises. I am more interested in the question of whether it is necessary or morally appropriate to make those compromises.

in a dumpster, his bacalao a la vizcaína and the group preparation it entails will remain out of reach for his vegan grandchildren. I will add that it is challenging to imagine most people making food for their families using roadkill or dumpster options unless food scarcity is a significant issue. I am also hard-pressed to see anyone in my family serving sandwiches leftover from the philosophy department lunch meeting at a holiday event or important family gathering. That just would not be in line with the other cultural values around food and hosting. All of that said, Millburn does not claim that these minimal compromise options are widely available. He asserts only that, when they are, it opens an opportunity for compromise on the part of vegan parents regarding their children's food intake.[23]

In contrast to Hunt's pro-compromise and Millburn's minimal compromise positions, Alvaro defends a zero parental compromise stance (2020). He argues that veganism is like religion and therefore not the kind of thing that can be compromised. His argument does not apply to what he terms "flexible vegans" who are already making compromises in their veganism (478). Instead, he has in mind vegans who adhere as strongly to their vegan values as religiously devout people do to their religious values. Unlike Hunt, who sees eschewing consumption of animal products as part of veganism, Alvaro takes the rejection of flesh-based foods as a "the core doctrine of veganism" and adds that "a vegan who intentionally eats animal products even once a year is by definition not a vegan" (480). I disagree with the second part of his claim considering some vegans will face food scarcity issues, lack of access to plant-based options, and so on, and I do not want to rule them out of identifying as vegans.[24] I do agree, however, that rejecting consumption of animal products is a central tenant of veganism. Compromising on that tenet does indeed seem impossible for most vegans outside of the most extreme conditions. This harkens back to Safran Foer's grandmother refusing to eat nonkosher meat even though she was starving. If certain norms and values guide your life because you take them to be the correct way to live and a manifestation of who you are as a person, compromising on those values would be exceptionally distressful. Alvaro does not ground veganism in a rights framework, so does not accept Millburn's minimal compromise position (481). He notes that there may be some room for compromise around in vitro meat, but he believes there are virtue-based reasons to reject that option (2019a, 2019b). Alvaro summarizes his zero-compromise position as follows:

> Consider the suggestion of regarding ethical veganism as more than a simple ethical view, but rather as a religion, one whose principal values are

---

[23]Whether these "unusual eating" options are ones a particular vegan will avail themselves of will depend largely on the moral underpinnings of their vegan values. Some ecofeminist vegans and virtue-based vegans like Alvaro, for example, would not find these options fit with their values.

[24]Food Empowerment Project, "Food Deserts*."

> non-violence, integrity of character, and aesthetic beauty, it is clear that there is no room for compromise. As such, there can be no room for compromise, whether it be three servings of fish per week or roadkill or cockroaches or ants. Consequently, there is no way that a co-parent could compromise without thereby attacking his or her ethical aesthetic, gustatory, and religious (as I proposed that ethical veganism be regarded as a religion or quasi-religion) convictions. (493)

I am sympathetic to Alvaro's point here. It is true that when one is committed to nonviolence and the integrity of one's moral character, it seems impossible to make compromises. This is true whether we are talking about veganism or a moral position against stealing. I once watched mortified as my grandfather gleefully removed a box of donuts from a store shelf, ate the donuts he wanted while shopping, then replaced the box on the shelf before paying for his other items. I am hard-pressed to imagine a world in which I allow my son to partake in that activity in service of building a relationship with my grandfather. I similarly would not permit my child to attend a rally of white supremacists even if my action deprived him of an opportunity to connect in the deepest possible way with his racist grandparent. Alvaro makes a strong case for zero compromise, and his position is echoed by some vegan parents who will not make compromises on their children's behalf (Amato and Partridge 232).

That said, Alvaro does not address the question of competing values. He writes as though vegans' sole value system is that of veganism. If ethical vegans' value systems include commitments to love, care, and respect for the cultural and religious values of our families and communities, then they will face a dilemma regarding compromise.[25] Is it really true that compromise is always unavailable to an ethical vegan? Certainly, their moral distress will be significant in the face of such deliberations, but could the ethical vegan parent be open to some compromise in service of other values? Since Alvaro defines the vegan who eats animal-based foods once a year out of being vegan, this is likely not a difficult question for him. As I reject the idea of defining veganism in such a rigid way, this remains a live question in my view.

The vegan parent's position becomes particularly complex when we consider legitimate concerns about how making compromises might impact our children's learning about moral stances. In response to the question "Can [your children] eat a single nonvegan cupcake or one slice of pizza?" at a special event, Robyn

---

[25]For example, a person raised in the Jain community with a commitment to ahimsa might feel as though compromising veganism on some occasions is part of that commitment. They might believe that one does harm to hosts when rejecting their food, which conflicts with the Jain practice of minimizing harm. Alternatively, they might not find that kind of harm to hosts compelling and adhere instead to their veganism (Tejas Mehta, personal communication, November 18, 2025). People from within the same religious or cultural communities may bring different approaches to competing values.

Moore, interviewed in Lindstrom's book, describes her zero-compromise policy as follows:

> No! I think allowing kids to have nonvegan foods once in a while sends the wrong message. It's like dropping your morals at the door and picking them back up after the party. It doesn't make sense. Especially at parties or special events, which is worse because it sets up the issue as "because we're at this special celebration, you get to do something special like have a nonvegan treat." It sends a mixed message—a nonvegan treat becomes a positive reward. It downplays the seriousness and importance of why our family is choosing this lifestyle. … We teach our children to make decisions on compassion, not convenience. (60)

Robyn Moore hits upon a genuine difficulty for vegan parents; we do not want to teach our children that moral commitments are to be jettisoned whenever it is convenient for us. The message cannot be that we care about the animals and humans impacted in the food system but that we set all that aside because the pizza looks especially delicious at our friends' gathering or because our friends' Persian kebab smells so good. Part of providing a moral education to one's children is demonstrating that moral principles do not give way to convenience.

That said, convenience is not the only competing value that arises in vegan parenting. Compromising on veganism because it is more convenient to do so is problematic. What, though, about compromising in the face of important relationships and our children's ability to connect to the larger familial and cultural communities around them? These considerations go well beyond convenience to concerns about identity, connection, relationships, love, care, and belonging.

Ecofeminism allows us to approach the difficult questions surrounding compromise with attention to context and nuance. One piece of that context is what makes up the ethical foundation of a family's veganism. If the ethical underpinning of their veganism is a utilitarian or consequentialist calculus, then Millburn's minimal compromise approach or even Hunt's pro-compromise approach might feel acceptable. Such a family might conclude that the harm has already been done to the chickens in the soup; they cannot prevent that from happening as it already happened. Hence, eating Grandma's chicken soup yearly at Rosh Hashannah could be seen as a reasonable balance between vegan values and values around identity, love, care, and belonging. If the ethical underpinning of their veganism is rooted in animal rights, then compromise may be less available. If the ethical underpinning is a pluralistic approach including considerations of rights, virtue, care, compassion, and so forth then compromise may be possible. Whether or not that is true will depend on other features of the context.

For example, considerations around the status of the specific child (or children) in question are highly relevant to these considerations. Is the child neurodivergent in some way that renders compromise particularly distressing or easy? Is the child different from other family members in some way that renders them vulnerable to other difficulties in developing a sense of belonging or connection with their relatives and cultural community. Parenting a child who identifies as LGBTQ+, for example, might complicate how much they can tolerate being differentiated from others in their family and community through their veganism. Would strictly adhering to veganism on special occasions make their already vulnerable situation worse? Would they find it even more challenging to connect to their aunts, uncles, cousins, and important community members if food on special occasions underscored their difference from others even more and added more distance to an already wide chasm? What is the relationship between the parents and other members of the family or community? Are these relationships where communication and working through these issues together are possible? Are methods of mitigation available? These questions and more about the specific child in question, and the parents' relationship with their extended family will strongly influence whether or how to compromise.

Another relevant feature of the context is whether the parents have the skills to have complex conversations about the question of compromise with their children. Clearly, those conversations will not be possible in the very early stages of childhood, but young children are capable of wondering about and discussing deep philosophical questions. If the parents are equipped to do so, their children may be able to think about the nature of compromise, its role in morality, and what they think is right or wrong much earlier than most adults give them credit for. These conversations can play a key role in both making decisions about compromise and building children's autonomy.

One more piece of the context regarding compromise is whether the situation in question involves eating or an activity. For example, one might consider compromise around their children eating special foods where they have already been prepared and one's objection to their presence at the gathering did not result in changes in the menu. Allowing one's child to go to the zoo, hunt or fish with the rest of the family, or participate in the family's tradition of attending the rodeo is different. This came up in the conversation about recreational hunting in Chapter 5. There is a different moral valence to situations where the harm to the animal has already been done and where the activity itself involves supporting an exploitative industry with one's money (e.g., zoo admission) or harming or killing an animal who would otherwise remain unharmed or living. The bull in the rodeo will of course be harmed whether one's child attends the rodeo or not but paying for that as a form of entertainment supports the rodeo and attending sends the message to those running the rodeo, the press covering the rodeo, and so on that they have the support of another generation. Moreover, vegan children may be particularly distressed by the violence, exploitation, and conditions of captivity animals face in these activities. Compromise may be less available in the case of activities than in the case of special foods.

Finally, a contextual approach to these questions will observe that not all conflicts are created equally. As Safran Foer notes, "It stinks to not eat food that was prepared for you … but how much does it stink?" "The relative importance of ethical eating and table fellowship will be different in different situations (declining my grandmother's chicken with carrots is different from passing on microwaved buffalo wings" (2009, 55). For each of us there will be differences in the relative importance of different foods and, I will add, different relationships. Assessing those relative importances and the qualities of different relationships can influence how we think about the potential for compromise in the face of a particular dilemma.

As we are thinking relationally about these conflicts of interest between obligations to animals and relationships of love and care, it bears mentioning that another important contextual element is whether relational moral attention is possible. As vegan parents make decisions about when, if ever, to compromise on their child's veganism in service of creating, maintaining, or supporting relationships of love and care, identity in particular religious or ethnic groups, and so forth, they might consider the specifics of the relationships (including their relationship with their child) and what, if any, opportunities for relational moral attention are or could be available. There may be no such opportunities as when a loved one faces a terminal illness, and we gather for her last Rosh Hashannah and last batch of chicken soup. Alternatively, there may be many opportunities for repair as well as a variety of stops along the continuum between zero opportunities and many. This information will need to play a role in decision-making regarding how to move forward. With this in mind, I turn shortly to the matter of relational moral attention. Before doing so, I want to address briefly the question of whether "humane meat" and in vitro meat offer potential opportunities for compromise.

Since I discussed the question regarding "humane" and in vitro meat in Chapter 4, I will quickly say that what I wrote there applies to vegan parenting situations as well. In 2025, it is not currently the case that in vitro meat is readily available. If it were, whether a parent sees it as a viable option will depend largely on the moral underpinnings of their veganism and the importance of the particular conflict they face. Consequentialist vegans may have no difficulty in availing themselves of the option of an in vitro chicken-based chicken soup. This may not be the case for ecofeminist or virtue-based vegans. While arguably less awful an experience for animals than industrialized animal agriculture, "humane meat" still involves cruelty, commodifying animals, premature death, and human supremacy. Hence, this option very likely remains off the table for most vegan parents.

6 Relational Moral Attention

Thinking back to the previous section on potential social and familial harms to vegan children, it is perhaps clear why parents must examine the impact of their decision to raise vegan children. This is not necessarily obvious to everyone, however. Alvaro, for example, thinks "a vegan diet in no way harms a child's social life" (2019, 659), and he minimizes the potential for a vegan child's distress at cultural and familial food-based functions. He also does not address at all the issue of activities and recreation that vegan children will miss out on or need to negotiate. Raising "resistors"—what Cole and Stewart call children and their carers who move against the status quo (82)—has an impact on them. Not all impact is negative, of course. Children who are raised to ask questions about that which is taken for granted by most people are better equipped to protect themselves and those around them through their questioning. They have a deep foundation in not taking on face value that which they are meant to accept without justification or reasoning. Being raised as a resistor will also build a kind of resilience that is perhaps not as necessary for young people raised in more culturally dominant ways. Children raised vegan may also grow into adults grateful for not having been complicit in animal exploitation.[26] They may feel that, as they face the existential threat of climate change, they have already taken one important step toward mitigating their impact on the environment just by being raised vegan. They will not face the hardships of conversion to veganism or the temptations that hamper those efforts for those raised as omnivores. These are some of the potential benefits of a vegan upbringing. No doubt the list is longer. I encourage those raised vegan to think about these benefits and what role they play in their sense of character, identity, and integrity. Nearly nothing has been written to address the potential negative impacts of raising vegan children (with the exception of concerns about nutrition), however, so I take up the issue of what vegan parents may owe to their children in terms of relational moral attention in order to start this important conversation.

When our vegan children come to us with hurt feelings, worries about social cruelties, and so forth we must turn to them with empathy and care. The world is nearly always harder for them than it is for adult vegans. That truth must guide our interactions. Rather than responding to difficult emotions with information reiterating why we have the values we have, parents must offer an empathetic ear and make space for our children's feelings. We must accept the uncomfortable reality that our decision to carry vegan values to the next generation can negatively impact our beloved children. We can work those feelings through in a therapeutic

[26]Alvaro worries that adults raised without vegan values may come to feel resentment toward their parents once they are old enough to understand the truth of what happens to animals (Alvaro 2020, 493).

setting, with friends, or even in an online forum but we must resist the urge to make our uncomfortable feelings disappear by telling our children they should not feel theirs or that taking the moral high ground will somehow assuage those feelings. If we do not undertake this important work within ourselves, we risk negating their experiences and gaslighting them into thinking they cannot accurately recognize when something is actually difficult emotionally or socially. What an important gift it is to model for our children how doing the right thing sometimes does not feel easy and how we can care for ourselves in those moments.

Assuming vegan parents have avoided indoctrination and have correctly cultivated the development of their children's autonomy, relational moral attention can focus on recognizing the harms that have resulted from the family's commitment to veganism, creating space in an age-appropriate way to openly discuss the child's experience, and taking responsibility for decisions that negatively impacted our children. This might seem obvious, but I suspect many of us know how often these ways of seeing and engaging with children are neglected by parents. It is all too easy for vegan parents to fall into a sense of moral righteousness about the necessity for their family's ethical veganism and then call up that moral righteousness whenever difficulty or dissent emerges. A child asks why they cannot eat a hot dog at the annual family reunion, and the parent responds with a rehearsal of the reasons they do not eat hot dogs, for example. Though on the face of it the question could be interpreted as asking for a reminder of what grounds our vegan values, it might actually be aimed at understanding why they cannot eat a hot dog right now, in *this* moment, when the whole family is eating Uncle Tim's famous hot dogs. We cannot know the true aim of the question if we fail to adopt a stance of curiosity and epistemic humility.[27] The parent raising a resistor carries the added responsibility of approaching these situations with care, curiosity, and attentiveness. We might ask our child "Are you having some feelings about not being able to join the family in enjoying Uncle Tim's hot dogs?" or "Are you wondering why we do not eat hot dogs generally or why we can't just eat Uncle Tim's hot dogs this one time, right now in *this* moment?" This approach generates a discussion that helps everyone understand what the child is feeling and how to address it. From here, a conversation about compromise might ensue with the child expressing their thoughts about moral compromise and the relative weights of veganism and familial connection through food.

Of course, some children may not respond well to this approach or may not wish to enter a philosophical discussion of when compromise is or is not appropriate. This is fine. A contextual relational approach emphasizes understanding the people and situation before you and attending to their needs. There is no

[27]This commitment to curiosity and epistemic humility is a central feature of the Philosophy for Children methodology. Oftentimes, we adults miss what children are actually asking about because we assume we have understood them when we have not.

one-size-fits-all method that will apply to all families across time, culture, and situation. The necessity for curiosity, good listening, attentiveness, patience, and thoughtfulness does, however, apply to all situations involving vegan children. These are elements of good parenting generally, to be sure, but again where moral values that run against societal norms are at issue it is crucial to keep this necessity at the forefront of one's mind. It's all too easy for those of us raising children with minority values to simply reassert the value and turn away from the experience of our children. I have done this at times. Now that my child is a young adult, I have come to recognize the mistake with grief and regret.

Finally, vegan parents must be understanding and flexible in the face of our children's mistakes and willful noncompliance with veganism. Mistakes will happen. Our child might accidentally eat something nonvegan or they might be told something is vegan when it is not. We must respond to these mistakes with patience and kindness. Admonishing children for mistakes is just bad parenting generally, but in the case of vegan parenting it is even more troublesome because of the amount of attention and self-control veganism requires. We also must be open when our children are at an age when they make choices to eschew vegan values. This is an important exercise of their autonomy and agency. Some of us may feel disappointment or ask ourselves, "Where did I go wrong?" Again, those responses are appropriate to share with our loved ones and mental health providers. Part of developing our children's autonomy is accepting when they exercise that autonomy (so long as their actions do not present a danger to themselves or others). Instead of reacting with anger or disappointment, we might respond with curiosity.[28] We could ask questions like: "How did it feel to go to the zoo?" "How do you decide when you want to adhere to veganism and when you want to try something new?" "What was it like eating a hamburger for the first time?" Curiosity helps us learn so much about our young people. Helping them see that making choices of their own is their birthright furthers their development as moral agents and lays fertile ground for them to ask questions about their own values without the emotional burden of fears about letting down or angering their parents. We may feel angry or let down, but that is ours to care for and manage.

These are at least some of the things vegan parents must do to support our vegan children in order to mitigate some of the social harms of being a vegan young person in a carnist and anthroparchal world. There may be more others can think of. Whatever we do, vegan parents cannot declare by fiat that because we pack vegan pizza for them or take them to a sanctuary rather than a zoo and

[28]Lindstrom discusses a couple who chose to let their vegan adolescent make their own choice about whether to go to the zoo. Those parents grounded their willingness to do so in the knowledge that they had imparted compassionate values to their children and because of this they could trust their children "to make sense of the trip in their own way, a way that is likely markedly different from their classmates" (136). Trust will also play a central role in embracing our children's decision-making process.

because our kids like vegan pizza and visiting sanctuary animals they do not potentially encounter significant social difficulties.

As part of our recognition that raising vegan children can cause relational harms to their connections with other important people in their lives, we must also ask ourselves whether compromise could be an option in any given situation. We may ask ourselves if something relationally important is at stake. If so, how does that relational consideration compare to our commitment to compassion, nonviolence, and care as manifested through our veganism? We also need to return to the context-building endeavors I articulated earlier: Who is this child right here in front of me (not a generic child but a specific one, Oliver)? What is his experience like? How is he impacted by lack of belonging? How does the family or community approach him generally? Does he have bandwidth for further separation caused by veganism? Is he capable of participating in discussion around compromise? If so, what does he say? We must then remain open to his input and be willing to discuss it regardless of the pain it may cause us to do so.

In addition to parents' responsibilities for their vegan children in the face of these conflicts, family members have obligations as well. These obligations are moral in character and not merely logistical or "just being nice." Given the moral nature of relationships, the considerations I lay out later involving how extended family members should approach vegan young people in their families are essential to ensuring the care and attention to need that are part of being in relationship with one another. I articulated many of these obligations in Chapter 4, but there are some that take on particular importance when in relationship with a young person who is vegan due to parental values. First, the responsibility to reconsider traditions and be open to new possibilities is especially great when a vegan child is in the family. Those who became vegan as adults already had an opportunity to build relationships with family members based on common practices and traditions. The child raised vegan from birth or early life has had no such opportunity. They are, thus, at risk of being an outsider from the very beginning. They will have fewer opportunities to bond over traditional foods and special meals or familial recreational interests that involve harm to animals. Brighouse and Swift make the point that raising one's child with the values one was raised with will help the child/grandparent relationship deepen.

> In the standard, three-generational case of grandparent-parent-child, it seems obvious that, other things equal, the relationship between grandparent and child will be richer and deeper if the parent has raised his child in ways informed by the values and beliefs that in turn informed his own upbringing. The gain here is not to the parent-child relationship but to the grandparent-child relationship. And something similar, albeit more attenuated, applies to other relationships with members of one's extended family. Cousins who have been brought up in ways that reflect their parents', and their grandparents' understandings of what

> matters in life, or perhaps simply of what is fun in life, will tend to understand each other better, will have the basis of a more substantial and affectionate relationship, than cousins whose parents have worked hard to shield their children from influences by a sense of the family's identity across generations. (2014, 160–1)

They go on to note that for adults who turn away from generational family values "at least there will be a continuing sense of something that was shared, if only in childhood, that has the potential to enrich those relationships if there is the will to continue them" (161). Brighouse and Swift raise this point to underscore why parents have an interest in shaping their children's values. This is relevant to the discussion here because it acknowledges the ways not sharing family values can weaken familial relationships for children raised with alternative, or resistor, values.

This is not a reason to avoid raising children with resistor values, but it is a reason for grandparents and extended family members to take seriously their role in aiding the child in forming those important connections and relationships. Certainly, they are not responsible for the decision to raise the child as an "outsider," but if they love the child, want to be in relationship with them in a meaningful way, have compassion for how challenging it can be to feel like an outsider, and take seriously that they want to have deep connections with the child then they have some work to do. Part of this work will involve openness to shifting traditions in the ways I discussed in the Chapters 4 and 5. By altering traditions and making them shared across the whole extended family, vegan children are not left on the sidelines while others enjoy the fruits of family belonging. Again, I do not expect this openness in cases where the alternative values of the young person's parents are harmful, disrespectful, or otherwise problematic. Where veganism is concerned, however, that is not the case.[29] Veganism is focused on compassion, care, justice, and connection. Veganism seeks to bring humans and animals into right relationship with one another—rejecting exploitation and marginalization within human and human/animal relationships. As Cole and Stewart note, shifting traditions to those that celebrate "respect, wonder and joy in our relations with other animals rather than the distancing objectification of instrumental knowledge" is what we are after (170). This is something others ought to be willing to embrace if they love and care for the vegans in their lives, especially when the vegan(s) in question is a young person.

[29]Determining whether the values in question are harmful, disrespectful, or otherwise problematic will not always be clear, of course. Whether they are so will sometimes be a matter over which reasonable people can disagree. In those cases, the discussions regarding disagreement should be aimed at the parents and not the children.

I have seen the effect of what Brighouse and Swift point to in my own child's life. In some familial relationships, he was set to the side and unable to participate in the activities that his cousins could—activities that formed the foundation of deep and lasting relationships with their grandparents. This chasm widened further when other differentiating elements of my son's identity beyond veganism came to the fore. He was at a distinct disadvantage with some of his grandparents in part because he could not rely on happy memories of sharing steak with his grandfather, for example. It seems silly for steak sharing to have such a hold on familial relationships, but where distance plays a factor, firm ideas about identity and masculinity take hold, and other shared values are hard to find something as simple as sharing steak can make a difference in whether a child is able to enjoy the goods of special relationships with their extended loved ones. I have also witnessed the potential for the kind of belonging and attachment that came into our son's life when family and friends have taken relational moral attention seriously. The difference is stark indeed.

In addition to owing a relational obligation to the child to reconsider traditions involving flesh-based foods and recreational activities that harm or exploit animals, family members must make good-faith attempts to work toward inclusivity and not merely accommodation. I borrow this language from disability studies and activism. Amai Hamraie describes accommodation as an approach that identifies the person with a disability as a "misfit" requiring accommodations that they must then advocate for and arrange for themselves (2016, 264) beyond certain legally required structural changes. Of course, legislation like the Americans with Disabilities Act does not apply to cases of intrafamilial handling of resistor values in their midst, but the idea that we loved ones can do better than mere accommodation does resonate.

In talking about families' and friends' obligations to their vegan loved ones, the "accommodationist" approach makes it the vegan's responsibility to ask for accommodations. This singles them out as a misfit.[30] What if the whole gathering were planned with the vegan in mind? What if people thought about which dishes naturally lend themselves to vegan recipes so that everyone eats vegan mashed potatoes, for example. What if vegans were included in thinking about how to lay out the food. Some might appreciate having "their food" set aside in a different area to avoid cross-contamination from utensils. Others might find having their food off to the side and announced as the "vegan food" ostracizing or otherwise upsetting. What if it were a conversation first? The conversation could take place with the vegan parents at first and then with the vegan child when they can advocate for themselves. There could be recognition that the child's preferences

[30]Sunaura Taylor makes the important point that unease with requiring accommodation or asking for what one needs is a privilege. People living with disabilities have had to cause disruption by asking for accommodation their whole lives (2017, 152).

may alter over time. As a young person, they may have no unpleasant feelings about food being set aside in a different area. As an adolescent or teen, however, they may find that kind of singling out particularly uncomfortable or unwelcome.

Framing in terms of inclusion rather than accommodation changes the feel of the experience from one of onerous attentiveness to the freakish needs of some subsection of the group to a collective effort to show up for one another in the spirit of receptivity and connection. Instead of coming from a list of what the vegan does not eat, how about coming from the idea of the abundance of what they can eat? Asserting that the vegan *can* eat flesh foods or visit the zoo but chooses not to is unwelcome. If I put food someone I love doesn't like out on the table after having invited them to my home and I say "well, you *can* eat green beans, you just choose not to" that would be considered rude and a failure of loving attention. Saying a vegan can eat lamb chops but chooses not to is like the vegan guest, upon hearing their host's sighs when facing cleaning up the meal, pointing out that the host could have an indentured servant to clean up after the meal but chose not to. People who choose not to commit a moral wrong are choosing, sure, but they are choosing the way of nonviolence, of care, of respect, so it seems impolite at best and a failure of relational care to point out what they could be eating as if they somehow need to recognize how their choices are limiting themselves. This is especially true when considering children and young people who are being raised vegan by their parents and may not have the agency or developmental capacity to make other choices.

To summarize, grandparents and extended family members have relational obligations to vegan children to mitigate the relationship-impacting consequences of the child's veganism.[31] Where relationships are loving and caring, there must be responsiveness to need and attentiveness to the unique factors that can put a loved one at more risk for relational harm than other members of the family. As a result, grandparents and extended family members (how extended will depend on the family) must try to reconsider food-based traditions and recreational activities that involve causing suffering to animals. They must strive for inclusivity rather than mere accommodation and take the time to reflect on their choices regarding these things, questioning whether they have moral grounds for their resistance. If not, then however uncomfortable it may be, they ought to make necessary changes in service of the relational well-being of a young and vulnerable person. This may generate resentment, but that resentment must be directed to the parents or dealt with in settings with other adults (with friends or in counselling). The kinds of support asked of families in some of the literature on vegan parenting is paltry at best. Conciliatory gestures Roth points to, for example, include "fewer instances of arguing or challenging the vegetarian's behavior, acquiring non-meat protein

[31]Though I cannot argue for it here, I believe this is true where the adults desire a close relationship with the child as well as in situations where they do not.

alternatives at family meals, inviting the vegetarian herself or himself to cook a dish for the meal and so forth" (2005, 197). Obviously, some of these gestures will be meaningless to young children—three-year-olds can't cook their own meals—but even for adults these gestures are thin. They are the very least a loved one can do in the face of a beloved's ethical veganism. I am suggesting a stronger obligation that goes beyond adding a vegan protein or holding back on argumentation, especially where vegan children are concerned. Relational moral attention in the form of love, care, and attention to need requires a deeper engagement with the vegan child's need to belong, build meaningful familial relationships, and have a sense that they are a cherished insider rather than a misfit outsider.

In addition to having relational obligations to children being raised vegan, families and close friends have such obligations to the vegan parents who, presumably, they value and care for. Most obviously, they have an obligation not to undermine their loved one's vegan values by engaging in acts of deception or subterfuge. Such acts include taking the vegan child out for nonvegan ice cream and not telling the parents, putting flesh food ingredients in the child's meal without disclosure, sneaking in visits to the zoo or aquarium if parents object to those visits, and so forth. Any action that shows disrespect for the vegan values underlying a child's veganism is a moral relational affront to the vegan parent. Whether family members have the right to do such things does not interest me here. I can imagine some rights-based argument for the idea that those caregiving in their own homes might be entitled to make certain decisions about what activities they choose or foods they offer in their own homes.[32] We can assert our rights and in doing so be terrible loved ones, however, violating all kinds of relational and care obligations. Whatever rights a good friend or family members has to choose the food and activities engaged in "on their watch," it is a breach of trust and care to make those decisions without consulting with and informing the child (when age-appropriate) and the parents in these situations.

Another area for loved ones (whether family or friends) to demonstrate care for their vegan beloveds is to consciously focus on limiting the situations where parents will face conflicts between their vegan values and their cultural or familial identity, important relationships, and desire to facilitate their child in building strong connections to others in their sphere. Of course, we cannot have relational obligations to reduce all dilemmas for our loved ones. That is (1) not possible and (2) not necessarily desirable. Some dilemmas are worth wrestling with, and occasional conflicts in values can be clarifying. Sometimes, however, opportunities to make relatively simple adjustments to special occasions or outings are missed or consciously rejected by family or friends resistant to vegan values. Some carnist

[32]In most cases, though, these rights would be limited in some regard, I would think. For example, temporary caregivers do not have the right to inflict bodily harm on children in their care no matter how much they enjoy practicing their Brazilian Jiu-Jitsu skills.

loved ones lean heavily into "that's their choice, so they should deal with the consequences." There is some sense in that claim, to be sure. Those of us who decide to live according to values that go against the norm and raise children with those resistor values do have a sense of what we are getting into and how we might face certain consequences. Thinking relationally, however, it is quite reasonable to expect the people who profess to love and care for us to make things easier when they are able. Perhaps the evening your vegan relations are coming to dinner on a random, nonholiday Saturday is not the night to offer lamb ribs to everyone else at the table. Even when providing a vegan option or welcoming the vegans to bring their own dish, why not demonstrate care by not subjecting them to dining with a group of people sucking meat off animals' bones? Indeed, why not? When I attempt to answer that question from a relational point of view, I cannot find an appropriate answer. There is no care in such an act, no respect, no attention to need, and no kindness. Where food is not a scarcity and options abound, it is a breach of relational ethics to put your vegan loved ones in such a position. Now, it is possible one does such a thing precisely to communicate that the relationship hitherto taken to be one of care and mutual regard is no longer so, but in that case it would be better to not invite the relatives over at all or to have a direct conversation with them to air and repair grievances before doing so.

Here again it is worth noting that vegan values are directed at making the world a better place, at increasing the sphere of compassion, and deepening connections to others. Making room for, demonstrating care for, and respecting these values should not be asking too much of those who love us. This is different than making room for values that are harmful or that undermine care and compassion. If our adult siblings raise their children to be hateful toward people of a different ethnicity, for example, we do not have a relational obligation to avoid inviting a friend from that ethnicity to our birthday party dinner the same evening our family comes over to celebrate with us. Now, we do have an obligation of care to that friend to offer full disclosure regarding who is attending when offering said invitation. We may even have a relational obligation of care to our racist loved ones to let them know this friend will be attending and explain what the boundaries are for engagement with them. That way, the racist family members can decide which values weigh more heavily in the situation—celebrating the birthday of a loved one or avoiding contact with people of a specific race or ethnicity. The party thrower, however, has no relational obligation to their racist family to exclude their friend to ease the evening for them.

One might push back here and ask why the relational obligations are different in this case than in the case of the vegan loved ones. Isn't it important to show respect, care, and attention to the needs of all the people with whom we are in loving relationships? It certainly is important to demonstrate respect, care, and attention to the needs of those we love and wish to be in relationship with. What that respect, care, and attention look like, however, will differ depending on context.

With values like racism, that make the world less caring, less compassionate, and aim at sowing division rather than connection, our relational obligations of care can be discharged by simply letting the racist family member know what will be happening and allowing them to make their own choices. Their choice may surprise or hurt us, but we have empowered them to make an informed decision, handling on their own the consequences of having values that make the world a more hateful place. We can decide not to accommodate values that run so contrary to our own where they are hateful, hurtful, and make the world a worse place for all.

With the vegan relatives, however, the context is different. First, vegans' values are centered on compassion, care, and a commitment to nonviolence (and perhaps ecofeminist and virtue considerations, which also aim for the good of all). Relational moral attention means making room for such values rather than critiquing and questioning them as one might do with hateful values. Second, resistance to vegan values is usually not rooted in some deep-seated values around the supremacy of humans over other animals and the importance of demonstrating that supremacy through acts of violence and suffering. At least in the dominant culture of the United States, for example, most carnists and most people who frequent animal-centered recreation (with the exception of some recreational hunting) have not questioned their values about such practices at all. Widespread speciesism and deeply rooted conceptions of human supremacy have made it so that carnism and animal exploitation is just what is done. The idea that exploitation and violence are involved may either not be thought of or in some cases not known. When the carnist family serves lamb ribs at the dinner party, they generally do so not because they have a deep-seated value around the importance of eating lambs but because it is what they like, what they do, and they do not really give it any thought (unless the food served is part of a traditional or ceremonial meal). For a family meal on a random Saturday, the issue for the hosting loved ones is not that the veganism offends them morally the way the racism offends them morally. The issue is that the veganism annoys them, makes them think about their own behavior in ways they find unappealing, is perceived as judgmental regarding their own behavior, and so forth or that making vegan food is a nuisance or beyond their culinary skills.[33] Hence, what happens for them is not a conflict of values as in the case of the birthday party and racist relatives. Rather, the issue is that veganism is bucking up against something they just normally do, and they find the call for accommodation or care burdensome or exasperating. Surely, when we love and care for people, part of demonstrating relational care and attentiveness

[33]See Adams (2009). They may also have concerns that veganism introduces a radical or subversive ideology into the family (Roth 2005). I have more sympathy for the latter concern but maintain that it is the family's or community's obligation to engage in relational moral attention and move past these concerns.

is asking ourselves how we might show care for our beloveds when their values are in service of making the world a more compassionate place and we do not have firmly set values that contrast with theirs (i.e., a moral value that it is morally required to eat animal flesh at every meal).

My little vegan family is fortunate to have friends and loved ones who go out of their way to show this kind of relational moral attentiveness. Even the most committed carnist in our midst makes concerted efforts to find restaurants where we can eat. He experiments with vegan cooking and prepares vegan foods to bring to our home. We have family who ensure there are vegan options for various holiday meals and who bake our son's favorite vegan desserts when we visit. These acts of care and compassion have been done by many people in our lives, and we have appreciated each one. Our relationships have grown closer as a result. Our lives have been made easier by not having to navigate conflicts that are so easily avoided. We have felt welcomed, seen, and loved each time this has happened.

Where our loved one's values are not in direct conflict with ours, where their values turn toward a more compassionate and caring approach to the world, and where we are situated logistically and financially to demonstrate care by reducing the hardships those loved ones face, then relational moral attention requires we do just that. To make this concrete in the case of vegan loved ones parenting a vegan child, that might mean making the random Saturday gathering a vegan meal everyone can enjoy together and talk about as a shared memory, it could mean planning their cousin's birthday party at a trampoline center instead of the zoo, so the vegan family members can easily attend (particularly if the birthday child has no real preference between the two venues). It might look like letting your vegan relatives know what you can and cannot do to make an event more accessible for them. One might ask one's vegan relatives questions regarding what they need or expect and then see what feels like an appropriate expression of care in one's response to those needs and expectations. It involves thinking *relationally* in the sense of acknowledging that, yes, their veganism is a choice they have made, but we are both individuals and a relational entity all together. Their veganism is important to me by virtue of that relationship. Seeing their needs and attending to them is important to me because I value the relationship. In this sense, we are not just individuals, we are a relational organism that needs care, compassion, and attentiveness to need in order to survive and thrive.

This organism requires relational moral attention from all parties to the relationship. It is important, then, for vegan parents to recognize their obligations to their families and friends in situations where vegan parenting creates conflicts. In Chapter 4, I articulated obligations vegans have to their relationships with carnist loved ones in cases where those relationships are challenged by the vegan's commitments. Many of those obligations will apply in the case of vegan parents but with some additional context in place. In Chapter 4, we discussed a vegan's own relationships with their carnist loved ones. In this chapter, we are thinking specifically about what relational attentiveness could mitigate the conflicts that arise between raising a vegan child and traditional, familial, or community values and norms. The fact that we are not merely acting on behalf of our own adult relationships with important others but also on behalf of our child's relationships adds urgency to the need for care and attentiveness. As I discussed earlier in this chapter, vegan children are vulnerable to bullying, teasing, and feeling like outsiders in their own families and communities. They face this situation because of choices their parents made for them (at least in the early years of their lives before they are able to choose for themselves), which gives parents a relational obligation to them to address the vulnerability of their situation directly. Additionally, because vegan parents are the parents of the child as well as the children of the grandparents, sibling of the aunts and uncles, and so forth, they have obligations of care to those other family members to help in facilitating meaningful relationships with their vegan child. In other words, insomuch as the choice to raise a child vegan can create relational difficulties for the child and the extended family, the vegan parent has relational work to do to attend to those difficulties. Doing this relational work is required of us when in relationships of love and care. It will also have the additional benefit of occasionally or even often reducing the instances of conflicts in values between veganism and those relationships. I begin with what those relational obligations are and then explain why I think this work will result in fewer conflicts.

Safran Foer writes: "However strong our intuitions about what's right for us personally and even about what's right for others, we all know in advance that our positions will clash with those of our neighbors. What do we do with that most inevitable reality? Drop the conversation, or find a way to reframe it?" (33). Dropping the conversation or finding a way to reframe it are, of course, options one can consider. I am suggesting that there are actions we can take that are morally salient in the moment and that have nothing to do with a conversation about harming animals. One such action is, as Roth suggests, to recognize the anger and fear our vegan values may cause loved ones (142). For all the reasons I articulated in Chapter 4 and earlier in this chapter, vegan values can be a frightening afront to family systems. In a situation where children are involved, those feelings may be more acute given the amount of hope for new and meaningful connection children can bring to a family or community. Remember Roth's point, discussed earlier in this chapter, that the family system will tend to organize itself toward homeostasis, or maintaining the status quo when disruptions are afoot. Vegan parents can help with this difficulty by being curious about and addressing their family's concerns.

In "Why Do Vegans Have Such Bad Reputations?," Tani Khara notes that vegans should extend the empathy and respect they have for animals to other humans who live according to different values or habits (2018). As a vegan for decades myself, I know how jarring this might sound. Why must we show empathy for those who make decisions to engage in behaviors harmful to animals, humans, and the environment? Why should that be our job? My response is that we are not showing empathy for the choices and values held by our loved ones. We are instead demonstrating care and empathy for the difficulty our decision to live according to other values creates in our relationship with them and, in the case of this chapter, the relationship they have or will be able to have with our children. We can stand on the peak of the righteous mountain of our vegan values and condemn those we love for remaining in carnist base camp, or we can tune into what it's like for them to contemplate the distance between us all and feel its impact in the form of fear, sadness, grief, and discomfort. Such feelings are all a part of being alive and we do not have obligations to, nor are we capable of, protecting loved ones from feeling these feelings. If we care about and love others, however, we do need to tune into what it is like to be them, what is going on with them, and find some way to respond that does not require us to give up too much of ourselves. In the case of vegan parenting, this can be as simple as acknowledging our loved one's feelings, showing empathy, and providing reassurance that there remains much common ground from which to build and maintain relationships with our vegan children. If we work together, find our shared values, make some adjustments to our norms and practices, and so forth we can create a foundation from which those relationships can flourish. Simply pointing out that our values are right and theirs wrong misses the point. We are not in an ethical debate about whether it is permissible to cause horrific suffering to animal others during these conversations. Rather, we are in a discussion about our relationships and how we will tend to them in the face of what is a significant disruption, whether it is justified or not.

In focusing solely on the whys and wherefores of ethical veganism we miss what our loved ones are telling us about their hurt, their fears, their uncertainty. That hurt, fearfulness, and uncertainty is not about whether animals are morally considerable. It is about what this all means for our relationships, our cultural traditions and norms, and so forth. When raising vegan children, relational moral attention requires us to address these feelings. This does not mean we must bend to the demands or tolerate the ill-treatment that stems from them. It means that our loved ones, through fear or just failure of creativity or lack of experience with building relationships without the common foundation of speciesist practices, need some empathy and care from us. We ought to give it to them since we are, after all, the ones introducing a huge wrench into the works even if we are morally justified in doing so.

Another, more tactical, position a vegan parent might take is doing what Erin Pavlina suggests and letting some things go. Thinking about a case where a friend or family member is planning a large, catered event (e.g., a wedding) and they will not accommodate veganism or allow the vegan to speak directly with the caterer, Pavlina suggests we "stop there." She says, "Remember, it's just one meal. There's no need to ruin a friendship or create family friction over one meal. The focus, after all, is the event itself" (117–18). Though I would add that the family member or friend in this case is in breach of relational obligations of care and attentiveness to need, I agree that relational care sometimes does require us to let such things go where the impact is temporary and easily managed. Here again, it might be particularly true where vegan children are involved. Vegan parents ought to take seriously that stubbornly pursuing accommodation in these cases, and causing rifts long term will impact their child's ability to be in relationship with the loved ones in question.

Here, as in Chapter 4, a concerted effort to focus on shared values can mitigate relational difficulties for our children and loved ones. Inasmuch as veganism can be described as reflective of and continuous with existing family values, relationships will have a greater chance to grow and thrive. Since vegans often remain in the stance of justice in conversations about their vegan values, opportunities are missed to focus on care. I am empathetic to the feeling that so much pain and suffering is on the line that we must explain and reexplain why our values are right, better, deserving of consideration, and so forth. When you are attuned to the suffering of billions of animals every year (as well as the humans who share fate with them), the fight for their lives is urgent and the desire to do something to effect change locally as well as systemically is so very strong. Still, we cannot turn a conversation about our important relationships into an argument about animal ethics. Rather, we should maintain focus on relational moral attention.

Pavlina says the following about how vegans might approach holidays or other occasions when others are eating flesh foods: you, as a vegan, of course have the right to refrain from eating at a table where others are eating meat, but "on the other hand, what right do you have to expect other people to conform to your lifestyle when they don't agree with it and they are perfectly content with their own?" (135–6). We of course have the right to sit or not at tables where loved ones are munching on the carcasses of dead animals. We of course have the right to refuse attending the rodeo with everyone else who is going. We do not have a right to dictate what our family and friends do about their own cooking and recreational behavior. This points, though, to how limited the rights perspective is in these cases. Asserting our rights does not always make us loving people. We see this all the time in people exercising their right to free speech. My loved one has a right to eat a burger on his way to my vegan house and ring me to tell me all about it. Why would he though? When he does it, my knowledge of his right to do so is no comfort at all. What hurts me is the failure of his care and compassion toward me. That is a failure of relational care and should be seen and discussed as such. When we think relationally rather than from a justice standpoint, key elements of these conflicts between veganism and familial and cultural traditions are revealed. Once revealed, they are available for resolution with attentiveness and care.

So far, I have made the case for relational obligations to our vegan children, on the part of our family members toward vegan parents and vegan children, and on the part of vegan parents toward the extended family or community. I have argued that all of these aspects of relational moral attention are important in the face of conflicts between vegan parenting and familial and cultural traditions. When we take the relational obligations seriously, we can in turn limit the occasions for conflict. If my family sees that making lamb ribs for a Saturday dinner is bound to cause unnecessary distress for my vegan child and single him out as different from his cousins and therefore make a vegan meal instead then the conflict dissipates. I no longer have to determine what compromise might be necessary in service of my child's relational well-being, for example. If I acknowledge my brother Tim's sorrow that my son will never experience his amazing hot dogs, then he and I can work toward finding a shared activity or food experience that will work. Instead of arguing about animals' moral standing, we are discussing who we are and how we want to be in relationship with one another.

I recognize, however, that there are some considerable obstacles to finding alternative activities or practices in some cases. It may be that relational care will hit a wall in what it can accomplish if, for example, there are no vegan alternatives at the local grocery store, or the broader community makes inclusivity challenging. If my extended family goes to the annual pancake breakfast in town every year on the morning after Thanksgiving and the organizers fail to consider vegan dietary restrictions, there is only so much to be done. This leads to the necessity for increased structural support for veganism in our broader social world. If our religious communities, for example, demonstrate leadership in veganizing holidays or gatherings that will lend support to both vegans and their family members. If our community organizations do so, that will broaden the potential for shared activities and chances for our children to bond with their extended family. Oscar Horta outlines how discriminatory practices against vegans are solidified by institutions by, among other things, failing to offer vegan alternatives to food and activities (Horta 2018). Imagine how much easier it could be to navigate conflicts between obligations to animals and relationships of love and care if veganism were normalized by institutions and systems as well as understood and supported more broadly in the world.

7 Conclusion

Raising vegan children brings more compassion and awareness into the world as well as opportunities to repair humans' relationships with both other animals and marginalized humans. Vegan children can thrive as vegans, enjoying many of the goods of life as they grow. At the same time, those who have written about raising vegan children have ignored the very real relational complications that arise when children are raised with values so different from the norms of their community and family. Vegan children and their parents will face a number of conflicts in values as the children grow up. We have options other than ignoring the existence of these conflicts or simply throwing up our hands and declaring vegan values must be compromised. If we engage in relational moral attention as vegan parents, as family members of a vegan child, and as vegans who are part of carnist families we can address many of the conflicts that arise. In doing so we may limit the frequency of such conflicts simply by demonstrating care and compassion for one another. As Nel Noddings wrote:

> It may well be that you care deeply for some plant, animal, or environment in which I have no interest. My carelessness may shock and offend you. Now my obligation as one-caring is to listen, to receive you in all your indignation. I do not give way because of political pressure and the might of your lobbying, but I listen carefully because you address me. What matters to you is of interest and concern to me. We do not draw the line at principle, choose sides, and confront each other across it. Rather, we receive each other, we allow ourselves to feel what the other feels, and then we reason together. "All this is of variable importance, but you still matter more." (2013, 150)

Where conflicts cannot be remedied in these ways, contextualized moral thinking can help us determine when compromise might be possible. We can also advocate for structural support for vegan families in the form of institutional attention to vegans' values and needs. All of this will help vegan parents address the complexities of raising vegan children in an anthroparchal world and support the children in developing the roots of relationships that will (hopefully) form the relational foundations for their lives.

7 CONCLUSION

When I began work on this book, I read the journalist Eli Saslow's book *Rising out of Hatred: The Awakening of a Former White Nationalist*. In it, Saslow tells the real-life story of Derek Black, a young man who had grown up heir to the white supremacist movement in the United States. Black's father, Don, was the founder of the hate-spewing website *Stormfront* and his godfather was David Duke, the prominent white supremacist and former Ku Klux Klan Grand Wizard. That's not "former" in the sense that Duke renounced his white nationalism but in that he rebranded himself in more socially acceptable language as part of a calculated effort to take the white nationalist movement more mainstream. It is an effort that has been frighteningly successful in the United States. Through meeting people at college who took an interest in Black, invited him into their spaces, and built relationships with him through compassion, empathy, and critique he eventually turned away from white nationalism ultimately giving up his family connections and the community in which he had grown and thrived all his young life.

On the face of it, this might seem an odd choice of book for someone writing on relational vegan ecofeminism. White nationalism is a topic that is not even tangentially related. Yet, the book called to me because I wanted to hear the story of someone who had turned their back on the values they had grown up with and how they had navigated that change within their own community. As it happens, that is not what I came to learn about in *Rising Out of Hatred*. Derek Black's family could not forgive him for his change in values; he became physically unsafe as members of the white supremacist movement sought to silence someone who was once considered their future leader, and he lost everything and nearly everyone he had known. Black changed his name and walked away forever. No relational repair was possible. What I learnt about instead was the power of relational moral attention in a very different sense. His is a story about the force of slow transformation through dialogue and inclusion. Derek was welcomed by, of all people, a group of Orthodox Jewish students. He ate Shabbat dinner with them, they got to know one another as humans, and Derek heard about the Holocaust and Jewish experiences in America. He also spoke with Cuban American students who generously shared their stories of migration, integration, and building a life in America. These demonstrations of inclusivity and empathy on the students' part are remarkable as is Derek Black's courage and openness to commune with people he had been told his entire life are vile and unworthy of life in society. It is a story of relational moral attention across viewpoints so disparate that one would think it an impossibility.

Matthew Stevenson, one of the students who welcomed Black to their Shabbat dinners, talked about the importance of "nonjudgmental inclusion." As Saslow puts it, "Instead of trying to build a case, Matthew began working to build a relationship in which Derek might be able to learn what the enemy was actually like." Matthew said, "The goal was really just to make Jews more human to him" (81). The idea, then, was to be in relationship with Derek, to turn toward him and to enable him to turn toward them, and, in doing so, to develop some mutual understanding and perhaps pave the way for Derek to see the world in a different, less hateful light. It worked. I am grateful for Derek's story for a number of reasons. It demonstrates how relational moral attention can, indeed, move us toward mutual understanding and more compassion and care. It highlights why some moments are not right for debate about the sources of disagreement but instead are better focused on finding our common humanity and shared values (nonjudgmental inclusion, indeed). Finally, it reminds us that change is possible even among people who have everything to lose in the face of that change—their sense of self, their family, their community, their plans for the future, their home—*everything*.

I am not suggesting that Derek's story taught me that relational moral attention is the panacea for all that ails us. We all look at the world and know that is just not true. However, his story helps ground an answer to a question that arises frequently when I discuss this project: Aren't you too optimistic about the value of this approach? Wouldn't it be more accurate to say that "in some cases relational moral attention might work" rather than "in some cases relational moral attention might not work"?[1] Aside from the reality that I have never been accused of courting too much optimism in my entire life, this line of questioning strikes me in a tender place whenever I hear it. In my darkest hours when I contemplate all the violence and pain that exists in the world, I can so very easily get drawn into this line of thinking. Then I think of Derek Black, the heir apparent of the white nationalist movement in the United States being invited to Shabbat dinner by a group of Jewish students and actually going! This in turn reminds me of the mundane, day-to-day, mostly unnoticed acts of relational moral attention that make life more compassionate, more caring, and more loving every single day. I am reminded that despite the apparent chasm between people, there is still loving attention, care, attentiveness to need, and that these are all acts of relational moral attention.

---

[1]My thanks to Todd Jones for phrasing the worry in this clear way when I gave a talk at UNLV on my hunting chapter.

They generally do not garner much public attention, which is unsurprising as care has long been relegated to the private rather than public sphere, but they occur throughout the day every day.

More concretely, I believe these questions around relational moral attention's potential to contribute to solutions to interanimal and intracultural conflicts of interest highlight the importance of how closely theory and practice are linked. We need to get the theory right. Relational moral attention will not work in all families or communities. Animal activism, however, is strongly driven by animal ethical theory,[2] and there is a significant chance that if those of us who do public philosophy can get the theory right then that will trickle to activists and from the activists to their communities and then substantive change becomes possible. If the approach we start from is rooted in context, understanding particulars, responding to need, and offering loving attention then there is more cause for hopefulness than if we start from focusing solely on the claims of justice. Whether the approach I have put together works for a particular individual and their family is less important than how vital it is that we all have the correct conversation about these conflicts of interest.

All of this relates closely to a related question that asks whether anything I have said is helpful in ending oppressive practices. The approach seems so focused on individual or small group dynamics that it is not clear how it can help take the number of animals killed annually in the United States by recreational hunters down from 100 million to zero, for example. If the view cannot help with that then, frankly, what is the point? It is rather important that we keep an eye on what counts as success in adjudicating interanimal and intracultural conflicts. It is a losing strategy to focus entirely on the numerical outcomes of these kinds of conflicts of interest—on whether there is a significant decrease in the number of animals we eat, wear, experiment on, and kill for sport or on how many people are converted to veganism or stop visiting Sea World. I hope it goes without saying that I would like to see those numbers come down to zero, to one day see animal sanctuaries close because we humans finally got in right relationship with our animal others and such places of refuge are no longer needed, to see animal agriculture become a relic of a confused past. When we think about interanimal and intracultural conflicts of interest, however, the main focus is on other, less quantifiable matters. What counts as success is an animal advocate feeling less torn in two by the tension between honoring their commitments to animals and their loved ones at the same time. Success is a family or community coming to the animal advocate in their lives in the spirit of curiosity and mutual understanding, perhaps offering to shift a tradition or alter a plan to better respect their values.

---

[2]I am thinking here of the long-standing influence of Peter Singer and Tom Regan's work on the grassroots animal rights movement as well as the more recent, and I think unfortunate, ways philosophical work on effective altruism has impacted the movement.

Success is meeting would-be vegans where they are and acknowledging rather than willing away the struggles they experience as they attempt to hold on to their ethnic or religious identity while extending their values of peace and nonviolence to animals. If we can ease the tension between honoring animals and our own identities and relationships with loved ones, then we will slowly make it easier for others to turn away from animal exploitation and anthroparchal institutions.

On a practical level, as I have alluded to before, animal activists should consider shifting tactics to be more in line with relational vegan ecofeminism. We need to take interests tied to identity and important relationships seriously and focus less on veganism as "purity" and more on context and relationships. When we do so, I believe that will shift the brutal realities for animals over time. When we look at people genuinely struck by a dilemma between competing important values, in this case the desire to defend animals without disappointing people, we need a better answer than "meat is murder!" or "if you really cared about animals you would not eat your Uncle Tim's hotdogs!" or "but that's such an inconsequential consideration in the face of animals' suffering!." I will own that I have given these answers myself during various stages of my own journey through animal advocacy. I feel the pain of how pressing is the fight for animals' lives. We do not help them, however, by pretending these very real conflicts do not exist or by trivializing them. Instead, we must take them seriously and offer empathy and support. Every time I find that difficult, I remember the students who invited Derek Black to Shabbat dinner and that Black accepted their invitation.

Success is also getting matters right ethically. As I argued in Part 1, other approaches to conflicts of interest fail to do so because they either entirely neglect contextualizing interests, they contextualize in the wrong ways, or they are underdeveloped contextual approaches. Relational vegan ecofeminism offers a more accurate understanding of humans' nonbasic but nevertheless highly valued interests and in turn provides an ethical approach that speaks to the pressing moral questions that arise. Thinking contextually and relationally is important for ethical accuracy. It is a moral success to approach conflicts of interest with a theory that tells the moral story with more precision and truth.

Another question shuffling around in the background of this book is whether, in the face of all of these challenges to defending animals without disappointing people, I am simply asking too much of everyone. Recall from Chapter 2 that Gary Varner's two-level utilitarianism included the conservative bias or inertia. Varner accounted for how demanding and challenging it is to go beyond the bounds of common morality by stating that to do so is supererogatory—it is permissible but not required. It may be, Varner said, that common morality needs to shift before we can begin to think about veganism as an ethical requirement. The related concern for the defending animals, disappointing people project is that the deeply contextual analyses I provided in Part 2 might point in the direction of inertia rather than relational moral attention. These conflicts are extremely challenging, so why wouldn't we simply default to the position that it is above and beyond the call of ethics at the moment to defend animals when we risk disappointing people. Simply eat your grandmother's soup, hunt with your grandfather, and let your child eat whatever everyone else is eating. Someday, matters will improve for animals and when they do, we will not face the tremendous obstacle of common morality and then we can tackle relational moral attention. In the meantime, there is no need to stretch oneself so painfully in service of a moral ideal. Perhaps the same could even be said of loved ones who have an animal advocate in their midst. It is simply too much to ask of them to show up in curiosity, care, and respect given that common morality seems to demand none of these with regard to valuing animals. Perhaps they just get to demand that we eat their soup, hunt with them, and have our children eat whatever animal flesh everyone else consumes.

There are a number of reasons I reject this idea. First, common morality is woefully inadequate steeped as it is in anthroparchal values. The idea that resisting against those norms is too much to ask of people is unimaginable to me. I cannot see how anything, anything at all, will change if we all go about our business thinking that it is not required of us to resist the common morality that appears to endorse exploitation, violence, and misery. Anthroparchy is real and the consequences for individual animals, for humans, and for our planet are dire. We must rouse ourselves no matter how hard. This will be an imperfect duty to be sure. Some people are struggling with daily survival, subject to enormous cruelties, and living under oppressive regimes. For those of us who are able, however, some form of resistance is vitally important to living a moral life. In a way, two-level utilitarianism's endorsement of the conservative bias and inertia is deeply sympathetic to the human condition. It can, indeed, be costly and painful to stand up against the moral norms of one's day. I can appreciate this concern for all of our well-being. At the same time, asserting that pushing beyond the bounds of current moral norms is above and beyond the call of duty (or of care, I would add) strikes me as tilling fertile ground for vice. People of moral integrity have courage, bravery, and a willingness to challenge the status quo in service of making our world a better place. Such traits are not supererogatory; they are at the foundation of what makes individuals people of moral character. Perhaps most importantly, relational vegan ecofeminism and relational moral attention address precisely the difficulty of how terribly challenging and lonely it can be to follow values unrecognized by others or by institutions. By not thinking relationally, two-level utilitarianism misses that if we use context to better understand one another and to engage in attending to one another in a caring way, then those challenges are diminished. We need not face them alone, allowing them to overwhelm us with their complexity and seeming insurmountability. When we fully contextualize conflicts and turn toward one another in the spirit of care, we build the strength needed to go against common morality ourselves and to support our loved ones in doing so. Perhaps we are not joined on the far side of common morality by our nearest and dearest, but if we can stay in caring relationships with one another, working relationally toward mutual understanding and mutual avowal, challenging the status quo is less daunting and less personally costly.

I see the ideas and the approach I put forth in this book as a contribution to what has been and, I hope, continues to be a long and enriching conversation about human-animal relationships. There is much more to be done. One option involves animal advocates and academics (these two groups are not mutually exclusive) applying the relational vegan ecofeminist approach in their own cultural, religious, and ethnic contexts. What does relational vegan ecofeminism and relational moral attention look like in situations I have not examined here? How might the approach help or fall short in those contexts? How might the deeply contextualized and relational approach be applied to situations outside of animal ethics? How might it help with other seemingly intractable tensions or dilemmas?

Some matters I was not able to satisfactorily address but invite others to think along with me about moving forward include fully articulating what relational moral attention would look like between humans and other animals. I have focused on the necessity and promise of thinking in terms of relational moral attention between humans as a significant part of approaching interanimal and intracultural conflicts of interest but only briefly addressed the matter of cross-species relational moral attention. Questions surrounding the possibility for cross-species relational moral attention, particularly around the issue of reparative moral attention, are central to fully considering how to adjudicate human/animal conflicts of interest. As I have said throughout the earlier chapters, whether and to what degree relational moral attention is possible ought to play a significant role in how we think about adjudicating such conflicts.

In Chapter 2, I briefly mentioned Paul Taylor's introduction of the Principle of Restitution into his system for conflict adjudication. Taylor believed firmly that restitution is required in cases where humans justifiably override other living beings' interests in service of their own highly valued interests. His principle tells us that the efforts we undertake to make restitution must "bring about an amount of good that is comparable (as far as can reasonably be estimated) to the amount of evil to be compensated for" (305). He claims that by following the principle of restitution we can relieve the burden of guilt we experience when we harm wild animals and plants in pursuit of human interests.[3] Taylor says,

> To set aside habitat areas and protect environmental conditions in [areas we have harmed] so that wild communities of animals and plants can realize their good is the most appropriate way to restore the balance of justice with them,

[3]Restitution is, of course, a complicated affair. There are lively debates in the ecological restoration literature, for example, about whether such restorations can count as a form of restitution (Almassi 2021; Elliot 2003; Katz 2003; Light 2003).

> for it gives full expression to our respect for nature even when we have done harm to living things in order to benefit ourselves. We can, as it were, return the favor they do us by doing something for their sake. Thus we need not bear a burden of eternal guilt because we have used them—and will continue to use them—for our own ends. There is a way to make amends. (1986, 306)

I wish I shared Taylor's conviction that such amends are widely possible. Interspecies repair and restitution are profoundly complicated even if we have access to the specific individuals harmed (Emmerman 2014). In cases where we have killed individual animals or they have been killed for us, Taylor suggests focusing on ecosystems as a whole (305). This approach likely will not work in cases of industrial animal agriculture or biomedical research as it is difficult to see how focusing on the ecosystem could "balance" the harm done to the animals used as tools for human ends. We will certainly fall far short of bringing about an amount of good equal to the harm we caused—we are quite far from making amends and assuaging our guilty burden. As a result, the challenges with interspecies restitution and relational moral attention point to reasons we humans ought to give up or at a minimum rethink some of our most highly valued interests.

Restitution in the form of compensation in the way Taylor suggests (304) is a fool's errand. Instead, we should think in terms of relational moral attention as we can never compensate the individual animals we have killed and it may be impossible to compensate those we have harmed in ways that do not cause them further harm (e.g., spending the rest of their lives in captivity). What interanimal relational moral attention entails specifically needs to be fleshed out. Lori Gruen's work on "entangled empathy" is a promising starting place for helping us think about what loving attention and care look like across species barriers (2015). Ben Almassi's *Environmental Reparative Justice in a World of Wounds* is also a helpful place to begin as Almassi examines thoroughly what repair in the environmental context entails. There is so much more to think about in this realm. What feels certain to me for now is that cross-species relational moral attention will require reflecting on the nature of human/animal relationships, which are different in many ways in both character and content than human/human relationships. What does it mean, for example, to "be in relationship" with the chicken raised and slaughtered to make your traditional chicken soup? The answer is certainly different from what it means to be in relationship with your best friend whether that being is a human or your beloved dog. Thus, it will not do to map what we say about caring in human relationships to the interspecies realm.

As Gruen notes, we must recognize that empathetic engagement in interanimal relationships has both a cognitive and an affective element (2015, 66–8). Empathetic engagement entails understanding animals' species-typical needs *and* their individual traits and needs. Jamie and Burrito chimpanzee at Chimpanzee Sanctuary Northwest both have needs as chimpanzees that are understood by learning about primatology and ethology. But Jamie loves boots and shoes whereas her pal Burrito does not. Jamie needs to see interesting footwear close up to feel enriched, and Burrito prefers noodling around and playing chase. Relational moral attention will involve understanding these differing levels of need. If you ask anyone who works in animal rescue, rehabilitation, or sanctuary contexts you will be struck by just how much expertise, time, patience, care, and financial resources are required to even approximate getting this work right. Finally, our efforts at interanimal relational moral attention will require a considerable amount of epistemic humility. Our efforts must involve minimizing unintended harms those efforts might generate while coming to grips with the reality that we are not always epistemically equipped to adequately anticipate or respond to those harms. We should strive to avoid reifying oppressive and marginalizing belief systems as much as possible, while also recognizing that the possibilities for interanimal relational moral attention will be limited by the anthroparchal structures in which these efforts take place.

The time is ripe to think more carefully about the possibilities and limits of interanimal relational moral attention because those possibilities and limits are germane to how we adjudicate conflicts. It is a central part of the contextual analysis we must do for both the humans we love and the animals we care for so deeply. In these chapters I have shown in some depth how relational moral attention can work interpersonally among humans, but this issue about interanimal relational moral attention requires careful reflection for a complete analysis. I look forward to talking and thinking with others about this in future.

Taylor's work has always surprised me because, for a person so heavily invested in an approach guided solely by principles, he was capable of recognizing that there will be situations in which the priority principles he offers will fail to help us identify priority in conflicts. In his characteristically thorough way, Taylor offers one last refuge in such cases by suggesting that we fall back on our vision of an ideal world order. In his case, that vision is informed by the attitude of respect for nature and is of a "world order on our planet where human civilization is brought into harmony with nature" (308). In the absence of clear guidance at the level of principle, Taylor asks us to remember that we always have guidance in the form of our vision for what the world should be like across all the many values we hold dear.

This guidance to be grounded at all times by our vision of bringing the world into more harmony is helpful. I would add, though, that what I think Taylor is getting at when he talks about harmony is being in right relationship with one another, and our understanding of right relationship is dangerously incomplete without the ethics of care. When we incorporate the ethics of care, we are not left only with the somewhat meager offering that we rely on our vision of how we wish the world to be. We in fact have at our disposal all of the relational moral attention involved in caring —loving attention, turning toward one another rather than away, thinking relationally instead of in terms of competition, and saying to one another "I care for you; therefore, I want to learn more about what you are going through." Or, as Noddings put it in the quote that heads this chapter, "What matters to you is of interest and concern to me." This is a plentiful offering full of potential for understanding, responsiveness, and empathy. It also offers opportunities for critique and dialog as a welcome part of a caring relationship, something central to so many loving and respectful friendships. As those of us lucky enough to have such beautiful relationships know, along with loving attention and compassion, caring involves questioning, challenging, and pushing those we love to reflect upon who they are, their beliefs, and their actions. These characteristics of relational vegan ecofeminism are what makes the defending animals, disappointing people tension both understandable and resolvable. Thinking contextually and relationally sheds light on the robustness of some seemingly trivial human interests, specifically those related to relationships of love and care. It also illuminates a way forward, guiding us toward living with integrity with respect to our love of both the animals with whom we share this earth and the humans with whom we share our lives.

REFERENCES

Aaltola, Elisa. 2005. "Animal Ethics and Interest Conflicts." *Ethics & the Environment* 10 (1): 19–48.

Aaltola, Elisa, and M. Oksanen. 2002. "Species Conservation and Minority Rights: The Case of Springtime Bird Hunting in Åland." *Environmental Values* 11: 443–60.

Abbate, Cheryl. 2020. "Veganism, (Almost) Harm-Free Animal Flesh, and Nonmaleficence: Navigating Dietary Ethics in an Unjust World." In *The Routledge Handbook of Animal* Ethics, edited by Bob Fischer. New York: Routledge, 555–68.

Abrell, Elan. 2018. "Defining Posthumanism." *ASI's Defining Human-Animal Studies* 18. https://www.youtube.com/watch?v=BiuU287BD0Y.

Acampora, Ralph. 2008. "Zoos and Eyes: Contesting Captivity and Seeking Successor Practices." In *The Animal Ethics Reader*, 2nd ed., edited by S. J. Armstrong and R. G. Botzler. New York: Routledge, 501–6. Originally published in 2005 in *Society & Animals* 13 (1).

Adams, Carol J. Spring 1991. "Ecofeminism and the Eating of Animals." *Hypatia* 6 (1): 125–45.

Adams, Carol J. 1994a. "Bringing Peace Home: A Feminist Philosophical Perspective on the Abuse of Women, Children, and Pet Animals." In *Feminism and Peace*, edited by Karen Warren and Duane L. Cady. Special issue of *Hypatia* 9 (2) (spring): 63–84.

Adams, Carol J. 1994b. *Neither Man Nor Beast: Feminism and the Defense of Animals.* New York: Continuum.

Adams, Carol J. 2009. *Living Among Meat Eaters: The Vegetarians Survival Handbook*, 2nd ed. New York: Lantern Books.

Adams, Carol J. [1990] 2010. *The Sexual Politics of Meat: A Feminist-Vegetarian Critical Theory*, 20th anniversary ed. New York: Continuum.

Adams, Carol. J., and Lori Gruen. 2014. *Ecofeminism: Feminist Intersections with Other Animals & the Earth.* New York: Bloomsbury.

Adams, Carol J., and Lori Gruen. 2022. *Ecofeminism: Feminist Intersections with Other Animals & the Earth*, 2nd ed. New York: Bloomsbury.

Adler, Rachel. 1983. *Engendering Judaism: An Inclusive Theology and Ethics.* Philadelphia, PA: Jewish Publication Society.

Afshari, Atoosa. 2026. "Culture and Meat-Eating: A Critique of Anthropocentrism in Animal Ethics." *The Ecological Citizen* 9 (1): epub-143.

Agar, Nicholas. 2001. *Life's Intrinsic Value: Science, Ethics, and Nature.* New York: Columbia University Press.

Akhtar, Sahar. 2011. "Animal Pain and Animal Welfare: Can Pain Sometimes Be Worse for Them Than for Us?" In *The Oxford Handbook of Animal Ethics*, edited by Tom L. Beauchamp and R. G. Frey. Oxford: Oxford University Press, 495–518.

Almassi, Ben. 2011. "The Consequences of Individual Consumption: A Defence of Threshold Arguments for Vegetarianism and Consumer Ethics." *Journal of Applied Philosophy* 28 (4): 396–411.

Almassi, Ben. 2021. *Reparative Environmental Justice in a World of Wounds*. Lanham, MD: Lexington Books.

Alvaro, Carlo. 2019a. "Lab-Grown Meat and Veganism: A Virtue-Oriented Perspective." *Journal of Agricultural and Environmental Ethics* 32: 127–41.

Alvaro, Carlo. 2019b. *Ethical Veganism, Virtue Ethics, and the Great Soul*. Lanham, MD: Lexington Books.

Alvaro, Carlo. 2020. "Vegan Parents and Children: Zero Parental Compromise." *Ethics and Education* 15 (4): 476–98. http://doi.org/ 10.1080/17449642.2020.1822610.

Amato, Paul R., and Sonia A. Partridge. 1989. *The New Vegetarians: Promoting Health and Protecting Life*. New York: Plenum Press.

Ankomah, William Sarfo. 2020. "Animal Studies: Let's Talk About Animal Welfare and Liberation Issues in Childhood." *Society & Animals* 28: 311–26.

Bailey, Cathryn. 2007a. "We Are What We Eat: Feminist Vegetarianism and the Reproduction of Racial Identity." *Hypatia* 22: 39–59.

Bailey, Cathryn. Spring 2007b. "'Africa Begins at the Pyrenees': Moral Outrage, Hypocrisy, and the Spanish Bullfight." *Ethics and the Environment* 12 (1): 23–37.

Barwick, Emily Moran. 2016. "Forcing Kids to Be Vegan? Parents Answer." *BiteSizeVegan.com*, https://bitesizevegan.org/forcing-kids-to-be-vegan-parents-answer/ (published April 20, 2016, accessed March 26, 2024).

Baur, Gene. 2008. *Farm Sanctuary: Changing Hearts and Minds About Animals and Food*. New York: Touchstone.

Beard, S., K. Freeman, M. L. Velasco, W. Boyd, T. Chamberlain, A. Latoni, D. Lasko, R. M. Lunn, L. O'Fallon, J. Packenham, M. M. Smarr, R. Arnette, C. Cavalier-Keck, J. Keck, N. Muhammad, O. Wilson, B. Wilson, A. Wilson, A. Wilson, and Darlene Dixon. 2024. "Racism as a Public Health Issue in Environmental Health Disparities and Environmental Justice: Working Toward Solutions." *Environmental Health* 23 (8). https://doi.org/10.1186/s12940-024-01052-8.

Bekoff, M. 2000. "Animal Emotions: Exploring Passionate Natures." *BioScience* 50 (10): 861–70.

Bishop, Sharon. 1987. "Connections and Guilt." *Hypatia* 2 (1): 7–23.

Borgoyn, Shannon. 2017. "Teen FAQ Question: How Do I Handle Bullying for Being a Vegetarian or Vegan?" *The Vegetarian Resource Group Blog*, June 14. https://www.vrg.org/blog/2017/06/14/teen-faq-question-how-do-i-handle-bullying-for-being-a-vegetarian-or-vegan/.

Brighouse, Harry, and Adam Swift. 2006. "Parents' Rights and the Value of the Family." *Ethics* 117 (1): 80–108.

Brighouse, Harry, and Adam Swift. 2014. *Family Values: The Ethics of Parent-Child Relationships*. Princeton, NJ: Princeton University Press.

Callicott, J. Baird. 2003. "The Case Against Moral Pluralism." In *Environmental Ethics: An Anthology*, edited by Andrew Light and Holmes Rolston III. Malden, MA: Blackwell Publishing.

Calvo, Erika. 2008. "'Most Farmers Prefer Blondes': The Dynamics of Anthroparchy in Animals' Becoming Meat." *Journal for Critical Animal Studies* 6 (1): 32–45.

Causey, Ann. 1989. "On the Morality of Hunting." *Environmental Ethics* 11 (4): 327–43.

Cherry, E. 2015. "I Was a Teenage Vegan: Motivation and Maintenance of Lifestyle Movements." *Sociological Inquiry* 85 (1): 55–74.

Ciochetti, Christopher. 2012. "Veganism and Living Well." *Journal of Agriculture and Environmental Ethics* 25: 405–17.

Cole, Matthew, and Kate Stewart. 2016. *Our Children and Other Animals: The Cultural Construction of Human-Animal Relations in Childhood.* London: Routledge.

Cowan, Lisa. 2014. "UW to Build Animal Research Lab Underground." *The Seattle Times*, August 4. https://www.seattletimes.com/seattle-news/uw-to-build-animal-research-lab-underground/.

Cuomo, Chris J., and Lori Gruen. 1998. "On Puppies and Pussies: Animals, Intimacy, and Moral Distance." In *Daring to Be Good: Essays in Feminist Ethico-Politics*, edited by Bat-Ami Bar On and Ann Ferguson. New York: Routledge, 129–42.

Curtin, Deane. 1991. "Toward an Ecological Ethic of Care." *Hypatia* 6: 60–74.

Curtin, Deane. 1992. "Recipes for Values." In *Cooking, Eating, Thinking: Transformative Philosophies of Food*, edited by Deanne Curtin and Lisa M. Heldke. Bloomington: Indiana University Press, 123–44.

Curtin, Deane. 2004. "Contextual Moral Vegetarianism." In *Food for Thought: The Debate over Meat Eating*, edited by Steve F. Sapontzis. Amherst, NY: Prometheus Books, 272–83.

Davis, Karen. 2012. "The Mental Life of Chickens as Observed Through Their Social Relationships." In *Experiencing Animal Minds: An Anthology of Animal-Human Encounters*, edited by J. A. Smith and R. W. Mitchell. New York: Columbia University Press, 13–29.

De Vries, Bouke. 2020. "Should Children Have a Veto over Parental Decisions to Relocate?" *Moral Philosophy and Politics* 7 (2): 321–34.

de Waal, Frans. 2016. *Are We Smart Enough to Know How Smart Animals Are?* New York: W.W. Norton.

Deckha, Maneesha. 2012. "Toward a Postcolonial, Posthumanist Feminist Theory: Centralizing Race and Culture in Feminist Work on Nonhuman Animals." *Hypatia* 27 (3): 527–45.

DeVault, Marjorie. 1991. *Feeding the Family: The Social Organization of Caring as Gendered Work.* Chicago, IL: University of Chicago Press.

Donaldson, Sue, and Will Kymlicka. Fall 2015. "Farmed Animal Sanctuaries: The Heart of the Movement? A Socio-Political Perspective." *Politics and Animals* 1 (1): 50–74.

Donaldson, Sue, and Will Kymlicka. 2019. "Children and Animals." In *The Routledge Handbook of the Philosophy of Childhood and Children*, edited by A. Gheaus, G. Calder, and J. De Wispelaere. New York: Routledge, 282–93.

Donovan, Josephine. Winter 1991. "Reply to Noddings." *Signs* 16 (2): 423–5.

Donovan, Josephine. 1993. "Animal Rights and Feminist Theory." In *Ecofeminism: Women, Animals, Nature*, edited by Greta Gaard. Philadelphia, PA: Temple University Press, 167–94.

Donovan, Josephine. 2007. "Attention to Suffering: Sympathy as a Basis for Ethical Treatment of Animals." In *The Feminist Care Tradition in Animal Ethics*, edited by Josephine Donovan and Carol J. Adams. New York: Columbia University Press, 174–97. First published in *Journal of Social Philosophy* 27 (1) (1996).

Donovan, Josphine, and Carol J. Adams. 2007. "Introduction." In *The Feminist Care Tradition in Animal Ethics*, edited by Josephine Donovan and Carol J. Adams. New York: Columbia University Press, 1–15.

Doyle, Catherine. 2017. "Captive Wildlife Sanctuaries: Definition, Ethical Considerations and Public Perception." *Animal Studies Journal* 6 (2): 55–85.

Dreier, Hannah. 2025. "Meatpacking Companies to Pay $8 Million for U.S. Child Labor Violations." *The New York Times*, January 16, 2025. https://www.nytimes.

com/2025/01/16/us/perdue-jbs-slaughterhouses-child-labor.html?searchResultPosition=1 (accessed May 27, 2025).

Edwards, Sachi. 2013. "Living in a Minority Food Culture: A Phenomenological Investigation of Being Vegetarian/Vegan." *Phenomenology & Practice* 7 (1): 111–25.

Egan, Sarah. 2014. "National Identity and Cultural Resonance in English Foxhunting Movements." *National Identities* 16 (1): 71–90.

Elliot, George. 2003. *The Mill on the Floss*. London: Penguin Books. Originally published 1860.

Elliott, Robert. 2003. "Faking Nature." In *Environmental Ethics: An Anthology*, edited by Andrew Light and Holmes Rolston III. Malden, MA: Blackwell. First published in *Inquiry* 25 (1982): 81–93.

Emmerman, Karen. 2012. *Beyond the Basic/Nonbasic Interests Distinction: A Feminist Approach to Inter-Species Moral Conflict and Moral Repair*. PhD diss., University of Washington.

Emmerman, Karen S. 2014. "Sanctuary, Not Remedy: The Problem of Captivity and the Need for Moral Repair." In *The Ethics of Captivity*, edited by Lori Gruen. Oxford: Oxford University Press, 213–30.

Emmerman, Karen S. 2019. "What's Love Got to Do with It? An Ecofeminist Approach to Inter-Animal and Intra-Cultural Conflicts of Interest." *Ethical Theory and Moral Practice* 22 (1): 77–91. https://doi.org/10.1007/s10677-019-09978-6.

Emmerman, Karen S. 2020. "Moral Arguments Against Zoos." In *Routledge Handbook of Animal Ethics*, edited by Bob Fischer. New York: Routledge, 381–93.

Emmerman, Karen S. 2022. "Interanimal Moral Conflict and Moral Repair: A Contextualized Ecofeminist Approach in Action." In *Ecofeminism: Feminist Intersections with Other Animals and the Earth*, 2nd ed., edited by Carol J. Adams and Lori Gruen Adams. New York: Bloomsbury Academic, 181–96.

Emmerman, Karen S. 2024. "Feminist Veganism." In *The Routledge Companion to Gender and Animals*, edited by Chloë Taylor. New York: Routledge, 141–51.

Fesmire, Steven. 2015. *Dewey*. London: Routledge.

Fesmire, Steven. 2024. *Beyond Moral Fundamentalism: Toward a Pragmatic Pluralism*. Oxford: Oxford University Press.

Fischer, Bob. 2020. *The Ethics of Eating Animals: Usually Bad, Sometimes Wrong, Often Permissible*. New York: Routledge.

Fischer, Bob, and A. Lamey. 2018. "Field Deaths in Plant Agriculture." *Journal of Agricultural and Environmental Ethics* 31: 409–28.

Fischer, Jeremy, and Rachel Fredericks. 2024. "Creating Carnists." *Philosophers' Imprint* 24: 18, 1–20. https://doi.org/10.3998/phimp.3235.

Fisher, Linda. 2011. "Freeing Feathered Spirits." In *Sister Species: Women, Animals, and Social Justice*, edited by Lisa Kemmerer. Urbana: University of Illinois Press, 110–16.

Fitzgerald, Amy J. 2010. "A Social History of the Slaughterhouse: From Inception to Contemporary Implications." *Human Ecology Review* 17 (1): 58–69.

Food Empowerment Project. n.d. "Chickens (Hens) Raised for Eggs." https://foodispower.org/hens-raised-for-eggs/ (accessed June 20, 2025).

Food Empowerment Project. n.d. "Environmental Racism." https://foodispower.org/environmental-and-global/environmental-racism/ (accessed June 23, 2025).

Food Empowerment Project. n.d. "Food Deserts*." https://food ispower.org/access-health/food-deserts/ (accessed February 10, 2025).

Food Empowerment Project. n.d. "Produce Workers." https://foodispower.org/human-labor-slavery/produce-workers/ (accessed June 19, 2025).

Food Empowerment Project. n.d. "Slaughterhouse Workers." https://foodispower.org/human-labor-slavery/slaughterhouse-workers/ (accessed June 23, 2025).
Food Empowerment Project. n.d. "VeganFilipinoFood.com." https://veganfilipinofood.com/ (accessed January 14, 2022).
Food Empowerment Project. n.d. "VeganMexicanFood.com." https://veganmexicanfood.com/ (accessed January 14, 2022).
Fox, Laura. 2024. "The Intersectionality of Environmental Justice, Other Societal Harms, and Farmed Animal Welfare." *Environmental Justice* 17 (2): 101–9.
Francione, Gary. 1996. *Rain Without Thunder*. Philadelphia, PA: Temple University Press.
Francione, Gary. 2004. "Animals—Property or Persons?" In *Animal Rights: Current Debates and New Directions*, edited by Cass R. Sunstein and Martha Nussbaum. Oxford: Oxford University Press, 108–42.
Freedman, Samuel G. 2007. "Rabbi's Campaign for Kosher Standards Expands to Include Call for Social Justice." *The New York Times*, May 19. https://www.nytimes.com/2007/05/19/us/19religion.html.
Friedman, Marilyn. 1989. "The Impracticality of Impartiality." *Journal of Philosophy* 86 (11): 645–56.
Friedman, Marilyn. 2003. *Autonomy, Gender, Politics*. Oxford: Oxford University Press.
Gaard, Greta. 1993. "Ecofeminism and Native American Cultures: Pushing the Limits of Cultural Imperialism?" In *Ecofeminism: Women, Animals, Nature*, edited by Greta Gaard. Philadelphia, PA: Temple University Press, 295–314.
Gaard, Greta. Winter 1997. "Toward a Queer Ecofeminism." *Hypatia* 12 (1): 114–37.
Gaard, Greta. 2001. "Tools for a Cross-Cultural Feminist Ethics: Ethical Context and Contents in the Makah Whale Hunt." *Hypatia* 16: 1–26.
Gaard, Greta. 2002. "Vegetarian Ecofeminism: A Review Essay." *Frontiers: A Journal of Women Studies* 23: 117–46.
Gaard, Greta, and Lori Gruen. 1995. "Comments on George's 'Should Feminists Be Vegetarians.'" *Signs* 21 (1): 230–41.
García, María Elena. 2013. "The Taste of Conquest: Colonialism, Cosmopolitics, and the Dark Side of Peru's Gastronomic Boom." *Journal of Latin American and Caribbean Anthropology* 18 (3): 505–24.
Gardiner, Stephen M. 2010. "Is 'Arming the Future' with Geoengineering Really the Lesser Evil? Some Doubts About the Ethics of Intentionally Manipulating the Climate System." In *Climate Ethics: Essential Readings*, edited by Stephen M. Gardiner, Simon Caney, Dale Jamieson, and Henry Shue. Oxford: Oxford University Press, 439–543.
George, Kathryn Paxton. 1994. "Should Feminists Be Vegetarians?" *Signs* 19 (2): 405–34.
George, Kathryn Paxton. 1995. "Reply to Adams, Donovan, and Gaard and Gruen." *Signs* 21 (1): 242–60.
Gillespie, Kathryn A. 2010. "Killing with Kindness? Reconceptualizing 'Humane Slaughter.'" Master's thesis, University of Washington.
Gillespie, Kathryn A. 2011. "How Happy Is Your Meat? Confronting (Dis)connectedness in the 'Alternative' Meat Industry." *The Brock Review* 12 (1): 99–128.
Gilligan, Carol. 1982. *In a Difference Voice: Psychological Theory and Women's Development*. Cambridge, MA: Harvard University Press.
Gluck, John P. 2016. *Voracious Science & Vulnerable Animals: A Primate Scientist's Ethical Journey*. Chicago, IL: University of Chicago Press.
Gragg, Roy Dallas. November 1986. "Why I Quit Hunting." *Animals' Agenda* 6: 34–5.
Grandin, Temple, and Catherine Johnson. 2009. *Animals Make Us Human: Creating the Best Life for Animals*. Orlando, FL: Houghton Mifflin Harcourt.

Grant, Juawana, and Brittni MacKenzie-Dale. 2016. "Lisa Simpson and Darlene Connor: Television's Favorite Killjoys." In *Critical Perspectives on Veganism*, edited by Jodey Castricano and Rasmus R. Simonsen. Switzerland: Palgrave Macmillan, 307–28.

Gray, Elizabeth D. 1979. *Green Paradise Lost*. Wellesley, MA: Roundtable Press. Quoted in Marti Kheel, "The Liberation of Nature: A Circular Affair." *Environmental Ethics* 7: 145.

Greenebaum, Jessica. 2012. "Managing Impressions: 'Face-Saving' Strategies for Vegetarians and Vegans." *Humanity & Society* 36 (4): 309–25.

Gruen, Lori. 1991. "Animals." In *A Companion to Ethics*, 2nd ed., edited by Peter Singer. Oxford: Blackwell, 343–53.

Gruen, Lori. 1993. "Dismantling Oppression: An Analysis of the Connection Between Women and Animals." In *Ecofeminism: Women, Animals, Nature*, edited by Greta Gaard. Philadelphia, PA: Temple University Press, 60–90.

Gruen, Lori. 1999. "Must Utilitarians Be Impartial?" In *Singer and His Critics*, edited by Dale Jamieson. Malden, MA: Blackwell, 129–149.

Gruen, Lori. 2001. "Conflicting Values in a Conflicting World: Ecofeminism and Multicultural Environmental Ethics." *Women & Environments International Magazine* 53 (53): 16–19.

Gruen, Lori. 2004. "Empathy and Vegetarian Commitments." In *Food for Thought*, edited by Steve F. Sapontzis. Amherst, NY: Prometheus Books, 284–92.

Gruen, Lori. 2011. *Ethics and Animals: An Introduction*. Cambridge: Cambridge University Press.

Gruen, Lori. 2012. "Navigating Difference (Again): Animal Ethics and Entangled Empathy." In *Strangers to Nature: Animal Lives and Human Ethics*, edited by Gregory R. Smulewicz-Zucker. Lanham, MD: Lexington Books, 213–34.

Gruen, Lori. 2014. *The Ethics of Captivity*. Oxford: Oxford University Press.

Gruen, Lori. 2015. *Entangled Empathy: An Alternative Ethic for Our Relations with Animals*. New York: Lantern Books.

Gruen, Lori. 2022. "Facing Death and Practicing Grief." In *Ecofeminism: Feminist Intersections with Other Animals & the Earth*, 2nd ed., edited by Carol J. Adams and Lori Gruen. New York: Bloomsbury Academic, 161–76.

Gruen, Lori, and Robert C. Jones. 2016. "Veganism as Aspiration." In *The Moral Complexities of Meat*, edited by Ben Bramble and Bob Fischer. Oxford: Oxford University Press, 153–71.

Hamraie, Amai. 2016. "Beyond Accommodation: Disability, Feminist Philosophy, and the Design of Everyday Academic Life." *philoSOPHIA* 6 (2): 259–71.

Hare, R. M. 1981. *Moral Thinking: Its Levels, Method, and Point*. Oxford: Oxford University Press.

Hare, R. M. 1999. "Why I Am Only a Demi-Vegetarian." In *Singer and His Critics*, edited by Dale Jamieson. Malden, MA: Blackwell, 233–46. Originally published in 1983.

Harper, A. Breeze. 2010. *Sistah Vegan: Black Female Vegans Speak on Food, Identity, Health, and Society*. New York: Lantern Books.

Hawkins, Ronnie. 2001. "Cultural Whaling, Commodification, and Culture Change." *Environmental Ethics* 23: 287–306.

Hawthorne, Mark. 2013. *Bleating Hearts: The Hidden World of Animal Suffering*. Alresford: Changemakers Books.

Hawthorne, Mark. 2016. *A Vegan Ethics: Embracing a Life of Compassion for All*. Alresford: Changemakers Books.

Held, Virgina. 1995. "Feminist Moral Inquiry and the Feminist Future." In *Justice and Care: Essential Readings in Feminist Ethics*, edited by Virginia Held. Boulder, CO: Westview Press, 153–78.

Held, Virginia. 2006. *The Ethics of Care: Personal, Political, and Global.* New York: Oxford University Press.

Hogan, Linda. 1996. "Silencing Tribal Grandmothers: Traditions, Old Values at Heart of Makah's Clash over Whaling." *The Seattle Times*, December 15. https://archive.seattletimes.com/archive/19961215/2365045/silencing-tribal-grandmothers----traditions-old-values-at-heart-of-makahs-clash-over-whaling.

Horiuchi, Mae. 2017. *Decolonizing Veganism: A Japanese Perspective.* Unpublished senior thesis, University of Washington.

Horta, Oscar. 2018. "Discrimination Against Vegans." *Res Publica* 24: 359–73.

Hribal, Jason. 2003. "Animals Are Part of the Working Class: A Challenge to Labor History." *Labor History* 44 (4): 435–53. https://doi.org/10.1080/0023656032000170069.

Hrynowski, Zach. n.d. "What Percentage of Americans Are Vegetarian?" https://news.gallup.com/poll/267074/percentage-americans-vegetarian.aspx (accessed January 1, 2022).

Hunt, Marcus William. 2019a. "Parental Compromise." *Critical Review of International Social and Political Philosophy* 25 (2): 260–80. https://doi.org/10.1080/13698230.2019.1644582.

Hunt, Marcus William. 2019b. "Veganism and Children: Physical and Social Well-Being." *Journal of Agricultural and Environmental Ethics* 32: 269–91.

Hursthouse, Rosalind. 1991. "Virtue Theory and Abortion." *Philosophy & Public Affairs* 20 (3): 223–46.

Hursthouse, Rosalind. 2006. "Applying Virtue Ethics to Our Treatment of Other Animals." In *The Practice of Virtue*, edited by Jennifer Welchman. Indianapolis, IN: Hackett, 136–55.

Hursthouse, Rosalind. 2007. "Environmental Virtue Ethics." In *Working Virtue: Virtue Ethics and Contemporary Moral Problems*, edited by Rebecca L. Walker and P. J. Ivanhoe. Oxford: Oxford University Press, 155–71.

Hussar, Karen M., and Paul L. Harris. 2010. "Children Who Choose Not to Eat Meat: A Study of Early Decision-Making." *Social Development* 19 (3): 627–41.

Jamieson, Dale. 2002a. "Against Zoos." In *Morality's Progress.* Oxford: Oxford University Press.

Jamieson, Dale. 2002b. "Zoos Revisited." In *Morality's Progress.* Oxford: Oxford University Press.

Johnson, Harriet McBryde. 2003. "Unspeakable Conversations." *The New York Times Magazine*, February 16. https://www.nytimes.com/2003/02/16/magazine/unspeakable-conversations.html?pagewanted=print&src=pm.

Jolma, Dena Jones. 1992. "Why They Quit Hunting: Thoughts from Ex-Hunters." *The Animals' Agenda* 12 (6): 38–40.

Jones, Miriam. 2014. "Captivity in the Context of a Sanctuary for Formerly Farmed Animals." In *The Ethics of Captivity*, edited by Lori Gruen. Oxford: Oxford University Press, 90–101.

Jones, Pattrice. 2004. "Crossing the Mammalian-Avian Line." *Satya.* http://www.satyamag.com/nov04/jones.html (accessed February 9, 2026).

Joy, Melanie. 2010. *Why We Love Dogs, Eat Pigs, and Wear Cows: An Introduction to Carnism.* San Francisco, CA: Red Wheel Press.

Katz, Eric. 2003. "The Big Lie: Human Restoration of Nature." In *Environmental Ethics: An Anthology*, edited by Andrew Light and Holmes Rolston III. Malden, MA: Blackwell, 390–7. First published in *Research in Philosophy and Technology* 12 (1988).

Kemmerer, Lisa. 2006. "Verbal Activism: 'Anymal.'" *Society & Animals* 14 (1): 9–14.

Kemmerer, Lisa. 2011. *Sister Species: Women, Animals, and Social Justice*. Chicago: University of Illinois Press.

Khara, Tani. 2018. "Why Do Vegans Have Such Bad Reputations?" *The Conversation*, https://theconversation.com/why-do-vegans-have-such-bad-reputations-103683 (published November 5, 2018, accessed February 6, 2024).

Kheel, Marti. 1985. "The Liberation of Nature: A Circular Affair." *Environmental Ethics* 7: 135–49.

Kheel, Marti. 1993. "From Heroic to Holistic Ethics: The Ecofeminist Challenge." In *Ecofeminism: Women, Animals, Nature*, edited by Greta Gaard. Philadelphia, PA: Temple University Press, 243–71.

Kheel, Marti. 1995. "License to Kill: An Ecofeminist Critique of Hunters' Discourse." In *Animals and Women: Feminist Theoretical Explorations*, edited by Carol J. Adams and Josephine Donovan. Durham, NC: Duke University Press, 85–125.

Kheel, Marti. 1996. "The Killing Game: An Ecofeminist Critique of Hunting." *Journal of the Philosophy of Sport* XXIII: 30–44.

Kheel, Marti. 2004. "Vegetarianism and Ecofeminism: Toppling Patriarchy with a Fork." In *Food for Thought*, edited by Steve F. Sapontzis. Amherst, NY: Prometheus Books, 327–41.

Kheel, Marti. 2008. *Nature Ethics: An Ecofeminist Perspective*. Lanham, MD: Rowman & Littlefield.

Kildal, Charlotee Lilleby, and Karen Lykke Syse. 2017. "Meat and Masculinity in the Norwegian Armed Forces." *Appetite* 112: 69–77.

Kim, Claire Jean. 2015. *Dangerous Crossings: Race, Species, and Nature in a Multicultural Age*. Cambridge: Cambridge University Press.

Kittay, Eva Feder. July 2009. "The Personal Is Philosophical Is Political: A Philosopher and Mother of a Cognitively Disabled Person Sends Notes from the Battlefield." *Metaphilosophy* 40 (3–4): 606–27.

Ko, Aph, and Syl Ko. 2017. *Aphro-ism: Essays on Pop Culture, Feminism, and Black Veganism from Two Sisters*. New York: Lantern Books.

Kumar, Rahul. 1999. "In Defense of the Moral Moderate." *Philosophy & Public Affairs* 28 (4): 275–309.

La Follette, Hugh. 1991. "Personal Relationships." In *A Companion to Ethics*, edited by Peter Singer. Oxford: Blackwell.

Lee, Angela. 2018. "An Ecofeminist Perspective on New Food Technologies." *Canadian Food Studies* 5 (1): 63–89.

Leopold, Aldo. 1966. *A Sand County Almanac, with Essays on Conservation from Round River*. New York: Ballantine Books.

Leopold, Aldo. 1989. *A Sand County Almanac and Sketches Here and There*, Commemorative ed. New York: Oxford University Press. First published 1949 by Oxford University Press (New York).

Light, Andrew. 2003. "The Case for a Practical Pluralism." In *Environmental Ethics: An Anthology*, edited by Andrew Light and Holmes Rolston III. Malden, MA: Blackwell.

Lindstrom, Eric. 2018. *Raising Vegan Kids: Lessons for Littles in Plant-Based Eating and Compassionate Living*. New York: Skyhorse.

Littlefield, Jon. 2006. "Subculture of Deer Hunters and the Negotiation of Masculinity: An Ethnographic Investigation of Hunting in the Rural South." PhD diss., Virginia Polytechnic Institute and State University.

Littlefield, Jon. 2010. "Men on the Hunt: Ecofeminist Insights into Masculinity." *Marketing Theory* 10 (1): 97–117.

Littlefield, Jon, and Julie L. Ozanne. 2011. "Socialization into Consumer Culture: Hunters Learning to Be Men." *Consumption, Markets, & Culture* 14 (4): 333–60.

Loftin, Robert W. Fall 1984. "The Morality of Hunting." *Environmental Ethics* 6 (3): 241–50.

Lucas, Sheri. 2005. "A Defense of the Feminist-Vegetarian Connection." *Hypatia* 20 (1): 150–77.

Lugones, María C., and Elizabeth V. Spelman. 1983. "Have We Got a Theory for You! Feminist Theory, Cultural Imperialism and the Demand for the 'Woman's Voice.'" *Women's Studies International Forum* 6: 573–81.

Luke, Brian. 1995. "Taming Ourselves or Going Feral? Toward a Nonpatriarchal Metaethic of Animal Liberation." In *Animals and Women: Feminist Theoretical Explorations*, 3rd ed., edited by Carol J. Adams and Josephine Donovan. Durham, NC: Duke University Press, 290–319.

Luke, Brian. Spring 1997. "A Critical Analysis of Hunters' Ethics." *Environmental Ethics* 19: 25–44.

Luke, Brian. Fall 1998. "Violent Love: Hunting, Heterosexuality, and the Erotics of Men's Predation." *Feminist Studies* 24 (3): 627–55.

Luke, Brian. 2007. "Justice, Caring, and Animal Liberation." In *The Feminist Care Tradition in Animal Ethics*, edited by Josephine Donovan and Carol J. Adams. New York: Columbia University Press, 125–52.

MacDonald, Mia. 2022. "Maximum Plunder: The Global Context and Multiple Threats of Animal Agriculture." In *Ecofeminism: Feminist Intersections with Other Animals and the Earth*, 2nd ed., edited by Carol J. Adams and Lori Gruen. London: Bloomsbury Academic, 355–372.

Mackenzie, Catriona, and Natalie Stolijar, eds. 2000. *Relational Autonomy: Feminist Perspectives on Autonomy, Agency, and the Social Self.* Oxford: Oxford University Press.

María, Gustavo A., Beatriz Mazaz, Francisco J. Zarza, and Genaro C. Miranda de la Lama. 2017. "Animal Welfare, National Identity, and Social Change: Attitudes and Opinions of Spanish Citizens Towards Bullfighting." *Journal of Agricultural and Environmental Ethics* 30: 809–26.

Marino, Lori. 2017. "Thinking Chickens: A Review of Cognition, Emotion, and Behavior in the Domestic Chicken." *Animal Cognition* 20: 127–47.

Marks, Stuart A. 1991. *Southern Hunting in Black and White: Nature, History, and Ritual in a South Carolina Community.* Princeton, NJ: Princeton University Press.

Masson, Jeffrey Moussaieff. 2003. *The Pig Who Sang to the Moon: The Emotional World of Farm Animals.* New York: Ballantine Books.

McAfee, Noëlle, Ann Garry, Anita Superson, Heidi Grasswick, and Serene Khader. Spring 2024. "Feminist Philosophy." In *The Stanford Encyclopedia of Philosophy*, edited by Edward N. Zalta and Uri Nodelman. https://plato.stanford.edu/archives/spr2024/entries/feminist-philosophy/ (accessed May 30, 2025).

McDonald, Barbara. 2000. "'Once You Know Something, You Can't Unknow It': An Empirical Look at Becoming Vegan." *Society & Animals* 8 (1): 1–23.

McGinn, Colin. 1999. "Our Duties to Animals and the Poor." In *Singer and His Critics*, edited by Dale Jamieson. Malden, MA: Blackwell, 150–61.

McKenna, Erin. 1994. "Feminism and Vegetarianism: A Critique of Peter Singer." *Philosophy in the Contemporary World* 1 (2): 28–35.
McKenna, Erin. 2021. *Living with Animals—Rights, Responsibilities, and Respect.* Lanham, MD: Rowman & Littlefield.
McKenna, Erin. 2023. "The Question of Veganism, the Dangers of Moral Extensionism, and a Pragmatist Ecofeminist Alternative." *Between the Species* 26 (1): 18–41.
Meyerding, Jane. Nov/Dec 1982. "Feminist Criticism & Cultural Imperialism (Where Does One End and the Other Begin)." *Agenda* 14–23.
Midgley, Mary. 1983. *Animals and Why They Matter.* Athens: University of Georgia Press.
Millburn, Josh. 2021. "Zero-Compromise Veganism." *Ethics and Education* 16 (3): 375–91.
Millburn, Josh. 2022. "Should Vegans Compromise?" *Critical Review of International Social and Political Philosophy* 25 (2): 281–93. https://doi.org/10.1080/13698230.2020.1737477.
Mohr Lone, Jana. 2021. *Seen and Not Heard: Why Children's Voices Matter.* London: Rowman & Littlefield.
Moritz, Bill. 2021. "Federal Wildlife Restoration Revenue Up, Evaluating Hunting's 'Covid Bump.'" *Wildlife Management Institute Outdoor News Bulletin* 75 (11). https://wildlifemanagement.institute/outdoor-news-bulletin/november-2021/federal-wildlife-restoration-revenue-evaluating-huntings-covid (accessed February 9, 2026).
Nagel, Thomas. 1986. *The View from Nowhere.* Oxford: Oxford University Press.
Ngqangashe, Yandisa. 2019. "Vegan and Vegetarian Communities in South Africa." In *To Eat or to Not Eat Meat: How Vegetarian Dietary Choices Influence Our Social Lives,* edited by Charlotte De Backer, Maryanne L. Fisher, Julie Dare, and Leesa Costello. Lanham, MD: Rowman & Littlefield, 149–57.
Noddings, Nel. [1984] 2013. *Caring: A Relational Approach to Ethics and Moral Education.* Berkeley: University of California Press. ProQuest Ebook Central, http://ebookcentral.proquest.com/lib/washington/detail.action?docID=1342614 (accessed March 3, 2025).
Noddings, Nel. Winter 1991. "Comment on Donovan's 'Animal Rights and Feminist Theory.'" *Signs* 16 (2): 418–22.
Nussbaum, Martha. 2004. "Beyond 'Compassion and Humanity': Justice for Nonhuman Animals." In *Animal Rights: Current Debates and New Directions,* edited by Cass R. Sunsteing and Martha C. Nussbaum. Oxford: Oxford University Press.
Ornelas, lauren. 2012. "Maturing of Activism." Paper presented at "Finding a Niche for All Animals: A Conference Honoring the Ecofeminist Work of Marti Kheel." Wesleyan University.
Oxford English Dictionary, "brainwashing (n.)," July 2023. https://doi.org/10.1093/OED/1045162308.
Oxford English Dictionary, "indoctrinate (v.)," December 2024. https://doi.org/10.1093/OED/1167396294.
Oxford English Dictionary, "indoctrination (n.)," July 2023. https://doi.org/10.1093/OED/7894631477.
Pachirat, Timothy. 2011. *Every Twelve Seconds: Industrialized Slaughter and the Politics of Sight.* New Haven, CT: Yale University Press.
Palmer, Clare, and Francis O'Gorman. 2003. "Animals, Power, and Ethics: The Case of Foxhunting." In *Moral and Political Reasoning in Environmental Practice,* edited by Andrew Light and Avner de Shalit. Cambridge, MA: MIT Press, 281–94.
Pavlina, Erin. 2003. *Raising Vegan Children in a Non-Vegan World: A Complete Guide for Parents.* Las Vegas, NV: VegFamily.
Pluhar, Evelyn. Summer 1991. "The Joy of Killing." *Between the Species* 121–8.

Plumwood, Valerie. Summer 1996. "Being Prey." *Terra Nova: Nature and Culture* 1 (3): 33–44.
Plumwood, Valerie. 2012. *Animals and Ecology*. Edited by Lorraine Shannon. ANU Press.
Preston, Julia. 2008. "Kosher Plant Is Accused of Inhumane Slaughter." *The New York Times*, September 4. http://www.nytimes.com/2008/09/05/us/05immig.html.
Raphaely, Talia, and Asher Meyerson. 2019. "Experience of a Vegan in the Australian Jewish Community." In *To Eat or Not Eat Meat: How Vegetarian Dietary Choices Influence Our Social Lives*, edited by Charlotte De Backer, Maryanne L. Fisher, Julie Dar, and Leesa Costello. Lanham, MD: Rowman & Littlefield, 49–58.
Railton, Peter. Spring 1984. "Alienation, Consequentialism, and the Demands of Morality." *Philosophy & Public Affairs* 13: 134–71.
Regan, Tom. Summer 1980. "Utilitarianism, Vegetarianism, and Animal Rights." *Philosophy & Public Affairs* 9: 305–24.
Regan, Tom. 2004a. *The Case for Animal Rights*, updated edition. Berkeley: University of California Press. First published in 1983 by the University of California Press.
Regan, Tom. 2004b. *Empty Cages: Facing the Challenge of Animal Rights*. Lanham, MD: Rowman & Littlefield.
Reilly. 2025. "What to Do If You're Bullied for Being Vegan." *Peta2.com*, September 29, 2025. https://www.peta2.com/help-animals/bullied-for-being-vegan/ (accessed February 9, 2026).
Riley, Shamara Shantu. 2022. "Ecology Is a Sistah's Issue Too: The Politics of Emergent Afrocentric Ecowomanism." In *Ecofeminism: Feminist Intersections with Other Animals and the Earth*, edited by Carol J. Adams and Lori Gruen, 2nd ed. London: Bloomsbury Academic, 89–105.
Robinson, Margaret. 2013. "Veganism and Mi'Kmaq Legends." *Canadian Journal of Native Studies* 33: 189–96.
Rollin, Bernard E. September 2007. "Animal Mind: Science, Philosophy, and Ethics." *Journal of Ethics* 11 (3): 253–74.
Roth, LuAnne K. 2005. "'Beef. It's What's for Dinner': Vegetarians, Meat-Eaters and the Negotiation of Familial Relationships." *Food, Culture, & Society* 8 (2): 181–200. https://doi.org/10.2752/155280105778055272.
Rubio, Julie Hanlon. 2014. "Animals, Evil, and Family Meals." *Journal of Moral Theology* 3 (2): 35–53.
Ruddick, Sara. 1989. *Maternal Thinking: Toward a Politics of Peace*. Boston, MA: Beacon Press.
Ryder, Richard. Autumn 2005. "The Case Against Hunting and for Democracy." *Think* 91–6.
Safran Foer, Jonathan. 2007. *Eating Animals*. New York: Little Brown.
Safran Foer, Jonathan. 2009. "Against Meat." *New York Times Magazine*, October 7, 2009. https://www.nytimes.com/2009/10/11/magazine/11foer-t.html?searchResultPosition=4 (accessed September 20, 2024).
Salsow, Eli. 2018. *Rising Out of Hatred: The Awakening of a Former White Nationalist*. New York: Anchor Books.
Sameth, Mark. 2011. "'I'll Have What She's Having' Jewish Ethical Eating." In *The Sacred Table: Creating a Jewish Food Ethic*, edited by Mary L. Zamore. New York: CCAR Press, 225–34.
Scheffler, Samuel. 1992. *Human Morality*. New York: Oxford University Press.

Schlosser, Eric. 2001. "The Chain Never Stops." *Mother Jones*, July/August. https://www.motherjones.com/politics/2001/07/dangerous-meatpacking-jobs-eric-schlosser/ (accessed August 14, 2025).

Schmidtz, David. 1998. "Are All Species Equal?" *Journal of Applied Philosophy* 15 (1): 57–67.

Shafran, Avi. 2012. "When Tzedek Isn't: The Conservative Movement Finds a Cause." *Cross Currents*, February 17. https://cross-currents.com/2012/02/17/when-tzedek-isnt-the-conservative-movement-finds-a-cause/ (accessed February 9, 2026).

Shapiro Samatha M. 2008. "Kosher Wars." *The New York Times Magazine*, October 9. http://www.nytimes.com/2008/10/12/magazine/12kosher-t.html.

Sheehan, George J. 2016. Introduction to *National Survey of Fishing, Hunting, and Wildlife-Associated Recreation*, by US Fish and Wildlife Service.

Sherratt, Anna. 2007. "Vegetarians and Their Children." *Journal of Applied Philosophy* 24 (4): 425–34.

Singer, Peter. 1972. "Famine, Affluence, and Morality." *Philosophy & Public Affairs* 1: 229–43.

Singer, Peter. 1973. "Animal Liberation." *New York Review of Books* 10–15.

Singer, Peter. 1979a. *Practical Ethics*. Cambridge: Cambridge University Press.

Singer, Peter. 1979b. "Killing Humans and Killing Animals." *Inquiry* 22: 145–56.

Singer, Peter. 1979c. "Not for Humans Only: The Place of Nonhumans in Environmental Issues." In *Ethics and the Problems of the 21st Century*, edited by Kenneth E. Goodpaster and Kenneth M. Sayre. Notre Dame, IN: University of Notre Dame Press.

Singer, Peter. 1989. "All Animals Are Equal." In *Animal Rights and Human Obligations*, 2nd ed., edited by Tom Regan and Peter Singer. Englewood Cliffs, NJ: Prentice-Hall, 73–86.

Singer, Peter. 1990. *Animal Liberation*, revised ed. New York: Avon Books.

Singer, Peter. 1993. *Practical Ethics*, 2nd ed. Cambridge: Cambridge University Press.

Singer, Peter. 1994. "Feminism and Vegetarianism: A Response." *Philosophy in the Contemporary World* 1 (2): 36–9.

Singer, Peter. 1999. "A Response." In *Singer and His Critics*, edited by Dale Jamieson. Oxford: Blackwell, 269–335.

Singer, Peter. 2002. *One World: The Ethics of Globalization*. New Haven, CT: Yale University Press.

Singer, Peter. 2008. "The Ethics of What We Eat." Filmed October 2008 at Williams College, Williamstown, MA. https://www.youtube.com/watch?v=UHzwqf_JkrA&t=3960s.

Singer Peter, and Jim Mason, eds. 2006. *The Ethics of What We Eat: Why Our Food Choices Matter*. Rodale.

Slicer, Deborah. Spring 1991. "Your Daughter or Your Dog: A Feminist Assessment of the Animal Research Issue." *Hypatia* 6 (1): 108–24.

Stanescu, Vasile. 2014. "Crocodile Tears, Compassionate Carnivores, and the Marketing of 'Happy Meat.'" In *Critical Animal Studies: Thinking the Unthinkable*, edited by John Sorenson. Toronto: Canadian Scholars' Press, 216–33.

Stone, Christopher D. 2003. "Moral Pluralism and the Course of Environmental Ethics." In *Environmental Ethics: An Anthology*, edited by Andrew Light and Holmes Rolston III. Malden, MA: Blackwell, 193–202.

Talbott, William J. 2005. *Which Rights Should Be Universal?* Oxford: Oxford University Press.

Taylor, Angus. Fall 1996. "Animal Rights and Human Needs." *Environmental Ethics* 18: 249–64.

Taylor, Angus. 2009. *Animals & Ethics: An Overview of the Philosophical Debate*, 3rd ed. Buffalo, NY: Broadview Press.

Taylor, Paul W. 1981. "The Ethics of Respect for Nature." *Environmental Ethics* 3: 197–218.

Taylor, Paul W. Summer 1984. "Are Humans Superior to Animals and Plants?" *Environmental Ethics* 6: 149–60.

Taylor, Paul W. 1986. *Respect for Nature*. Princeton, NJ: Princeton University Press.

Taylor, Sunaura. 2017. *Beasts of Burden: Animal and Disability Liberation*. New York: New Press.

Thompson, Gabriel. 2012. "New Rules Mean New Hardship for Poultry Workers." *The Nation*, published May 14. https://www.thenation.com/article/archive/new-rules-mean-new-hardship-poultry-workers/ (accessed February 10, 2025).

Tobin-Taylor, Elizabeth. 2023. "Intimate Partner Violence, Firearm Injuries and Homicides: A Health Justice Approach to Two Intersecting Public Health Crises." *Journal of Law, Medicine & Ethics* 51: 64–76.

Torres, Bob. 2007. *Making a Killing: The Political Economy of Animal Rights*. Oakland, CA: AK Press.

Twine, Richard. 2014. "Vegan Killjoys at the Table—Contesting Happiness and Negotiating Relationships with Food Practices." *Societies* 4: 623–39.

Twine, Richard. 2016. "Negotiating Social Relationships in the Transition to Vegan Eating Practices." In *Meat Culture*, edited by Annie Potts. Boston, MA: Brill, 243–63.

Twine, Richard. 2021. "Emissions from Animal Agriculture—16.5% Is the New Minimum Figure." *Sustainability* 13 (11): 6276. https://doi.org/10.3390/su13116276.

Twine, Richard. 2022. "Ecofeminism and Veganism: Revisiting the Question of Universalism." In *Ecofeminism: Feminist Intersections with Other Animals and the Earth*, 2nd ed., edited by Carol J. Adams and Lori Gruen Adams. New York: Bloomsbury Academic, 229–46.

Twine, Richard. 2024. *The Climate Crisis and Other Animals*. Sydney: Sydney University Press.

US Fish & Wildlife Service. 2011. *National Survey of Fishing, Hunting, and Wildlife-Associated Recreation*.

US Fish & Wildlife Service. 2016. *National Survey of Fishing, Hunting, and Wildlife-Associated Recreation*.

US Fish & Wildlife Service. 2022. *National Survey of Fishing, Hunting, and Wildlife-Associated Recreation*.

Vanderhoof, Erin. 2021. "Brigitte Bardot Is Handed Her Sixth Fine for 'Inciting Racial Hatred.'" *Vanity Fair*, November 5. https://www.vanityfair.com/style/2021/11/brigitte-bardot-fined-for-inciting-racial-hatred?srsltid=AfmBOop_qNtGzT7Ax7uWH4dpz4pVYmVp-Dj7HetjpBEDaz0S2b0y2CoC (accessed May 27, 2025).

VanDeVeer, Donald. 1979. "Interspecific Justice." *Inquiry* 22: 55–79.

Varner, Gary E. 1998. *In Nature's Interests*. Oxford: Oxford University Press.

Varner, Gary E. Winter 2003. "Review of *Life's Intrinsic Value*, by Nicholas Agar." *Environmental Ethics* 25: 413–16.

Varner, Gary E. Fall 2010. "A Harean Perspective on Humane Sustainability." *Ethics and the Environment* 15 (2): 31–49.

Varner, Gary E. 2012. *Personhood, Ethics, and Animal Cognition: Situating Animals in Hare's Two-Level Utilitarianism*. Oxford: Oxford University Press.

Vitali, Theodore. Spring 1990. "Sport Hunting: Moral or Immoral?" *Environmental Ethics* 12 (1): 69–82.

Vitello, Paul. 2008. "Label Says Kosher: Ethics Suggest Otherwise." *The New York Times*, December 10. http://www.nytimes.com/2008/12/11/nyregion/11kosher.html.

Walker, Margaret Urban. 1989. "What Does the Different Voice Say?: Gilligan's Women and Moral Philosophy." *Journal of Value Inquiry* 23: 123–34.

Walker, Margaret Urban. 1995. "Moral Understandings: Alternative 'Epistemology' for a Feminist Ethics." In *Justice and Care: Essential Readings in Feminist Ethics*, edited by Virginia Held. Boulder, CO: Westview Press, 139–52. First published in *Hypatia* 4, no. 2 (1989): 15–28.

Walker, Margaret Urban. 2006. *Moral Repair: Reconstructing Moral Relations After Wrongdoing*. Cambridge: Cambridge University Press.

Warren, Karen J. 1990. "The Power and the Promise of Ecological Feminism." *Environmental Ethics* 12: 125–46.

Warren, Mary Anne. 1997. *Moral Status: Obligations to Persons and Other Living Things*. Oxford: Oxford University Press.

Warren, Mary Anne. 2003. "Moral Status." In *Blackwell's Companion to Applied Ethics*, edited by R. G. Frey and Christopher Heath Wellman. Malden, MA: Blackwell, 439–50.

Weaver, Matthew. 2024. "Pro-Foxhunting Group Says UK Hunters Should Be Protected Ethnic Minority." *The Guardian*, https://www.theguardian.com/uk-news/article/2024/aug/12/pro-foxhunting-group-says-uk-hunters-protected-ethnic-minority (accessed April 24, 2025).

Williams, Bernard. 1965. "Ethical Consistency." *Proceedings of the Aristotelian Society, Supplementary Volumes* 39: 103–24.

Williams, Bernard. 1973. "A Critique of Utilitarianism." In *Utilitarianism for and Against*, edited by J. J. C. Smart and Bernard Williams. Cambridge: Cambridge University Press, 77–150.

Williams, Bernard. 1981. *Moral Luck*. Cambridge: Cambridge University Press.

INDEX